Donated In Honor of

Kate Parks Kitchin
By
Class of 1940
Rocky Mount High School

Critical Essays on
ROBERT BROWNING

CRITICAL ESSAYS ON BRITISH LITERATURE

Zack Bowen, General Editor
University of Miami

Critical Essays on
ROBERT BROWNING

edited by
MARY ELLIS GIBSON

G. K. Hall & Co. / New York
Maxwell Macmillan Canada / Toronto
Maxwell Macmillan International / New York Oxford Singapore Sydney

Copyright © 1992 by Mary Ellis Gibson

All rights reserved. No part of this book may be reproduced or transmitted in any form or by any means, electronic or mechanical, including photocopying, recording, or by any information storage and retrieval system, without permission in writing from the Publisher.

G. K. Hall & Co.
Macmillan Publishing Company
866 Third Avenue
New York, New York 10022

Maxwell Macmillan Canada, Inc.
1200 Eglinton Avenue East
Suite 200
Don Mills, Ontario M3C 3N1

Macmillan Publishing Company is part of the Maxwell Communication Group of Companies.

Library of Congress Cataloging-in-Publication Data

Critical essays on Robert Browning/edited by Mary Ellis Gibson.
    p.   cm. – (Critical essays on British literature)
   Includes bibliographical references and index.
   ISBN 0-8161-8861-0
   1. Browning, Robert, 1812–1889—Criticism and interpretation.
I. Gibson, Mary Ellis, 1952–   . II. Series.
PR4238.C74   1992
821'.8—dc20   91-47110
                                                                          CIP

The paper used in this publication meets the minimum requirements of American National Standard for Information Sciences—Permanence of Paper for Printed Library Materials. ANSI Z3948-1984.∞™

10 9 8 7 6 5 4 3 2 1

Printed in the United States of America

Contents

◆

General Editor's Note	vii
Publisher's Note	ix
Introduction	1
MARY ELLIS GIBSON	

ESSAYS

Dramatic Monologue and the Overhearing of Lyric HERBERT F. TUCKER	21
Notes on Some Structural Varieties and Variations in Dramatic "I" Poems and Their Theoretical Implications RALPH W. RADER	37
Consciousness as Writing: Deconstruction and Reading Victorian Poetry E. WARWICK SLINN	54
Reading the Reader in Robert Browning's Dramatic Monologues JOHN MAYNARD	69
The Divided Subject LOY MARTIN	79
Projection and the Female Other: Romanticism, Browning and the Victorian Dramatic Monologue U. C. KNOEPFLMACHER	100
Browning's Female Signature ADRIENNE AUSLANDER MUNICH	120
"Cleon" and Its Contexts ANTONY H. HARRISON	139

Browning's *Sordello* and the Parables of Modernist Poetics 161
CHRISTINE FROULA

Genre and Poetic Authority in *Pippa Passes* 186
DAVID G. RIEDE

Browning and the Primitive 202
DOROTHY MERMIN

Browning's *Strafford* and the History of the Present 226
DAVID E. LATANÉ, JR.

"The Englishman in Italy": Free Trade as a Principle of Aesthetics 243
ROBERT VISCUSI

Index 267

General Editor's Note

◆

The Critical Essays on British Literature series provides a variety of approaches to both classical and contemporary writers of Britain and Ireland. The formats of the volumes in the series vary with the thematic designs of individual editors, and with the amount and nature of existing reviews—criticism augmented, where appropriate, by original essays by recognized authorities. It is hoped that each volume will be unique in developing a new overall perspective on its particular subject.

Mary Ellis Gibson's Browning collection is primarily concerned with the variety of cultural approaches to Browning by the contemporary critical community. Her introduction addresses both Browning's contemporaries and our own on the central, if unspoken, question of why Browning should be read at all. Both Gibson's introduction and the essays stress the interaction of readers with Browning's poetry, on such questions as Browning's varying appeals to egalitarian popular audiences and to intellectuals challenged by his later obscurity. Putting the critical assessment of Browning into historical perspective, Gibson then offers us a selection of the most recent criticism.

ZACK BOWEN
University of Miami

Publisher's Note

♦

Producing a volume that contains both newly commissioned and reprinted material presents the publisher with the challenge of balancing the desire to achieve stylistic consistency with the need to preserve the integrity of works first published elsewhere. In the Critical Essays series, essays commissioned especially for a particular volume are edited to be consistent with G. K. Hall's house style; reprinted essays appear in the style in which they were first published, with only typographical errors corrected. Consequently, shifts in style from one essay to another are the result of our efforts to be faithful to each text as it was originally published.

Introduction

Mary Ellis Gibson

Robert Browning's poetry has the unusual quality of anticipating the intellectual problems of its readers. Critics have often remarked on the way Browning's *Sordello* in all its difficulties reflects upon itself and directs the terms of its reading. This is true not only in Sordello's advocacy of poet and reader cooperating to understand a "brother's speech," but even in the poem's commentary on the social uses of art.

In Book 3 of *Sordello* the poet in propria persona reflects upon his characters, contrasting the man of action Salinguerra with the poet Sordello, who by this point seems reduced to a life only of contemplation:

>Not so unwisely does the crowd dispense
>On Salinguerras praise in preference
>To the Sordellos: men of action, these!
>Who, seeing just as little as you please,
>Yet turn that little to account,—engage
>With, do not gaze at,—carry on, a stage,
>The work o' the world, not merely make report
>The work existed ere their day! In short,
>When at some future no-time a brave band
>Sees, using what it sees, then shake my hand
>In heaven, my brother! Meanwhile where's the hurt
>Of keeping the Makers-see on the alert,[1]

The poet imagines a time when action and art might be perfectly congruent, but this, he acknowledges with bitter irony, is some "future no-time." Meanwhile, he solaces himself with a Maker-see "on alert" and certain to meet with no very kind reception.

Contemporary critics are still answering the questions the poet raises in *Sordello*: What is the social significance of art in any particular time? Is a poet's vision central or marginal to his or her culture? What are the responses and the responsibilities of readers?

Many of the essays collected here address these questions directly. In this emphasis and in their approaches to questions of theory, these essays represent the significant changes in literary studies during the past ten or fifteen years. Because of the fruitful dialogue among the critics whose work is represented here and because many of these critics have reconsidered their own earlier positions, I have limited my selection to essays written or published between 1980 and 1990, and I have arranged them in a thematic rather than chronological order. In this way the collection offers an integrated survey of new directions in the criticism of Browning's poetry and of Victorian culture.

Though I have tried to choose essays that discuss a broad range of texts in the enormous Browning canon, to represent criticism on the whole of Browning's work is beyond the scope of a single volume. The more important emphasis here is on essays that represent new ways of understanding the relationships among genre, reading practices, and culture. I have searched for a mix of essays that focus on theoretical issues and those that engage in detail the historical particularities of Browning's art. The goal of this collection is to represent Browning studies as at once a process of theoretical reflection and a project of cultural criticism.

The poet and poetry that emerge from this examination are claimed by several of the essayists here to have anticipated concerns with language, representation, gender, and ideology that are central to much criticism since the advent of poststructuralism. Browning is seen at once as eminently Victorian and as eminently interesting to his postmodern successors. These essays provide, consequently, an appropriate context for considering what the shape of cultural studies might become and how such an endeavor might make use of previous work on Browning's poetry.

Criticism in Context: Browning's Victorian and Contemporary Audiences

John Maynard hypothesizes in his essay here that the Browning Societies themselves may well have been an agent of modern critical practice, of close reading and consideration of poetry that eventually became institutionalized in the practice and pedagogy of the New Criticism. If reading, criticism, and pedagogy are indeed so intimately connected, it may be useful to speculate further on the present cultural meanings of Browning's poetry and of the terms in which it is discussed or not discussed, read or left unread.

Even as we celebrate the persistence of Browning's poetry, however, we might usefully remember that Elizabeth Barrett Browning, despite the fluctuations in her critical reputation, still outdistances her spouse in general popularity. Thanks to the continued appeal of *Sonnets from the Portuguese*, Barrett Browning's poetry is a fixture even on the shelves of chain bookstores. It may scarcely seem necessary to question the meaning of this popularity. A more sobering experience awaits the undergraduate teacher who has been well schooled in the delights of ambiguity and paradox or the dilemmas of dissolving selves and authors and who finds students more immediately responsive to Barrett Browning's autobiographical poetry than to her husband's indirections. The practices of more or less ordinary readers reading, say, "My Last Duchess" and Barrett Browning's "Bertha in the Lane" provide an interesting context for theoretical speculation on how to approach Victorian poets or on why we should.

As Robert Browning's poems are taught in new contexts—as his work is read in the context of postmodern culture and communication conglomerates and as the student readers of Browning, at least at the postsecondary level, are predominantly female—the most useful and pressing critical questions necessarily change. So do the possibilities of reading. Recent changes in reading and publishing have made it increasingly difficult to find accessible classroom copies of either Robert's or Elizabeth's long poems; what one can ask about either poet in the classroom is shaped by the persistent "out of stock" or "out of print" status in the United States of both *Aurora Leigh* and *The Ring and the Book*.

There are then various constraints on reading Browning's poetry, but perhaps because of the questions arising from new social contexts of reading, scholarship on Browning is flourishing. As critics more self-consciously ask questions about literary canons and the cultural meanings of art, they are confronting anew the question of why read Robert Browning at all. While no critic whose work appears here addresses this question in the bald way I have put it, various answers may be deduced from their critical approaches and from the history of the reception of Browning's work.

From the beginning, Browning himself and the criticism of Browning raised the question of whether poetry was marginal to its culture. The split between popular and elite reading cultures was taking its modern shape in the very period of Browning's career.

Reading Browning—and reading nineteenth-century reactions to Browning—can give us a measure against which to situate and judge our own cultural productions. The case of Browning in the Victorian period is a particularly good one, because his poetry was—in the limited arena of argument over poetics—quite controversial. Browning's poetry served as something of a litmus test of a Victorian critic's taste and standards, and it created an arena for debate in which critics argued, directly or indirectly, about the nature of the audience for poetry. In the view of many critics, poetry, ideally, could become part of a new (but ostensibly old) ideological glue, binding together the disparate classes, genders, and interests of Victorian society. But Browning's poetry manifestly provided no such glue.

As a poet Browning worked uneasily amid these expectations and their contrary, a notion of poetry as the spiritual prerogative of select souls. Browning's poetry itself raises the question of readers and reading on numerous occasions (most elaborately in *The Ring and the Book* where we are admonished to devolve our own meanings from multiple texts). David Latané in his monograph *Browning's Sordello* has shown how the problem of reading affected Browning's early work, especially what many readers took to be the willful obscurity of *Sordello*. As Latané, Lee Erickson, Christine Froula, and John Woolford have shown, Browning demanded in essence that his readers complete his poems through their active participation.[2]

Victorian readers and reviewers often resisted this imperative, and their resistance was interpreted in part as Browning's eccentric obscurity and in part as the situation of an elite poet before a split audience. By any number of reviewers this audience was felt to be, though not often explicitly acknowledged to be, divided by differences of education, gender, class, and even nationalist prejudice. Contemporary students of Browning could most conveniently begin thinking about these difficulties by reading the selections from Victorian criticism included in *Browning: The Critical Heritage*.[3] The reviewers of Browning's *Men and Women* give particularly interesting evidence of this cultural construction of the meanings of poetic obscurity at mid-century, and the reviews, on the whole, were particularly disturbing for Browning, who in his collection of 1855 was, if not actively courting public approbation, at least expecting a more positive response.

The *Athenaeum* constructed its discussion of Browning's obscurity along lines that indicate the marginality of the "modern" Victorian poet—"who can understand this stuff or wants to?" is the subtext of the reviewer's complaints. The reviewer complains that modern poets rely too much on the sympathy of the reader. Indeed, he exclaims, "a large proportion of modern verse is not verse at all, by reason of its licence [sic] and assumption. The artists show themselves, by their exigencies, to be less masterly than the artists of old, who had their fullest praise from the few, but their full praise also from the many. . . . Our poets now speak in an unknown tongue,—wear whatever unpoetic garniture it pleases their conceit or their idleness to snatch up; and the end too often is, pain to those who love them best. . . . and to the vast world, whom they might assist, they bring only a mystery and receive nothing but wonder and scorn."[4] This review of course nostalgically posits a time when poets were readable and the "vast world" and the "few" were united in their tastes. Now even the few are asked to tolerate too much, and the many (novel readers perhaps?) have forsaken poetry almost altogether.

The general complaint was shared by the reviewer for the *Saturday Review* who argued that the "demon" of bad taste "now seems to hold in absolute possession the fashionable masters of our ideal literature." Unlike many reviewers who compared Browning unfavorably with Tennyson, the

Saturday Review commentator lumped the two poets together as modern examples of misguided artists, and he compared Browning's experiment on the "public patience" to Tennyson's *Maud* and to the Spasmodics.[5] In the view of the Victorian critics who linked Browning to the Spasmodics, Browning was like other modern poets contemptuous of his audience and their due.

If some Victorian reviewers saw themselves living in an age when poetry had become marginal through the willful obscurity of the poets themselves, others attributed this situation to the Victorian reader. Those who defended Browning often did so by chiding readers, as George Eliot did when she declared that Browning makes us "feel that what we took for obscurity in him was superficiality in ourselves."[6] W. B. Donne, reviewing Browning's volume of selections in 1863, was prepared to chide not Browning but the "indolent and luxurious readers of the nineteenth century." He compared Browning favorably to Longfellow, whom he called a "thoroughly accomplished versifier and something more." Mr. Longfellow, Donne said, has "taken the young ladies of England by storm. Now, in our judgment . . . Mr. Browning contains within himself a mass of solid metal which might be beaten thin into a couple of Longfellows at least."[7] Young ladies—and the middle-class but not classically educated reader by extension—can hardly be expected to appreciate the "lightness" with which, the reviewer says, Mr. Browning dances in his "self-imposed fetters" of style.

In a favorable review, David Masson simply dismissed the notion that mass appeal (or general middle-class appeal) should be a central criterion of judging a poet's success: "That . . . much of Mr. Browning's poetry is and must always remain 'caviare to the general' must of course be admitted; but we have yet to learn that a man may not be a great poet, and yet be 'caviare to the general.' It may be that the greatest poets of all are those whose genius enables them to thrill the most universal human emotions, and so to command the largest constituencies; but surely, if the select and most cultured minds of a time can have a poet all to themselves, or nearly so, handling the questions which they handle, and leading them out in new tracks which have for them all the interest of blended curiosity and familiarity, that is also a great gain to the community."[8]

Divisions of taste and selections of reading depend not only on gender, class, and education (Browning's style, so unappealing to "young lady" readers of Longfellow, is often remarked to be masculine), but on national propensity. And this category may be said to crosscut the other three. Browning's reviewers brought to bear the category of nationality or national taste to defend or to dismiss his poetry. Browning's defenders characterized what most took to be his singular un-Englishness as a mark of his broad learning and of his readers' provinciality; Browning's critics attributed it to a lack of consideration for the tastes of the age. David Masson recounted the feeling, probably among the London intelligentsia, that Browning himself and his sympathies "rarely had to do with those circles of our British society where authors most do congregate."[9] Masson of course takes this as no real diminution of the poet's powers—on the contrary. Another essayist, E. P. Hood praised Browning in *The Eclectic and Congregational Review* for not succumbing to the "cant of Church-of-Englandism" and for the virtues of his independence from the "sneers of fine gentlemen-critics." But Hood explained Browning's lack of a fame commensurate with his abilities in what may be an oblique reference to Tennyson's greater Englishness. Neither Elizabeth Barrett nor Robert Browning was sufficiently admired, Hood said, because "England and English scenes and English life never seem to enter into the texture either of their genius, their sympathies, or their writings. . . . He writes for men—for men and women—but not for Englishmen. He unconditions himself from those circumstances which would attract English readers, lives in other ages, and other countries, and with a power we believe to be felicitously transparent and clear he seems to determine on making himself obscure . . . A second thought shows us that this is indeed very natural to his peculiar genius."[10] Like other Victorian critics, Hood judged Browning's work partly in terms of his contribution to the Victorian sense of national identity.

Hood's essay and other less sympathetic ones allow us to see in Victorian culture the complex forces underlying the creation of canons. Invoking various divisions of audience—popular versus elite, male versus female, classically educated versus poorly educated, the self-consciously intellectual versus the unintellectual, the nationalist versus the cosmopolitan—invoking these differences Browning's Victorian critics did not of course create a reading audience that fit neatly into these categories; this was surely impossible as the categories themselves were relatively incongruent. Certainly many a woman or a self-educated man admired Browning's poetry and read it with pleasure. And certainly the critics of Browning's obscurity did not prevent his canonization as a major Victorian poet; indeed against their wills they contributed to his fame. Nonetheless, the critical discourse surrounding Browning's art was conducted in terms that have significantly shaped contemporary understandings of poetry's place. Particularly clear in these Victorian polemics is a nostalgia for a previous age when, it was implied, artists spoke clearly to an undivided and admiring public.

These observations about Browning's reception are investigated from another point of view in this volume by Loy Martin, who discusses the cultural demands of Browning's poetic language. In his essay, published as a chapter in *Browning's Dramatic Monologues and the Post-Romantic Subject*, Martin accounts for Browning's uses of specialized vocabulary in the monologues in terms of the specialized competing elites of the Victorian middle and upper classes. In Browning's monologues, Martin argues, we find distinct vocabularies of "interest groups, of aristocracies, of scientific and aesthetic elites, of distant cultures, both primitive and exotic, of the educated in rhetoric or in logical processes." What appears in the poems, then, is a "dialectic of discourses" where poetic discourse is opposed to other specialized discourses, where specialized discourses are opposed to popular or colloquial Victorian speech, and where any speaker's language can become profoundly idiosyncratic. Finally, Martin concludes, this multiplication of languages and the fragmentation of the subject raise "complex and difficult questions about the nature of communication."

What Martin calls dialogical or dialectical language, Victorian reviewers called obscurity. My brief story of Browning's audience, and its fragmentation, focuses on the other side of the communicative process, on the side of the multiple recipients of Browning's poetic language. What Martin so ably describes in his essay as the specialization of languages in Victorian culture can also be understood as the fragmentation of audiences.

This double analysis of communication and Browning's poetry is a testimony to the importance of reading Browning's poetry in the late twentieth century, where specialized discourses have become ever more powerful and the fragmentation of reading audiences ever more acute. We may see in the not-too-distant mirror of Victorian Britain parables for contemporary art and culture. At the same time, this historical focus brings home to the critic the way contemporary critical discourse, specialized as it is, perpetuates relations of power. The opposite possibility, an ideal of a transparent mutual discourse in a unified culture, has its own problems. Like Browning and his Victorian readers, contemporary readers of Browning are caught, for good or ill, in a situation where nostalgia for unified language or culture principally serves established power relations and has become a form of discourse used by the powerful for their power's self-perpetuation. The scene of Browning's reception enables us to take the measure of our own reading practices and possibilities.

Yet the importance of Browning's reception as a significant instance inviting comparison to contemporary cultural relations provides but an initial reason for reading Browning at this point in our cultural history. Various critics represented here have found further motivations, most recently in the discussion of Browning and various political and cultural forms—national politics, sexual politics, the cultural uses of the primitive, the place of Browning's liberalism in the connections between art and economics. Robert Viscusi's essay " 'The Englishman in Italy': Free Trade as a Principle of Aesthetics" directly engages the problems of reading Browning with explicit attention to politics. There is little to be gained, Viscusi implies, by critics functioning as thought police to bring writers to judgment at the bar of history. Viscusi suggests in his wittily written essay that we can resist the charms of "attack against a dead man for the crime of belonging fully to his own moment."

Yet the questions of poetic tradition and aesthetic judgment that Viscusi raises, based as they are in Browning's politics, allow us to interrogate what it might mean to belong as fully, if ambivalently, to our own moment as Browning belonged to his. To take an analogy, reading Browning has become for a number of his critics like a particularly disturbing form of historical tourism. We visit the foreign country, admire it and deplore it, debate or describe its faults—its sexism, its racism, its too easy answers to questions that perplex us—and we are diffident about the virtues of our own country, willing to see its faults as well. Then the moment comes when we realize that we expect those we meet to speak our own language better than we speak theirs. My analogy suggests that an element of poststructuralist irony and political darkness be added to any more brightly lit hermeneutic model of reading Browning. We have no transparencies of sender and receiver, poet and audience, either in the Victorian age or in our own. If there is a fusion of horizons between dead poet and modern reader, it comes without moral and historical guarantees.

But if the political reading of Browning in contemporary America is something like guilty tourism, reading Browning now, as in Victorian Britain, also has its pleasures. Surely this is the most lasting reason for the continuing influence of Browning on poets writing in English, for the profusion of Browning studies, and for Browning's persistent appeal even to students who have a phobia about poetry. Though actually counting Browning's late twentieth-century readers would be a most difficult sociological project, it would be fair to say, in the United States at least, that the majority of those who read Browning are students and the scholars who assign them Browning's poetry. Any good teaching and even the most recondite scholarship begin with the interest of the casual reader.

Browning's poetry still interests because it evokes a response to character, to the representation of hypocrisy, domination, delight, self-delusion we so often recognize in others if not in ourselves. A fascination for character, and its construction, is not lost on contemporary critics, even those resistant to the illusions of identity or of individual self-sufficiency in literature or life. This fascination for character—whole or insistently dissolving—is apparent in the frequency with which recent theoretical discussions of form and ideology return to what have long been thought the great monologues. The scholarly reader, however she or he can expose the illusions of character or stable meaning, does not escape the guilty pleasures of vicariously experiencing what Browning perhaps disingenuously called "so many utterances of so many imaginary persons, not mine."[11]

Recent Criticism of Browning's Poetry

The essays collected here represent some, though by no means all, of the excellent criticism on Robert Browning published during the last ten years. With one exception, I have chosen essays that have not been published in the numerous recent books on Browning. That exception is Loy Martin's essay, which I have included here not only for its intrinsic importance but because Martin has not published further work on Browning. The essays by Adrienne Munich and Antony Harrison are taken from their broadly defined books on Victorian art and culture. Munich's *Andromeda's Chains* examines Browning's poetry as part of a much broader consideration of art, iconography, and gender in Victorian culture. Harrison's essay, " 'Cleon' and Its Contexts," is taken from his study of intertextual connections among Victorian poets and between these poets and their predecessors. The remainder of the essays were first published in critical journals or collections of essays, excepting those by Maynard, which first appeared in Italy, and Latané, published here for the first time.

The essays in this collection both respect and depart from the work of previous scholars. Though it was commonplace in the 1960s and 1970s to lament the paucity of good criticism on Browning, and indeed on much Victorian poetry, the situation has changed for the better. Nonetheless, a careful reading of these essays suggests just how important earlier work has been for scholars currently publishing on Browning.

Thirty years after its publication, Robert Langbaum's *The Poetry of Experience* remains crucial for discussion of the dramatic monologue.[12] Langbaum's theory of reading has had a lasting influence and has provided a standard by which later critics measure their work, however different it may be. First published in 1957, Langbaum's book offered a convincing account of how one reads a monologue, and this focus on the process and nature of reading has had much to do with his study's lasting importance. Langbaum's notion that we approach the monologues through a combination of sympathy and judgment has provided an important point of departure for succeeding critics, who may criticize unitary notions of character or of readers, who may destabilize the texts more than Langbaum ever does, but who share his concern with the poem and its reading as process. Langbaum, too, has been influential in shaping our understanding of Browning's importance for modernism both in *The Poetry of Experience* and in his essay "Browning and the Question of Myth," published in *The Modern Spirit* (New York: Oxford University Press, 1970).

Along with Langbaum's work, especially important in the 1960s were Park Honan's *Browning's Characters* (1961), W. David Shaw's *The Dialectical Temper: The Rhetorical Art of Robert Browning* (1968), James Loucks and Richard Altick's *Browning's Roman Murder Story* (1968), J. Hillis Miller's *The Disappearance of God: Five Nineteenth-Century Writers* (1963), and Robert Preyer's essay "Two Styles in the Verse of Robert Browning" (1965).[13] The work of Honan, Shaw, and Loucks and Altick provided important readings of many of Browning's major poems. Honan's focus on the complexities of Browning's characters still has important implications. While most contemporary critics would probably dissent from Shaw's argument that Browning's later work is a progression toward the central truth of a pure white light in *The Ring and the Book* and is "free from the limitations of perspective that mar his early poetry," many contemporary studies of Browning start from Shaw's notion that Browning's poetry is significantly a rhetorical art, at once dialectical and ironic. With the more limited focus of *The Ring and the Book* Loucks and Altick offered historical and critical notions about the poem that subsequent critics have had to take into account.

Preyer's and Miller's studies, though quite different in focus, suggest paths into the Robert Browning who has been created in the critical discourse of the last fifteen years. Both critics in essence destabilize any unitary vision of the poems, Preyer by identifying competing styles as characteristic of Browning's art and Miller by stressing Browning's decentered multitudinousness in poetic practice and in such theology as he could manage.

This critical matrix was further complicated in the 1970s as critics and biographers examined relatively neglected aspects of Browning's life and art. Particularly notable were two biographies, William Irvine and Park Honan's *The Book, the Ring, and the Poet* (1974), which still remains the best single biography of the poet, and John Maynard's *Browning's Youth* (1977), which provided valuable new information on and interpretation of the poet's early years.[14]

Among a number of essays and books of note, three are particularly important for examining relatively neglected texts and questions. The fullest consideration to date of Browning's complex relationship to the Higher Criticism of the Bible came in Elinor Shaffer's fascinating essay on "A Death in the Desert."[15] Eleanor Cook's *Browning's Lyrics* is still the only book to focus exclusively on Browning's lyric poems, and it offers subtle commentary on Browning's techniques and on a great many of his best lyrics. Browning's later poetry was surveyed by Clyde Ryals, who cautioned readers against simply treading again the familiar paths of the Browning canon. Ryals argued persuasively that Browning's later poetry complicates any facile pronouncement based on his work up to and including *The Ring and the Book*. The grotesqueness of these late poems, Ryals showed, functioned as what Browning called in "Parleying with Christopher Smart" "Art's response / To earth's despair."[16] In concluding his study, Ryals developed the starting point for his own future work and for the criticism of the next decade: "We should recognize in the contrivances of [Browning's] art—his quirkish diction, his manner of proceeding by fits and starts, his arbitrary shifts of direction—a way of signaling us that art is play and only a feigned image of things, that speech is a precious gift which nevertheless belies the ineffable."[17] Ryals raised issues of art, of the play of meaning, and of artifice which became significant concerns of Browning criticism in the 1980s.

The centenary of Browning's death in 1989 alone provided the occasion for publication of much excellent work, most notably a special double issue of the journal *Victorian Poetry* (volume 27, numbers 3–4). There were, in addition, special conferences and sessions at professional meetings both in the United States and in England and a special issue of the journal of the Australian Modern Language Association. These activities closed out a period particularly rich in Browning studies, a period in which the various critical developments succeeding the New Criticism made themselves felt in very interesting ways. In the last decade virtually every year has brought the publication of one or more important books on Browning, not to mention numerous interesting articles. Although or because critics have been taking notable risks in exploring often complex theses, the quality of recent publications in general has been quite high. I can mention here only a small number of recent publications on Browning, a number of them books by the authors in this volume.

The decade in criticism was inaugurated by Herbert F. Tucker's *Browning's Beginnings*, the first major study of Browning's poetry with an avowedly poststructuralist approach. Tucker's brilliant discussions of *Sordello* and of "Cleon," among other poems, present us with texts always in process, always deferring closure. Meaning is always processual, and the pure light of truth or even the stability of a meaning temporally frozen and immutable is unavailable. When Browning's dramatic speakers most long for closure, time most decidedly betrays them; Cleon is the perfect example. His monologue becomes necessarily "a glittering, consistently untrustworthy fabric of reductive self-interpretations."[18]

Like Tucker, other critics in the eighties emphasized the unstable nature of Browning's texts. E. Warwick Slinn, in 1982, focused on the very fabric of self-referentiality, of artifice, of which Cleon is only too conscious. Slinn used this approach to criticize a too easy assumption of the unitary nature of identity or of a unitary experience unambiguously connected to reality.[19] Lee Erickson, in *Robert Browning: His Poetry and His Audiences*, also emphasized process, but for him Browning's process of identifying, responding to, and reconceiving audiences was most important. Erickson's discussion of Browning's ambivalence toward popularity is particularly significant, and his treatment of the relationship between Robert Browning and Elizabeth Barrett took seriously Barrett Browning's influence on her husband. In Erickson's presentation, Browning's definition of poetry and of audience was always under revision. Clyde Ryals further contributed to the discussion of Browning and process. In focusing on Browning's early poetry he argued for Browning as practicing a kind of Romantic irony in which "everything is simultaneously itself and something other."[20] Though Ryals's romantic irony is unstable, he refrains from pushing Browning into a poststructuralist abyss; in sympathy with Browning's endless aspiration, Ryals invokes a never-ending "transcendental process" that from a poststructuralist view must be placed always under suspicion.

In the second half of the decade, scholarship on Browning has sought to unite these arguments about process, irony, meaning, and form to historical and political questions. I have already mentioned Loy Martin's *Browning's Dramatic Monologues and the Post-Romantic Subject*, which brings together these two strands of critical analysis. David Latané's monograph on *Sordello* examines the notions of an interaction between reader and poem as they developed in the particular historical context of the 1830s. My own book *History and the Prism of Art: Browning's Poetic Experiments* was the first extended study of Browning's understanding of history in the cultural contexts of Victorian and modern notions about historicity. I trace the connections between Browning's contextualist view of history and his poet-personae, his synchronous narratives, his historical ironies and the "unpoetic" language that made Victorian readers wince.[21]

Historical considerations provide a background rather than a central concern in two other studies of the decade that might be mentioned. John Woolford's tracing of Browning's relationship to his audience contributed to our knowledge of that problematic area by focusing on the way Browning revised his poetics in response to his reception; even more useful than particular readings of poems is Woolford's argument that Browning deliberately ordered his shorter poems by the time of *Men and Women* in a form he calls the "structured collection." Woolford's observations might be usefully combined with Eleanor Cook's comments on Browning's practice of pairing poems.

Oddly the decade has brought no full-scale feminist reassessment of Browning's poetry, perhaps because such analysis is so daunting or so elusive. In addition to the essays published here, particularly notable was Ann Brady's argument for Browning's feminism in her book *Pompilia: A Feminist Reading of Browning's "The Ring and the Book."* Nina Auerbach took a different and more critical view of the poet's presentation of women and his relationship to Elizabeth Barrett in her essay "Robert Browning's Last Word."[22]

In sum the 1980s saw a tremendous outpouring of critical scholarship on Browning. And this work, good as it is, has been equaled in importance by work in textual and biographical scholarship. Recent years have brought publication of new and splendidly annotated editions of Browning's poetry, of a careful reconstruction of the Brownings' collections of books and art, and—at last—the first volumes of the complete edition of Robert and Elizabeth Barrett Brownings' letters. Studies of Robert Browning have also benefited directly and indirectly by recent publication of several important critical works on Elizabeth Barrett Browning and on the relationship between the two poets.[23] Browning studies, then, are richer for historical and textual work, for the introduction of new theoretical dimensions to old debates, and for recent efforts to understand Browning's poetry in the social and cultural contexts of its time.

The essays in this collection represent the effort in the last decade to specify relationships among genre, reading, and historical circumstances.

The first five essays here are particularly concerned with genre and form and with the difficult task of accounting for poetic forms culturally and theoretically. They emphasize, not surprisingly, the dramatic monologue. In these five essays, critics take issue not only with each other but with their own earlier positions. Herbert Tucker's essay discusses the genesis of the monologue form and demonstrates how the form treads the fine line between character and text. Just as Tucker is in some measure revising his earlier presentation of textuality in Browning, so Ralph Rader more explicitly revises his earlier theory of poetic forms and gives it current critical point: he defends the stabilities of reading that are entailed in formal differences. Warwick Slinn's essay in some ways counters Rader's, and yet like Tucker, Slinn takes a middle course between a single-minded emphasis on textuality and self-referentiality and a naive notion of reading as empathy. John Maynard's essay posits what he, too modestly, calls a "poor man's reader response" to account for the ways we read ourselves as readers when we encounter a dramatic monologue. Form and textuality, as I have suggested, also provide central concerns of Loy Martin's essay, even as he relates the form of the monologue to Victorian ideology.

The remaining essays in this volume are less concerned with the monologue form and with effects of poststructuralist criticism on our ways of reading monologues; they focus more directly on Browning's poetry in its cultural context even as they also interrogate form and language. The essays here by U. C. Knoepflmacher and Adrienne Munich raise questions about Browning's feminism or antifeminism as it is refracted through his female characters, through Victorian iconography, and through his relationship, personal and poetic, to his wife. Christine Froula and Antony Harrison are concerned with Browning's place in literary history, his complex relationships to Arnold and the Spasmodics, and his importance for Ezra Pound's poetics. David Riede opens to new consideration Browning's often neglected *Pippa Passes* by suggesting that the experimental nature of the poem is intimately connected to Browning's quarrel with authoritarian politics. Dorothy Mermin takes us deeply into Browning's later poems by examining the fascination for and cultural meanings of the primitive in the second half of the nineteenth century. The final two essays by David Latané and Robert Viscusi are both more theoretically motivated and somewhat more polemical than Mermin's work. Latané's avowedly new historicist essay shows how Browning's *Strafford* was an event in the political history of 1837; Latané demonstrates that the play is deeply engaged with the significant terms of early Victorian political debate. Viscusi's essay, similarly, draws attention to the overlooked nationalist and political dimensions of Browning's poetry. The net effect of these essays is to show us how ostensibly historical poems are intimately enmeshed in Victorian circumstances and how ostensibly apolitical poems have political implications.

Cultural Criticism and the Classroom

Many of the essays in this volume are part of the recent trend in Browning studies toward a cultural criticism broadly engaged with questions of art and politics. An equally telling indication of this trend is the restructuring in the 1990s of *Browning Institute Studies* into a new journal, *Victorian Literature and Culture*. Despite these developments, teaching Browning's poetry in the context of cultural studies remains a challenging and not altogether straightforward task. It is a far cry from an examination of the social commentary of, say, Tennyson's *Maud* or *The Princess* to an examination of Browning's poetry in the context of crucial Victorian texts and issues. Browning's poems obviously invite speculation on the meaning of and possibility of meaning, the labyrinths of epistemology, the nature of dissolving selves, the paths of historical irony. To trace Browning's filiation to the complex historical, ideological, and material circumstances of Victorian society, however, is difficult indeed, in part because of Browning's own resistance to presenting himself in his poems as a representative man, a representative Englishman.

There is a certain paradox here. Browning did comment in his poetry without reluctance on various religious and theological matters (in "Rabbi Ben Ezra," for example). But aside from the offhand comment or the occasional poem ("Why I am a Liberal" or "The Lost Leader") one finds little poetry explicitly evoking current political and social concerns. There was no laureateship in hand or seriously in prospect to evoke such effusions as Tennyson's militaristic poems, and Browning, for complex reasons of literary, political, and religious affiliation, never self-consciously set out, as Arnold did, to cast himself in a representative role. To trace out the complex relationships of Browning's poetry to its culture, then, means to follow Browning's own rather circuitous paths. The paradox of this effort arises in the truth that Browning, in refusing the role of representative commentator, was yet necessarily enmeshed in the presuppositions and ideological contests of his own culture. As we have seen in the instance of Browning's Victorian reception, to choose not to be clear, transparent, representative is still to choose within the possibilities of one's time and, thus, is also to have choices made for one. This tension between the ineluctable individuality of Browning's art and the power of various Victorian discourses to set the terms of that art makes Browning's poetry an interesting litmus test for the possibilities of cultural criticism.

Many of the essays collected here provide points of departure for such study. They suggest ways we might make better and more extensive use of Victorian writing in areas such as science, politics or law. Political controversy, the discourse of English nationalism, the invention of anthropology and elaboration of the primitive—all of these provide possible connections. But, as these essays have indicated, Browning's poetic practices, and particularly his focus on historical or foreign subjects, means that we must almost always consider Browning's poems as a history of the Victorian present at one remove, and a remove more complex than Tennyson's medievalizing strategies in *The Princess* and *The Idylls*. This remove, if we can be so lucky, will require a cultural criticism as canny as Browning's own ability to elude our grasp.

What shapes might further forays in cultural criticism take? I would like to conclude by briefly sketching examples of three possibilities. The first possibility invites us to take more seriously those poems that obviously do have a political point. We might especially keep in mind the complex dimensions of nationalism that Robert Viscusi has sketched and that we see operating in the discourse about Browning's obscurity. It would be fascinating, for example, to reread "Prince Hohenstiel-Schwangau" against Robert and Elizabeth's arguments over Napoleon III and against Marx's *Eighteenth Brumaire of Louis Bonaparte*. Such a comparison might provide a basis for further investigation of irony in nineteenth-century poetry and historiography (in Pater or Hardy, Burckhardt or Nietzsche). It could lead further to a consideration of how continental revolutions were treated in the popular English press, to a reading of the Arnoldian response to upheaval in *Culture and Anarchy*, and to more detailed consideration of British political context of the poem. At the same time, the initial discussion of an overtly political poem like "Prince Hohenstiel-Schwangau" could suggest further consideration of nationalism and political authority as it is treated in Browning's poetry.

A second possible direction for cultural criticism would be an investigation of gender, genre, and audience as they are connected in Browning's poetry and in Victorian culture. Feminist criticism of Browning is now more complex than the assessment of Browning's female characters as a test of his feminism or lack thereof. As criticism pushes further, it would be interesting to ask how female readers responded to Browning's poetry and whether or not one sees any distinctive pattern of difference based on gender. More complex still is Browning's relationship to the novel and to the gendering of literary pursuits and pleasures in Victorian Britain. These issues can in turn be linked to other cultural issues—the gendering of "serious" poetry or, as Adrienne Munich suggests, the presentation of the body in Victorian culture. For instance in a recent essay, "The Criminal Body in Victorian Britain: The Case of *The Ring and the Book*," I have argued that the poor law amendment act, various penal reforms, the rise of the sensation novel in the 1860s, and the presentation of "morbid anatomy" in Browning's long poem are intimately connected: as Guido offers to anatomize Pompilia's ring-finger joint by joint, issues regarding gender, reading, and the body become thoroughly intertwined.[24]

Yet a third possibility for examining Browning's connections to his culture could be approached through a pedagogy that organizes its questions on the model of concentric circles. One might begin with a poem whose political and social implications are not at all obvious and move out from this text toward questions of broader cultural relations. I have for years enjoyed in a beginning literature survey contrasting Tennyson's and Browning's versification by analyzing short lyrics. If we contrasted "The Splendor Falls on Castle Walls" from *The Princess* with "Home Thoughts from Abroad," we could begin with a discussion of versification, of the sense of music in Tennyson's and Browning's poetry, and of Browning's complex metric, which runs two predominant metrical patterns in a kind of counterpoint. These poems easily invite such comparison and seem to deflect cultural and social questions because both are self-reflexive to an extraordinary degree. "Home Thoughts" especially is a rare attempt at imitative form. The two strophe poem recapitulates in its form the music of the "wise thrush" who "sings each song twice over." The poem has a certain self-circling, if not self-congratulatory aspect, as the reader is assured the thrush redoubles his song "Lest you think he never could recapture / The first fine careless rapture!" Tennyson's lyric too is musically complex; it attempts to recreate the acoustic quality of a hunting horn and its echoes. Yet when these poems are most resistant to an interpretation that draws directly on their cultural contexts, they may paradoxically be most revealing. One could easily reread "Home Thoughts" from the perspective of Robert Viscusi's comments on the cultural meanings of Italy and England for Browning and from the perspective of Victorian constructions of the garden and of domesticity; it would be fruitful also to discuss the fine ambivalence of the poem's conclusion in which good English buttercups will be "Far brighter than this gaudy melon-flower!" Similarly, Tennyson's lyric, a tour de force of musical experiment, can lend itself to broader speculations, beginning with its placement in *The Princess*, moving on to its evocation of a nostalgia for ancient poetry and custom, and finally to its evocation of Irish castles at the end of the decade of the hungry forties. Versification, then, could provide in this context a point of return for broader social and cultural questions.

The essays in this collection provide many such moments, revealing to us the cultural meanings of Browning's writing and of our own reading. At the same time they simply tell us more about Victorian culture and art than we knew before. As we pass from the centenary of Browning's death toward the bicentenary of his birth, it is hard to foretell the course of criticism or even the organization of English studies. It is safe to imagine that even if we do modify significantly our disciplinary boundaries and create a flexible and yet meticulous new cultural criticism, Browning's poetry will continue to pose for its readers both a pleasure and a challenge.

Notes

1. Robert Browning, *Sordello, Robert Browning: The Poems*, edited by John Pettigrew and Thomas A. Collins (New Haven: Yale University Press, 1981) 1: 222, lines 917–28. All further references to Browning's poetry are to this edition. For their help and suggestions, in this project I thank Herbert F. Tucker and Adrienne Munich.
2. David Latané, *Browning's* Sordello *and the Aesthetics of Difficulty*, English Literary Studies Monograph Series, no. 40 (Vancouver, Canada: University of Victoria, 1987); Lee Erickson, *Robert Browning: His Poetry and His Audiences* (Ithaca, New York: Cornell University Press, 1984); John Woolford, *Browning the Revisionary* (New York: St. Martin's Press, 1988). See also Christine Froula's essay in this volume.
3. Boyd Litzinger and Donald Smalley, eds. *Browning: The Critical Heritage* (New York: Barnes and Noble, 1970).
4. Unsigned review of *Men and Women*, *Athenaeum*, 17 November 1855, quoted in Litzinger and Smalley, 155–56.
5. Unsigned review of *Men and Women*, *Saturday Review*, 24 November 1855, quoted in Litzinger and Smalley, 158. Antony Harrison discusses Browning's relationship to the Spasmodics in the essay reprinted here.
6. George Eliot, review of *Men and Women*, *Westminster Review*, January 1856, quoted in Litzinger and Smalley, 174–75.
7. W. B. Donne, review of *Selections from the Poetical Works of Robert Browning*, *Saturday Review*, 7 February 1863, quoted in Litzinger and Smalley, 204.
8. David Masson, review of *Men and Women*, *British Quarterly Review*, 23 (1856), quoted in Litzinger and Smalley, 182.
9. Masson, quoted in Litzinger and Smalley, 178.
10. E. P. Hood, "The Poetry of Robert Browning," *Eclectic and Congregational Review*, 6th series, no. 4 (1863), quoted in Litzinger and Smalley, 209–210.
11. Note to *Dramatic Lyrics* (1842), 1: 347.
12. Robert Langbaum, *The Poetry of Experience: The Dramatic Monologue in Modern Literary Tradition* (London: Chatto and Windus, 1957).
13. Park Honan, *Browning's Characters: A Study in Poetic Technique* (New Haven: Yale University Press, 1961); W. David Shaw, *The Dialectical Temper: The Rhetorical Art of Robert Browning* (Ithaca: Cornell University Press, 1968); James Loucks and Richard Altick, *Browning's Roman Murder Story* (Chicago: University of Chicago Press, 1968); J. Hillis Miller, *The Disappearance of God: Five Nineteenth-Century Writers* (Cambridge: Harvard University Press, 1963); Robert Preyer, "Two Styles in the Verse of Robert Browning," *ELH* 32 (1965): 62–84.
14. William Irvine and Park Honan, *The Book, the Ring, and the Poet: A Biography of Robert Browning* (New York: McGraw-Hill, 1974); John Maynard, *Browning's Youth* (Cambridge: Harvard University Press, 1977).
15. Elinor S. Shaffer, *"Kubla Khan" and "The Fall of Jerusalem": The Mythological School in Biblical Criticism and Secular Literature, 1770–1880* (London: Cambridge University Press, 1975).
16. Eleanor Cook, *Browning's Lyrics: An Exploration* (Toronto: University of Toronto Press, 1974); Clyde de L. Ryals, *Browning's Later Poetry, 1871–1889* (Ithaca: Cornell University Press, 1975), 246.
17. Ryals, *Browning's Later Poetry*, 246–47.
18. Herbert F. Tucker, Jr., *Browning's Beginnings: The Art of Disclosure* (Minneapolis: University of Minnesota Press, 1980), 212.
19. E. Warwick Slinn, *Browning and the Fictions of Identity* (Totowa, New Jersey: Barnes and Noble, 1982).

20. Clyde de L. Ryals, *Becoming Browning: The Poems and Plays of Robert Browning, 1833–1846* (Columbus: Ohio State University Press, 1983), p. 4.

21. Mary Ellis Gibson, *History and the Prism of Art: Browning's Poetic Experiments* (Columbus: Ohio State University Press, 1987).

22. Ann Brady, *Pompilia* (Athens: Ohio University Press, 1988); Nina Auerbach, "Robert Browning's Last Word," *Victorian Poetry* 22 (1984): 161–73.

23. For an excellent survey of textual scholarship in the 1980s, see John Maynard, "The Decade's Work in Browning Studies," *Victorian Poetry* 27 (1989): 5–28. On Robert Browning and Elizabeth Barrett, see Daniel Karlin, *The Courtship of Robert Browning and Elizabeth Barrett* (New York: Oxford University Press, 1985); Dorothy Mermin, *Elizabeth Barrett Browning: The Origins of a New Poetry* (Chicago: University of Chicago Press, 1989); Helen Cooper, *Elizabeth Barrett Browning: Woman and Artist* (Chapel Hill: University of North Carolina Press, 1988); Angela Leighton, *Elizabeth Barrett Browning* (Bloomington: Indiana University Press, 1986).

24. Mary Ellis Gibson, "The Criminal Body in Victorian Britain: The Case of *The Ring and the Book*," *Browning Institute Studies* 18 (1990): 73–93.

ESSAYS

Dramatic Monologue and the Overhearing of Lyric

Herbert F. Tucker

> His muse made increment of anything,
> From the high lyric down to the low rational.
> —*Don Juan* III. lxxxv. 5–6

> I would say, quoting Mill, "Oratory is heard, poetry is overheard." And he would answer, his voice full of contempt, that there was always an audience; and yet, in his moments of lofty speech, he himself was alone no matter what the crowd.
> —*The Autobiography of William Butler Yeats*

I

"Eloquence is *heard*, poetry is *overheard*. Eloquence supposes an audience; the peculiarity of poetry appears to us to lie in the poet's utter unconsciousness of a listener. Poetry is feeling confessing itself to itself, in moments of solitude." "Lyric poetry, as it was the earliest kind, is also, if the view we are now taking of poetry be correct, more eminently and peculiarly poetry than any other."[1] Thus wrote John Stuart Mill in 1833, with the wild surmise of a man who had lately nursed himself through a severe depression, thanks to published poetry and its capacity to excite intimate feeling in forms uncontaminated by rhetorical or dramatic posturing. One listener Mill's characteristically analytic eloquence is likely to have found at once was Robert Browning, who moved in London among liberal circles that touched Mill's and who in the same year published his first work, the problematically dramatic *Pauline: A Fragment of a Confession*, to which Mill drafted a response Browning saw in manuscript. Browning's entire career—most notably the generic innovation for which he is widely remembered today, the dramatic monologue—would affirm his resistance to the ideas about poetry contained in Mill's essays. Indeed, as early as *Pauline* Browning was confessing to the

Reprinted from Herbert F. Tucker, "Dramatic Monologue and the Overhearing of Lyric," in *Lyric Poetry: Beyond the New Criticism*, edited by Chaviva Hosek and Patricia Parker. Copyright © 1985 by Cornell University Press. Used by permission of the publisher.

open secret of spontaneous lyricism, but in ways that disowned it. What follows is emphatically the depiction of a bygone state:

> And first I sang as I in dream have seen
> Music wait on a lyrist for some thought,
> Yet singing to herself until it came.
> (ll. 377–79)

In this complex but typical retrospect the poet of *Pauline* figures as an eavesdropper on his own Shelleyan juvenilia, themselves relics of a dream of disengaged and thoughtless youth from which the sadder but wiser poet has on balance done well to awaken. Browning's enfolding of a lyrical interval into a narrative history sets the pattern for the establishment of character throughout his subsequent work, a pattern knowingly at odds with the subjectivist convention that governed the reading of English poetry circa 1830 and to which Mill's essay gave memorable but by no means unique voice.[2]

To the most ambitious and original young poets of the day, Browning and Alfred Tennyson, the sort of lyricism Mill admired must have seemed "overheard" in a sense quite other than Mill intended: heard overmuch, overdone, and thus in need of being done over in fresh forms. Among their other generic experiments in the lyrical drama (*Paracelsus, Pippa Passes*), the idyll ("Dora," "Morte d'Arthur"), and the sui generis historical epic form of *Sordello*, during the 1830s Tennyson and Browning arrived independently at the first recognizably modern dramatic monologues: "St. Simeon Stylites" (1842; written in 1833) and the paired poems of 1837 that we now know as "Johannes Agricola in Meditation" and "Porphyria's Lover." These early monologues were not only highly accomplished pieces; within the lyrical climate of the day they were implicitly polemical as well. The ascetic St. Simeon atop his pillar, exposed to the merciless assault of the elements, stands for an exalted subjectivity ironically demystified by the historical contextualization that is the generic privilege of the dramatic monologue and, I shall argue, one of its indispensable props in the construction of character. Browning's imagination was less symbolically brooding than Tennyson's and more historically alert, and he launched his dramatic monologues with speakers whose insanities were perversions, but recognizably versions, of the twin wellheads of the lyrical current that had come down to the nineteenth century from the Reformation and the Renaissance. The historical figure Johannes Agricola is an antinomian protestant lying against time as if his soul depended on it; and Porphyria's lover, though fictive, may be regarded as a gruesomely literal-minded Petrarch bent on possessing the object of his desire. Each of Browning's speakers, like St. Simeon Stylites, utters a monomaniacal manifesto that shows subjectivity up by betraying its situation in a history. The utterance of each stands revealed not as poetry, in Mill's terms, but as eloquence, a desperately concentric rhetoric whereby, to adapt Yeats's formulation from "Ego Dominus Tuus," the sentimentalist deceives himself.

What gets "overheard" in these inaugural Victorian monologues is history dramatically replayed. The charmed circle of lyric finds itself included by the kind of historical particularity that lyric genres exclude by design, and in the process readers find themselves unsettlingly historicized and contextualized as well. The extremity of each monologist's authoritative assertion awakens in us with great force the counter-authority of communal norms, through a reductio ad absurdum of the very lyric premises staked out in Mill's essays, most remarkably in a sentence that Mill deleted when republishing "What is Poetry?": "That song has always seemed to us like the lament of a prisoner in a solitary cell, ourselves listening, unseen in the next."[3] ("Ourselves"? How many of us in that next cell? Does one eavesdrop in company? Or is that not called going to the theater, and is Mill's overheard poetry not dramatic eloquence after all?) Tennyson's and Browning's first monologues imply that Mill's position was already its own absurd reduction—a reduction not just of the options for poetry but of the prerogatives of the unimprisoned self, which ideas like Mill's have been underwriting, as teachers of undergraduate poetry classes can attest, for the better part of two centuries. Tennyson and Browning wanted to safeguard the self's prerogatives, and to that extent they shared the aims of contemporary lyrical devotees. But both poets' earliest dramatic monologues compassed those aims through a more subtle and eloquent design than the prevailing creed would admit: a design that might preserve the self on the far side of, and as a result of, a contextual dismissal of attenuated Romantic lyricism and its merely soulful claims; a design that might, as Browning was to put it in the peroration to *The Ring and the Book* (1869), "Suffice the eye and save the soul beside" (XII. 863). St. Simeon, Johannes, and Porphyria's lover emerge through their monologues as characters: poorer souls than they like to fancy themselves but selves for all that, de-and re-constructed selves strung on the tensions of their texts.

II

Both Tennyson and Browning proceeded at once to refine their generic discoveries, though they proceeded in quite different directions. While Tennyson kept the dramatic monologue in his repertoire, he turned to it relatively seldom; and with such memorable ventures as "Ulysses" and "Tithonus" he in effect relyricized the genre, running its contextualizing devices in reverse and stripping his speakers of personality in order to facilitate a lyric drive. Browning, on the other hand, moved his dramatic monologues in the direction of mimetic particularity, and the poems he went on to write continued to incorporate or "overhear" lyric in the interests of character-formation.

"Johannes Agricola" and "Porphyria's Lover" had been blockbusters, comparatively single-minded exercises in the construction of a lurid character through the fissuring of an apparently monolithic ego. The gain in verisimilitude of Browning's later monologues is a function of the nerve with which he learned to reticulate the sort of pattern these strong but simple monologues had first knit. The degree of intricacy varies widely, but the generic design remains the same. Character in the Browningesque dramatic monologue emerges as an interference effect between opposed yet mutually informative discourses: between an historical, narrative, metonymic text and a symbolic, lyrical, metaphoric text that adjoins it and jockeys with it for authority. While each text urges its own priority, the ensemble works according to the paradoxical logic of the originary supplement: the alien voices of history and of feeling come to constitute and direct one another. Typically Browning's monologists tell the story of a yearning after the condition of lyric, a condition that is itself in turn unimaginable except as the object of, or pretext for, the yearning that impels the story plotted against it.[4]

What we acknowledge as the "life" of a dramatic monologue thus emerges through the interdependence of its fictive autobiography and its *élan vital*, each of which stands as the other's reason for being, and neither of which can stand alone without succumbing to one of two deconstructive ordeals that beset character in this genre (and that arguably first beset the self during the century in which this genre arose). The first ordeal lies through history and threatens to resolve the speaking self into its constituent influences, to unravel character by exposing it as merely a tissue of affiliations. At the same time, character in the dramatic monologue runs an equal but opposite risk from what certain Romantic poetics and hermeneutics would assert to be the self's very place of strength and what we have been calling, after Mill, the privacy of lyric. A kind of sublime idiocy, lyric isolation from context distempers character and robs it of contour, as Socrates said long ago in the *Ion* (lyric poets are out of their minds), and as Sharon Cameron, with an eye on Greek and earlier origins of lyric, has said again more recently: "the lyric is a departure not only from temporality but also from the finite constrictions of identity."[5] We find this lyric departure superbly dramatized in the valediction of Tennyson's Ulysses, that most marginal of characters, whose discourse poises itself at "the utmost bound of human thought" (l. 32). Insofar as we find Ulysses transgressing that bound—as for me he does in the final paragraph, with its address to a bewilderingly mythical crew of Ithacan mariners and with the concomitant evanescence of its "I"—we find Tennyson trangressing the generic boundary of dramatic monologue as well.

One good reason why the dramatic monologue is associated with Browning's name rather than with Tennyson's, who technically got to it first, is that in Browning the lyrical flight from narrative, temporality, and identity appears through a characteristic, and characterizing, resistance to its allure. Browning's Ulysses, had he invented one, would speak while bound to the mast of a ship bound elsewhere; his life would take its bearing from what he heard the Sirens sing, and their music would remain an unheard melody suffusing his monologue without rising to the surface of utterance.[6] Such a plot of lyricism resisted would mark his poem as a dramatic monologue, which we should be justified in reading as yet another allegory of the distinctive turn on Romantic lyricism that perennially recreated Browning's poetical character. "R. B. a poem" was the title he gave in advance to this allegorical testament, in the fine letter, virtually an epistolary monologue, that he addressed on the subject to Elizabeth Barrett; and by the time of "One Word More" (1855) he could proudly affirm his wife's lyricism as the privately silencing otherness his public character was to be known by.[7]

Dramatic monologue in the Browning tradition is, in a word, anything but monological. It represents modern character as a quotient, a ratio of history and desire, a function of the division of the modern mind against itself. Our apprehension of character as thus constituted is a Romantic affair; in Jerome Christensen's apt phrase for the processing of the "lyrical drama" in Romanticism, it is a matter of learning to "read the differentials." As a sampling of the dozens of poetry textbooks published in recent decades will confirm, the dramatic monologue is our genre of genres for training in how to read between the lines—a hackneyed but valuable phrase that deserves a fresh hearing.[8] In the reading of a dramatic monologue we do not so much scrutinize the ellipses and blank spaces of the text as we people those openings by attending to the overtones of the different discourses that flank them. Between the lines, we read in a no-man's-land the notes whose intervals engender character. Perhaps the poet of the dramatic monologue gave a thought to the generic framing of his own art when he had the musician Abt Vogler (1864) marvel "That out of three sounds he frame, not a fourth sound, but a star" (l. 52). The quantum leap from text to fictive persona (the dramatic "star" of a monologue) is no less miraculous for being, like Abt Vogler's structured improvisation, "framed," defined and sustained as a put-up job. That such a process of character-construction tends to elude our received means of exegesis is a contributing cause for the depression of Browning's stock among the New Critics. But one way to begin explicating a dramatic monologue in the Browning tradition is to identify a discursive shift, a moment at which either of the genre's constitutive modes—historical line or punctual lyric spot—breaks into the other.

III

Since the premier writer of dramatic monologues was, as usual in such matters, the most ingenious, it is difficult to find uncomplicated instances in Browning that are also representative. We might sample first a passage from "Fra Lippo Lippi" (1855), a sizeable blank-verse monologue that happens to contain lyric literally in the form of *stornelli*, lyrical catches Englished in italics that Browning's artist monk emits at odd intervals during the autobiography he is improvising for the night watch. In the following lines Lippo is taking off those critics whom his new painterly realism has disturbed:

> "It's art's decline, my son!
> You're not of the true painters, great and old;
> Brother Angelico's the man, you'll find;
> Brother Lorenzo stands his single peer:
> Fag on at flesh, you'll never make the third!"
> *Flower o' the pine,*
> *You keep your mistr . . . manners, and I'll stick to mine!*
> I'm not the third, then: bless us, they must know!
> Don't you think they're the likeliest to know,
> They with their Latin?
>
> (ll. 233–42)

The gap for interpretation to enter is, of course, the middle of the second italicized line, marked typographically by ellipsis and prosodically by the wreckage of the embedded snatch of song. Amid Lippo's tale of the modern artist's oppression by his superiors, by religious and representational traditions, and by the Latin learning that backs up both (poetry as overseen?), the apparently spontaneous individual talent bursts forth in a rebellious chant—which is then itself interrupted by a reminder, also apparently spontaneous, of Lippo's answerability to the authorities right in front of him. Lippo's lyric flower breeds a canker: the poetry we and the police thought we were overhearing turns out to be, through versatile revision or instant overdubbing, a rhetorically canny performance. Or, if we take a larger view, it turns out to have been rhetoric all along, Lippo's premeditated means of affirming solidarity with the unlettered night watch by ruefully policing his own speech in advance and incorporating this police action into the larger speech act that is his monologue.

The passage is intensely artificial yet intensely realistic, and we should note that its success does not rely on our deciding whether the monologist has forecast his occasion or stumbled upon it. The twist of the lyrical line against itself nets a speaking subject who is tethered to circumstances and, for that very reason, is anything but tongue-tied. Here as throughout the Browningesque monologue, character is not unfolded to comprehension but enfolded in a text that draws us in. Even after nearly four hundred lines we do not grasp Lippo's character as an essence and know what he is; but if we have negotiated the text we know how he does. In the terms of the passage in question, we know his *manners*, not least his manner of covering up his *mistr*. . . . Lippo's character arises, in the differentials between vitality and circumstances, as a way of life, a mazing text, a finely realized, idiosyncratic instance of a generic method.

A similarly punctuated digression from story, or transgression into lyric, occurs at the center of Browning's most famous monologue, "My Last Duchess" (1842):

> She had
> A heart—how shall I say?—too soon made glad,
> Too easily impressed; she liked whate'er
> She looked on, and her looks went everywhere.
> Sir, 't was all one! My favour at her breast,
> The dropping of the daylight in the West,
> The bough of cherries some officious fool
> Broke in the orchard for her, the white mule
> She rode with round the terrace—all and each
> Would draw from her alike the approving speech,
> Or blush, at least. She thanked men,—good! but thanked
> Somehow—I know not how—as if she ranked
> My gift of a nine-hundred-years-old name
> With anybody's gift.
>
> (ll. 21–34)

The framing hesitations of "How shall I say?" and "I know not how" may or may not come under the Duke's rhetorical control; but a comparable tic or stammer invades his discourse more subtly with the appositional style of the middle lines, which do here with syntax the work done otherwise in Fra Lippo's *stornelli*. Halfway through the monologue, these lines constitute a lyrical interlude around which the Duke's despotic narrative may be seen to circle, with a predatory envy that escapes his posture of condescension. Anaphora and grammatical suspension, time-honored refuges of lyric, harbor recurrent images of the daily and seasonal cycle, of natural affection, and of sexual generation that not only contradict the Duke's potent affiliation with art, culture, and domination but show these contradictions within the text to be contradictions within the Duke. Or rather, to discard the figuration of inside and outside that dramatic monologue at its best asks us to do without, it is these textual contradictions that constitute the Duke's character. The polymorphous perversity he here attributes to his last Duchess is as much an attribute of his own character as is the different, monomaniacal perversity with which he has put a stop to her egalitarian smiles. Each perversity so turns on the other as to knot the text up into that essential illusion we call character. Hence the Duke's characteristic inconsistency in objecting to the "officious fool" who, in breaking cherries for the Duchess, was not breaking ranks at all but merely executing his proper "office" in the Duke's hierarchical world. Hence, too, the undecidable ambiguity of "My favour at her breast": the phrase oscillates between suggestions of a caress naturally given and of an heirloom possessively bestowed, and its oscillation is what makes the star of dramatic character shine. Such a semantic forking of the ways, like the plotting of spontaneity against calculation in Fra Lippo's *"mistr . . . manners"* revision, blocks reference in one direction, in order to refer us to the textual production of character instead.

Because in grammatical terms it is a paratactic pocket, an insulated deviation from the syntax of narrative line, the Duke's recounting of his Duchess's easy pleasures wanders from the aims of the raconteur and foregrounds the speech impediments that make her story his monologue.[9] Moreover, the Duke's listing is also a listening, a harkening after the kind of spontaneous lyric voice that he, like the writer of dramatic monologues, comes into his own by imperfectly renouncing. Lyric, in the dramatic monologue, is what you cannot have and what you cannot forget—think of the arresting trope Browning invented for his aging poet Cleon (1855), "One lyric woman, in her crocus vest" (l. 15)—and as an organizing principle for the genre, lyric becomes present through a recurrent and partial overruling. This resisted generic nostalgia receives further figuration intertextually, in "My Last Duchess" and many another monologue, with the clustering of allusions at moments of lyric release. Here "The dropping of the daylight in the West" falls into Browning's text from major elegies, or refusals to mourn, by Milton ("Lycidas"), Wordsworth ("Tintern Abbey," "Intimations" ode), and Keats ("To Autumn"); and the Duchess on her white mule so recalls Spenser's lyrically selfless Una from the opening of *The Faerie Queene* as to cast the Duke as an archimage dubiously empowered.

Amid the Duke's eloquence the overhearing of poetry, in this literary-historical sense of allusion to prior poems, underscores the choral dissolution that lurks in lyric voice. Furthermore, it reinstates the checking of such dissolution as the mark of the individual self—of the dramatic speaker and also of the poet who, in writing him up, defines himself in opposition to lyrical orthodoxy and emerges as a distinct "I," a name to conjure with against the ominous: "This grew; I gave commands" (l. 45). Toward the end of his career, in "House" (1876) Browning would in his own voice make more explicit this engagement with the literary past and would defend literary personality, against Wordsworth on the sonnet, as just the antithesis of unmediated sincerity: " ' *"With this same key / Shakespeare unlocked his heart,"* once more!' / Did Shakespeare? If so, the less Shakespeare he!" (ll. 38–40). Poetry of the unlocked heart, far from displaying character in Browning's terms, undoes it: Browning reads his chief precursor in the English dramatic line as a type of the objective poet, the poetical character known through a career-long objection to the sealed intimacies of the poem à clef.

IV

In 1831 Arthur Hallam gave a promising description of the best of Tennyson's *Poems, Chiefly Lyrical* (1830) as "a graft of the lyric on the dramatic."

The Victorian dramatic monologue that soon ensued from these beginnings was likewise a hybrid genre, a hardy offshoot of the earlier hybrid genre in which the first Romantics had addressed the problem of how to write the long modern poem by making modern civilization and its discontents, or longing and its impediments, into the conditions for the prolonging and further hearing of poetry: the "greater Romantic lyric." The genre M. H. Abrams thus christened some years ago has by now achieved canonical status, but a reconsideration of its given name from the standpoint of the dramatic monologue may help us save it from assimilation to orthodox lyricism by reminding us that the genre Abrams called "greater" was not more-lyrical-than-lyric but rather more-than-lyrical. Despite a still high tide of assertions to the contrary, the works of the first generations of Romantic poets were on the whole much less lyrical than otherwise.[10] Once we conceive the Romantic tradition accordingly as a perennial intermarriage, which is to say infighting, of poetic kinds, we can situate the Victorian dramatic monologue as an eminently Romantic form. In correcting the literary-historical picture we can begin, too, to see how fin-de-siècle and modernist reactions to the Browningesque monologue have conditioned the writing, reading, and teaching of poetry, literary theory, and literary history in our own time.

At the beginning of Browning's century Coleridge remarked, "A poem of any length neither can be, nor ought to be, all poetry." By the end of the century Oscar Wilde, looking askance at Browning's achievement, took up Coleridge's distinction, but with a difference: "If he can only get his music by breaking the strings of his lute, he breaks them, and they snap in discord. . . . Meredith is a prose Browning, and so is Browning. He used poetry as a medium for writing in prose."[11] The difference between Coleridge's and Wilde's ideas of what a poem should be is in large part a difference that the dramatic monologue had made in nineteenth-century poetry, a difference Browning inscribed into literary history by inscribing it into the characteristic ratios of his texts. Wilde and others at the threshold of modernism wanted Mill's pure lyricism but wanted it even purer. And through an irony of literary history that has had far-reaching consequences for our century, the Browningesque dramatic monologue gave them what they wanted. Symbolist and imagist writers could extract from such texts as *Pauline* and "Fra Lippo Lippi"—and also, to sketch in the fuller picture, from the Tennysonian idyll and most sophisticated Victorian novels—lyrical gems as finely cut as anything from the allegedly naive eras, Romantic or Elizabethan, upon which they bestowed such sentimental if creative regard. The hybrid dramatic monologue, as a result of its aim to make the world and subjectivity safe for each other in the interests of character, had proved a sturdy grafting stock for flowers of lyricism; and the governing pressures of the genre, just because they governed so firmly, had bred hothouse lyric varieties of unsurpassed intensity. These lyrical implants it was left to a new generation of rhymers, scholars, and anthologists to imitate, defend, and excerpt in a newly chastened lyric poetry, a severely purist poetics, and a surprisingly revisionist history of poetry.[12]

The fin-de-siècle purism of Wilde, Yeats, Arthur Symons, and others was polemically canted against the example of Browning; yet it remained curiously, even poignantly, in his debt. Consider, for example, Symons's resumption of a rhetoric very like Mill's, as he praises Verlaine in *The Symbolist Movement* (1899) for "getting back to nature itself": "From the moment when his inner life may be said to have begun, he was occupied with the task of an unceasing confession, in which one seems to overhear him talking to himself."[13] The pivotally wishful "unceasing," which distinguishes Symons's formulation from Mill's, also betrays a kind of elegiac overcompensation. Mill had dissolved audience in order to overhear poetry as if from an adjacent cell; Symons, writing at an appreciable historical remove from the achievements of Verlaine, is by contrast trapped in time. Symons's overhearing of poetry resembles less Mill's eavesdropping than the belated Browningesque audition of a poignant echo, and the symbolist movement he hopes to propel is fed by an overwhelming nostalgia that creates from its own wreck the thing it contemplates. The nostalgia for lyric that throbs through the influential versions of the poetic past Symons and his contemporaries assembled sprang from a range of cultural causes we are only beginning to understand adequately.[14] But we can observe here that the rhetorical pattern into which their lyrically normed historiography fell was precisely that of the poetic genre that had preeminently confronted lyricism with history in their century: the dramatic monologue. It is as if what Symons championed as the "revolt against exteriority, against rhetoric,"[15] having repudiated the "impure" Browning tradition in principle, was condemned to reiterate its designs in writing. The symbolist and imagist schools wanted to read in their French and English antecedents an expurgated lyric that never was on page or lip. It was, rather, a generic back-formation, a textual constituent they isolated from the dramatic monologue and related nineteenth-century forms; and the featureless poems the fin-de-siècle purists produced by factoring out the historical impurities that had ballasted these forms are now fittingly, with rare exceptions, works of little more than historical interest.

Virtually each important modernist poet in English wrote such poems for a time; each became an important poet by learning to write otherwise and to exploit the internal otherness of the dramatic monologue. When the lyrical bubble burst within its bell jar, poetry became modern once again in its return to the historically responsive and dialogical mode that Browning, Tennyson, and others had brought forward from the Romantics.[16] And upon the establishment of Yeats's mask, Pound's personae, Frost's monologues and idylls, and Eliot's impersonal poetry, it became a point of dogma among sophisticated readers that every poem dramatized a speaker who was not the poet. "Once we have dissociated the speaker of the lyric from the personality of the poet, even the tiniest lyric reveals itself as drama."[17] We recognize

this declaration as dogma by the simple fact that we—at least most of us—
had to learn it, and had to trade for it older presuppositions about lyric
sincerity that we had picked up in corners to which New Critical light had
not yet pierced. The new dogma took (and in my teaching experience it takes
still) with such ease that it is worth asking why it did (and does), and
whether as professors of poetry we should not have second thoughts about
promulgating an approach that requires so painless an adjustment of the
subjectivist norms we profess to think outmoded.

The conversion educated readers now routinely undergo from lyrical to
dramatic expectations about the poems they study recapitulates the history
of Anglo-American literary pedagogy during our century, the middle two
decades of which witnessed a great awakening from which we in our turn
are trying to awaken again. Until about 1940 teachers promoted poetry
appreciation in handbooks and anthologies that exalted lyric as "the supreme
expression of strong emotion . . . the very real but inexplicable essence of
poetry," and that throned this essential emotion in the equally essential
person of the poet: "Lyrical poetry arouses emotion because it expresses
the author's feeling."[18] By 1960 the end of instruction had shifted from
appreciating to understanding poetry, and to this end a host of experts
marched readers past the author of a poem to its dramatic speaker. John
Crowe Ransom's dictum that the dramatic situation is "almost the first head
under which it is advisable to approach a poem for understanding" had by
the 1960s advanced from advice to prescription. In Laurence Perrine's widely
adopted *Sound and Sense* the first order of business is "to assume always that
the speaker is someone other than the poet himself." For Robert Scholes in
Elements of Poetry the speaker is the most elementary of assumptions: "In
beginning our approach to a poem we must make some sort of tentative
decision about who the speaker is, what his situation is, and who he seems
to be addressing."[19]

That such forthright declarations conceal inconsistencies appears in the
instructions of Robert W. Boynton and Maynard Mack, whose *Introduction
to the Poem* promotes the familiar dramatic principle but pursues its issues to
the verge of a puzzling conclusion. The authors begin dogmatically enough:
"When we start looking closely at the dramatic character of poetry, we find
that we have to allow for a more immediate speaker than the poet himself,
one whom the poet has imagined speaking the poem, as an actor speaks a
part written for him by a playwright." But then Boynton and Mack, with a
candor unusual in the handbook genre, proceed to a damaging concession
that dissolves the insubstantial pageant of the dramatic enterprise into thin
air: "In some instances this imagined speaker is in no way definite or distinctive; he is simply a voice." (When is a speaker not a speaker? When he is a
"voice," nay, an Arnoldian "lyric cry.") With this last sentence Boynton and
Mack offer an all but lyrical intimation of the mystification inherent in the
critical fiction of the speaker and suggest its collusion with the mysteries of

the subjectivist norm it was designed to supplant.[20] It may well be easier to indicate these mysteries than to solve them; what matters is that with our New Critical guides we seem to have experienced as little difficulty in negotiating the confusions entailed by the fiction of the speaker as we have experienced in converting ourselves and our students from lyrically expressive to dramatically objective norms for reading.

Why should we have made this conversion, and why do we continue to encourage it? Why should our attempts at understanding poetry through a New Criticism rely on a fiction that baffles the understanding? These are related questions, and their answers probably lie in considerations of pedagogical expediency. One such consideration must be the sheer hard work of bringing culturally stranded students into contact with the historical particularities from which a given poem arises. Life (and courses) being short, art being long, and history being longer still, the fiction of the speaker at least brackets the larger problem of context so as to define a manageable classroom task for literary studies. To such institutional considerations as these, which have been attracting needed attention of late, I would add a consideration more metaphysical in kind. The fiction of the speaker, if it removes from the study of poetry the burden, and the dignity, of establishing contact with history, puts us in compensatory contact with the myth of unconditioned subjectivity we have inherited from Mill and Symons in spite of ourselves. Through that late ceremony of critical innocence, the readerly imagination of a self, we modern readers have abolished the poet and set up the fictive speaker; and we have done so in order to boost the higher gains of an intersubjective recognition for which, in an increasingly mechanical age that can make Mill's look positively idyllic, we seem to suffer insatiable cultural thirst. The mastery of New Critical tools may offer in this light a sort of homeopathic salve, the application of a humanistic technology to technologically induced ills.

The thirst for intersubjective confirmation of the self, which has made the overhearing of a persona our principal means of understanding a poem, would I suspect be less strong if it did not involve a kind of bad faith about which Browning's Bishop Blougram (1855) had much to say: "With me, faith means perpetual unbelief / Kept quiet like the snake 'neath Michael's foot / Who stands calm just because he feels it writhe" (ll. 666–68). The New Criticism of lyric poetry introduced into literary study an anxiety of textuality that was its legacy from the Higher Criticism of scripture a century before: anxiety over the tendency of texts to come loose from their origins into an anarchy that the New Critics half acknowledged and half sought to curb under the regime of a now avowedly fictive self, from whom a language on parole from its author might nonetheless issue as speech. What is poetry? Textuality a speaker owns. The old king of self-expressive lyricism is dead: Long live the Speaker King! At a king's ransom we thus secure our reading against the subversive textuality of what we read; or as another handbook from the 1960s puts it with clarity: "So strong is the oral convention in poetry that, in the absence of contrary indications, we infer a voice and, though we know we are reading words on a page, create for and of ourselves an imaginary listener."[21] Imaginative recreation "for and of ourselves" here depends upon our suppressing the play of the signifier beneath the hand of a convention "so strong" as to decree the "contrary indications" of textuality absent most of the time.

Deconstructive theory and practice in the last decade have so directed our attention to the persistence of "contrary indications" that the doctrine espoused in my last citation no longer appears tenable. It seems incumbent upon us now to choose between intersubjective and intertextual modes of reading, between vindicating the self and saving the text. Worse, I fear, those of us who are both teachers and critics may have to make different choices according to the different positions in which we find ourselves— becoming by turns intertextual readers in the study and intersubjective readers in the classroom—in ways that not very fruitfully perpetuate a professional divide some latter-day Browning might well monologize upon. I wonder whether it must be so; and I am fortified in my doubts by the stubborn survival of the dramatic monologue, which began as a response to lyric isolationism, and which remains to mediate the rivalry between intersubjective appeal and intertextual rigor by situating the claims of each within the limiting context the other provides.

In its charactered life the dramatic monologue can help us put in their places critical reductions of opposite but complementary and perhaps even cognate kinds: on one hand, the transcendentally face-saving misprisions that poetry has received from Victorian romanticizers, Decadent purists, and New Critical impersonalists alike; on the other hand, the abysmal disfigurements of a deconstruction that would convert poetry's most beautiful illusion—the speaking presence—into a uniform textuality that is quite as "purist," in its own way, as anything the nineteenth century could imagine. An exemplary teaching genre, the dramatic monologue can teach us, among other things, that while texts do not absolutely lack speakers, they do not simply have them either; they invent them instead as they go. Texts do not come from speakers, speakers come from texts. *Persona fit non nascitur.* To assume in advance that a poetic text proceeds from a dramatically situated speaker is to risk missing the play of verbal implication whereby character is engendered in the first place through colliding modes of signification; it is to read so belatedly as to arrive only when the party is over. At the same time, however, the guest the party convenes to honor, the ghost conjured by the textual machine, remains the articulate phenomenon we call character: a literary effect we neglect at our peril. For to insist that textuality is all and that the play of the signifier usurps the recreative illusion of character is to turn back at the threshold of interpretation, stopping our ears to both lyric cries and historical imperatives, and from our studious cells overhearing nothing.

Renewed stress upon textuality as the basis for the Western written character is a beginning as important to the study of poetry now as it has been for over a century to the writing of dramatic monologues and to the modern tradition they can illuminate in both backward and forward directions. But textuality is only the beginning.

Notes

1. John Stuart Mill, *Essays on Poetry*, ed. F. Parvin Sharpless (Columbia, S. C., 1976), pp. 12, 36. The quotations come from two essays of 1833, "What is Poetry?" and "The Two Kinds of Poetry."

2. Ideas like Mill's abound, for example, in Macaulay's 1825 essay "Milton," in *Critical and Historical Essays* (London, 1883): "Analysis is not the business of the poet" (p. 3); "It is the part of the lyric poet to abandon himself, without reserve, to his own emotions" (p. 6); "It is just when Milton escapes from the shackles of the dialogue, when he is discharged from the labour of uniting two incongruous styles, when he is at liberty to indulge his choral raptures without reserve, that he rises even above himself" (p. 8). Comparing Mill's writings with T. S. Eliot's "The Three Voices of Poetry" (1953), Elder Olson, *American Lyric Poems* (New York, 1964), p. 2, concludes that "the study of the question has not advanced much in over a hundred years." Olson's conclusion retains its force after two decades. See Barbara Hardy, *The Advantage of Lyric* (Bloomington and London, 1977), p. 2: "Lyric poetry thrives, then, on exclusions. It is more than usually opaque because it leaves out so much of the accustomed context and consequences of feeling that it can speak in a pure, lucid, and intense voice."

3. *Essays on Poetry*, p. 14.

4. Genre theorists have often observed this distinction, though usually in honoring the exclusivity of lyric. For Babette Deutsch, *Potable Gold* (New York, 1929), p. 21, the essential distinction lies between prose and poetry: "The one resembles a man walking toward a definite goal; the other is like a man surrendering himself to contemplation, or to the experience of walking for its own sake. Prose has intention; poetry has intensity." According to Kenneth Burke, *A Grammar of Motives* (1945; Berkeley and Los Angeles, 1969), p. 475, "The *state of arrest* in which we would situate the essence of lyric is not analogous to dramatic action at all, but is the dialectical counterpart of action." Olson, "The Lyric," *PMLA*, 1 (1969), 65, says of lyrics that "while they may contain within themselves a considerable narrative or dramatic portion, that portion is subordinate to the lyrical whole. . . . Once expression and address and colloquy become subservient to a further end as affecting their form as complete and whole in themselves, we have gone beyond the bounds of the lyric." For a recent view of Browning opposed to that of the present essay see David Bergman, "Browning's Monologues and the Development of the Soul," *ELH*, 47 (1980), 774: "For Browning, historicity only prettifies a work. . . . History, the creation of a concrete setting, has never been a major focus for Browning." I would reply that history is indeed a major focus for Browning—one of the two foci, to speak geometrically, that define his notoriously elliptical procedures.

5. *Ion* 534; Sharon Cameron, *Lyric Time* (Baltimore and London, 1979), p. 208. See also the quirky Victorian theorist E. S. Dallas, *Poetics* (London, 1852), p. 83: "The outpourings of the lyric should spring from the law of unconsciousness. Personality or selfhood triumphs in the drama; the divine and all that is not Me triumphs in the lyric."

6. Although Browning never wrote such a monologue, he glanced at its possibility in "The Englishman in Italy" (1845), with its vision of "Those isles of the siren" (l. 199) and its audition of a song "that tells us / What life is, so clear"; "The secret they sang to Ulysses /

When, ages ago, / He heard and he knew this life's secret / I hear and I know" (ll. 223–27). Life's secret, needless to add, goes untold in Browning's text.

7. Letter of 11 February 1845, in *Letters of Robert Browning and Elizabeth Barrett Barrett, 1845–1846*, ed. Elvan Kintner, 2 vols. (Cambridge, Mass., 1969), 1:17.

8. Jerome Christensen, " 'Thoughts That Do Often Lie Too Deep for Tears': Toward a Romantic Concept of Lyrical Drama," *Wordsworth Circle*, 12:1 (1981), 61. For an appropriately genealogical testimonial to the pedagogical virtues of the dramatic monologue see Ina Beth Sessions's postscript to "The Dramatic Monologue," *PMLA*, 62 (1947), 516n.: "One of the most interesting comments concerning the dramatic monologue was made by Dr. J. B. Wharey of the University of Texas in a letter to the writer on January 17, 1935: 'The dramatic monologue is, I think, one of the best forms of disciplinary reading—that is, to use the words of the late Professor Genung, "reading pursued with the express purpose of feeding and stimulating inventive power." ' " Among the earliest systematic students of the genre in our century were elocution teachers; their professional pedigree broadly conceived goes back at least to Quintilian, who recommended exercises in impersonation (*prosopopoeia*) as a means of imaginative discipline. See A. Dwight Culler, "Monodrama and the Dramatic Monologue," *PMLA*, 90 (1975), 368.

9. David I. Masson, "Vowel and Consonant Patterns in Poetry," in *Essays on the Language of Literature*, ed. Seymour Chatman and Samuel R. Levin (Boston, 1967), p. 3, observes that "where lyrical feeling or sensuous description occurs in European poetry, there will usually be found patterns of vowels and consonants." For more general consideration of the linguistics of lyric, see Edward Stankiewicz, "Poetic and Non-poetic Language in Their Interrelation," in *Poetics*, ed. D. Davie et al. (Gravenhage, 1961), p. 17: "Lyrical poetry presents the most interiorized form of poetic language, in which the linguistic elements are most closely related and internally motivated." Note that Stankiewicz, following the Russian Formalists, here refers not to psychological inwardness but to the nonreferential, auto-mimetic interiority of language itself.

10. Arthur Hallam, "On Some of the Characteristics of Modern Poetry, and on the Lyrical Poems of Alfred Tennyson," in *The Writings of Arthur Hallam*, ed. T. Vail Motter (New York, 1943), p. 197; M. H. Abrams, "Structure and Style in the Greater Romantic Lyric," in *From Sensibility to Romanticism*, ed. Frederick W. Hilles and Harold Bloom (New York, 1965), pp. 527–60. On the Romantic mixture of lyric with other genres see Cameron, *Lyric Time*, p. 217; Christensen, " 'Thoughts,' " pp. 60–62; Robert Langbaum, "Wordsworth's Lyrical Characterizations," *Studies in Romanticism*, 21 (1982), 319–39. Langbaum's earlier book *The Poetry of Experience* (1957; rpt. New York, 1963), which places the dramatic monologue within Romantic tradition, should be consulted, as should two responses that appeared, almost concurrently, two decades later: Culler, "Monodrama," and Ralph W. Rader, "The Dramatic Monologue and Related Lyric Forms," *Critical Inquiry*, 3 (1976), 131–51.

11. Coleridge is quoted in Frederick A. Pottle, *The Idiom of Poetry* (Ithaca, 1941), p. 82. Wilde's comments occur in "The Critic as Artist" (1890), in *Literary Criticism of Oscar Wilde*, ed. Stanley Weintraub (Lincoln, Neb., 1968), p. 202.

12. Victorian writers were divided as to the chronological priority of lyric over other genres. For Dallas, as for Mill, "Lyrics are the first-fruits of art" (p. 245), while Walter Bagehot contends that "poetry begins in Impersonality" and that lyric represents a later refinement ("Hartley Coleridge" [1852], in *Collected Works*, ed. Norman St. John-Stevas, I [Cambridge, Mass., 1965], pp. 159–60). As to the normative status of lyric, however, the later nineteenth century had little doubt. Summaries and bibliographical aids may be found in Francis B. Gummere, *The Beginnings of Poetry* (New York, 1901), p. 147; Charles Mill Gayley and Benjamin Putnam Kurtz, *Methods and Materials of Literary Criticism* (Boston, 1920), p. 122; W. K. Wimsatt, Jr., and Cleanth Brooks, *Literary Criticism: A Short History*

(New York, 1966), pp. 433, 751–52. For representative belletristic histories of poetry from a nostalgic, fin-de-siècle perspective see John Addington Symonds, *Essays Speculative and Suggestive* (London, 1893), pp. 393 ff.; Edmund Gosse, "Introduction" to *Victorian Songs: Lyrics of the Affections and Nature*, ed. E. H. Garrett (Boston, 1895); and Arthur Symons, *The Symbolist Movement in Literature* (1899; rpt. New York, 1958) and *The Romantic Movement in English Poetry* (New York, 1909). On the influence of F. T. Palgrave's *Golden Treasury* (1861; rev. 1981), an anthology that "established, retroactively and for the future, the tradition of the English lyric," see Christopher Clausen, *The Place of Poetry* (Lexington, 1981), p. 67.

13. Symons, *The Symbolist Movement*, p. 49.

14. Marxian approaches now offer the most promising and comprehensive explanations of the fortunes of lyric as a product of industrial culture, yet recently published Marxian analyses evaluate the social functions of lyric very differently. For Theodor W. Adorno, "Lyric Poetry and Society" (1957; trans. Bruce Mayo, *Telos*, 20 [Summer 1974], 56–71), "The subjective being that makes itself heard in lyric poetry is one which defines and expresses itself as something opposed to the collective and the realm of objectivity" (p. 59); in contrast, Hugh N. Grady, "Marxism and the Lyric," *Contemporary Literature*, 22 (1981), 555, argues that "the lyric has become a specialized, though not exclusive, genre of Utopian vision in the modern era."

15. Symons, *The Symbolist Movement*, p. 65.

16. Olson, "The Lyric," p. 65, in distinguishing the "verbal acts" of lyric from those of more elaborated forms, himself acts fatally on the strength of a simile: "The difference, if I may use a somewhat homely comparison, is that between a balloon inflated to its proper shape, nothing affecting it but the internal forces of the gas, and a balloon subjected to the pressure of external forces which counteract the internal." But a balloon affected only by internal forces (i.e., a balloon in a vacuum) would not inflate but explode. That the "proper shape" of a poem, as of a balloon, arises not from sheer afflatus but as a compromise between "internal" and "external" forces is precisely my point about the framing of the dramatic monologue—as it is, I think, the dramatic monologue's (deflationary) point about the lyric.

17. Wimsatt and Brooks, *Literary Criticism*, p. 675; see also Cleanth Brooks and Robert Penn Warren, *Understanding Poetry* (1938; rev. ed. New York, 1950), p. liv. Don Geiger, *The Dramatic Impulse in Modern Poetics* (Baton Rouge, 1967), pp. 85–95, provides a capable overview of the persona poetics of the New Criticism.

18. Oswald Doughty, *English Lyric in the Age of Reason* (London, 1922), p. xv; Walter Blair and W. K. Chandler, eds., *Approaches to Poetry* (New York, 1935), p. 250.

19. Ransom is quoted in William Elton, *A Glossary of the New Criticism* (Chicago, 1949), p. 38. *Sound and Sense*, 2nd ed. (New York, 1963), p. 21; *Elements of Poetry* (New York, 1969), pp. 11–12.

20. Robert W. Boynton and Maynard Mack, *Introduction to the Poem* (New York, 1965), p. 24. On p. 45, to complete the circuit, the authors equate the "voice" with "the poet." They thus return us through a backstage exit to Clement Wood's definition of lyric in *The Craft of Poetry* (New York, 1929), p. 189, as "the form in which the poet utters his own dramatic monolog." Compare the dramatic metaphor in Benedetto Croce's 1937 *Encyclopedia Britannica* article on "Aesthetic": "The lyric . . . is an objectification in which the ego sees itself on the stage, narrates itself, and dramatizes itself" (quoted in Wimsatt and Brooks, *Literary Criticism*, p. 510). For Geoffrey Crump, *Speaking Poetry* (London, 1953), p. 59, the reverse seems true: "an element of the dramatic is present in all lyrical poetry, because the speaker is to some extent impersonating the poet."

21. Jerome Beaty and William H. Matchett, *Poetry: From Statement to Meaning* (New York, 1965), p. 103.

Notes on Some Structural Varieties and Variations in Dramatic "I" Poems and Their Theoretical Implications

RALPH W. RADER

This essay is intended as a sequel to, and refinement of, an earlier attempt to question some of the prevailing assumptions about the ways in which readers experience the "I" in monodramatic poems, particularly the notion that this "I" is uniformly given as an autonomous speaker who stands free of any determinate relation either to the creating poet or the world outside the poem.[1] Building upon while reformulating Robert Langbaum's important distinction between the dramatic monologue and the dramatic lyric, I emphasized the very different relations between poet, speaker, and reader which those forms manifest, and went on to argue that still further conceptual categories of "I" poems were required for fullness and accuracy in this and other descriptive respects. For the benefit of readers not familiar with my earlier argument, I will begin by recapitulating some of its main points before embarking on some further observations and conclusions about structural variations and varieties in dramatic "I" poems as they can be illustrated through an exploration of the formal characteristics of three poems that in different significant ways do not fit the specifications of the categories previously developed.

I

In my earlier effort, I tried to clarify the basis of the distinction between the dramatic monologue and the dramatic lyric by pointing out that in the former, as an inescapable condition of rendering the text intelligible, the reader must imagine the speaker as an outward presence, as we in our bodies register others in their bodies, from the outside in, whereas in the dramatic lyric we are imaginatively conflated with the speaker, understanding him from the inside out, seeing with his eyes and speaking with his voice as if on our own behalf. This distinction is reflected in the fact, invariant for all readers, that in a "cinematic" projection of our imaginative visualization of the two kinds of poems, the dramatic monologue speaker will be seen displayed directly on the screen, with the words of the poem issuing from his mouth, while in the dramatic lyric we see not the speaker but rather an outward scene that he is understood as seeing, with the camera implicitly taken as his eyes, through which we also look, and the words of the poem registered voice-over as articulating his inner act of perception.

In neither kind of poem is the apparently autonomous speaker actually self-existent but stands in different kinds of fixed relationship to the implicit constructive act of the poet. The most striking instance I have discovered of the poet's presence behind the speaker in the dramatic monologue is the fact that in "My Last Duchess" we both hear the duke speaking and hear the rhymes in the poem, but do not hear the duke as speaking the rhymes. Thus our imaginations locate pre-analytically—in their complex but not contradictory "let's pretend" operations—what the analysis of critics and linguists commonly does not recognize, that sentences can be construed by the mind as expressing two agents (here the explicit speaker and the implicit creating author) simultaneously. The distinctness of represented speaker and representing poet in the dramatic monologue seems correlated with the often-noted fact that the speaker is projected as a person "other" than the poet with a mental process cleanly separate from his. In the dramatic lyric, in contrast, the conflation of mental processes often results in structural confusion between poet and speaker, or more accurately, poet and actor, as in Gray's "Elegy" with its puzzling shifts of reference between the character musing in the twilight and the poet writing the lines of the poem. This kind of confusion can be explained on the hypothesis that in dramatic lyrics the represented actor is a recreation from memory of the poet's own experience, which he reenters imaginatively as he constructs in the poem an image aesthetically adequate in the present to his memorial sense of the structure and significance of a past cognitive event. The situation is such that only in the course of his reconstructive act does he perhaps first fully discover and articulate the felt significance of the experience, so that the poet's remembered act and his reconstruction of it may tend to merge. This is particularly likely to be the case in dramatic lyrics where the representation is in the present tense, as in the "Elegy" or Keats's "Ode to a Nightingale" or Hopkins' "Windhover," in contrast to those where it is in the past tense, as in Hardy's "Darkling Thrush," or is given as the actual speech act of the actor within the scene, as in Arnold's "Dover Beach."

This assumption about the relation between poet and actor in the dramatic lyric cogently accounts for the consistent "behind the eyes" effect in these poems and for the fact that the reader, following the poet, is imaginatively conflated with the speaker's represented subjective act, as for the moment he dwells in the image of the poet's spirit. The assumption accounts also for the fact that though the dramatic lyric speaker has no name or specified identity, unlike dramatic monologue speakers who do have names and specified personal identities, we are hesitantly prompted to call him by the name of the poet, because of our intuitive sense that the poem reflects the poet's actual experience at a real point in space/time beyond the poem. Nevertheless, the fact that the poems are manifestly artificial constructions—the man in the churchyard cannot be writing a poem and we cannot be there with him as we seem to be—makes us properly hesitate to make a simple identification of poet and actor. (Wordsworth nicely catches the quality of a dramatic lyric as an artificial reconstruction of a personal visual experience when he says that, in "With Ships the Sea Was Sprinkled Far and Nigh," "I am *represented* . . . as casting my eyes" [my emphasis] on the given scene.)[2] Thus though based in a time-bound event, such poems may be said to transcend time by translating a temporal into an eternal moment, escaping the contingency of the experienced real moment by fully articulating its felt significance in a poetic construct.

In addition to these two classifications of dramatic poems, I located a third, the mask lyric, instanced in many famous nineteenth-and twentieth-century poems, and also a fourth, the expressive lyric, of which I will speak below. Splitting off the mask lyric from the dramatic monologue (under which rubric the poems it points to are normally included) is intended to permit explicit recognition and provide a guide for analysis of a kind of poem in which an artificial personage—Ulysses, Childe Roland, J. Alfred Prufrock—is the vehicle of the poet's lyrical expression. Whereas lyrical elements in a dramatic monologue proper tend to dilute our sense of its formal purity as a rendering of an autonomous other, as in Browning's "Fra Lippo Lippi," in the mask lyric we understand the art of the poem as involving the poet's sophisticated attempt to express, while at the same time objectifying and limiting, an aspect of his own subjective situation. So it is that we can understand Eliot's "Prufrock" as a dramatic construct which permits the poet at once to express and escape from his own personality while projecting himself into Prufrock's as he characterizes and delimits it. The crucial point of contrast with the dramatic monologue is that the reader experiences Prufrock lyrically, feeling his situation as he feels it, including his self-irony, within an appreciation of Eliot's deliberate deployment of Prufrock as a calculated artificial construct, a mask. (A mask, we remember, is an artificial semblance which a real person can use both to hide behind and speak through.) The reader joins the poet in the mediation of the mask as he projects himself into, and limits his expression to, the character and his situation.

This differentiation of the mask lyric from the dramatic monologue, though it complicates the simplicity of Langbaum's original dual conception of the dramatic monologue and dramatic lyric, is I think justified by the conceptual clarification and additional explanatory power it offers. Like the other two concepts it fits a whole range of poems quite sharply, revealing closely analogous formal features, including the typically irreal, fluid, and symbolic scene of the mask lyric, so clearly in contrast with the wholly natural though fictive probability of the dramatic monologue scene and the quasi-actual scene of the dramatic lyric. Langbaum uses his two concepts so flexibly and applies them to individual poems with such sensitivity, accuracy, and brilliance, that the student, in attempting to extend the application of the concepts himself, may have difficulty seeing that they do not in themselves provide a clear basis for keeping sufficiently constant and unambiguous, across different applications, what are significant differences and contrasts. For instance, Langbaum says in his primary formulation that the dramatic monologue characteristically involves a "tension between sympathy and moral judgment," so that "we understand the speaker of the dramatic monologue by sympathizing with him, and yet by remaining aware of the moral judgment we have suspended for the sake of understanding" him.[3] But he can then describe Tennyson's "Tithonus" as allowing "us no reserve of judgment" (p. 89), an accurate description which departs without acknowledgment from the idea that the dramatic monologue involves a necessary "tension" between sympathy and judgment. The quality pointed to may be located less equivocally by describing "Tithonus" as a mask lyric in which the poet employs an artificial person as a means of expressing and delimiting a personal emotion.

We shall be returning below to the matter of dual awareness in dramatic monologues. For the moment it may be sufficient to say that this departure from the ambiguities of Langbaum's "sympathy and judgment" terminology is meant to assert clearly that the basis of our imaginative commerce with the poems in this field is our in-built cognitive capacity to read from the mind/body of the "self" into that of the "other," a capacity which allows us by extension to register and discriminate different kinds of creative relations between dramatic figures and the mode in which they are constructed or projected from the immanent creating poet. This emphasis on the assumption that we read poems as we read the world, that is, as written by beings like ourselves rooted in the natural and historical conditions ineluctably incident to such beings, stands in contrast also with Langbaum's view of the modes as essentially autonomous artistic "strategies" not internally manifesting a defining connection with the implicit presence of a "real" poet.

Directly relevant in this connection is a fourth category, the expressive lyric, which I felt it necessary to develop in my earlier exposition in order to make clear how Wordsworth's "Tintern Abbey," originally Langbaum's paradigm instance of the dramatic lyric, could not be accurately described in the structural terms that applied so well to other poems he had indicated by the same name. The leading fact is that in "Tintern Abbey" there is plainly no built-in artful contrast between the poet as an actor and the poet as representer of the actor, but rather the sense that the articulation of the poem was achieved as the poet's unfolding, emergent response to the stimulus of the scene. Unlike "With Ships the Sea was Sprinkled Nigh and Far," the poem is not a recreation in memorial tranquillity of a feelingful perception but rather a sublimely successful attempt to articulate toward completed catharsis the urgent burden of overflowing feelings. One imaginative consequence of this implicitly registered constructive situation is that, in contrast with our uncertain identification of actor and poet in the dramatic lyric, our sense of the speaker's identity is such that we must call him Wordsworth, with no hesitation or ambiguity, and may further, indeed almost must, go beyond the strict limits of the poem to call the speaker's "dear sister" "Dorothy."

II

The appearance of a fourth distinctive structure in my set of dramatic "I" forms clearly portends the imminent possibility of discriminating still further distinct types of structure, and in illustration of this possibility I will later be pointing to a complex fifth one, without any sense (rather the opposite) that one wouldn't need to develop many more beyond in order to do precise analytical justice to the structural workings of dramatic poems not here considered, particularly post-modern ones. The indicated situation comports with my assumption that all the forms under consideration are based, as indicated above, directly on our natural capacity as human creatures to image and understand ourselves and others. But it very much needs to be emphasized that to make vital and seemingly autonomous images of our selves and of others, real and fictional, by means of representation in words, was not itself a capacity given and automatically available in our natural endowment but only a creative potentiality that had to be historically discovered, articulated, and developed. This way of conceiving the origins of the forms in question yields quite a different view of individual poems and the interrelations of the formal sets and subsets involved from that envisaged by structuralist or archetypal theories which would see all literary works as cleanly assimilable to a finite number of pre-existing patterns revealing themselves in individual works. Categories of poems are not like categories of biological species which locate the uniform characteristics of whole ranges of individuals, nor (to employ an analogy closer to structuralist usage) are they like sentences in a language which can all unequivocally manifest a finite number of basic grammatical structures. Resemblances among poems need to be understood, on the one hand, as resulting from the emergent discovery of natural creative possibilities and on the other in terms of the subsequent historical development, with variation and extension, of such possibilities.

The historical continuity of literary forms is often attributed to convention, when not to structural archetypes, but this point of view usually does not involve a sufficient recognition of the pre-conventional objectifying base that forms have in our common cognitive endowment, nor does it often involve an appreciation of the nature of generic conventions themselves as specifically invented, inherited, and redeployed with creative variation by the succession of writers working with them.

Further, though deeply conditioned by nature and history, literary forms have to be considered, in their individual manifestation, as ultimately ad hoc, contingent and personal in a sense which, despite our current bias toward the pre-and transpersonal, we all intuitively understand: we do realize, when we think about it, that if Browning had not written "My Last Duchess," that great poem, despite all the conventions and structures and other poets in the world, despite all the rest of history and nature, would just not have been.

But the masterpiece distinctiveness of such a structure as "My Last Duchess" is closely akin to its status as a particularly "pure instance," a paradigm instance, of the dramatic monologue form. This leads to the further observation that, even as there are an indefinite number of potential formal principles derivable from the structure of the natural imagination, there are necessarily (given the notion of a work as a personal and therefore finally contingent construct) different degrees of fullness of constructive realization of a particular formal potentiality, conditional on the author's powers operating within the terms of particular constructive situations. The methodological consequence is that, in the application of formal principles to the interpretations of individual works, the conception of the principle needs to be kept clear and distinct, so that its degree of "fit" to the work can be given perspicuous statement. When concept and work are not congruent, the critic can then conclude either that the principle is not the principle of the work and hypothesize a new, more adequate principle for it (as in my reconception of "Tintern Abbey" as an expressive rather than a dramatic lyric) or take the incongruence as an objective indication of the work's only approximate realization of a formal potentiality and conduct his analysis and evaluation accordingly.

Since such variant possibilities are more easily illustrated than generalized about, the space remaining will be devoted to consideration of three masterpiece poems whose formal characteristics do not in some way fit those of any of my developed categories—Browning's "Porphyria's Lover," Yeats's "Leda and the Swan," and Tennyson's *In Memoriam*—and indicate how the first can be analyzed as realizing while to some degree departing from the full formality of the dramatic monologue, how the second can be effectively described by an extension of the dramatic lyric conception, while the third has to be seen as displaying a more complex formality than can be described in terms of the other formal notions.

Browning's three supreme monologues—"My Last Duchess," "The Bishop Orders His Tomb," and "Andrea del Sarto"—are all developed as speech acts deeply motivated in the actor's represented situation, in contrast with the normal mode in dramatic lyrics where the words of the actor do not constitute a speech act but are a "worded" objectification of his inner cognitive process, so that one might be tempted to see the outward speech act/ inner cognitive act contrast as locating the essential characteristics of the forms.[4] But both clearly retain their distinctive imaginative character even when the normally characteristic speech modalities are not present (a fact which supports my fundamental assumption that literary forms, though always realized in language, are never subject to merely linguistic definition). Arnold's "Dover Beach," which has all other properties of a dramatic lyric, is articulated as the speaker's speech in the scene to his lover, whereas Browning's "Porphyria's Lover" is not literally voiced speech but must be understood as implicitly giving the speaker's stream of memory and reflection after the represented action has taken place. Even these anomalies confirm the underlying structuring presence of the respective forms, however, since the "Dover Beach" actor's speech must be taken as inner-thought-in-consequence-of-perception moving into speech, perhaps not even actually voiced, and if at all, only at "Ah, love, let us be true / To one another!" We do not see him as an outward presence but look through his eyes at the registered scene, and orient ourselves through him toward the (implicit) presence of the lover; we enter the speaker's act and engage with him in his heartfelt appeal. (I leave this description in place, as instructively illustrating the fact that it may not be quite accurate. The editor of this volume, Linda Shires, tells me that she has tested the description with a group of student readers who unanimously report that they see the reader as an outward presence at the same time that they orient themselves through him. My general claim that we "conflate" ourselves with the actor in the dramatic lyric implies the participation of our identity in his, and this notion of a merging duality can accommodate the possibility of a slight disjunction between the reader and the "Dover Beach" actor coordinate with the sense of him as not merely perceiving but speaking in the scene. In a cinematic projection, this may register as an "over the shoulder" view, still allowing us to dwell in the actor and his act; certainly we cannot imagine ourselves as seeing him face-to-face as an other.)

In contrast, though a cinematic projection of "Porphyria's Lover" also shows us an outward scene by means of the "voice-over" wording of the lover projecting his inner image of the action (as in the dramatic lyric), he is registered by our imaginations from the outset as peculiarly "other." It is as though we stood outside his body and mind, privy to his stream of thought from an outward perspective (as if he were speaking to or toward us), but not to its sensed inner meaning, hidden within his embodied mind. This correlates with the fact that we "hear" his unvoiced speech as if in the distinctive voice of "another" person.

Beyond this, we can uncover the fact of our awareness of the indwelling quasi-invisible poet, who from the outset generates a subliminal sense of the unbalance of the lover through the odd abab*b* rhyme scheme, just as the muted rhymes of the couplets in "My Last Duchess" suggest the Duke's dissembled purpose (see "The Dramatic Monologue and Related Lyric Forms," pp. 138–139). But of course the Lover's whole memorial recapitulation of the early action is developed with the greatest skill by the poet so as to maintain the perspective of the "other." Browning achieves this perspective not only through the Lover's dramatically significant pathetic fallacy whereby he projects his paranoid fears onto the setting, but by displaying in Porphyria's seemingly autonomous action the signs by which we form a judgment of her independent of the speaker's, register as excessive his motivating fear that she is fickle and faithless, and thereby judge him. From the fact that she enters wordlessly without knocking, the reader infers her status as his intimate. At the same time, her spontaneous act of making a fire in the cheerless grate (before doing anything else) and soiling her gloves in the process suggests her concern for his comfort and her complete lack of pride as the lady the gloves (and the later reference to the "gay feast") indicate she is. The fact of her "dripping cloak" and "damp hair" (ll. 11, 13) confirms the imaginative premise of the rainy night established in the opening and draws upon it further to emphasize the extraordinary devotion required to bring her to him from the feast, as the Lover notes, "through wind and rain" (l. 30); so that, all in all, we have good grounds for seeing his estimate of the quality of her love as having its basis more in his fears than in her character, so "Perfectly pure and good" (l. 37).

The disjunction between the Lover's and our own estimate of Porphyria's character needs to be sharp, for the more the reader sees the Lover's fearful reading of her as objectively justified, the less mad he will seem, and the less accordingly the impact of the poem. We may therefore admire the skill by which Browning allows the Lover to confirm our positive estimate of Porphyria without either disrupting our sense of his consistency or qualifying the basis of our (retrospective) judgment that his motivation is insane. Thus his strongly positive concessions about her occur, as already in part noticed, in contexts that confirm them and undermine his qualifications, as when he says that it was just a "sudden thought" (l. 28) that prompted her determined foray through the stormy night or that her manifest devotion to him was only to last "That moment" (l. 36).

Yet not all readers, or at least not all interpreters, will agree without equivocation that the Lover's negative assertions about Porphyria are unjustified, just because the necessary complexity of the representation made it so difficult for Browning to keep the terms of the contrast clear. For that matter, fully establishing Porphyria's character is not required by the primary objective of the poem, and though she is persuasive enough in our concrete awareness, the further we ponder her character outside our immediate encounter with it in the poem, the more we may be inclined to doubt, not that she could be faithful to the Lover, but that, given her vitality and goodness, she could have been attracted to him at all, since nothing we learn suggests how this moping solitary could have been so overwhelmingly attractive to her. Our sense of the depth and cogency of Porphyria's motivation in its ultimate relation to our sense of the Lover's action, as perhaps of that action itself, does not go so implicitly deep as our sense, for instance, of the Duke's innocent last Duchess, or Andrea's Lucrezia, or even of the Bishop's so briefly represented mistress of the glittering eyes; and this may have something to do with our feeling that "Porphyria's Lover," for all its brilliant economy of representation and insight, is not so great a poem as the generality of readers surely feel the three others to be.

Browning's problem in unequivocally establishing the Lover's unreliability from the outset connects with another problem, his need to prevent the reader from too early inferring the Lover's murderous insanity while at the same time clearly developing its probability. His achievement, and the impact of his achieved effect, can be cleanly located in terms of the reader's response to the lines where the Lover's murderous action and his insanity are jointly revealed:

> I found
> A thing to do, and all her hair
> In one long yellow string I wound
> Three times her little throat around,
> And strangled her.
> (ll. 37–41)

We can locate the structure of the strong effect by saying that, at the end of the next-to-the-last line, the reader has no anticipation of what the Lover's intention is, whereas after the following phrase he realizes that this act is completely consistent with everything that has gone before. The paranoid projection of the opening, the confession that he listened with "heart fit to break" (l. 5), his strange passivity sitting alone in the cold, cheerless cottage, his even stranger self-conscious failure to answer her call ("When no voice replied" [l. 15]), the ominous oddity of "I found / A thing to do" (ll. 37–38), at once portending and coyly concealing his imminent act, all subliminally fill out our registration, in the midst of our focus on Porphyria, of the Lover's derangement. The effect turns, of course, on the presence of the unconcealed but entirely unsuspected weapon of her long, yellow hair, the damp hair she let fall on her gliding entrance which, with her "smooth white shoulder bare" (l. 17), defines her as so completely not for killing.

Yet it is just because of her overwhelming attractiveness and supportive love, as a stay against the threatening world beyond the cottage, that the lover does decide to kill her. After the insanity is established at the point of the strangling, the focus is simultaneously on the horror of the act and on the reasonableness of the Lover's action from his insane point of view (cf.

Langbaum, p. 88): he has killed her in order to fix her in her love for him forever, and as the poem moves to its end we continuously understand what we see simultaneously in his terms and ours. So, when he "warily" opens her eyelids to see her laughing "blue eyes without a stain" (l. 45), we understand, in visual terms, that he can register as thus alive the eyes that we see as those of a very dead woman. Similarly, we understand the "bright blush" he takes as a response to his burning kiss to be the result of the blood rushing back into her face as he releases the strangling hair, and her head, propped and drooping upon his shoulder, as manifesting a limp lifelessness which he reads as expressing her willing dependence on him.

This duality of awareness is the sine qua non of the dramatic monologue structure that Langbaum located in his famous and widely echoed phrase "sympathy and judgment." My own view, already in part indicated, is that this dual effect is based on our in-built capacity to empathize with the innerness of another person when we stand as the uninvolved external observer of his speech and bodily action, at the same time that we necessarily retain the anchoring perspective of our mind in our own body.[5] But if this explanation is clearer and more explanatory than the "sympathy and judgment" formulation in locating the common reference of both, I would underline the importance of Langbaum's emphasis on the fact that, in his terms, sympathy predominates over judgment in our experience of the dramatic monologue, or, to put it in mine, that we are absorbed in our focal empathy with the dramatic monologue character, whereas our awareness of the in-built disjunction is subsidiary; we are in short rapt in our outside act of understanding the "other." This agrees with and glosses Langbaum's statement, quoted above, that "we understand the speaker of the dramatic monologue by sympathizing with him, and yet by remaining aware of the moral judgment we have suspended for the sake of understanding." Langbaum speaks as if more deliberate choice were involved than I do in my insistence on the in-built pre-structuring of our cognition of the "other," but in saying of the Duke that "we prefer to participate in [his] power and freedom" (p. 83) rather than hold ourselves in disjunctive judgment, Langbaum locates rightly the side to which our awareness of these poems must incline if we are to achieve full aesthetic appreciation of them. The point is particularly useful for teachers who might wish to articulate the source of a problem students develop more frequently with the Bishop of St. Praxed's than with the Duke, as they hold themselves judgmentally aloof from the urgent flow of the Bishop's errant and sensual spirit and quite miss the enchanting access the poem offers to his strange but nonetheless deeply human point of view (cf. "The Dramatic Monologue and Related Lyric Forms," pp. 139–140).

It is in fact the consistent mark of the dramatic monologue character that he should, in his otherly mystery, be distinctly understandable. The characters are normally extreme instances just so understanding will not be easily available through assimilation to our own "perspective of the normal," but the ultimate beauty of the poems depends on the fact that the poet provides, the more covertly though clearly the better, a representation which fixes the rationale of the character and allows us literal *in*-sight through his speech and action into the structure of his motive, so that our act of rapt sympathy can begin in aroused curiosity and end in the release of full insight and understanding. (This is equivalent in reference to the familiar but inadequate and incomplete characterization of the dramatic monologue as involving a "study" of "character.") In presenting the character as if autonomous and actual, the dramatic monologue poet may risk obscuring the reader's understanding of the peculiar motivation which objectively characterizes him, but the need for implicit intelligibility is a necessary corollary of the poet's creative control of his two-sided enterprise; he could not focus his mysterious other without some key to his mystery. It is accordingly no accident that we can discover that the Duke's entire action is grounded in his imperious wish that his pride be respected without his seeming to stoop to insist on it; or that the key to the Bishop's character and action is that, desiring eternal life, he cannot conceive immortality as spiritual but only as material; or that, as noticed above, Porphyria's Lover's mad act has its rationale in his thought that he can preserve Porphyria's love for him only by killing her.

Whereas in the dramatic monologue the fact of "character" and the need for an implicit external notion of its rationale are inseparable from the fact that the represented character is an "other" of whom we seek sympathetic understanding, in the dramatic lyric, in contrast, the registered actor has no "character" as he has no name: he lacks both because a self in its self-inhabitation and self-understanding does not need to locate itself with a name, just as it acts out of its identity rather than directs its understanding toward it, so that it is an undefined indwelt ground rather than a defined outward object. What is outward for the dramatic lyric actor is the external world as the object of his understanding.

An essential feature of the dramatic lyric is its power to bring before the reader's imagination a visually objective scene which is yet perceived as instinct with discovered subjective meaning. Gray's initiating achievement in the "Elegy" is truly remarkable for the sense it gives of seeing and hearing the objects of the churchyard scene in the gathering dusk, and its structural anomalies can in fact be explained as produced by its rigorous commitment to the probability of the actor seeing in the scene.[6] The scenic sense in the poem, however, is nonetheless somewhat diluted by the meditative development, and the natural tendency of later poets was to work in more reduced compass for more continuous and sharply realized visual effect, as does Arnold in the open moonlit seascape of "Dover Beach," framed by the flickering light on the French coast and the bright belt of the moonlit beach, both so charged with the felt meaning of the poem. But "Dover Beach" in turn is not so fully informed by intricate visual probability as Hardy's

"Darkling Thrush," where so many details—the tangled bine stems that score the sky, the wintry dregs of the clouds, the sun as the "weakening eye of day," the "sharp features" of the distant landscape—evoke and confirm the sense of seeing the scene in the distinct outline produced by the reduced ambient light of the winter day, so that one needs an account of the workings of vision like that developed by J. J. Gibson in his revolutionary but already classic *The Senses Considered as Perceptual Systems* (Boston, 1966) to articulate fully the registered structure of the visual situation as Hardy makes it manifest through the words of the poem. Hardy follows Gray, Arnold, and also Keats in developing the auditory correlate of the visual dimension of his poem, perhaps with no greater affective power but with more integrating technique than Gray and Arnold, as the significance of the poem bursts with the thrush's song more probably and surprisingly from the scene. In this progression, if it is that, we see the development of the possibilities of an invented and inherited form realized in permanent aesthetic instances, each based on and appealing to universal cognitive resources but at the same time articulating the unique personal experience of each writer.

Considered off-hand, Yeats's "Leda and the Swan" would seem quite an unlikely work to think of as a dramatic lyric, for how can a portrayal of a mythological figure be related to a tradition of poems which are implicitly reconstructions of actual cognitive experience? But it is just this apparent contradiction which leads to a fruitful use of the concept to locate the source of power in this great poem. The crucial point is that we are given the scene not, as would have been conventionally quite possible, in a free flight to literary never-never land, but that we see it rather, through our imaginative absorption in the poet-speaker, as if in the twentieth-century present. The rape is shown us not as if told or imagined but in rigorously visual terms as if literally seen—so that we infer Leda's (and the swan's) inward state exclusively from external signs, as from the sight of "those terrified vague fingers" attempting to push the "feathered glory" from "her loosening thighs"; we infer from what we see of Leda's body that her mind is not in command of her body's compelled acquiescence to the swan's assault. But yet simultaneously with our restrictedly visual perspective, we know that it is Leda and the swan as Zeus that we see; we know the event perceived in the present as nonetheless fixed in the mythological past, and we know with the speaker what the sequel of the rape will be ("engenders there / The broken wall, the burning roof and tower / And Agamemnon dead"), though it has already been. And this knowledge we are also able to read in what we see, as the "great wings" and "feathered glory," mimetically descriptive of a swan, bespeak the presence of the god; indeed, the swan's represented action is only intelligible as Zeus's. Yet the poet-speaker's independent knowledge of the myth does not include knowledge of Leda's and the swan's inner consciousness, hidden and only to be guessed at in the objective presence of their bodies ("Did she put on his knowledge with his power / Before the indifferent beak could let her drop?"). In sum the reader experiences the poem not as a fictive entry into a fabulous past but as Yeats's recreation of his vision of the fabulous as impinging objectively on his awareness in the real present, like Keats's nightingale or Hopkins' windhover, though Yeats's is an inwardly present scene without setting or sound. A great deal has been written about the relation of Yeats's odd beliefs to his poetry, and treating this poem as a dramatic lyric helps us to be clearer about dealing with the problem. "Now as at all times I can see in the mind's eye / . . . the pale unsatisfied ones," Yeats says in the opening of "The Magi"; in that poem and in others, as in "Leda," he induces us to share the fact and inward act of his visionary belief.

The reader's tacit experience of "Leda" then turns out to be surprisingly if covertly dependent on his sense of the relation of the matter of the poem to Yeats's experience in a way quite out of keeping with doctrines of autonomous speakers and the "textuality" of poems, but we are so used to thinking of a poem like *In Memoriam* as obviously and unproblematically connected with the poet's experience that we are likely not only to forget how grossly such assumed connection contradicts accepted doctrines of autonomous textuality but also to lose sight of the fact that the biographical elements in the poem are not a matter, first of all, of external knowledge but are inseparable from the intrinsic intelligibility of the poem as immediately read and experienced, so that, more strongly than the dramatic lyric, and more complicatedly than "Tintern Abbey," it requires the presumptive identification of the speaker/actor in the poem with the creating poet Tennyson. (External knowledge of course has to fill in the formal implication of the poem. The "A.H.H." whose initials and date of death are given epigraphically and the person mourned as "Arthur" in the text constitute a conjunction of incomplete terms which we must take as converging on a real and not fictional referent, but this referent has to be externally glossed for us as the historical Arthur Henry Hallam, analogous to the way we might need to be told by a mutual acquaintance that an unknown person who has come under our palpable observation as actually existing is in fact "Frank Smith," with such and such a personal history.)

Although the individual lyrics of the poem have clear affinities with the dramatic and expressive lyric forms, our experience of the individual structures is developed within the force field of the larger structure of the whole, which is in fact the primary cause of our reading the poem as inherently autobiographical in substance and diaristic in form. The poem displays overall coherence only if we interpret the speaker/actor in the lyrics as effectively identical, though (as we shall see) to some degree in contrast, with the real poet conceived as articulating himself in the poem. This identity is most strikingly implied in such features as the speaker's later reference ("Let this not vex thee, noble heart!" [LXXIX]) to his brother's reaction to the lines in the poem asserting that Hallam, was "More than my brothers are to me" (IX), where the mutual internal/external reference of the poem is implicit.

A further implication of this and cognate references is that the poem must be understood as diaristic, so that to grasp the movement of the poem and feel its beauty, we must react to the individual lyrics as expressive constructs artistically achieved and in place before the completion of the whole; there is necessarily a sense throughout of the poem as a serially staged existential projection into time, in which the later stages were not for poet, any more than for the speaker/actor, foreseen at the earlier stages. Consider in this connection the force of the Proem as looking back upon the whole recorded experience, including the recording poems themselves, as "the long result" of time, with itself, the beginning of the poem, as the last (retrospective) temporal point in its series.

The fact that the poem must be registered as created emergently, with the parts complete before the resolution of the whole was achieved or in view, is not inconsistent with the assertion that the poem has also to be simultaneously understood as a pre-envisioned construct. Though Tennyson no doubt wrote some of the early poems, as he said, with no initial thought of putting them into a larger work, it was then very fortunate that he cast them all in the same verse form; and indeed we know that he did not contribute to Henry Hallam's memorial volume because he already hoped at this early date (February, 1834) to construct some larger tribute to his friend; this was surely the *In Memoriam* project.[7]

The homogeneous aesthetic quality of the poem also has to be conceived as fixed from the outset. This quality involves a continuity of effect dependent upon our lyrical participation in the poet's continuously achieved serenity—shadowed and weighted, momentary and tentative in the earlier part, increasingly stable and enduring in the later and in the whole—as he struggles to assert by fiat of faith, completely against all evidence, the presence of a divine purpose in the universe; so that the "Believing where we cannot prove" in the fourth line of the poem should be seen as defining the basis of the continuouous emotional effect of the whole rather than as merely a statement of religious "idea" or belief. This emphasis (which is perhaps what Eliot meant to convey when he spoke of the quality of the doubt in the poem being more important than the quality of its faith) is proper to our understanding of a work not of philosophy but literature, whose raison d'etre is its power to move rather than its validity as thought; but at the same time it is the enacted validity of the assertion as rooted in earnest belief which gives it its emotional power. If the belief were felt to be generated by the poet's search for effect rather than the other way around, the effect would be sentimental, whereas the avoidance of sentimentality is the mark of Tennyson's signal success in this poem which, so precariously based in personal feeling, is consistently articulated in aesthetic dispassion. The quality of unfounded affirmation, one may note, finds expression even in the metaphorical detail of the poem, as in "God's finger touched him, and he slept" (LXXXV), where the emotional force of the statement depends on the reader's measuring its calm assertion that Hallam's death was the result of God's benevolent act against his well-developed coordinate awareness of the spiritual anguish the loss has earlier wrought in the speaker; the overriding emotional denial of brute fact through faith in what is invisible and doubtful is an enactment which generates an emotional effect pervasively characteristic of the poem. A parallel example is "the great world's altar-stairs" that "slope through darkness up to God" (LV), which so persuasively postulates secure support and direction within the space of complete objective uncertainty. The effect of course culminates in the confident grandeur of the final assertion, understood by poet and reader as assertion but felt as truth, of the "one far-off divine event, / To which the whole creation moves" ("Epilogue," ll. 143–144).

Our awareness of the poem as based in and reflecting real experience while having a complementary status as an aesthetically homogeneous artificial construct enables us to understand and accept the fact that Tennyson wrote various of the poems at times different from their implied chronology and inserted them into an earlier or later sequence. This can be theoretically glossed in terms of the fact that the poet's act of construction is in principle separate from the experience he expresses or reconstructs, so that he can fill out or complete his construct in terms of its unity and effect in ways that prevent it from being anything like a reflexive response to his raw "experience," while at the same time it is expression as close to his "real" experience as the total creative situation permitted.

There is something of a paradox here. It was the sense of the unavoidable disjunction from his experience that expressing it in a poem involved which caused Tennyson to say that the poem displayed more optimism than he actually felt, or that the voice of the poem was not always his but "the voice of the human race speaking thro' him":[8] From one perspective of the analysis offered here, this statement is not so much the self-important pomposity it seems as a consequence of the constructive inevitabilities implicit in the logic of writing such a poem. At the same time, one can see from another perspective of the analysis that the objective act of writing the poem which disjoined him from his actual experience also implicated him personally because of its inevitable opposite tendency to become intertwined with the experience it recorded. It is no wonder, then, that we find as an integral part of the poem the assertion, in contrast with his later external one that it is not his personal self speaking, that "I sometimes hold it half a sin / To put in words the grief I feel" (V). The idea of halfness is accurate: the poems only half express his real grief because they do not present immediate real experience but artistic objectifications of memories of real experience, and this double aspect of the poems, as at once objective constructs and serially completed expressions of personal emotion, is just the character so accurately and beautifully attributed to them from within the work as "these brief lays, of Sorrow born . . . Short swallow-flights of song, that dip / Their wings in tears, and skim away" (XLVIII). (The reflexive consciousness of itself as a poem stands in contrast with the directly "expressive" mode of "Tintern Abbey" and the Immortality Ode and even with the closer integration of artifice and experience in the dramatic lyric, just because the artistic reconstruction is so manifestly long-term, independent, and separate from the experience.)

As a final brief illustration of the comprehensive way in which the overarching structure of the poem as the progressive artistic reenactment of the poet's moments of personal grief governs the reader's registration of the component lyrics, thus giving them a phenomenological dimension that by themselves they would not have, notice Section XXXI, "When Lazarus left his charnel-cave." Nowhere in this lyric is there any reference to the poet and his personal situation or any implication about him other than that he is, as in any poem, the author of the lines we are reading. Removed from its context, the poem would be a generalized meditation on resurrection vis-a-vis Lazarus. But of course we do read it in the very powerful context of the whole, and readers take it and deeply feel it, universally and unreflectively, not as meditation but as marking one in the continuing series of stages of the poet's lament for his friend, though neither of them is in any explicit way implicated by the language.

I would apologize for belaboring the obvious in this analysis of *In Memoriam*, as of other poems earlier, except that it is just the inescapably obvious, the ground of our ordinary reading experience and our practical critical operations, which has to be explicitly laid out in its experienced objectivity and brought into full conceptual focus if effective challenge and counterclaim is to be offered to the powerful theoretical denials of significant connection between poetry and experience, text and world which currently hold sway in the literary critical arena. The kinds of imaginative stabilities and invariants of our literary experience which I have been pointing to throughout are, I would claim, the underlying though usually not clearly conscious basis of our sense of generic distinctions and of the structure of significance and value in individual poems. A systematic account of such imaginative facts is the most meaningful test that can be offered of the application and validity of critical theories. Even more important, explicit theoretical reconstruction of the implicit basis of literary works in the definite though various constructive intentions of authors—their intelligible purposes as human beings rooted in their personal grounds of reality—can invigorate our sense of literature as movingly meaningful to us as likewise rooted in the pre-existent realities of our experience in and of the world.

Notes

1. See "The Dramatic Monologue and Related Lyric Forms," *CritI*, 3 (1976), 131–151.
2. *The Letters of William and Dorothy Wordsworth*, ed. Ernest de Selincourt; 2nd ed., rev. Mary Moorman (Oxford, Univ. Press, 1969), II, 148.

3. *The Poetry of Experience: The Dramatic Monologue in Modern Literary Tradition* (New York, 1957), pp. 85, 96.

4. Cf. Ann Banfield, *Unspeakable Sentences: Narration and Representation in the Language of Fiction* (London, 1982), pp. 178–179 and 306n.

5. See "The Dramatic Monologue and Related Lyric Forms," pp. 133–135 and also my "Exodus and Return: Joyce's *Ulysses* and the Fiction of the Actual," *UTQ*, 48 (1978), 149–171, and "The Logic of *Ulysses*, or Why Molly Had to Live in Gibraltar," forthcoming in *CritI* (June, 1984), where I extend the application of the concept to Joyce's representation and projection of himself in *Ulysses*, climaxing in his abandonment of the "anchoring perspective" in the creation of Molly.

6. See my essay, "The Concept of Genre and Eighteenth-Century Studies," in *New Approaches to Eighteenth-Century Literature*, ed. Phillip Harth (New York, 1974), pp. 94–99.

7. See Tennyson, *Works*, ed. Hallam Lord Tennyson (London, 1913), p. 954.

8. Hallam Lord Tennyson, *Alfred Lord Tennyson: A Memoir By His Son* (London, 1897), I, 305.

Consciousness as Writing: Deconstruction and Reading Victorian Poetry

E. Warwick Slinn

Readers of Victorian literature will be familiar with the difficulty which Victorians felt when required to respond to new evolutionary models of the world, models which provided a view of change and development as intelligible, that is recognizable and explicable, and yet essentially unauthored, without defined origin or providential plan. Change, transformations, apparently occurred without any determinable cause or discernible intent other than the amoral, pragmatic aim of continuing the existence of organic life. Such a view was a shock to a society dominated by a religious ethos which explained all events in terms of divine origins and teleological purpose. A world without god was a world without an author or plot.

Currently a similar model is being provided for writing, not in terms of evolutionary development, but in terms of a process which exists without beginning or end, without author or reader in their traditional roles as the instigator and receiver of independent messages. What is at stake is no longer god, but consciousness: it is not that consciousness is being denied, but its status and function is being considerably redefined. In one sense, human consciousness in the twentieth century has explored its relationship to language and discovered to its amazement that there is no relationship to explore, since man and language are inseparable. Without separability there cannot, strictly speaking, be a relationship, that is between man as conceptually constituted and language as the mode of conception. Within this context the post-structuralist metaphor of consciousness as writing becomes an inevitable analogy for explaining such discoveries (or constructions), but while the problematics of consciousness are of general epistemological interest in the study of literature, the concern here is necessarily more specific. The implications drawn from one example of this metaphor, taken from a passage in Derrida, may provide a means of continuing to read Victorian poetry, and specifically "Two in the Campagna," in terms of the "representations" of the processes of consciousness, yet without falling into some of the traps of empirical assumptions. The underlying assumptions are the propositions that the monologue form in particular already contains, thematically and in

Reprinted from *Victorian Poetry* 25 (1987): 67–81, with permission.

its epistemological paradoxes, the modern dilemma about the relationship between language and consciousness; and that Victorian poetry in general, insofar as it is concerned even in its larger forms (perhaps most of all in the larger forms) with the existence of a self which is constituted within the forms and conventions of lyric verse, is dominated by the problems of awareness and knowing—if not consciousness *as* writing, at least consciousness *in* writing.

I

Consider these two extracts from *Empedocles on Etna*:

> Before the sophist-brood hath overlaid
> The last spark of man's consciousness with words—
> Ere quite the being of man, ere quite the world
> Be disarrayed of their divinity—
> Before the soul lose all her solemn joys,
> And awe be dead, and hope impossible,
> And the soul's deep eternal night come on—
> Receive me, hide me, quench me, take me home!
> (II.i.29–36)

> But mind, but thought—
> If these have been the master part of us—
> Where will *they* find their parent element?
> What will receive *them*, who will call *them* home?
> But we shall still be in them, and they in us,
> And we shall be the strangers of the world,
> And they will be our lords, as they are now;
> And keep us prisoners of our consciousness,
> And never let us clasp and feel the All
> But through their forms, and modes, and stifling veils.
> (II.i.345–354)[1]

These lines present two anxieties about consciousness: the fear that it may be lost or obliterated in language, "overlaid / . . . with words," and the fear that the speaker may be shut forever within consciousness, imprisoned within its forms and modes. Also, these two contradictory fears involve two assumptions about the status of consciousness: that it is separate from language and that it is a distinguishing feature of individual knowing whereby it is the means through which the individual is separated from the world. Impelling Empedocles' fears is the desire to find some means of retaining the sense of a consciousness which remains free from the controlling forces of abstract thought or linguistic structuring. This is what remains perhaps of the Romantic desire for an independent selfhood or transcendent ego, the desire for the power of origination, the desire not to be subsumed into a process without authorship or telos. It is of course one of the devastating ironies of Empedocles' predicament that the only alternative is to commit himself to an external process which is potentially just that. He does not know what death entails, whether an end or merely a repetition, but the crucial difference is the act of death itself, that it be committed by a free individual, an independent consciousness. It is the act, not the product or the significance, the vision accompanying it, which constitutes the fact of independence for Empedocles.

On the other hand, consider these two extracts from Nietzsche:

> *consciousness has developed only under the pressure of the need for communication.* . . . Consciousness is really only a net of communication between human beings. . . . only this conscious thinking *takes the form of words, which is to say signs of communication*, and this fact uncovers the origin of consciousness.
>
> Consciousness plays no role in the total process of adaptation and systematization.[2]

Consciousness here has been linked totally to language; it has been denied as having any power to authorize action at any significant level in human or social affairs, and it has been assigned only a communicative function. It is through consciousness as language that we are linked, in this model, to other members of the community: it is a "net" of communication, the web by which we are interwoven. Clearly this proposition is what Empedocles fears, and it has been expanded recently in structuralist and post-structuralist theory, where consciousness is not some entity separate from language, but is inscribed in language, and where it does not originate meaning or thought—it is itself "written" in and through language.[3] Jacques Derrida, for instance, sustains the corollary of Nietzsche's point about consciousness as a net of communication by saying that writing as an iterative structure becomes "cut off . . . from *consciousness* as the ultimate authority" and that writing is not therefore "a communication of consciousnesses or of presences."[4] If the process of communication is itself constitutive of consciousness, there cannot be separate consciousnesses which perform the communicating.

Derrida's point here is to stress that speakers and their consciousnesses are not required to be present for communication to occur; indeed, quite the contrary is the case. It is the absence of the speaker which is the necessary condition for signs to function as signs. However, while his point involves the absence of separateness, not the absence of consciousness, it is worth noting that the consciousness which Nietzsche and Derrida locate within the process of language as communication is always known as the process within a singular, or seemingly singular, mind. While consciousness may be tied ontologically to language, it is known epistemologically in terms of the combined illusion of singularity and separation. This is an understandable illusion arising from the subject's identification of the web of communication with the weft of his biological independence (which is presumably another illusion even in biological terms), and in terms of the context of this discussion, it is the meeting point between the texts of Arnold and Nietzsche. Nietzsche's web of communication is experienced by Empedocles as the location of his separate awareness. This illusion is also a means of explaining why Empedocles is caught in his contradictory fears about consciousness: he experiences consciousness as the defining quality of his separate being and yet he senses that it is constituted in terms of its own modes and "stifling veils."[5] The consciousness which is known as an intrasubjective process is yet tied to forms which define intersubjectivity.

The increasing post-Romantic recognition of these problematics of awareness and of the sense in which experience is an unreliable source of human understanding (exposed in Browning's monologues, for instance, through various disjunctions within his speakers' discourse and structures) has led Ann Wordsworth recently to challenge the reading of Victorian monologues in terms of an empirical base which ties them to speech acts and to assumptions about the originary qualities of character.[6] We are to beware of assumptions about the universality of experience and its necessary meaningfulness and to remain cautious about explaining poems in terms of their apparently referential context when all we have is language and what Ann Wordsworth calls its "textual mobility." She points to the dissolution of identity within language and to the way writing may then "reinvent the self as multiple projections of textuality" (p. 9). There is no need to disagree with these propositions. Victorian monologues, in particular (as well as the long lyric poems), involve a "textual mobility" which produces a weaving and unweaving of identity, and therefore a precariously realized process of awareness. But this mobility of language, or "pure unaccountability of writing," need not disallow interpretative acts which read the "linguistic performance" of a poem as including the action or nonaction of a simulated subject, as the process, that is, by which a consciousness is simultaneously active and passive within the field of its constitution. While it is entirely correct that Ann Wordsworth should challenge the prevailing assumptions about the empirical reading of Victorian poetry, there is a point when her method, necessarily polemical, moves toward a reverse privileging of the structures of language over the function of a subject in the act of writing (whether the subject as reader, as author, or as speaker). Writing as the model for speech acts, which is what Derrida suggests may be the case, is a paradoxical process: communication is not a communication of consciousnesses, but communication is not denied ("Signature," p. 181); the subject is situated, but not destroyed;[7] intention no longer governs the whole scene, but intention is not removed or denied ("Signature," p. 192). What is required is a more thorough consideration of what is involved with the image of writing in its (non)relationship to consciousness. The image of consciousness as writing emerges from Derrida's essay on "Freud and the Scene of Writing," notably from the last section on Freud's piece of wax, or Mystic Pad; using the example of "Two in the Campagna," this image might be applied to Victorian poetry.

II

In "Freud and the Scene of Writing," Derrida traces the development of Freud's search for an appropriate model for the processes of memory, a model which would combine the possibility of indefinite preservation with an unlimited capacity for reception.[8] The usual image of writing was inadequate, since a sheet of paper as the receptacle for impressions was limited in size and once filled could not be reused. Eventually Freud explored an analogy between a certain writing apparatus and the perceptual apparatus of the human psyche, and in this analogy Derrida observes the elements of the idea of consciousness as a form of writing. The writing apparatus in question is the child's "Mystic Pad," a device which consists of a transparent sheet with two layers, one celluloid and one piece of thin waxed paper, which is placed over a block of dark resin or wax. When marks are made on the top piece of celluloid, writing appears. These marks are etched in the piece of wax, but the waxed sheet can be lifted in order to remove the signs of writing and allow for more writing to be registered. At the same time the marks in the wax are retained and may still be legible under certain conditions. Thus the device includes the requisites of both retention and reception. For my purposes there are four main points to be drawn from Derrida's account of Freud's use of this analogy.

1. *Temporality as spacing.* The image of the Mystic Pad illustrates the interruption and restoration of contact between various layers of the psychic process. Specifically, the image is spatial (the writing occurs on a defined space) and at the same time temporal (the perception exists for the time it remains in that space, until the sheet is lifted, which it inevitably must be in order to allow for more writing to occur). The temporal aspect thus disrupts the homogeneity which would be implicit in a model purely spatial, and the mixed elements are represented by Derrida in terms of a theatrical metaphor: we find "only the differentiated duration and depth of a stage, and its spacing" (p. 225). Such drama images are worth noting, since they suggest a potential analogy between psychic process and literary staging, the point where psychic action and literary action coincide as a theatrical performance.[9]

2. *Perception as already a representation.* Pure perception does not exist, because what is perceived is what is written on the space of writing. Perception is thus the product of an act of writing which has already occurred, with

its complications of spacing, deferring, and erasure: " 'perception,' the first relation of life to its other, the origin of life, had always already prepared representation" (p. 226). All perception is thus located within the already existing structures which allow perception as a meaningfully understood activity to occur, but what is also involved is its essential multiplicity—it is not a singular act. One of the marks of the temporality of the machine of the Mystic Pad, for instance, is that it is operated with two hands; it requires "a system of gestures, a coordination of independent initiatives," so that it is "an organized multiplicity of origins" (p. 226). Insofar as the model involves this multiplicity of agencies in its functioning, it represents the fracturing of any belief in writing and perception as a single originary action: "We must be several in order to write, and even to 'perceive.' The *simple* structure of maintenance and manuscript, like every intuition of an origin, is a myth" (p. 226).

3. *The subject as system.* It follows from the previous point that neither is the subject of writing a singular entity; the subject does not exist if we mean "some sovereign solitude of the author" (p. 226). Derrida is careful to refer to the subject of writing, which is to be distinguished from the subject as biological or psychic organism. This subject, then, the subject of writing, is a system, "a *system* of relations between strata: the Mystic Pad, the psyche, society, the world" (p. 227). It is also a system which is characterized by the paradox of an action, in writing, which is passive, being written: "We are written only as we write, by the agency within us which always already keeps watch over perception" (p. 226). Jeffrey Mehlman's translation of this crucial passage provides slightly different phrasing: "We are written only by writing [*en écrivant*], by the instance within us which always already governs perception" (p. 113). The original phrase, *en écrivant*, contains the ambiguity of a process which is both active and passive: we write and are thereby written. The difficulty in English is to capture that ambiguity, but it is important to register its presence, or it may be thought that this passage renders the subject entirely passive, given up totally to the powers of writing as other. That is not the case, however, and the proposition is rather to confront us with the paradox of the active/passive, the action of a subject who writes, and yet who in writing is written as a self produced by the multiple agencies which precede perception. The active and passive elements of this action are not to be conceived as opposite sides of conflicting forces, but as inseparable components of the process of writing and, in terms of the psychic metaphor which is the concern of this discussion, inseparable components of the process of consciousness. Derrida's paradox here is a version of an earlier attempt by Charles Sanders Peirce to represent the double process of a perception which is at once actively engendered and passively received: "Every cognition involves something represented, or that of which we are conscious, and some action or passion of the self whereby it becomes represented." Walter Benn Michaels points out that Peirce's strategy "is to collapse the distinction between the

interpreter and what he interprets," and the consequence is "not only that the self interprets but that the self is an interpretation."[10]

4. *The erasure of selfhood.* An important condition of the machine or tool of the Mystic Pad is that its contents are subject to continual removal, to the raising of the covering sheet from the wax slab. The marks of writing always exist, therefore, under the threat of erasure: "Traces . . . produce the space of their inscription only by acceding to the period of their erasure" (p. 226). They exist within the conditions of repetition and disappearance. Indeed, traces "are constituted" by repetition and erasure (p. 226), and the possibility of erasure is a condition of the trace as sign: "An unerasable trace is not a trace, it is a full presence, an immobile and uncorruptible substance" (p. 230). Writing is characterized by iterability and loss. To be committed to writing is to be committed to the paradox of a constitution which is dissolution, a "representation" which is "death" (p. 227). To come into being in the writing which is consciousness is at once to be committed to the repetition and deferral which is the death that is a sign of life. Consciousness as writing involves, therefore, the conception of the self as under erasure: "The trace is the erasure of selfhood, of one's own presence, and is constituted by the threat or anguish of its irremediable disappearance, of the disappearance of its disappearance" (p. 230).

It should be apparent, then, that the self as constituted in language is attached to images which are part of the temporizing and mobility of the trace. The self is attached to itself as always other, to the elusiveness and mobility of the signifier, so that it is attached to a process which guarantees its loss at the moment in which it is brought into being. The threat or anguish of its disappearance may be seen consequently in terms of a fear of nonexistence which leads, paradoxically, to an identification with the very source of the anxiety, with the trace which is the doubling of the self in language, the metaphor which denies full presence, the illusion of a continuity which is bound to process and thus to "irremediable disappearance."

III

The indivisibility of consciousness from the elusiveness and mobility of signifiers provides a useful transition to reading "Two in the Campagna,"[11] a Victorian poem where the elusiveness of signification and the mobility of thought as image become main themes with devastating consequences for the consciousness defined by their predicament. In part a love poem, it nevertheless moves beyond the traditions of expressiveness in love lyrics to suggest both the underlying lack which impels all desire and the futile attempts of consciousness to understand the source and nature of its own processes. The poem approaches the humiliating discovery of self-consciousness that it can never recover the source or origin which seems always to be implicit in its own utterance. The moment of feeling is lost in the act of its representation which is also the act of its discovery. Bound to the temporality of utterance, thought is irrecoverable, ever absent in the moment of its apparent presence, and the voice in this poem finally confronts the limits of its finitude with the unlimited desire which those limits generate, the yearning to recover lost presence, or the desire of all lovers to obliterate through union with the beloved that absence or lack which makes them lovers. In approaching this moment of crisis, the speaker epitomizes the predicament of all those Victorian poems which seek to fix a self within or against the mobility of a discourse which cannot be fixed.

The poem begins with a differentiated consciousness which is able only to speculate about its counterpart ("I wonder do you feel to-day / As I have felt") and which engages immediately in temporal and figurative play: the intermingling of past and present as the speaker places feelings from the immediate past ("As I have felt") against the potential feelings of the beloved in an ongoing present ("feel to-day"), and the intermingling of literal and figurative (they "sat down" in order to "stray / In spirit"), which is also an interfusion of the finite ("sat") with the potentially unrestricted ("to stray"). The second stanza moves even further into a mixing of past and present, and singularity and multiplicity, through recalling the continuing moments of a thought which "Has tantalized" and the one moment when the speaker apparently "touched" it. The act is both recollection and repetition. This stanza also introduces the theme of thought as image: the thought which "tantalized" is "Like turns of thread" thrown by spiders. It is immediately a problematic image, for it is the tantalizing quality of the thought as much as the thought itself which is like the thread that is thrown "Mocking across our path," and therefore the referent of the image is essentially inseparable from the qualities of the image: the thought does not exist, has no definition, other than as the teasing insubstantiality of a spider's web. The thought is literally the web, and the web is figuratively the thought. The thought is known in no other way than in terms of this conflation of literal and figurative. Such an uncertainty of signification leads "thought" as signified to point to its signified not as *a* thought existing outside the utterance, but to thought as indeterminate trace, to signification itself, the process in the poem of attempting to fix the trace, and yet with only an analogy, the analogy of the spider's web, as method. There is, then, no thought, only the image for it, and what these first two stanzas establish is a context where referentiality is undermined, where the literal is continually presented as figure. The imperatives of present action in the third stanza ("Help me to hold it!") occur, therefore, within a context where the present is not simply itself but is a repetition of the past, and where the literal tracing of the weft among the fennel and brickwork is a figurative retracing of a web which is itself a figure for the traces of a thought that is known only as a figure. We enter thus a network of signifiers. Even the brickwork is not just brickwork but the sign of "Some old tomb's ruin" (l. 14), and the speaker's attempt to act positively by calling on his companion to help him seize the weft is also paradoxically a sign of passivity in his inability to seize it himself. His active attempt to grasp the thread is thus inseparable from the futility of the effort and from the passive process of following where he is led. He is led to the expansiveness of "The champaign," where its unending "fleece / Of feathery grasses" suggests both an enduring possibility of harmony and value, of "Silence and passion, joy and peace," and a prospect of endless mobility, "An everlasting wash of air," a future that always contains the past, "Rome's ghost" (ll. 21–25).

Within this context, the process of figuration seems to take on a life of its own, so that the erotic energies of natural processes are the juxtaposed "naked forms of flowers" and "miracles" of "letting nature have her way" (ll. 26–28), and the force of this energy and activity leads the speaker to question the freedom of personal action: "How is it under our control / To love or not to love?" (ll. 34–35). Amidst the play of uncertain reference the purpose of this question is ambiguous. One effect of its rhetoric is to urge his companion to relinquish coyness, to be "unashamed" and submit to the forces and passions of nature—they have no choice; it is not under their control. But it is also a question about origins and may refer equally to the speaker's own sexual desire, his urge to overcome the obstacles of difference. What follows the question, for instance, is not further argument for submission to external forces but an emphatic statement of desire to fulfil internalized will: "I would that you were all to me" (l. 36). And these statements of intent are juxtaposed with more questions about origins ("Where does the fault lie?", l. 39), questions which make explicit the sense of inevitable failure ("What the core / O' the wound, since wound must be?", ll. 39–40).

There is a subtle blend of elements here. The lover is caught among forces and desires which seem to take over, leading to the inevitability of sexual union, and yet those desires are accompanied by a sense that they will never be satisfied, so that desire and failure, yearning and futility already coexist. At the same time, this consciousness also emerges from the rhetoric of persuasiveness, from the attempt to convince the companion that there is no need to be morally restrained, and thus the "core / O' the wound," the center of yearning, is quite blurred: what seems to be part of "letting nature have her way" (l. 29) may simply be the product of a rhetoric which signifies no more than personal need (albeit itself a part of nature). The origins and signification of concept and feeling are impossible to fix, and the speaker's questions are unanswerable, although that very feature may act as part of their rhetorical persuasiveness. All that seems certain is the repetition of desire—"I would I could adopt your will" (l. 41)—a desire that is overwhelming, that would exceed the constraints of physical and social inhibition, and yet which is impossible to realize, where the inevitability of the failure is inseparable from the way that desire is conceived. Such desire would also exceed the constraints of knowing through possession. The line "Nor yours nor mine, nor slave nor free!" (l. 38) may refer equally to the beloved's indeterminate state of being "just so much, no more" (l. 37), belonging to neither of them, having neither choice nor compulsion, or to the speaker's yearning for an ideal union where neither of them would be privileged over the other. Read in the latter sense, the consummation of the speaker's purpose would involve the obliteration of all differentiation. But of course the condition of consciousness is that it exists through differentiation; consciousness is brought into being through the separation of the self as subject from the other as object so that while consciousness remains such desires can never be fulfilled. He may touch the beloved, kiss her cheek, but inevitably the "good minute" is lost (l. 50)—temporizing intrudes. The speaker is forced back to the earlier confrontation with a process without origin and without end, and the return is signaled through a question which confronts the impossibility of a center:

>   Must I go
> Still like the thistle-ball, no bar,
>   Onward, whenever light winds blow,
>   Fixed by no friendly star?
>   (ll. 52–55)

The attempt to fix thought fails: "Where is the thread now? Off again!" (l. 57). To utter the image which represents thought is to gain it and lose it in the same instant. Thus, when consciousness and desire are constituted in language, when they become part of the attempt to pursue meaning, they are alike in their submission to a temporality which allows no fixed moment, no teleological fulfillment.

The last lines finally provide a climactic paradox:

>   Only I discern—
>   Infinite passion, and the pain
>   Of finite hearts that yearn.
>   (ll. 58–60)

What is provided here is an overt act of consciousness, a discernment in the sense of its original Latin (*discernere*: to separate), whereby something has been differentiated. In a context of configuration, the speaker finally "sees" figuratively in a perception that is at once a conception and what is seen is a concept about his own condition, about its paradoxically divided nature, caught between the desire for infinitude which is realized in consciousness and the inevitable restriction which is at the same time part of that realization. This is the ironic trap of consciousness: its ability to utter this conception—to become conscious of it—is the condition which renders any attainment of that conception impossible. In this context the process of communication leads to an irony of communication: the discourse which links (we presume) the two people is also able to indicate the basis for their separation. In other words, the communicative function which defines consciousness, in Nietzsche's sense, is also a means whereby consciousness is brought to confront its own separation. Or, as stated earlier, consciousness is an intersubjective form which is known as an intrasubjective experience, and that is why the consciousness of a lover, who yearns to escape the bounds of intrasubjectivity and enter entirely the forms of intersubjectivity, is ideally suited to representing such a disjunctive condition.

So far this thematic account of the poem has led to statements about the speaker's awareness of the contradictions inherent in his own condition, where he exists in a precarious state of elusive configuration, ever chasing the disappearing thread of representation. It should be clear by now that the poem in this reading is very close to containing, almost overtly, the elements of Derrida's metaphor of writing, but it remains to indicate how those elements can be traced in the poem more directly, adding a further dimension to the interpretation. The concept of temporality as spacing, for instance, clearly explains the combination of time and space in the image of the thread as thought. Thought is spatially conceived, represented in the image of a web which exists in space, but which also, in being perceived, *moves* through space and so is subject to process, the conditions of time. Just as the Victorians were thrust by evolution into an organic process without aim or telos, so the speaker in "Two in the Campagna" is placed within a process of representation, of writing (thought as image), without determinable origin or conclusion—except for the momentary distinction of a paradox of process.

The concept of perception as already a representation is also contained in the image of thought as a spider's thread, an image already available, already written on the mind of the speaker. The various elements of dislocated tenses, shifts between stanzas, entering into a process of thought already begun and the ambiguity of rhetorical questions also suggest the dissolution of singularity. There develops thus a complex interrelationship between several levels and disruptions: recollected feeling, wondering about the companion's feelings, past attempts to capture the thread, present attempts to repeat the process, present desire, the will to aspiration, expectations, confirmation of thwarted desire, statements of intent, statements of abstract questioning, and the movement toward an awareness which attempts to arrest the whole by encompassing it within a philosophical statement about emotional contradiction. Such are the marks of the multiplicity of perception. They are also the marks of the subject as system, and it is clear that varying forces are at work in the production of the subject of consciousness in this text: the speaker's desire for sexual union, the more conceptualized desires for a recovery of lost thought, on the one hand, or for a moment of realized bliss on the other; the imposing atmosphere of the campagna, with its mixture of "Silence and passion, joy and peace"; the erotic energies of the natural world and the inexorable temporizing which characterizes all conscious experience under textual conditions. These forces combine to construct the multiple system of a subject in process.

The double action of a subject which writes and is thereby written is also indicated in the present action of tracing a thread which has already been arranged, by past attempts, in terms of the metaphor for thought, and by the external actions of a spider, in terms of the literal placing of an image within an already existing environment. In tracing the path of the weft, the speaker is being traced by its configuration, both literal and figurative. The same doubleness is contained in the act of "discerning." This is the act of consciousness that is constituted in that act by the differentiation which sees (a seeing which is a construction as it is a perception) the nature of its own condition. But the condition and the speaker's awareness of its quality were conditioned by an array of elements, by the experience of the countryside, by the relationship with a lover, and by reflection on mental processes, and all these in turn were differentiated through the figurative powers of language itself. These powers are both within the poem in the process of tropes which present and shape all perception and outside the poem in its antecedents and contemporary contexts. To repeat the actions of the text and trace the origins of the speaker in earlier love poetry is beyond the scope of this discussion, but one obvious instance of this textual writing is the image of the rose: "I pluck the rose / And love it more than tongue can speak— / Then the good minute goes" (ll. 48–50). Richard Altick has already noted that this image echoes Othello's similar sense that the delight of the moment cannot stay:

> When I have pluck'd the rose
> I cannot give it vital growth again,
> It must needs wither.[12]

And as a Petrarchan convention the rose has always been a sign of passion that fades, of beauty that, in Keatsian phrase, "must die," so that in writing of his brief kiss as a plucked rose, the speaker is thereby written into the texts of all lovers who found that ecstasy did not last. The speaker must speak—without that action there is no utterance and no constitution of the subject—and the constituted subject interprets, separates off the condition of its feelings. But the subject is also itself an interpretation, a figure within the conditions allowed by utterance itself. In a text such as this it becomes comparatively easy for a reader to observe Peirce's principle that the self is a compromise, for the process of the text is to move through conflicting elements, juxtaposed phrases, toward an abstraction which "represents" the speaker's consciousness as compromise, as the paradoxical conception of a temporal space where interdependent opposites contend: "Infinite passion, and the pain / Of finite hearts."

Of course the commitment to being written is the commitment to temporal dissolution which is what the text states, and the self under the constant threat of erasure is contained thematically in the futile attempt to grasp the thread which is thought, to seize the moment which is now. Each image is committed to the double process of writing which is both inscription and erasure, the lifting of the paper on the Mystic Pad to clear the space for more writing. There is also in the poem a desire for a life which would mean death, that is, as previously indicated, the desire for a union with the beloved which would mean the loss of the separate self. Such a union would be an identification with the other which would involve loss of identity for the self as separate consciousness: "I would I could adopt your will, / See with your eyes" (ll. 41–42). Such a loss is seen, however, as a potential gain, as physical and spiritual ecstasy, a transportation out of the self which would allow an escape from the threat of erasure through transcending the conditions of that threat. It is the life in death that is the goal of all lovers whose essential lack leads to the desire for reconstitution. It is the paradox of the lover's desire, as indicated in this poem, that it earnestly seeks what would deny its separate seeking. In a sense we are returned to Empedocles, to his desire not for sexual union but for a more elemental union with natural forces which would save consciousness from the dissolutions of language. The paradox of the desire is similar: the way to preserve consciousness from the threat of death is to die. The desired death is not, of course, in either case, read as obliteration; it is read as a transformation, as the loss of an identity which is then reconstituted through a different identification—the transformation of self through sexual union or through union with organic process. Such are the signs of the self as it exists within the conditions which threaten erasure.

IV

One of the purposes of this discussion has been to suggest that the metaphor of consciousness as writing provides a way of reading the subtleties of the portrayal of consciousness in texts such as "Two in the Campagna." It is an idealist reading, but part of the point is to suggest that many Victorian poems are peculiarly suited to such analysis (the metaphor would apply theoretically to all texts), particularly since so many of them represent speakers in contexts where they confront the failure of the transcendent ego, whether through the devastation of grief, as in *In Memoriam*; through the loss of the beloved as the object of identification, as in "Evelyn Hope" or "Too Late"; through the suspected failure of personal talent, as in "Pictor Ignotus" or "Andrea del Sarto"; through the fragmentation of unity in "Childe Roland to the Dark Tower Came"; through the inability of Empedocles to resolve the oscillations between society and solitude; through the bitter fancies which threaten to destroy the speaker in *Maud*; or through the dehumanizing public identity of "Mr Sludge, 'the Medium'." In so much Victorian poetry there is the represented process of selves who attempt to fix the self against the forces which have questioned their authority or center. The lyrical medium which constitutes such speakers constantly suggests the metaphor of writing for the context of their attempted survival, their attempt to restore the illusion of a singular identity.

All of these concepts separated off from Derrida—temporality as spacing, perception as already a representation, the subject as system, the erasure of the self in its utterance—are contained within the metaphor of writing as consciousness. We need to attend to textual mobility and to the unaccountability of writing when reading Victorian poetry, but if we are to do that in the way suggested by Ann Wordsworth, we should do so with regard to the full complexity of what is involved with such processes. Linguistic performances in lyric and dramatic poetry can still be read as presentations of the processes which constitute human consciousness, provided that we take full account of the paradoxes and contradictions that are inherent in those processes.

Notes

1. Matthew Arnold, *The Poems of Matthew Arnold*, ed. Kenneth Allott; 2nd ed. Miriam Allott (London, 1979); all quotations from the poem are from this edition and will be cited within the text.
2. Friedrich Nietzsche, *The Gay Science*, trans. Walter Kaufmann (New York, 1974), pp. 298–299; *The Will to Power*, ed. Walter Kaufmann (New York, 1967), p. 285. All italics here and elsewhere are Nietzsche's.
3. Nietzsche also anticipates such a proposition: "In brief, the development of language and the development of consciousness (*not* of reason but merely of the way reason enters consciousness) go hand in hand" (*The Gay Science*, p. 299).
4. "Signature Event Context," *Glyph*, 1 (1977), 181.
5. Again this conception can be found in Nietzsche: "Fundamentally, all our actions are altogether incomparably personal, unique, and infinitely individual; there is no doubt of that. But as soon as we translate them into consciousness *they no longer seem to be*" (*The Gay Science*, p. 299).
6. " 'Communication Different'," *BSN*, 13, No. 1 (n.d.), 4–18. This essay in *BSN* is part of a growing concern among critics with the importance in Victorian poetry of language as theme, the textualization of experience, consciousness and the self as illusion: see also articles by Harold Bloom and Ann Wordsworth in *Robert Browning: A Collection of Critical Essays*, eds. Harold Bloom and Adrienne Munich (Englewood Cliffs, New Jersey, 1979); Herbert F. Tucker, Jr., *Browning's Beginnings* (Minneapolis, 1980); E. Warwick Slinn, *Browning and the Fictions of Identity* (Totowa, New Jersey, 1982); Isobel Armstrong, *Language as Living Form in Nineteenth-Century Poetry* (Totowa, New Jersey, 1982); Timothy Peltason, "Supposed Confessions, Uttered Thoughts: The First-Person Singular in Tennyson's Poetry," *VNL*, 64 (1983), 13–18; Tucker, "From Monomania to Monologue: 'St. Simeon Stylites' and the Rise of the Victorian Dramatic Monologue," *VP*, 22 (1984), 121–137; Slinn, "Some

Notes on Monologues as Speech Acts," *BSN*, 15, No. 1 (1985). Clyde de L. Ryals' book, *Becoming Browning* (Columbus, Ohio, 1983), in its use of romantic irony and F. Schlegel's dialectics as a context for reading Browning is also directly relevant.

7. Derrida, in *The Structuralist Controversy*, eds. Richard Macksey and Eugenio Donato (Baltimore, 1972): "The subject is absolutely indispensable. I don't destroy the subject; I situate it" (p. 271).

8. In *Writing and Difference*, trans. Alan Bass (Chicago, 1978), pp. 196–231. In this section of the discussion, references to this essay will be cited within the text by page number.

9. In the notes to his own translation of "Freud and the Scene of Writing," Jeffrey Mehlman observes that "Derrida presses in the direction of a theatre of writing," in *YFS*, 48 (1972), 73.

10. "The Interpreter's Self: Peirce on the Cartesian 'Subject'," *GaR*, 31 (1977), 401. The quotation from Peirce is cited on the same page in Michaels' article.

11. All quotations from "Two in the Campagna" are taken from *Browning: Poetical Works 1833–1864*, ed. Ian Jack (London, 1970), and will be cited within the text.

12. Richard D. Altick, "Lovers' Finiteness: Browning's 'Two in the Campagna'," *PLL*, 3, No. 1 (1967), 79.

Reading the Reader in Robert Browning's Dramatic Monologues

JOHN MAYNARD

For a long time now, it seems that Browning studies have been widely engaged in a religious quest for the one true interpretation of each dramatic monologue. Many an academic career begins with another Child Roland finding his or her way off the traveled road of interpretation, raising his or her slughorn, and pronouncing, to the ring of gathered peers, what? . . . a new reading of the Duke of "My Last Duchess." No sooner pronounced, than he, she, or we wonder: Is this *another* failed quest? Are we bound to be a band of failed questers by something difficult and unsettling in the very soil of Browning studies—those abundant weeds and rank growth: the dramatic monologues themselves. No center seems to hold anymore. Each traditional reading of each monologue falls sooner or later to a new inverse or perverse interpretation.

You remember when the Duke became the hero. You recall how Gismond's chivalric dame came under suspicion for playing him double. You know the Grammarian is buried nowadays with a pedant's last rites, not a scholar-hero's. You have perhaps heard of Lippo's new role as the culpable libertine of art. You may yet hear the Lost Leader *accused* of being a liberal at the Thatcher-Bush Browning Society. I would like to suggest that we might now profitably stop arguing over interpretation of speakers of monologues. I submit that we might admit that these interpretations that are so fiercely argued in the journals like schoolboy debates are *not* stable, that we all move regularly from one position to another unless we are very committed to something we wrote or very uninterested in the poems.

When it comes to interpretation of individual texts we all stand in a guilty relation to the New Criticism. Like sons or daughters of bad conscience, we renounce our fathers and mothers regularly while living on the inheritance they left us. The elders, those called New Critics in the gladness of their now distant youth, were not fools. I dare say that again: they were not fools. They, if not their disciples, had thought hard about the problems of reading literature. They, you will recall, wanted to free themselves from

---

Reprinted from *Browning e Venezia*, Sergio Perosa, ed. (Florence, Italy: Leo S. Olschki, 1991). Reprinted with permission of the Cini Foundation.

the tradition of historical context of the nineteenth century. They, as you know, sought an opening for an interpretation of their time (what now might be called a contemporary horizon). They invented a thing called a text—an illusion mightily revived by Yale deconstruction. Meaning was in the page somehow, not in the two places where it usually was located: that is, on one side, in the author or in the historical time of the creation, the horizon of the historical context, or, on the other side, as Wolfgang Iser, Fish, and Tompkins have been telling us, in all that we can know of the text, our own reading of it or that of others.

From the New Critical view each of these perspectives falls off miserably from the saving myth of the text as text. An older colleague of mine in a broadly New Critical tradition often speaks, for instance, of affect. I finally got up my courage to ask him if the word "affect" meant to him an effect in or on the reader—that is, an affect felt in the reader. "No, indeed," he thundered, "It is *in the text*: a marker of emotional intensity in the work itself." From their point of view New Critics were rightly suspicious of historical scholarship. For they could see in the accumulation of scholarship not merely more useful knowledge but a competing idea of interpretation. The context—the historical with-read—is really another kind of reader—one of Fish's communities, if you will. This reader is not in fact the diverse real readers of the day, who often seem merely the sum of bad, because too immediate and involved, too interested, readings. For instance, the reading, sponsored even by Browning and his close friends, that "The Bishop Orders His Tomb" was a hit at the Oxford Movement; or that "Blougram's Apology" was an attack on the revived English Catholic Church; or that "The Englishman in Italy" was an assault on the Corn Laws, a view encouraged by Browning's own assertion that it is—coded into the poem itself! Despite even the author's sometime authorization, such contextual readings represent too narrow horizons in which to view the poems.

Our contextual reading creates instead an imaginary community made up of a kind of ideal reader of the time. We manufacture an historical reading that displays the balance and breadth of vision that is precisely denied those caught in the historical moment. It is, in short, a special reading, the assumption of an horizon, the putting on of special glasses. The point is that any step, the least one, from the myth/illusion of the text brings us into a world that changes the idea of interpretation. If there is a text, we can argue over its one correct interpretation. If there is a reading, whether an attempt at its contextual, historical meaning (in E. D. Hirsch's sense of meaning), or any kind of response of the reader (whether in Iser's, Holland's, Fish's, or Bleich's sense), we have one, two, many readings. The Intentional and Affective Fallacies are one. Interpretation as reading is many.

I have not myself been able to stand comfortably in the two-dimensional world of the text. Either I have fallen over into biographical and historical readings of the text in its genesis, or, no sooner up, I fall over on the other side into the multiplex life of the text as readings. Of course, I haven't been alone. Only deconstruction has staged an important defense against the invading democratic voices of many readers, many communities of reading, whether historical, metaphysical, Freudian, mythological, perverse, individual. Deconstruction preserved the illusion of the text—even while it paid the price for keeping it from fragmenting and disintegrating it. Not surprisingly, Paul de Man was one of the first to express alarm at Fish's practical criticism. In Browning studies the move to deconstruction actually only had the effect of inserting more individual interpretations in an already overcrowded playing board. Herbert Tucker's brilliant work, Warwick Slinn's interesting but more relentless deconstruction of language and systems of character gave us new interpretations of a text that was now, simultaneously, rigid—only a text—and now pulsating and disintegrating under its alternating current of conflicting interpretive pulses.

Look at the idea of interpretation—itself really an idea we can place historically, something created by the move to free the text from ideology and context and to allow some kind of "pure" meaning apart from all interested, horizoned approaches at the text. As the text is only an ideal space (an idea, a place for a necessary fiction, an impossibility), so an interpretation is necessarily ideal: a raid on the impossible with whatever shabby literary-critical equipment we and our generation possess in order to create a meaning that we expect nonetheless to be *the* meaning. And so we make another attempt at a final interpretation of "My Last Duchess." All experience is against our finding it. All theory used to be in favor.

What, really, do we have when we evaluate critical interpretation at the moment? Let's call it the cosmopolitan community. We are not one interpretive approach but an amalgam of competing ones. We may dream of some simpler life where we hear only one voice in some critical Tahiti or other Gigadibsian Antipodes. We choose to remain in our universities and cities where we hear many voices. You will recall how Norman Holland tried to avoid the implications of his pluralistic focus on readings by shrinking the readers—giving *them* one interpretation. And how quickly he was attacked (by Culler and others) for essentializing the reader after de-essentializing the text. Or look at the idea of one historical contextual reading as *the* meaning. This in effect essentializes our knowledge, as historians and literary historians of the period, as an answer to a de-essentialized text. Yet anyone who writes biography or history knows there are infinitely more patterns in *that* enormous carpet than in the strands of any single text. We are offended by those (*other* historians, curse them) who claim to know the Victorian period, Victorian man and woman, Victorian values, the Victorian family, etc. We know that such assurance of the Bradford millionaires of criticism will only offer us partial views dished up as *the* correct historical meaning: Brownings's poems are *about* the Protestant religious myth (the Central Truth); they are *about* the Patriarchal Victorian world (whether Browning was in favor or against it is still in dispute); they are *about* liberalism and its attack on the ancien régime, whether in London or in Italy; no, they are *about* Victorian political, economic, and cultural hegemony (the imperialist *pax Britanniae* of Casa Guidi). They all help; let knowledge grow; but none alone will do. Who are we as interpreters? Heirs to the ages, multipersons created on the cosmopolitan multicultures in which we live today.

Browning's texts explicitly engage the difficulties and anxieties of reading and being read. David Latané has written an excellent study of the reader in *Sordello* that provides a model for Browning's conception of his reader. Drawing on Romantics' ideas of a reader challenged by hard works of literature, Latané persuasively suggests that the young Browning looked to a reader who would welcome difficult works that made him or her cooperative in the labor of the imagination. The reader, almost in Iser's own words, was to connect the stars of the work into the constellations of his reading: "were my scenes stars it must be his co-operating fancy which, supplying all chasms, shall connect the scattered lights into one constellation—a Lyre or a Crown" (Preface to *Paracelsus*). The notorious difficulties, as well as the great successes of *Sordello*, derived from a strategy in which the reader was expected to be nothing less than great—like those Paladins, including even Sidney himself, incorporated in the text as figures for readers.

The next step in the story is of course reading the reader in the dramatic monologues. I have already tried to explore elsewhere why it is so difficult to read a dramatic monologue in two dimensions—as merely a text. In the meantime that kind of reading has been being discredited everywhere after the New Criticism as mere formalism. The thing to say about Browning studies is that there was in any event very little to discredit. New Criticism notoriously failed to leave any really important monuments of interpretation of Browning monologues. The problem was not that the bag of tricks was not useful. One looks for tone of voice, a dramatic persona, vivid metaphor, striking effects of sound in Browning and finds them with great ease. It could even be said that these poems, with their very clear creation of a persona—"so many utterances of so many imaginary persons, not mine"— were the ideal model for the entire New Critical enterprise. We know how profoundly Browning affected the form of the modernist poem generally. It isn't surprising that the New Critics, who paid little attention to him, nonetheless created a form of analysis that especially fit the persona poem par excellence. Robert Frost, who, like Pound, actually wrote dramatic monologues, made a convenient stand-in for the Victorian originator in their critical analyses.

I think it is not even too farfetched to think of Browning's poems as playing an important role in the modern focus on interpretation. The Browning Society discussions, aimed initially at finding one answer to the problems of faith of the day that were left unanswered by Tennyson, led eventually to one of the first large-scale debates over interpretations of individual texts. Just because the poems were so opaque on the subjects of faith, science, progress for which they were interrogated, they opened up an accidental space for debates over interpretation. And indeed, since those first New Critical classrooms, Browning has never failed the quester for ambiguity: many of his portraits were early perceived to bear Mona Lisa smiles, haunting, in their ability to tease interpretation out of thought. No, the problem was not fit but surplus. There was always something major in the Browning monologue that left direct New Critical assaults on the poems dead on the field.

It was of course that damned (blessed) dramatic quality. The problem could be stated as a problem of the poet's relation to the poems. One solution could then be to ignore the obvious dramatic quality and prove, as Hillis Miller's phenomenological approach once tried to, that all the monologues were only so many Robert Brownings. After all, Browning did love to imagine himself into all those bright creatures God sets up for themselves. On another occasion he spoke of his well-known love of vermin—thus allowing one to explain even the criminal types as further identifications. But it is hard to progress from this extreme situation of negative capability to reading individual poems as versions of the poet's complex sensibility in the New Critical manner. At best one could suspend that quest for wholeness of artistic sensibility until all the poems were read and mastered. Then we might think of all those men and women and Calibans as one large poem equal to the "R.B. a Poem" that Browning said he could never write. Many of us who study Browning and note his modest/grandiose assertions about the difference between his work and Elizabeth's on the ideal of the objective/subjective poet may still dream of that one big text of all Browning's texts—a kind of Browning world. But what a prodigy of massive and mighty sensibility we have then to appreciate in our interpretation of that poem!

The more obvious problem is not the gap between poet's sensibility and poet's texts but the problem of the reader. The poems don't sit there waiting for a Fish or an Iser to come along and sketch on top of the text a third dimension. They fairly shout out at us their full-bodied existence beyond the flat ideal space of the text. Even where there is a poet's persona preserved in the speaker of *Sordello*, there are ideal readers shunting in and out of the poem like jet age scholars in and out of conferences. In the dramatic monologues the poet is nowhere to be seen, but the reader has become far more obtrusive—in a quite different incarnation. Having learned the limits of his real readers by the reception of *Sordello*, Browning now dismissed his guest-star readers, Sidney and the rest, and brought into his monologues (hitherto pure monologues or soliloquies) a collection of very ordinary readers. They are the unfortunate versions of ourselves in the poem (Caliban forced to see himself in Browning's mirror) who can in no way be overlooked. They strike us immediately as so many fools suffering gladly the greater verbal power and passion of the speakers themselves. Our instinct is of course to assert emphatically that these are so many readings by so many readers, *not ourselves*. They are Browning's others—his gallery of lesser creations to set beside the great ones of the monologuists, the "Karshish, Cleon, Norbert and the fifty . . . Lippo, Roland or Andrea." They—the listeners—are the silent ones: mostly targets for bores or downright patsies, envoys from the Count, Gigadibses, dogberrian night watchmen, with only here and there an unpassive person of spirit equal to her verbal besieger, such as Andrea's motile Lucrezia.

Most of these generally too open fax receivers provoke our contempt. Hearing the silence audible of the listener, we break into our own noisy response. It is almost as if Browning has found a poetic gadget to provoke reader response: a much simpler, more economical and effective mechanism than the palpable hold he takes of readers and the reader in *Sordello*. If we look back to the prototypes to the dramatic monologue—the two Madhouse poems of the 1830s—we can see Browning already inserting prominent hooks to pull the reader into action. Both "Johannes Agricola in Meditation" and "Porphyria's Lover" are so blatantly, aggressively, and brilliantly mad that we in no way allow them to soliloquize in a cool flat distance from us: we are driven to our own aggressive response. "Porphyria's Lover," the one that seems to anticipate the later monologues best, already has in effect two proto-listeners in the poem. There is the *very* passive listener, a true conversational target, a warning, to make us shout out of the ultimate consequences of letting ourselves be dominated by strong romantic voices. "And yet God has not said a word!" is almost too heavy with provocations to the reader. God as listener raises the entire world of ethical response against the totalitarian solipsistic amorality of the speaker. It also tells us that *we* had better react and speak because the withdrawn God of the poem's world refuses to speak for us. It underlines the interpretive problem at the very beginning of the Browning dramatic monologue: God doesn't offer definitive reader responses and interpretations. In his silence, we will rush forward with our own interpretations. But if God won't, who will authorize the one standard meaning?

That there may be two or too many interpretations is the unpalatable truth reader-oriented criticism offers. And as a theoretical enterprise it seems to lead all but its most blithe Bleichian laissez-faireists into deeper waters than they are comfortable swimming in. So we find in Iser or Fish rather desperate attempts to clamber out: with normative readings dictated by a rhetorical structure in the text or elaborate concepts of communities developed to stabilize responses. I hope I won't seem to be pushing myself in among the confusions of my betters in this field if I confess the same experience with my attempts at applications to Browning. Having once turned on the new gadget, I realized I was betraying myself into the pluralistic world we would-be apostles of high culture like to shun. *This* radio broadcast not one BBC interpretation—*my* interpretation—but band after band of interpretation-jockeys spinning their own disks.

This was hard to take. And so I found a thing to do: use the listener in the poem as a firm point to take a fix on the reader in the poem. My idea was a little like Renaissance perspective points in painting that were supposed to give a fixed and single place from which a viewer would view a scene (and you can see in that concept how far back in Western thinking our instinct for one right interpretation goes). My idea was also a bit like trigonometry and plotting of coordinates: with the speaker and listener in the poem proving two points of a triangle that would project out of the ideal medium of the text to a real-life but determinate (and thus also ideal) reader. We read a dramatic monologue by reacting to the (failed or inadequate) response of the listener in the poem to the speaker, then are directed to a third position that is neither that of speaker or listener. For instance, the envoy's silence and compliance in "My Last Duchess" allows us to objectify and criticize our own tendency merely to submit to the strength of the Duke's rhetoric—thus provoking us to a middle position, combining respect for hypnotically powerful language and moral distance and criticism.

I still like that way of thinking about a Browning dramatic monologue. It really takes us back to the kind of criticism that has uniquely survived from New Critical days just because it projected the experience of the poem off the page of the text into a reader. I refer, of course, to the now classic work of Robert Langbaum in *The Poetry of Experience*. In the present context we can now see that success as implicitly a position on interpretation: the establishment of a reader, the vehicle of that response of sympathy and judgment that Langbaum uses so well. Sympathy and judgment are indeed a limited case, a kind of ideal formulation itself of the entire spectrum of readers' responses to a dramatic monologue. We might, for instance, be merely overwhelmed, as poor Gigadibs seems to be at times; or moved to anger, disgust—any one of those human reactions that Browning's father loved to catalog in his caricature drawings. The main point is that we read a monologue by reading ourselves as readers as part of the experience. We don't just explore a poetic sensibility but necessarily have our sensibilities brought into play.

The trouble with my reading of the reader, as with so much early reader response work, was that it didn't face clearly the problems of pluralism of responses. Indeed my *math* was wrong! Two points determine a straight line but they don't determine where a third point will go to make a triangle. It is really a case for calculus, and I had never gotten that far. Wherever you imagine the reader as the third point of speaker and listener you can draw a useful triangle of relations. But the point itself can shift boldly from place to place.

So where does that leave us? I would now say it leaves us reading the reader not to define the ideal interpretive position, but to explore the range of response—experiences—the poem generates. Readers and readings are provoked by the thesis, antithesis, of speaker and listener in the poem. But we who stand at the latest point in time only throw a great heritage to the winds if we perversely insist on inserting our response as the last word. Better to see the poem as a system that includes a reading of many readers reporting many experiences. The art of reading is to be compared not to a dead camera that takes one perspective on a theatrical scene but rather to an entire caravanfull of television monitors with a variety of shots, some left, some right, some close-up, some distant. The experience of the mixer or viewer does not consist in picking one shot and throwing away the rest. Rather, he or she shifts and mixes until the performance *is* its many receptions.

Two final points: First, if we begin with the listener in the poem in order to decide where to position the cameras of our various readers, we had better be prepared for a variety of listeners as well. They are often vague, only faintly realized. They provoke many readings of their readings even before they provoke readings of the speaker. Witness Gigadibs, who can appear as a passive fool—in the arsenal of contemporary American-British conservative rhetoric, the liberal made of vague feelings and nothing to say (his loose deck of cards). Or does he find true grit within and live out the life of a bolder liberal of action, building a better society in a new world? And how will we nail down his so clever conservative opponent's effect on us when we can't even locate his effect on Gigadibs?

Second: I've been so far outlining a poor man's reader response, no theoretical breakthroughs but at least a way to think about what we do when we read dramatic monologues. Let me add a poor man's deconstruction of the dramatic monologue. The system of the dramatic monologue with its many sightings of listener and reader; the situation of the dramatic monologue in what I've been speaking of metaphorically as a three-dimensional space embracing text and reader: these are the aporia and *mise en abîme* all in one. Go into the poem this way: you won't come out alive with just one interpretation and you may hardly find your way out at all. Welcome to Browning's fun house, where we find ourselves only by losing our single-minded interpretation in a hall of mirrors filled with ourselves reading ourselves.

As an example, "The Bishop Orders His Tomb at Saint Praxed's Church," taken whole and after some readings, provokes us to go through something like the general process I have described. There are as listeners in the poem those silent "nephews." And we can try to decide if they do merely disregard all this rhetorical claptrap to get to the main point: this old man is dying; we will soon possess his possessions; nothing else matters. Or are they a more neutral audience of passive listeners like old Gandolf, there merely to act as foils by their passivity to the brilliance and eccentricity of this Renaissance man? And then, where should the reader be? Neither with the graspers (weak parodies of the virile bishop who fathered them) nor with the impassive pre-Renaissance starers-on.

We may project ourselves in history—as Ruskin certainly did when he read the poem—and create ourselves as *not* like those nephews or competing bishops of that time but as a modern sensibility of some sort that can historicize the Bishop—as Browning certainly encourages us to do by his dating and splendid paraphernalia of local color. We may read ourselves as the moral and religious readers: providing the authentic spiritual world that the Bishop so obviously materializes with his incense and cigar smoke, his naughty nymphs and madonna's breast. We may read ourselves as the psychological reader: psyching this odd combination of sensuality and pomposity, indulgence and sublimation, in some Freudian system. We may read ourselves as the deconstructive reader (Warwick Slinn, for a name), breaking the apparent solidity of the Bishop's character into so many words signifying in their self-contradiction (and there is a great deal of that here) little but themselves, until the Bishop becomes wholly a man of words.

Even before that formal process of interpreting our interpretations there is the immediate experience of being the readers who must respond as we are confronted by the poem. And this is a wonderful violence of shove and response: a kind of boxing ring of art experience in which we lunge and hop from spot to spot, trying to get in our own responses and trying not to be KO'd by our opponents' brilliant hits. He opens with a roundhouse bishop's morality: "Vanity, saith the preacher, vanity!" We counter with confused little jabs: wise? hypocrite? man of your times? He answers with last business—"Draw round my bed"—but what last business! He lands us a huge verbal and visual confection, his order for a tombstone to pass all tombstones. We respond: this fellow's an artist; this fellow's a fake; this is a bad bishop; this fellow does extraordinarily strange things, both acts and speech acts. Here is a unified premodern sensibility; but *what* a sensibility! By the time we have read thirty lines we are punch-drunk, tired, reeling, overwhelmed.

In case our attempts at identifying with those silent and inscrutable nephews/sons are not perplexing enough, we are given three other perspective points, all confusing. We are to imagine the Bishop (dying in bed at night) imagining himself dead: "Do I live, am I dead?" Then we imagine ourselves with the Bishop imagining we are a stone statue in the church, somehow listeners to ourselves describing a warm pastoral life in death. And we also almost listen with old Gandolf, mocking still from his shrewd snatch from out the corner South. And then, with the irresistible godfather command, "Draw close," he destroys our critical distance and delivers a series of drubbing punches. We are made complicit in arson and theft. With the nephews, we are bribed and cajoled with everything from villas to Greek manuscripts. We doubt his sanity but have to admire his Latin. And then he throws us the knockout. He exposes himself to us in those remarkable lines in which all hopes of immortality turn to nasty "Gritstone, a-crumble! Clammy squares which sweat / As if the corpse they keep were oozing through." He lets us, forces us, to see him dead—really dead. And for a moment we have the experience of hearing a man capable of deep feeling and deep fear. Or—we move position again—is he only manipulating those impassive nephews by bathos?

The three-dimensionality of the Browning dramatic monologue creates a brilliant life of readers reading their own readings from the moment we engage with the poem. First reading, close reading, anticipates and engages the continuum of readings we work out more fully when we try to interpret the poem. Once we see the poem working in this way to engage the reader as part of its existence/performance, we necessarily read ourselves and our many selves, the readers before us. Instead of tooting our slughorns in the wilderness, we will be directing an entire orchestra.

The Divided Subject

Loy Martin

I

The contradiction between person-as-object and person-as-process that I discussed in the last section may be read as a single discursive dialectical movement. In the dramatic monologue, the person-as-thing appears as an abstraction, as someone's thought about himself or about a particular other. Over against this abstraction stands the "real" person-as-process, which is manifested in the material productivity of speech. The monologue itself, as text, cannot choose between the material and the ideal person, either morally or epistemologically. No more can it elevate the ideal to the level of a transcendent signified. What the monologue signifies is the contradiction itself in its discursive unfolding. The material person is always being produced, but it cannot be produced by any process that does not also produce a contradictory idea of the unitary self. This process of production leaves its traces in a kind of textual discourse that I have been calling "The Being Written."

One needn't look far to see that this distilled and visible contradiction is one of the most powerful, though often hidden, contradictions of a more generalized ideology. Bourgeois individualism hardly requires documentation here. But the sovereignty of the individual never exists as a monolithic conviction, and it takes historically specific forms in large part from its relation to the concepts that oppose it at any given time. In England, during the magnificent expansion of industrial and scientific progress, the antithesis to individualism arises from the inescapable sense of progress and decay, of the unfinished nature of any moment's achievement, and of the desire for continuity that I discussed in the last chapter.[1] The individual dissolves into the kind of movement in human time that Walter Pater describes in his conclusion to *The Renaissance*. "That clear, perpetual outline of face and limb," he says, "is but an image of ours, . . . a design in a web, the actual threads of which pass out beyond it."[2] The dramatic monologue, while presenting a "clear image," continually attempts to suggest the presence of

Reprinted from *Browning's Dramatic Monologues and the Post-Romantic Subject*, Chapter 4 (The Johns Hopkins University Press, 1985). Reprinted by permission of the publisher.

those "actual threads" as they extend out beyond the image in both time and space. There are many ways of facing the irreducibility of the opposition, but Pater's almost wistful sadness is among the most moving:

> Analysis . . . assures us that those impressions of the individual mind to which, for each one of us, experience dwindles down, are in perpetual flight; . . . To such a tremulous wisp constantly reforming itself on the stream, to a single sharp impression, with a sense in it, a relic more or less fleeting, of such moments gone by, what is real in our life fines itself down. It is with this movement, with the passage and dissolution of impressions, images, sensations, that analysis leaves off—that continual vanishing away, that strange, perpetual weaving and unweaving of ourselves.[3]

A present that is felt to be insubstantial, "a tremulous wisp" forever fading, "dwindling down" to nearly nothing under scrutiny, needs, and must project, a past and future that give meaning to the "perpetual weaving and unweaving of ourselves." The other side of this need is the fear that the past is alienated, has been somehow lost or severed from the present. Pater describes the past chiefly as loss in the individual's perception of his own life; writers like John Stuart Mill and Matthew Arnold expressed the plight of an entire culture. In *The Spirit of the Age*, Mill writes,

> Before men begin to think much and long on the peculiarities of their own times, they must have begun to think that those times are, or are destined to be, distinguished in a very remarkable manner from the times that preceded them. Mankind are then divided, into those who are still what they were, and those who have changed; into the men of the present age, and the men of the past. To the former, the spirit of the age is a subject of exultation; to the latter, of terror; to both, of eager and anxious interest.[4]

Mill describes with high precision the contribution made by a perceived alienation from the past to interpersonal alienation within a contemporary community. These forms of division were, I believe, a subject of "eager and anxious interest" for many Victorians. An early portrait of the self-made genius, hermetically isolated from both his contemporaries and from a meaningful past, is Carlyle's Professor Teufelsdröckh:

> Had Teufelsdröckh also a father and mother; did he at one time, wear drivel-bibs, and live on spoon-meat? Did he ever, in rapture and tears, clasp a friend's bosom to his; looks he also wistfully into the long burial-aisle of the Past, where only winds, and their low harsh moan, give inarticulate answer?[5]

Teufelsdröckh is "a Pilgrim, and Traveller from a far country," whose past, whatever it may be, bears little relevance to the knowable individual confronted by the "Editor" of *Sartor Resartus*. It is this way of perceiving the individual self as temporally, culturally, and in the end, spatially disjoined that the dramatic monologue juxtaposes against that other view in which the boundaries of the individual are a mere illusory image.

It would, however, be a mistake to read this juxtaposition as symmetrical, as an equal balance. In its ideological form, the dyad is unbalanced by the fact that the autonomy of the individual usually appears as a positive value, while the absorption of the individual into a totality beyond itself is most often seen as a dehumanization. In the dramatic monologue, Browning raises the contradiction to consciousness in part by showing how this hierarchy of values might be reversed, how the individual might become in fact more fully human in a loss of discrete unity. The logic of this reversal begins from the premise that the essence of the human is language, and language fragments the speaking subject. In the terms of *Sordello*, the subject that is whole is one constituted in homogeneous "perception," while the subject-in-language is one constituted in heterogeneous "thought." At first, Sordello attempts to resolve the contradiction by constructing language as clothing, or armor, for perception. But this fusion proves unstable:

> Piece after piece that armour broke away,
> Because perceptions whole, like that he sought
> To clothe, reject so pure a work of thought
> As language: thought may take perception's place
> But hardly co-exist in any case,
> Being its mere presentment—of the whole
> By parts, the simultaneous and the sole
> By the successive and the many.
> —*Sordello*, 2.588–95

The dramatic monologue has fairly well abandoned the project of "presenting" an underlying wholeness. It recognizes the self-destroying quality of the idea of wholeness, an idea that can only be realized in discourse. The idea of wholeness is self-destroying in Browning because the subject of its discourse—the discourse of the dramatic monologue—can never be a discrete entity.[6] As we have seen, that subject lacks discreteness because it lacks fixed boundaries, but it also lacks discreteness because it is, in itself, split. It is not only "successive"; as we began to see in "Pictor Ignotus," it is also "many."

II

In my discussion of "My Last Duchess," I raised the traditional issue of the division between the poet and the speaker in dramatic monologues. I said that the duke and his creator interpret life differently, and this implies that

I can tell the difference between the "voices" of two subjects for a single discourse. This assumption about Browning has gone virtually unchallenged from the time the poet himself commented on his work to the present. As most readers know, Browning characterized his poems as "always dramatic in principle, and so many utterances of so many imaginary persons, not mine," and said, "These [idylls] of mine are called 'Dramatic' because the story is told by some actor in it, not by the poet himself."[7] Modern critics have generally followed this lead. B. W. Fuson defined the dramatic monologue in 1948 as "an isolated poem intended to stimulate the utterance not of the poet but of another individualized speaker," and more recently, in one of the best essays on the genre, Michael Mason defines a monologue in part as "a poem of which the versified part is devoted almost entirely to the imaginary utterances of some person other than the author."[8] After all of this unanimity, and after my own apparent participation in it, I wish to argue that this inferred division between poet and speaker is not in itself essential to the dramatic monologue. My argument is not a refutation but rather a complication of the traditional assumption, and for authority, I can return to Browning himself:

> Love, you saw me gather men and women,
> Live or dead or fashioned by my fancy,
> Enter each and all, and use their service,
> Speak from every mouth,—the speech, a poem.
> ("One Word More," 129–32)

Not all of the figures in *Men and Women* are imaginary, and Browning says that he has entered them and spoken in his own person from their mouths. I do not think that Browning is being inconsistent. The division between the voice of the poet and the voice of the imaginary speaker is based on a reader's willingness to construe them both equally as "persons." If these persons are imagined to be corporeal, then they must be discrete, mutually excluding entities. But if they are voices and merely voices, can they not in some sense be both different and the same? Lacan, among others, has suggested ways to think of being-in-language as both a selfhood and an otherness; does this not mean that the clear differentiation of individual speakers derives from an ideology that is subject to revision? This ideology is certainly a part of the dramatic monologue's repertoire of subject matter, but I think that formally, the monologue challenges the limitations of traditional Cartesian epistemology in precisely this regard. One of its effects is to divide the subjectivity of poetic discourse but not to divide it, as by mitosis, into two equally unitary subjects where before there was one. There is still only one discourse that constructs and locates its subject; all we can say is that the subject in question is bivalent, split but not multiplied. This is why the division between "speaker" and "poet" is only one version of the essential doubleness of the monologue, and an ambivalent version at that. My purpose here is to describe the monologue's doubleness in its more generalized form.[9]

One of the monologue's goals is to show how individualized or specialized language may function as an alienating force. Yet the monologue does not stop at recognizing the alienation. Its imaginative leap is to fuse these differentiating idioms into a seamless utterance, thus calling into question even the radical capacity of historical time to insist on the mutual "otherness" inherent in separate acts of speech. This chapter examines the monologue's treatment of specialized language, whether the boundaries of that specialization are those of an elite group like "poets," an idiosyncratic individual, or a particular geographical or historical location. The first step is to describe some of the formal features that lead most readers to hear two voices in dramatic monologues.

In "My Last Duchess," the differentiation of speaker from poet is not entirely dependent on the irony of the duke's equating a painted image to a living person; it may also be inferred from the fact that the duke "speaks" in rhymed couplets. Ralph Rader has described Browning's use of the couplet convention in the following terms:

> We may ask ourselves whether in reading we imaginatively hear the words of the poem as spoken by the Duke, and of course we reply that we do. We may then ask ourselves if we understand the rhymes that we hear in the poem as part of the Duke's speech, and we discover that we do not. This shows that prior to any conscious analysis our imaginations register and respond to the presence of two agents in the intuitive act of constructing the poem—a created actor, the Duke, and the immanent creator Browning.[10]

These seem reasonable things to say, though in a later article, Rader appears to argue somewhat differently. Instead of identifying the couplets as a sign of the presence of Browning, he tells us "that the couplets have a very definite function—to give a sense of submerged pattern running, like the Duke's hidden purpose, through the whole."[11] I am not sure whether Rader is really revising here, but even if he is, his two statements share a common feature. Whether we say that the structure of rhymed couplets points to a subjectivity other than that of the speaker or that it reveals a level of motive beneath the linguistic surface of a single speaker's discourse, we are observing a doubleness or bifurcation of the text.

The iambic pentameter line, even without rhyme, produces one kind of closure; syntactic periods produce another kind of closure. In a form like the Augustan couplet, these closures coincide, with the result that the relation of poetic convention to sentence structure is the relation of rhetoric to message. The couplet may generate emphasis, parallelism, or antithesis as well as a number of other modifications and effects, such as irony. "End-stopped" couplets are not, as some have imagined, a rigid convention. What they do imply, though, is a direct relationship of some kind between verse form and sentence form, leading us to read the entire discourse as an integrated whole. Between the couplet and the sentence in "My Last Duchess," however, there is no consistent relationship. Some lines are end-stopped, some are not, and the rhetorical periodicity of the duke's speech appears to draw little if anything from the verse form. This is why Rader is correct in saying that we do not hear the couplets as part of the duke's speech. Whether we wish to say that they point to the presence of the poet or to an unstated motive behind the speaker's address, we are assuming that the discourse of the poem exists for a divided subject rather than a unitary one. Rader's remarks illustrate that this doubleness can be recognized as a feature of the discourse independently of inferences we make about the separation of poet from speaker in the poem. Again, it may contribute to our inference of that separation (it usually does in the early monologues of the 1840s), but it also may have a number of other effects. My argument here is that it is discursive splitting or textual bifurcation itself, and not any of its particular effects, that helps us to recognize dramatic monologues.

Dramatic monologues call attention to the fact that language within their domain seems to operate both at a level that is consciously "poetic" in some traditional sense and at a separate syntactic, semantic, or merely "message" level. And these two levels give at least the initial impression that one is independently variable with respect to the other. This implies, for one thing, an ontological division between what language *is* as an artificial and malleable aesthetic medium and what it *says* as a constant medium of human communication. The self-conscious doubleness of the dramatic monologue points out, in other words, an alienation between poetry and discourse; between specialized usage and generalized usage; between trained language producers like poets and unspecialized language consumers like carousing monks, worldly bishops, Renaissance nobles (Browning's duke has no "skill in speech"), and, not least important, readers.[12]

The most simply articulated confrontation between poetic convention and sentence structure emerges in examples like "My Last Duchess." As a versifier, Browning was restless, constantly experimenting with different line and stanza forms, rhyme patterns, and metrical norms. He has no particular loyalty to a single prosodic or verse convention. The Spenserian stanza, the Elizabethan love sonnet, Miltonic blank verse, the heroic couplet—all of these became part of the stylistic signatures of their respective practitioners. The organizing power of balance and antithesis in Pope's couplets can be analyzed as integrally related both to the genres he writes in and his linguistic style in general. No such exercise is possible for Browning. He adapts his language to a wide variety of verse conventions, and he adapts those conventions at will to the dramatic monologue.

Nevertheless, a great many monologues seem to have some clearly definable, even obtrusive, metric, rhyme, or stanzaic scheme that relates to the poem's syntax much as the couplet did in "My Last Duchess." The discourse of "Any Wife to Any Husband," for example, is built of syntactic continuities quite independent of the stanzaic form with its complicated *a a b c c b* rhyme scheme. William Cadbury notices a similar phenomenon in "Childe Roland to the Dark Tower Came." He says that the "tone" of that poem

> is created from two plaited strands. Stanza pattern and metre in "Childe Roland" support our distance, while the run-on lines which undercut the stanza pattern, and the rhythm which works against the metre, create our involvement. Stanza pattern is carefully interlocked, coming always to a full and predictable close and emphasizing by its recurrence the integrity of each stanza; but rhythmical stress is varied freely in each line and run-on lines predominate.[13]

Cadbury's remarks can alert us to the fact that poetic discourse constructs more than just a subject of its own origin. It also locates a subject for its own intelligibility, a subject for the destination of its meaning. And the monologue effectively splits or fragments the subjectivity of "the reader." On the one hand, there is the "distanced" reader, the discriminating consumer of aesthetic commodities, while on the other, there is the "involved" reader, affected and moved by the essential human identification that the poem invites. These are not projected as two different subjects; they are a single subject constituted in contradiction, a fundamental contradiction of market economies in which a product is the fruit of real human labor and meets real human needs while at the same time it is alienated from both producer and consumer. These contradictions cannot be "resolved" within the culture for which Browning wrote—the Pictor Ignotus, we may recall, could not solve his situation either by identifying with his product or by isolating himself from it and the market that brings art into being. They can only be unveiled through a splitting of the subject itself, and this is a large part of the monologue's task.

The task is in no way a narrow one, and Browning shows us how richly serious and, indeed, how playful its various executions can be. "Love Among the Ruins," for example, employs a stanza in which rhymed couplets consist of alternating long and short lines resulting in a marked pause over the short lines. Despite this coercive focus, however, a great many of the short lines could be deleted without interrupting the grammatical flow of the sentences:

> Where the quiet-colored end of evening smiles,
>   Miles and miles
> On the solitary pastures where our sheep
>   Half-asleep
> Twinkle homeward thro' the twilight, stray or stop
>   As they crop—
> Was the site once of a city great and gay,

> (So they say)
> Of our country's very capital, its prince
>   Ages since
> Held his court in, gathered councils, wielding far
>   Peace or war.
>   (1–12)

The stanza is at once made of a language-to-make-stanzas and a language-to-make-sentences, and it is nearly possible to read them both separately but concurrently. This is not to say that the stanza would have exactly the same meaning without the short lines—this is where Browning draws back from simply multiplying or embellishing coherent discourses. The short lines emphasize the distance between the tranquil present and a turbulent past that, since its events transpired so many "ages since," is known only in the tenuousness of legend. This alternation of attention between the lost past and the present continues throughout the poem and is repeatedly reenforced in the short lines. The short lines are clearly indispensable to the sound patterns of the poem, yet often dispensable from the point of view of syntax. How much the poem's meaning relies on them is a matter of uncertainty, varying from stanza to stanza. The poem as a whole implies, without fully resolving, a fundamental question: Does poetry, in so far as it displays an ornamental artifice, communicate something that unspecialized or "ordinary" language does not?

The poem that explores this dialectical uncertainty perhaps more directly than any other is "A Toccata of Galuppi's." Generated out of the distinction between music as abstractly ordered patterns of sound and music as the medium of a message, the central question of the poem is posed at the beginning of the seventh stanza:

> What? Those lesser thirds so plaintive, sixths
>   diminished sigh on sigh,
> Told them something?

Thirds and sixths describe the technical, abstract order of Galuppi's music. Do they also "mean"? Do they "tell" their listeners something?[14] Browning asks the question about music and about poetry simultaneously, not just through the poem's thematic treatment of music, but also through the function of meter in the verse itself.

The rhythmic regularity of Browning's three-line stanza form is established at the outset:

> Oh, Galuppi, Baldassaro, this is very sad to find!
> I can hardly misconceive you; it would prove me deaf
>   and blind;

> But although I take your meaning, 'tis with such a
> heavy mind!

The metric form is a headless iambic line of eight feet. Traditionally, prosodic analysis moves between two levels of description. Recognizing the tendency of most English verse toward alternating lightly and heavily accented syllables, we measure the regularity of this pattern by scanning the poem's "meter." On the second level, we describe the "rhythm" as the range of variability within metrical regularity. Occasionally, however, a poem may display a pattern of accentual regularity that is not described by the metrical scansion yet is the principal source of repeating patterns of stress in the poem. This pattern is a kind of "sur-meter." It is not meter per se, since it can vary while the meter remains regular or remain regular while the meter varies. Yet the concept of rhythm must be reserved for describing variations in this sur-meter just as it does for meter itself. In the stanza from "A Toccata of Galuppi's," the most prominent stress pattern is one of four heavy beats per line, and this pattern is far more regular than that measured by the iambic meter. Hence using traditional accentual notation for the meter and the symbol x for a four-beat dominant sur-metric pattern, we get a scansion like this:

> Oh, / Galúp/pī, Bál/dăssá/rŏ, thís / ĭs vér/ў̆ sád / tŏ fínd!
>
> Í / căn hard/lў̆ mís/cŏncéive / yŏu; ĭt / woŭld próve / mĕ déaf / aňd blínd;
>
> Bút / although / Ĭ táke / yoŭr méa/nĭng, 'tís / wĭth súch / ă héa/vў̆ mínd!

This double regularity of meter and sur-meter creates the repetitional effect of the lines' music, an effect that persists as long as the four heavy beats remain in the standard position, are of nearly equal weight, and are substantially heavier than any of the other metrically heavy accents. This structure breaks down, however, in stanzas like the eighth:

> "Were you happy?"—"Yes."—"and are you still as happy?"
> "Yes. And you?"
> "Then, more kisses!"—"Did *I* stop them, when a million
> seemed so few?"
> Hark, the dominant's persistence till it must be
> answered to!
>
> (22–24)

To be regular, the four heavy stresses in the first line should fall evenly on the first syllable of "happy," the verb "are," the first syllable of the second "happy," and the final syllable of the line. Although echoes of this norm do remain, however, the heaviest stresses in the line fall on the two "yeses," the fifth and thirteenth syllables of the line, and both of these affirmatives are separated from the first syllables of their respective metrical feet by dialogical pauses. Moreover, though the metrically stressed "are" is regular within its own foot, it is sur-metrically unstressed, even in relation to "still." The three feet within the third set of quotation marks provide a crescendo of increasingly heavy stresses quite unlike the metronomic alternation pattern of the first stanza. Looking back at the first stanza, we can see that speech rhythms and exclamations were not absent, but they were rhythmically dominated by the verse. Conversely, in the first two lines of the eighth stanza, the sur-metrical norm is almost entirely obliterated by the irregular rise and fall, hesitation, and acceleration of natural speech. This is, of course, the familiar dialectic we have seen in other poems. Verse convention and sentence structure are fused beyond separation, but they remain discernible poles of verbal strength, as Browning reminds us by returning to the dominant both technically and thematically in the third line of the eighth stanza: "Hark, the dominant's persistence till it must be answered to!" This line is a near pun. Technically the "dominant" is a musical chord that must be "answered" by resolving to another chord later on. But the phrase "answered to" carries a connotation of moral accountability that later emerges again in the poem's thematic resolution.

The first six stanzas of "A Toccata of Galuppi's" have essentially the anaphoric function that I discussed in the last chapter. As in "My Last Duchess," however, the elements operative in deixis establish both an immediate past and a relatively distant past. The immediate past is continuous with the poem's moment in which the speaker is, and has been, listening to Galuppi's music: "Oh, Galuppi, Baldassaro, *this* is very sad to find!" The relevant distant past is the world of Baroque Venice, and it is temporally located by deictics like "thus" (l. 5) and "these" (l. 7), clusters of definite determiners (ll. 5–7), and by process forms like "once" (adverbial, l. 5) and "used to wed" (habitual aspect, l. 6). The music, then, is to the speaker both an immediate sensual experience (the rhythm of the poem might even be conditioned by that of the toccata) and a vivid conveyor of historical knowledge: "I was never out of England—it's as if I saw it all." Already implicit in this opening is a desire to repair historical discontinuity. The speaker fantasizes a verbal exchange between himself and Galuppi; his own side of the exchange is the monologue itself, while for Galuppi's part, he projects a verbal content onto music. This desire to deny the divisions of time is, of course, intimately connected with the desire to deny death. In the crudest terms, a Galuppi who could speak and answer questions through his music would, in some sense, be alive, thus sympathetically mitigating the finality of death for his interlocutor as well. A meaningless music, on the other hand, would more nearly signify the unbridgeable chasm between the dead composer and the living listener.

For music to be capable of speaking across centuries, it must first be capable of speaking to Galuppi's contemporaries. It must have said something to the Venetian court, and that "something," appropriately, is the impossible suggestion that death may be an illusion:

> What? Those lesser thirds so plaintive, sixths
>   diminished, sigh on sigh,
> Told them something? Those suspensions, those
>   solutions—"Must we die?"
> Those commiserating sevenths—"Life might last!
>   we can but try!"
>
> (19–21)

It is at this point that the musical structure of the stanza form begins to give way to the rhythms of speech; the conspicuous mode of aural *being* becomes faint as the possibility of aural *saying* seeks to predominate. And the semantic content of the projected dialogue in stanza eight is the denial of temporal displacement. The repetition of "yes" helps accomplish this denial as it gestures toward a homogeneous and consistent condition (happiness) that is as it was and that is signified by a virtual infinity of kisses, acts so repetitional as to mask or abolish the sense of linear time. It has also, as I said, temporarily abolished the sense of regular musical rhythm, suggesting that somehow the diachronic experience of music is a reminder of displacement and death and needs to be resisted by the projection of a fixed verbal meaning, a transcendent signification. This implication begins to explain the ominous quality of the return to the metrical norm in the third line of the eighth stanza, of the "dominant's" disturbing "persistence" toward a moment in time when an inevitable accounting must be made. This is the first time in the poem that the rhythmic or technical aspect of the music / verse becomes explicitly described as directional in time, although the rapid tumbling quality of the verse rhythm has perhaps suggested an energy impelled toward its own exhaustion from the outset.

Stanzas ten and eleven tell us what is obvious, that the life-loving Venetians have died; and the speaker begins to lose his hold on the fantasy that Galuppi's "old music" had generated:

> But when I sit down to reason, think to take my
>   stand nor swerve,
> While I triumph o'er a secret wrung from nature's
>   close reserve,
> In you come with your cold music till I creep thro'
>   every nerve.
>
> (31–33)

The impact of the music has changed—the merely "old" has become "cold"—although it still speaks a message similar to the one it spoke before:

"Butterflies may dread extinction,—you'll not die, / it cannot be!" Now the music is telling the speaker that he will not die just as it had the Venetians. But the message of this toccata has been insidious; it has spoken as much of loss as of hope by recalling distant Venice, and this ambivalence begins to be apparent in the relation between "message rhythm" and speech rhythm in the later stanzas. The quotation marks reappear; Galuppi is speaking again, but now the speech rhythms fail to overcome the dark verse rhythms as radically as they did in stanza eight. Hark the dominant's persistence—

> Dust and ashes, dead and done with, Venice spent
> what Venice earned.
> The soul, doubtless, is immortal—where a soul can
> be discerned.
> Yours for instance: you know physics, something
> of geology,
> Mathematics are your pastime; souls shall rise in
> their degree;
> Butterflies may dread extinction—you'll not die,
> it cannot be!
>   (35–39)

—till it must be answered to. In the phrases "Dust and ashes, dead and done with" are resolved the dialectic between music that says something and music that does not. The projected "argument" of the toccata tries to justify itself by a feeble appeal to the deathlessness of soul, a metaphysical commodity that the Venetians must not have had, since they died, but that the speaker of the monologue surely does have. But by this time, the message has irrevocably become one with the implied displacement of the on-rushing rhythm. The speaker knows it. The saying and the being of both music and poetry point toward only one kind of stasis or completeness beyond the end of the present dramatic moment: death itself. Lines 20–23 may be read almost as a miniature dramatic monologue within the larger one called "A Toccata of Galuppi's":

> . . . "Must we die?"
> . . . "Life might last! We can but try!"
> "Were you happy?"—"Yes."—"And are you still as
> happy?"—"Yes. And you?"
> —"Then, more kisses!"—"Did *I* stop them, when a million
> seemed so few?"

We hear, to be sure, more than one voice, but the passage has all the necessary features of the monologue: reference to an indefinite past and future, the doubling of speech and poetic elements, and structures of [social] exchange. That "monologue" was a fragment in a pair of lives that ended, a projection of meaning onto music for two people who found their timelessness only in "dust and ashes." The meaning of such a discourse is always double, although it cannot be factored out into two irreducible elements. And it is also always fused. Similarly, all of the subjects for this kind of discourse are at once double and unfactorable. It is both the Venetians and Galuppi who speak, and it is both Galuppi and the "speaker" of the poem for whom the intelligibility of meaning is in question. In the terms of Bakhtin and Kristeva, then, the Venetian fragment, like citation in the novel, is fully "dialogical."[15]

The enclosing dramatic monologue is similar in a way that characterizes the genre, though at times, the monologue's subject of utterance so overshadows the implicit subject of enunciation that the possibility of dialogical or ambivalent meaning seems endangered. These are the poems that often seem doctrinal or programmatic or "optimistic" to Browning's readers. The monologue so attractively invokes the ideology of the unified individual that by also invoking the possibility of discourse as dialogical or ambivalent, it only displays a contradiction rather than resolving or naturalizing it in a consistent convention, as realist fiction naturalizes the split between monological narrative and dialogical citation.

"A Toccata of Galuppi's" is a classic dramatic monologue. Nevertheless, there is one major difference between the function of the traditional poetic artifice in this poem and in a poem like "My Last Duchess." In the duke of Ferrara's monologue, the bifurcation of discourse contributed to the implication of a speaker's identity separate from the poet's identity. This was necessary to the irony of that particular poem. In "A Toccata of Galuppi's," though the subject is still divided, no such function appears. Is the speaker Robert Browning or someone else? We learn that whoever he is, he has an interest in physics, geology, and mathematics. Are we to search Browning's biography to solve the formal problems posed by the poem and the genre? I think this would contribute little to the interpretation of either. Just as the narrator in fiction may, in some cases, also be the character whose speech is cited, so the poet may or may not be the same person as the speaker of the poem. In the case of fiction, a distinction still exists between a subject of utterance and a subject of enunciation, the latter being the one who creates a second meaning (even for his own reported speech) in dialogue with an implied reader. In the same way, the subject of enunciation in "A Toccata of Galuppi's" offers a meaning for the speaker's words that is different from the speaker's meaning if only by virtue of the fact that the speaker addresses his words to someone other than the reader of the poem. Whether that speaker (subject of utterance) and the subject of enunciation are the "same person" is irrelevant; all that matters is that the discourse itself formally locates two different centers of intelligibility through its own bivalent structure.

One of the persistent mysteries of Browning's style lies in the distinctness with which it is both always the same and always different, always Browning's very Victorian English and always capable of particularizing speakers as different as Bishop Blougram and Caliban. To observe this is different from observing the linguistic range of Shakespeare creating Prospero and Caliban or Hyppolita and Bottom. Style in the Renaissance is neatly ordered in different levels, levels that may easily be used to signify different social groups. Movement from one level to another within a single play tells us something about the relative sophistication of different characters and about how seriously we are to take them and their dilemmas. The poet who is a master of style can move thoroughly from one level to another as a means of creating interactions among the characters within the single work. Indeed, as T. S. Eliot pointed out long ago, one measure of an Elizabethan writer's genius is his ability to make his own linguistic idiosyncrasies disappear as he moves among the different voices of his fictional world.

As the Elizabethan habit of thinking in hierarchies of plateaus disappeared, so too did the skills appropriate to that organization. This is one reason why after the seventeenth century, Shakespeare's range of characterization is not to be found in English drama. The conceptual and philosophical framework within which a poet learns several distinctly different styles has lost too much of its former influence. From the eighteenth century until the middle of the nineteenth, no comparable force of linguistic diversification is to be found. Among major poets, only Wordsworth attempted sustained experiments in the imitation of unfamiliar voices, and neither his reasons for doing so nor his results clearly foreshadow the innovations of Browning and Tennyson.

If the Elizabethan playwright leaves the fewest possible traces of his own speech in the speech of his characters, a Victorian poet like Browning carefully leaves his mark on each of his fictional "men and women." Robert Langbaum has discussed the dramatic monologue as a "piece" of an Elizabethan-type drama with its context of action stripped away.[16] This allows him to write persuasively about the illusion of fragmentariness generated by the genre, but it prevents him from investigating the continuity among different monologues. Dramatic action or interaction among the speakers of different styles creates continuity in a Shakespearean play. Often it takes a character like Prince Hal, who can speak both the language of drawers and the language of kings, to effect the social resolutions that the play requires. This kind of continuity is unavailable to the Victorian poet (witness Browning's disastrous career as a dramatist), but Browning found another kind of continuity among his speakers, one that makes the dramatic monologue *collection* as important to the history of genres as the structure of the individual monologue itself. Browning's speakers cannot speak to one another; they would be wholly isolated voices were it not for the insistent markers of a familiar Victorian language that at once translates and integrates the several voices of several times and places. Browning says in "One Word More" that he has "gathered" disparate men and women in order to "speak from each mouth," and this formal act of gathering has been too little emphasized in Browning studies. In time, he discovered a fictional framework within which he could "gather" and relate dramatic monologues without returning to the futile attempt at writing plays. This resolution was *The Ring and the Book*. Indeed, it is useful to consider the outline of Browning's poetic career as a movement from the failure to write successful plays to the invention of a short form that could gesture toward dramatic continuity without recovering it, and finally to a gathering of the shorter forms in artificially integrated collections, a process that culminated with the invention, in *The Ring and the Book*, of a governing fiction for the collection itself.

The key formal device in this evolution is, I think, the doubleness of language that so emphatically keeps the Victorian poet's own style before us even as each successive speaker reveals the extremities of his own specialized voice. The enclosing fiction of *The Ring and the Book* provided thematic means for the manifestation of such idiosyncrasies; we call them different "perspectives" on the murder case. Accordingly, Browning's stylistic variations are less necessary and less radical there than in the earlier monologues.

One does not, of course, in reading the monologues, consciously separate familiar contemporary traits of speech from those that give a particular speaker his memorable individuality. It is not just two voices but the fusion of two voices that Browning's poems force us to entertain. This fusion may recognize and resist the discontinuity between the present and the remote past, between the clergy and the lay public, between the well-educated and the common man, between the poet and his audience, or even between two different aspects of a single personality. In general, the isolated and the special production or consumption of language is acknowledged and then absorbed into the gathering of the monologues in Browning's collections.

III

The issue of the poet / specialist's alienation from the speaker as ordinary man is a special case of a problem that haunted many Victorians. In poetics, we have seen it emerge in the distinction between a potentially ornamental artifice in language and the "useful" capacity of language to convey messages. Antitheses between style and utility are, of course, old in literary tradition by the nineteenth century; indeed, they were very old when Ben Jonson justified the Elizabethan plain style as representing "language such as men do use." But in the nineteenth century, the association of ornamental style with the oppressive power of great wealth gained in force and thus intensified the social and economic alienation of style and use. In a recent book on Victorian design, for example, Herwin Schaefer has ably demonstrated what he calls a "two-track" tradition in the production of everything from fine instruments and great machines to the most common consumer goods: "the one [track] utilitarian, functional, matter-of-fact, the other a matter of prestige, of aesthetic, and social differentiation." Schaefer cites Rousseau and, later, Thorstein Veblen among those who deplored the separation of beauty from function. On the other side, he calls our attention to commentators who celebrate it and lament the opportunity for "persons to assume a semblance of decoration far beyond either their means or their station."[17] In this disagreement, both the egalitarian and the aristocratic sides assume the polarization of beauty and function, and Schaefer goes on to discuss numerous examples of designers in the nineteenth century, like Horatio Greenough, who attempt to resolve the antithesis. The most common model for the reconciliation was, not surprisingly, nature itself, in which form and function seemed ideally indistinguishable. This simple association can, of course, alert us to less obvious manifestations of the problem of aesthetic specialization. Darwin comes immediately to mind, in those often tortured passages in which he tries to reconcile the fine plumage of birds to the essentially utilitarian premise underlying the concept of natural selection. Or we may well think of the lifelong desire of John Stuart Mill to accommodate the strict Benthamite training of his mind to his undeniable spiritual response to natural beauty.

Many more examples might be cited, but these few can at least indicate how frequently the alienation of aesthetic values vexes the various departments of Victorian thought. For Browning, as we have seen, the nearest analog to poetry in this regard is music, and he returns to the relationship between music and communication in a number of poems about poets, singers, and musicians. One of the most interesting cases is "Saul." Like "A Toccata of Galuppi's," "Saul" is a poem in which music says something. David recounts how he sang to Saul and revived the great king, and the language displays the doubleness I have been describing. The regular periodicity of the anapestic rhymed couplets contrasts with the irregular accelerations and hesitations of the speech rhythms:

> Then I played the help-tune of our reapers, their
>   wine-song, when hand
> Grasps at hand, eye lights eye in good friendship,
>   and great hearts expand
> And grow one in the sense of this world's life.—
>   And then, the last song
> When the dead man is praised on his journey—
>   "Bear, bear him along
> With his few faults shut up like dead flowerets!
>   Are balm-seeds not here
> To console us? The land has none left such as
>   he on the bier.
> Oh, would we might keep thee, my brother!"
>   (49–55)

As in so many other poems, the verse units may or may not coincide with syntactic and rhetorical units; the relationship appears to be random. If we ask, as Ralph Rader asks about the duke of Ferrara, whether we hear the structure of the verse as part of the speaker's voice, we shall be bound to answer, as Rader does, that we do not. But this poem contains a complication that is not found in the earlier poem. After eight verse paragraphs of narration, David repeats the actual song that he sang to Saul, and this song too is rendered in anapestic rhymed couplets. This time, however, it is not at all certain that the regularity of the verse is a thing apart from the act of speech attributed to David. As easily as we can ask whether verse conventions constitute a part of David's speech or a part of Browning's poetry, we can also ask whether they constitute a part of David's speech or of David's own poetry. Browning is careful to frustrate the attempt to answer the latter question. The transition from speech to music in the poem is marked and yet seamless:

> And I bent once again to my playing, pursued it unchecked,
> As I sang,—
>
> IX
> "Oh, our manhood's prime vigor! No spirit
>   feels waste,
> Not a muscle is stopped in its playing nor sinew unbraced."
>   (67–69)

There is not any doubt that David's description of what happened occurs in stanza eight, while his reenactment of the song is wholly contained in stanza nine. Nevertheless, this division is not observed when it comes to the verse line. The final line fragment of stanza eight, "As I sang," is completed by the first line of the song in stanza nine. If we ask, therefore, whether the narrative and the song are discrete or continuous with one another, we shall get conflicting answers depending on whether our frame of reference is the verse stanza or the verse line. We cannot answer the question categorically for the poem as a whole. Accordingly, if we ask whether a given feature, such as anapestic meter, is a part of poetry or a part of speech, we will also be denied a conclusive answer, and this latter condition will also draw to our attention the impossibility of finally attributing some features to Browning's voice and some to David's.

    In poem after poem, Browning's magic lies in his ability to offer an illusion of an idiosyncratic voice dividing men from men and to make that illusion waver before our eyes as the voice of each of his men and women is, however ambivalently, "gathered" into that one voice that rings most clearly when all the poems have been read. It would be misleading merely to raise this final voice to a higher level of idiosyncrasy by calling it Browning's voice. It is the voice of a hypothetical language, one that displays the dialectic between the idiosyncratic and the generally shared. Thus the central contradiction of the dramatic monologue sets, as it did in "Pictor Ignotus," the private interest of the coherent individual against the general interest of the entire community. These interests are mutually exclusive, but in Browning they appear dialectically as a single ideological necessity.

Of course, ideology is also designed to obscure or veil something that is not itself, and Marx has shown in *The German Ideology* how the antithesis between private interest and general interest veils the reality of class interest. Browning brings contradiction to consciousness in the monologue in two forms, but it is in the slight nonalignment of these two forms that we can see the class interest that supports and perpetuates the contradictions. The two forms may be represented by two oppositions: *specialized discourse / unspecialized discourse* and *idiosyncratic voice / the language of the community*. The latter is perhaps most familiar as the distinction between speech production (*parole*) and language as an abstract system or code (*langue*), but it is distinctly not identical to the first antithesis. This inequality stems precisely from the fact that, while the idiosyncratic voice represents the mythical individual, specialized discourse represents a class interest.

In Victorian England, an individual's ability to improve his competitive posture toward his fellows increasingly became linked to the class credential of his education. One marker of a person's education was his speech, including his command of prestige uses of language like the poetic. The roots of social differentiation according to cultivated speech characteristics reach back to well before the nineteenth century; the relation of "prescriptive grammar" to social change in the eighteenth century has been described by Elizabeth Traugott in the following terms: "Perhaps the main social factor in the development of prescriptive grammars was the rise of the middle class. In urban communities the gentry felt threatened and sought ways to keep themselves apart from the middle class. They looked for overt behavioral tokens by which to single themselves out from others, tokens which would create barriers between themselves and the middle class. Language was an obvious vehicle for such an aim."[18] From this beginning, and within the middle class itself, a more complex system of specialized language grouping developed in the nineteenth century. The organization of these groups was not always clearly hierarchical, but fine distinctions, especially in the region of vocabulary, served increasingly to differentiate a plurality of competing elites: scientific, literary, diplomatic, financial, and so on. This development away from a simple gentry / commoner division toward a more complex and compartmentalized social structure derives in part from the division of labor and knowledge in the industrial world and in part from a concept of progress according to which certain collectives can attain or strive for a status superior to that of their predecessors. One result of these distinctions and ambitions is the formulation of interest groups with characteristic voices in the system of political thought that produced the parliamentary reform of 1832. That act may be seen as simply the most visible marker of a number of social transformations designed to elevate the status of a given class (e.g., industrial workers) or a given region (e.g., the cities). In the case of parliamentary reform, the new status directly entailed the right to present a new class-determined voice in adversary debate with established ruling interests.

The elitism of interest groups and the specialization of their languages are also allied with both nationalistic and racial pride. In particular, historically and geographically distant cultures, once revered for aesthetic or intellectual sophistication, could now become the objects of condescension based on England's scientific and industrial prowess. Charles Morazé has pointed out that Chinese culture, such a paragon of achievement to the eighteenth century, "revealed" to the nineteenth its inadequacy to compete with Western scientific progress due to its lack of a specialized language of logical reasoning.[19]

All of these distinct vocabularies—of interest groups, of aristocracies, of scientific and aesthetic elites, of distant cultures, both primitive and exotic, of the educated in rhetoric or in logical processes—all of these idioms appear in one form or another in Browning's monologues. Nearly every speaker projected by these poems can be identified according to his or her inclusion in or exclusion from a particular elite with its own hierarchy of values.

The dialectic of discourses in the dramatic monologue is thus a complex one. Literature itself had become, as Raymond Williams tells us, "a specialized and selective category," consciously distinguished both from other specialized discourses like the scientific and from general or "popular" discourse even in printed books.[20] In the monologue, therefore, we find the opposition of poetic discourse to other specialized discourses; the opposition of specialized discourse itself to generalized, popular, or even colloquial Victorian speech; and the opposition of generalized discourse to idiosyncratic discourse. This profoundly dialogical language, along with the fragmentation of the subject that it entails, raises, as we have seen, complex and difficult questions about the nature of communication. The model of communication questioned by the monologue is that of reciprocity or exchange. "Exchange" in a market system implies the existence of discrete and coherent subjects or private interests. The question addressed in the next chapter is what happens to communication as exchange when the subject of the monologue's discourse is paradoxically both individual and, at the same time, unboundaried and divided.

Notes

1. For a useful summary of these attitudes in the Victorian decades, see Jerome H. Buckley, *The Triumph of Time* (Cambridge: Harvard University Press, 1966).
2. Walter Pater, *The Renaissance* (London, 1914), p. 234.
3. Ibid., pp. 235–236. The recognition of this dialectic of attitudes toward the "self" now seems preferable to J. Hillis Miller's claim that "in Browning's day, and in England the idea of the indeterminacy of self-hood was a scandalous notion." Nevertheless, Miller's discussion of Browning's lack of a "definite, solid self" is one of the best moments in modern Browning criticism. See *The Disappearance of God* (Cambridge: Harvard University Press, 1963), pp. 103ff.
4. John Stuart Mill, *Essays on Politics and Culture*, ed. Gertrude Himmelfarb (New York: Doubleday, 1962), p. 3.
5. Thomas Carlyle, *Sartor Resartus* (New York: Dutton, 1975), p. 57.
6. In his chapter on Browning in *The Disappearance of God*, Miller properly perceives these qualities as functions of subjectivity. Furthermore, he also sees that Browning never finally repudiates the ideal of wholeness: "The habit of 'Still beginning, ending never' is one of the central characteristics of Browning's thought. Even at the last minute of life he will still be moving, still rejecting the latest expression of the indivisible whole, and still starting over indefatigably to make another, which will only be rejected in its turn" (p. 87). Miller also approaches an apprehension of the splitting of the subject in Browning, but by saying that the poet himself "oscillates within the poem back and forth between contradictory impulses," Miller cannot finally abolish the unitary subject; he merely moves it around.
7. See Browning's note to *Dramatic Lyrics* in the *Complete Works* 3:197. The second remark is quoted in William Clyde DeVane, *A Browning Handbook* (New York: Appleton-Century-Crofts, 1955), p. 430.
8. B. W. Fuson, *Browning and His English Predecessors in the Dramatic Monologue* (Iowa City: University of Iowa Press, 1948), pp. 11–12; Michael Mason, "Browning and the Dramatic Monologue," in *Robert Browning*, ed. Isobel Armstrong (Athens: Ohio University Press, 1975), p. 232. See also Park Honan, *Browning's Characters* (New Haven: Yale University Press, 1961), p. 122. An interesting group of recent theoretical statements on the nature of the dramatic monologue may be found in *Victorian Poetry* 22, no. 2 (1984). The most thorough and efficient collections of Browning's own statements supporting the conventional view appear in Philip Drew, *The Poetry of Browning: A Critical Introduction* (London: Methuen, 1970), pp. 12–14.
9. For an illuminating account of the origins of Browning's split subject in earlier poems, see Herbert Tucker's reading of the recognition of Eglamor at the end of *Sordello* in *Browning's Beginnings* (Minneapolis: University of Minnesota Press, 1980), pp. 16–29.
10. Ralph W. Rader, "The Concept of Genre and Eighteenth-Century Studies," in *New Approaches to Eighteenth-Century Literature*, ed. Philip Harth (New York: Columbia University Press, 1974), pp. 91–92. Rader's observation is, of course, simply an elaboration of a commonplace familiar at least since William Lyon Phelps compared Browning's couplets to those of Pope and Keats in 1912. See Phelps, *Robert Browning* (New York: Archon Books, 1968), pp. 170–72.
11. Ralph W. Rader, "The Dramatic Monologue and Related Lyric Forms," *Critical Inquiry* 3, no. 1 (1976): 139.
12. Browning's early uneasiness about these oppositions is expressed in his explanation of the title "Bells and Pomegranates": "I only meant by that title to indicate an endeavor towards something like an alternation, or mixture, of music with discoursing, sound with sense, poetry with thought" (from the preface to *A Soul's Tragedy* in *The Complete Works*, 5:4).
13. Cadbury, "Lyric and Anti-Lyric Forms: A Method for Judging Browning," *Browning's Mind and Art*, ed. Clarence Tracy (New York: Barnes and Noble, 1970), p. 38.

14. This queston is, of course, a transformation of the Shelleyan questions about the skylark's song that I discussed in chapter 2. For a transitional example, where the "meaning" of the music is, as for Shelley, more metaphysical than textual, see *Pauline*, lines 412–16, where Browning characterizes the task of reading Shelley: "To disentangle, gather sense from song; / Since, song-inwoven, lurked there sense which seemed / A key to a new world the muttering / Of angels, something yet unguessed by man" (quoted in John Hollander, "Robert Browning: The Music of Music," *Robert Browning: A Collection of Critical Essays*, ed. Harold Bloom and Adrienne Munich [New York: Prentice-Hall, 1979], p. 102). Hollander's essay is especially useful on the subject of Browning's music poems, as is George M. Ridenour's "Browning's Music Poems: Fancy and Fact," *PMLA* 78, no. 4 (1963): 369–77. See also Wendell Story Johnson, "Browning's Music," *Journal of Aesthetic and Art Criticism* 12, no. 2 (1963): 203–7.

15. For the relation between dialogical literary language and the presentation of open-ended time frames of the kind I have described in chapter 3, see M. M. Bakhtin, *The Dialogical Imagination, Four Essays by M. M. Bakhtin*, ed. Michael Holquist, trans. Caryl Emerson and Michael Holquist (London and Austin, Texas: University of Texas Press, 1981), pp. 7ff.

16. Robert Langbaum, *The Poetry of Experience* (New York: Norton, 1957), esp. chap. 6.

17. Herwin Schaefer, *Nineteenth-Century Modern* (New York: Praeger, 1970), p. 66.

18. Elizabeth Closs Traugott, *The History of English Syntax* (New York: Holt, Rinehart and Winston, 1972), p. 163.

19. Charles Morazé, *The Triumph of the Middle Classes* (New York: Doubleday, 1968), pp. 114–15.

20. Raymond Williams, *Marxism and Literature*, (Oxford: Oxford University Press, 1977), p. 51.

Projection and the Female Other: Romanticism, Browning, and the Victorian Dramatic Monologue

U. C. KNOEPFLMACHER

> We shall become the same, we shall be one
> Spirit within two frames, oh! wherefore two?
> —Shelley, *Epipsychidion*

> What I see is that I have become Total-Image, which is to say, Death in person; others—the Other—do not dispossess me of myself, they turn me, ferociously, into an object, they put me at their mercy, at their disposal, classified in a file, ready for the subtlest deceptions.
> —Barthes, *Camera Lucida*

Browning's 1864 monodrama "James Lee's Wife" contains a remarkable passage in its ninth and last section, "On Deck." The "ill-favored" female speaker, ready to annul herself by migrating "Over the sea," has "conceded" the failure of her union with James Lee, the object of her desire. The speaker accepts her self-exile from the apathetic "mind" of the man she continues to worship: "Nothing I was" will, she has now come to realize, ever find a "place" in that masculine mind. And yet, boldly and unexpectedly, she imagines a future moment in which a depleted James Lee "might" fade into

> a thing like me,
> And your hair grow these coarse hanks of hair,
> Your skin, this bark of a gnarled tree,—
> You might turn myself!
> (ll. 368–371)[1]

The metamorphosis the speaker envisions is neither the natural outcome of aging nor a wishful act of supernatural witchery. Her visionary casting into the future is a projection (from *pro-jacere*: to throw ahead). But what is involved is not the kind of "projection" that led a Paracelsus or an Agrippa, those alchemist-transformers with whom Percy Shelley and Browning identified, to cast powders into a crucible. It is, instead, a purely mental act.

What James Lee's Wife, the woman without a name of her own, envisions, then, is nothing less than a mental restoration of the identity she has lost. Though physically alive, she has become obliterated in James Lee's mind and hence has become more radically excluded than the extinguished Porphyria and Last Duchess whose outward forms are at least remembered by the male minds who drained their vitality. Like still another martyred female, Pompilia, James Lee's Wife requires an acknowledgement of kinship to take place in the mind of her denier. She can be animated only through such a rebirth of consciousness. She thus assigns herself a role somewhat like that played by the mute Dorothy whose "wild eyes" allow her brother to behold "in thee what once I was." But James Lee is not an eager Wordsworth. To conquer his obdurate resistance, his Dorothy does not merely wax silent but also resolves to place herself out of the reach of any "word" or "look" from him. She understands that only by evading him can she ever hope to force him to grasp her true import. Her removal may cause James Lee to re-imagine—and re-image—his own selfhood; only then will he be able to take the next step and recognize his wife's image as a specular analogue or epipsyche of himself:

> Strange, if a face, when you thought of me,
>   Rose like your own face present now,
> With eyes as dear in their due degree,
>   Much such a mouth, and as bright a brow,
> Till you saw yourself, while you cried "'Tis She!"
>   (ll. 353–357)

The young Browning who more than thirty years earlier had addressed the figure of Pauline as the equivalent of Wordsworth's Dorothy or of Shelley's Emilia Viviani had also tried to see himself in a female mirror:

> And then I was a young witch whose blue eyes,
> As she stood naked by the river springs,
> Drew down a god: I watched his radiant form
> Growing less radiant, and it gladdened me.
>   (ll. 112–115)

Still, the female impersonations of the *Pauline* poet who repeatedly likens himself to a "girl" were but a spasmodic expression of his "wild dreams of beauty," those yearnings after a complementary otherness which, like Shelley's search for an inconstant "Intellectual Beauty," were destined to remain unfulfilled. Although James Lee's Wife despairs of fusion as much as the *Pauline* poet, her self-removal frees her from the impotence that marks his mental agitations. She thus is actually closer to the figure of Pauline herself, the Frenchwoman who distances herself from the Romantic effusions of *"mon pauvre ami"* in a footnoted prose gloss to the poem (Browning's first experimentation with a female voice). She hence is even close to Browning's own distancing intelligence, especially as it had begun to operate, significantly enough, in "Porphyria's Lover" (1836) and "My Last Duchess" (1842), where Browning returned to the motifs of *Pauline* by ironically exposing a male speaker's inadequate attempts mentally to possess a Female Other.

When Browning renamed as "James Lee's Wife" the poem he had four years earlier titled "James Lee," he signified his full understanding of the reversal he had produced through the creation of still another layer in a multi-layered sequence. That sequence went back from poems in *Men and Women* (1855) in the previous decade to earlier dramatic monologues such as "Porphyria's Lover" and "My Last Duchess," and from these to his youthful *Pauline*, and beyond, to the Romantic conversation poem and to those lyrics and narratives by Shelley and "by a Mr. John Keats, which were recommended to [Browning's mother] as being very much in the spirit of Mr. Shelley."[2] To understand the genesis of the dramatic monologue and to appreciate also the impact that Browning's development of the monologue had on latter-day Romantic seekers of a female Muse—Rossetti, Morris, and Swinburne—the critic must carefully unravel each of these strands and assess their full interrelation.

I

It is no coincidence that "James Lee's Wife" should have been conceived after the death of Browning's own wife, that female "moon of poets," only one of whose "two soul-sides" her worshipful, Endymion-like mate had been able to extol "out of my own self" in "One Word More," at the end of *Men and Women*. Both in her poetry as well as in her own person, Elizabeth Barrett had tried to maintain that Keatsian "central self" she has Aurora Leigh adopt. Barrett thus furnished Browning with a further link to the Romantic idealization of a female complement who might restore an incomplete male self. She was his Mary Godwin, his Emilia Viviani. As I have briefly shown elsewhere, his elopement with Elizabeth was a self-conscious reenactment on the part of both lovers of Percy Shelley's own flight aboard, thirty-two years before, with another daughter shackled by a father.[3] Yet long before the famous letter of January 10, 1845, in which he offered his worship to the unseen "dear Miss Barrett," Browning had been what, around the same time, George Henry Lewes called Shelley, *"par excellence,* the 'poet of women'."[4] The elopement, after all, merely confirmed him in the role of liberator of an imprisoned Muse he had all along assumed in his verses. It was a fantasy come true. He could become the Perseus who was destined to "save" the alluring Andromeda-figure coveted by the impotent *Pauline* poet ("But change can touch her not—so beautiful / With her fixed eyes, earnest and still" [ll. 658–659]). He could be the manly Count Gismond, a St. George figure, who rescues from opproby and defamation the damsel he will marry. Pauline's successors had proliferated in the 1842 *Dramatic Lyrics*. In the same volume in which he reprinted "Porphyria's Lover" and for the first time published "My Last Duchess," "queen-worship" vies with the depiction of thwarted lovers, Cristina, the Lady of Tripoli, Artemis, Siora, Gertrude. With the publication in 1845 of the *Dramatic Romances and Lyrics*, their number had greatly multiplied.

Yet Browning's lifelong urge to represent the imaginative possession of a female epipsyche was punctured, in true Romantic fashion, by severe doubts. And these doubts were exacerbated by dissatisfactions with the lyric and narrative forms he had also inherited from his precursors. In his own lyrics and romances, severance and betrayal abound. Incompleteness is far more prominent than the fusion of complementary selves. But only in the form of the dramatic monologue first developed in "Porphyria's Lover" was Browning able to scrutinize that incompleteness without melodramatic overtones that made "In a Gondola" so inadequate a revision of Keats's "Isabella" and without the sentimentality that marred an otherwise unimpeachable lyric such as "The Lost Mistress." And, whereas his early female speakers remained two-dimensional (one would never think of "Count Gismond" as "Count Gismond's Wife," despite its female voice), it was in those monologues in which Browning parodied his own male desire to flatten women into the "fixed" and immoveable Andromedas of graphic art—in poems such as "Porphyria's Lover" and "My Last Duchess," once again, but also in "Andrea del Sarto," "The Bishop Orders His Tomb," and even "Fra Lippo Lippi"— where his own art suddenly became powerfully and magically three-dimensional.

"Porphyria's Lover" and "My Last Duchess"—more closely analyzed in the next section—feed on the very incompletion they depict. They still render the appropriation of a Female Other who is portrayed as elusive and silent; at the same time, however, they introduce a critical distance that was absent in the lyrics and the dramatic romances. Removed as either lyricist or narrator, Browning now ironizes the act of projection by which a devouring male ego reduces that Female Other into nothingness. Animations of a process of deanimation, these monologues thus self-consciously mock the poet's very own enterprise. Though an ironist, the poet also acts as abettor and accomplice, for he too flattens a female anima into a mere image, a representation, an object of art.

Still, if the Browning who animates the pathological windings of the Lover's and the Duke's minds ostensibly partakes of their suppression of the Female Other, he actually maneuvers the reader into becoming that suppressed Other's chief ally. Even more than Andrea's Lucrezia or the dying

Bishop's long-deceased, yet still jealously hoarded mistress, Porphyria and the Duchess have become deformed into static images. They thus assume the inertness of those frozen and "fixed" photographic stills which Roland Barthes reads as emblems of a cruel art (of nineteenth-century origins) of depersonalization.[5]

But Porphyria and the Duchess have lost more than a freedom of motion. Imprisoned as they are within a male's rhetoric of justification, they have also become bereft of a voice of their own. It is their very voicelessness, however, that stirs in us the process of identification that James Lee's Wife hopes to produce, through her absence and silence, in her husband's mind. It is because they are mute that the reader is prompted to adopt the same role of liberator that Browning delegated to chivalric surrogates such as Count Gismond. Unless rescued by the reader, Porphyria and the Duchess remain the perennial captives of masculine speech.

Thus, just as Barthes the reader of fading photographs is provoked into restoring to the photographer's subjects the motions and identities that they have lost, so is the reader of "Porphyria's Lover" and "My Last Duchess" stimulated into reanimating what Browning's speakers have deanimated. We are drawn into a process of restitution and reconstitution. Whether consciously or not, Browning thus cleverly delegates to his readers a task that neither he nor his Romantic predecessors had been able to represent to their full satisfaction.

It was a brilliant solution to a plaguing problem that went back, before *Pauline*, to the beginnings of the century. For, as a lyric poet manqué, Browning was able to profit from the experimentations of those Romantic subjectivists who had sadly discovered that their desire for fusion with another could all too easily convert that Other into a mere projection of the lyricist's male self. Hence, before we can assess the full achievement of "Porphyria's Lover" and "My Last Duchess," we must wind back to those earlier beginnings and try to unravel some further layers in this complicated genealogy.

Robert Langbaum was surely correct when, in *The Poetry of Experience*, he stressed the "movement toward objectivity" inherent in the productions of Romantic poets for whom "subjectivity was . . . the inescapable condition."[6] Yet whereas in 1957 Langbaum still felt compelled to rescue Romanticism from the "charges" made by Modernists overeager to signal their "independence" from their nineteenth-century roots, we no longer need to mount such a defense. Indeed, in the intervening quarter of a century, the emphasis has shifted in exactly the opposite direction. The influence of critics such as Harold Bloom has made us too disposed to read the poetry from Blake to Stevens as a smooth, uninterrupted continuum. If, as Bloom repeatedly would have it, Browning is a latter-day Shelley,[7] there are nonetheless highly important formal differences that sharply separate Browning's from preceding efforts at overcoming the "inescapable condition" that Langbaum so well describes: the plight of an individual ego "isolated within himself," bereft of an "objective counterpart" for his subjective will and feelings (p. 28). These differences become most notable when we specifically look at the Romantic search for a "counterpart" of the opposite gender, a topic that strangely seems to interest neither Langbaum nor Bloom, for all its centrality to their respective concerns.

"Be thou me!" an "impetuous" Shelley urged the "Maenad"-like West Wind. The famous apostrophe could just as well have been uttered by all those equally impetuous Romantic seekers who coveted an Eve in order to replenish the vacancies experienced by a solitary Adamic self. Whether factual or mythified, alive or dead, human or immortal, the Romantic epipsyche became an increasingly problematic emblem that allegorized the male's unsatiated desire for fusion. In the very first conversation poem, Coleridge could ask "pensive Sara" to act as a counterweight for his flights of fancy by having her recline her cheek against him in their "Cot" (a posture that Browning was to reverse carefully in his macabre parody of this idyllic cottage scene in "Porphyria's Lover"). Soon, however, the silent helpmeet on whose "more serious eye" Coleridge's speaker projects his own misgivings about the unbridled use of the imagination (in Miltonic double negatives that might have been used by admonishing archangels but hardly by Sara Fricker) fades out altogether. She is so much "at rest" in "Frost at Midnight" that her restless mate can appropriate her maternal role by bestowing a new Edenic birth on their infant son; she becomes replaced as a "woman beyond utterance dear" by her namesake in "To Asra"; both she and that namesake lose their individuality in "Dejection: an Ode," where the subjective capacity for projection (as in Browning's " 'Childe Roland' ") becomes a curse and where the speaker parades the isolation produced by this dubious gift before the "Dear Lady" to whom, in earlier drafts of his great poem, Coleridge had given the names of William and Edward.

This pattern of denying to the female the position to which she had first been exalted was to become a paradigm. If in Wordsworth's earlier poems, as Margaret Homans has perceptively suggested, "the quietude," not just of Dorothy the living sister but also of dead sister-spirits such as Lucy Gray or the Margaret of the Ruined Cottage, "verifies the power of the poet's performative words,"[8] the feminine Pagan sources of that power become dissipated in the later poetry when the Female Other once again turns into a male Christian deity. In "She Was a Phantom of Delight," the gleaming "Apparition" that glided, Porphyria-like, into the poet's field of vision dissolved into a mundane woman engaged in "household motion," who is acknowledged to retain at best "something" of the "angelic light" formerly conferred on her by the poet's recoiling imagination. Masculine history and masculine religion take over in the later books of *The Excursion* and in the "Victorian" revisions of the 1805 *Prelude*.

In Byron's poetry, too, whether in the obsessive lyrics of parting such as "Fare Thee Well" and "To Augusta," or in dramas like *Manfred* (where the male protagonist can receive nothing more than an echo of his own name from Astarte's shade), and, most persistently, in *Don Juan*, where all romantic liaisons come to naught, the desired Female Other can never be embraced. Haidée, whom Juan still worships as his lode-star before he is forced to enter the harem in woman's clothing, but whom he quickly forgets thereafter, can neither live nor expire in his arms. The only fusion possible is between Haidée and another male, the piratical father who causes her death:

> I said that they were alike, their features and
>   Their stature, differing but in sex and years;
> Even to the delicacy of their hand
>   There was resemblance.
> —*Don Juan*, IV.xlv

Female victim and male victimizer can blend in death, equally forgotten by memory, resting in unvisited tombs. In Byron's masculine world, the Female Other must necessarily be sacrificed. Not until "James Lee's Wife" and its pendant-piece "Dîs Aliter Visum," significantly subtitled "Le Byron de nos Jours," and, most significantly in "Pompilia," would Browning counter this dispiriting vision by restoring to Byron's silent Haidée a genuine voice of her own.

It was the immediate precedent of the younger Romantics, however, as Harold Bloom rightly insists, which was most forcefully engraved in the mind who moved from *Pauline* (modelled after confessional romances such as *Alastor, Epipsychidion*, and *The Fall of Hyperion*) to the dramatic monologue spoken by Porphyria's deranged lover. Bloom perceptively recovers some of the Shelleyan "sub-texts" that lurk in Browning's poetry. But his Oedipal emphasis on masculine rivalry leads him to miss one of the chief attractions which Shelley, that "poet of women," held for the young Browning and leads him also to underestimate the significance of a Keats he casts as Tennyson's, but not Browning's, poetic "father" (pp. 177, 143–174 passim).

Let us consider first the case of Keats. "Porphyria's Lover" can be seen as a deliberate revision of "The Eve of St. Agnes"—or, to indulge in Browning's macabre joke, what might be called an "Eve of St. Agnes" with a "twist." The ironies and ambiguities imbedded in Keats's semi-allegorical treatment of projection are sharpened by the psychological realism of a poem in which the active Porphyro turns into Porphyria and the illusions of the hoodwinked Madeline turn into the delusions of a mad male fantasist. But it is not just Keats's single poem that provides a Bloomian "sub-text" for "Porphyria's Lover." The Boccaccian Porphyro who penetrates Madeline's bower is merely one of many Lovers whose recurrence throughout Keats's entire canon Browning also rescrutinized.

Whether it is the Endymion with whose search for Cynthia the early Keats had already identified in "I Stood Tip-Toe" ("He was a Poet, sure a lover too, / Who stood on Latmus' top" [ll. 193–194]), or the "Bold Lover" on the Urn who must remain content with a "She" who cannot fade (ll. 17, 19), or the ever-smitten Hermes who can blend with the nymph who, "like a moon in wane, / Faded before him" (*Lamia*, ll. 136–137), or the acolyte who wrests Psyche away from Cupid's embrace in order to place her into "some untrodden region of my mind" (l. 51), the figure of the Lover persistently acts as Keats's chief agent for the satisfaction of his desire to blend sexual consummation with the stasis of immortality. That stasis is associated either with godhead (as it also will be in the closure of "Porphyria's Lover") or with the permanence of art (as it will be in "My Last Duchess"). Yet the lyrical reconciliation of the mutable and the permanent can only be expressed as a subjective wish fulfillment. Only wishfulness can combine, in Keats's last great sonnet, a simultaneous enjoyment of the "steadfast" and "unchangeable" qualities of the distanced "Bright Star" and of the breathing motions of a living woman's warm, white "breast" against which the reposing lover can lie "pillow'd" (the original version read "*cheek*-pillow'd").

Browning must have recalled some of these Keatsian touchstones in "Porphyria's Lover" (where Porphyria makes the Lover recline his "cheek" against her bared "white" shoulder). But he invokes them more directly in the sixteenth section of "One Word More," where he questions the fulfillment of the wish that Cynthia might "turn a new side" to her mortal gazers. "Unseen" by herdsman, huntsman, steersman, the other face of that female moon remains

> Blank to Zoroaster on his terrace,
> Blind to Galileo on his turret,
> Dumb to Homer, dumb to Keats—him, even!
> (ll. 162–165)

Browning's doubts, however, were fully anticipated by Keats himself. His skepticism is evident in the ironic treatment of a Porphyro who violates the "chamber of maiden thought" or of a Lycius incapable of sustaining the vision that is Lamia.[9] Keats was as aware as Browning of the dangers of subjectivity. If that subjectivity could happily result in Endymion's transfiguration or in the internalization of Psyche, it could also deanimate and kill. The "pale knight" who fails to read the "language strange" of a Belle Dame Sans Merci, the entranced Lycius who must die depleted, or the weak "dreaming thing" apostrophized by Moneta are all exemplars of the self-destructiveness inherent in a desire based on projection. In "Porphyria's Lover," Browning simply reverses the process by having the Lover kill the very object of his desire.

Although in "Porphyria's Lover" Browning was able to accentuate ironies already inherent in Keats's narratives, his infatuation with Shelley's own cult of the woman was not easily shaken. Not until after the 1852 "Essay on Shelley" did he discover the full record of the infidelities of the Sun-Treader whose idealizations of the Female Other he had earlier emulated. Browning's reluctant dissociation from *Alastor* and *Epipsychidion* in *Pauline* had been artistic, not emotional. Yet in the 1855 " 'Childe Roland to the Dark Tower Came'," that hallucinatory and "de-idealizing" monologue (Bloom, p. 175), the dissociation had become more profound. It is significant that there should be no females in that poem of pure projection. The knight who journeys to the Dark Tower is not charged with the mission of rescuing an immured female. He is not St. George about to free a chained maiden, no Perseus rescuing Andromeda, no chivalric Count Gismond or a Gareth or Lancelot (as in Tennyson's or in Morris' poems). Yet it is precisely the *absence* of a female object that makes the quest so gripping as an exercise in pure projection.[10] Absence *is* Presence, as Browning would have James Lee's Wife discover.

By the time Browning came to write "James Lee's Wife," a poem which, by his own account, interestingly enough, was to dwell on "people newly-married," trying futilely "to realize a dream of being sufficient to each other, in a *foreign land* (where you can try such an *experiment*) and finding it break up,—the man being *tired* first, and tired precisely of the love:—"[11] the repudiation had become complete. He could at last see Shelley plain. Browning was now wholly disenchanted with the experimental love-ethic of a poet who had tried to share Harriet Westbrook and Mary Godwin, or, later, Mary and Emilia Viviani, or, later still, Mary and Jane Williams. It was an affront to the widowed Browning's Victorian respectability. But it was more. Despite its negative emphasis, "James Lee's Wife" reinstates that Female Other which Browning now felt Shelley had tarnished. Browning had already fashioned critiques of a male's denial of the feminine in "Porphyria's Lover" and "My Last Duchess." But whereas Lover and Duke had at least tried to possess the Female Other, the "tired" James Lee rejects fusion altogether. As Browning now knew, Shelley too had wearied in his quest for an ideal he despaired of finding in any living woman.[12]

Like James Lee, and unlike the Browning who clung to a remembered happiness with Elizabeth Barrett, Shelley had never been satiated in his search for Intellectual Beauty. The Alastor poet who impales himself on the threshholds of consciousness could at best encounter a reflection of his own eyes. The speaker of *Epipsychidion*, who also dies in the course of his quest, similarly despairs of a female projection of his own self: "I measure / The world of fancies, seeking one like thee, / And find—alas! mine own infirmity" (ll. 69–71). Neither Emilia the Sun nor Mary the blotted Moon "whose pale and waning lips" shrink "as in the sickness of eclipse" (ll. 309–310), nor even Clare Clairmont, that other astral body so abruptly introduced as a Comet "beautiful and fierce" (1. 368), could satisfy an ever-hungry Astrophel. But if Keats questioned that hunger, Shelley relished it as a means of propulsion until, wearied, he turned away from the Female Other with something of the same disgust with which Victor Frankenstein destroys the half-completed Monsteress he had tried to fashion. In one of the last letters he was to write before he immolated himself like the poets of *Alastor* and *Epipsychidion*, he provided a fitting epitaph for his culmination of the Romantic quest for an epipsyche:

> The "Epipsychidion" I cannot look at; the person whom it celebrates was a cloud instead of a Juno; and poor Ixion starts from the centaur that was the offspring of his own embrace. If you are anxious, however, to hear what I am and have been, it will tell you something thereof. It is an idealized history of my life and feelings. I think one is always in love with something or other; the error, and I confess it is not easy for spirits cased in flesh and blood to avoid it, consists in seeking in a mortal image the likeness of what is perhaps eternal.[13]

In "James Lee's Wife," Browning gave a voice to the "something or other" Shelley treats as an abstraction. In part eight of the poem, he added a stanza in which the Wife adopts Shelley's bitterness as well as some of his phrasing:

> I have my lesson, understand
>   The worth of flesh and blood at last.
> Nothing but beauty in a Hand?
>   Because he could not change the hue,
>   Mend the lines and make them true
> To this which met his soul's demand—
>   Would Da Vinci turn from you?
>   (ll. 294–300)

Leonardo the artist, she conjectures, would not dismiss a spirit cased in "flesh and blood" for an unrealizable ideal. But James Lee has dismissed her. And so, as Browning reluctantly came to admit, would have Percy Bysshe Shelley.

II

In "Porphyria's Lover," as in Keats's "The Eve of St. Agnes," we are presented with a contrast between a cold outside world and a warm interior. Yet, in each poem, it is the passionate outsider penetrating that interior who brings warmth to the immobile dreamer within: just as Porphyria immediately kneels to make "the cheerless grate / Blaze up, and all the cottage warm" ("PL," ll. 8–9), so does her namesake, "burning Porphyro," with "heart on fire," try to melt the "chilly nest" he has invaded ("EA," ll. 159, 75, 235). Their efforts, however, are half-successful at best. If Porphyria cannot thaw her unresponsive lover by placing his "arm about her waist" and by pillowing his cold cheek on her "smooth white shoulder bare" ("PL," ll. 16–17), Porphyro cannot rouse the sleeping Madeline by sinking. "His warm, unnerved arm" on her "pillow" ("EA," ll. 280, 281).

The coldness of the outside world and its instability somehow cling to each of these intruders. Death's pallor envelops them, for all their warmth and vigorous movement. Kneeling before Madeline, Porphyro sinks "pale as smooth-sculptured stone"; when, on awaking, she sees him as "pallid, chill, and drear!" he becomes associated with the "pallid moonshine" in which her taper "died" (ll. 297, 311, 200). Even when, "flush'd," he springs back into motion, Madeline's fears seem borne out by ominous details wedged into the narrative: the blowing frost-wind, iced gusts, and setting moon undermine Porphyro's "impassion'd" professions of eternal devotion. Yet Porphyria's Lover is warier than Madeline. Though Porphyria assures him that the "thought of one so pale / For love of her" has caused her to brave the elements and try to free her "struggling passion," the Lover finds insufficient comfort in the knowledge that "passion *sometimes* would prevail" ("PL," ll. 28–29, 23, 26, italics added). Instead, he stares guardedly at Porphyria's damp clothes and "soiled gloves" before deciding to convert that "sometimes" into a "forever," a moment of eternity. He will not risk the fate of his Romantic predecessor.

Hence, while Madeline resorts to trustfulness, Porphyria's Lover remains suspicious. Madeline accepts Porphyro's assurance that what he calls an "elfin-storm from faery land" ("EA," l. 343) sanctions their joint removal from the "bloated wassaillers" at the feast (l. 346). She thus submits to her abductor and vanishes in the chilly exterior: "And they are gone: aye, ages long ago / These lovers fled away into the storm" (ll. 370–371). Porphyria's Lover, on the other hand, will not venture beyond his mental cell. He fears that he will be no more able to "restrain" Porphyria than did "to-night's," momentarily deserted, "gay feast" (l. 27). If Madeline comes to disregard the blowing "frost-wind," Porphyria's Lover considers the "sullen wind" to which he has listened "with heart fit to break" as an emblem of the instability that might again engulf this brief "moment" of communion (ll. 2, 5, 36). The woman who found it so difficult to "dissever" herself from the stormy world without may prove to be as unreliable as Porphyro; while alive, she can at best momentarily "shut the cold out and the storm" (ll. 24, 7). Thus, only by freezing her into a stony permanence can this pale Lover preserve her temporary fire. Though he will tell us that the "cheek" of the woman he has strangled still blushes "bright beneath [his] burning kiss," he has conferred on her his own deathly pallor (ll. 47, 48). The Lover who resembled Madeline has transformed himself into Madeline's possessor.

Browning's poem thus inverts Keats's narrative: the external coldness into which Porphyro ominously transports "so pure a thing" ("EA," l. 225) becomes internalized by the Lover who wants to preserve Porphyria's purity by making her permanently "mine, mine, fair, / Perfectly pure and good" ("PL," ll. 36–37). Yet Browning also has the Lover internalize the skepticism which in Keats's poem is presented through a "negative capability" that relies on imagery and multiple points of view. Porphyro's name (as well as Porphyria's) is derived from the Greek word for purple (as Keats knows when he alludes to the "purple riot" in Porphyro's heart); as such, the name suggests a warm hue, as well as a high station.[14] But the vermilion dye of porphyry is obtained by pulverizing ("porphyrizing") a hard red shell or equally hard red slab of rock (as Keats again suggests when he describes Porphyro as a "smooth-sculptured stone," a "throbbing star," a "vermeil dyed" shield for Madeline's beauty ["EA," ll. 297, 318, 336]). Madeline's warm lover, regarded by Angela as "liege-lord of all Elves and Fays" (l. 121), may thus well be a cold-blooded immortal like Lamia or Merlin's "Demon" (l. 171).

What Porphyria's Lover fears, however, is not the draining of his life-blood by a vampiric immortal but rather the mutability of the mortal woman he identifies with the raging wind. Stony and still, unresponsive to her overtures, he awaits the moment in which he can rob Porphyria of her animated movements. Porphyro devises a quick stratagem to bypass the revelers at the feast and enter the "maiden's chamber": "Sudden a thought came like a full-blown rose" ("EA," ll. 139, 187, 136). Similarly, a "sudden thought" has prompted Porphyria, according to the Lover's account, to leave the gay feast and venture into his chamber ("PL," l. 28). But her "thought" was a mere impulse, destined to be—or so he fears—short-lived. It is his own mind that searches for a stratagem as he, outwardly still passive and virginal, debates "what to do" until he lights upon the "thing" that might allow him to preserve her (ll. 35, 38). By draining Porphyria of her life, he can assume the mental control of a Porphyro. The "Bold Lover" forever frozen on Keats's stony Urn can never kiss his unfading "She": "though thou hast not thy bliss, / For ever wilt thou love, and she be fair!" (ll. 19–20). In the stony tableau devised by Porphyria's Lover, however, that "bliss" becomes attainable. The necrophilic Lover kisses the dead woman; but, what is more, he can now impose his own mental processes on the mind whose inconstancy he had earlier feared:

> I propped her head up as before,
> Only, this time my shoulder bore
> Her head, which droops upon it still:
> The smiling rosy little head,
> So glad it has its utmost will,
> That all it scorned at once is fled,
> And I, its love, am gained instead!
> —"PL," ll. 49–55

Converted into an "it," Porphyria's head no longer has the power of volition; instead, "its will" is that of her subjective interpreter. She has become an object for the Lover's projection, for he can now impute to her his own wishes without any fear of contradiction.

The mechanism of projection was also at work in "The Eve of St. Agnes," where Porphyro played on Madeline's wishful and childish trust in the "visions of delight" promised to virgins on St. Agnes' Eve. Yet Madeline had come to sense a disparity between subject and object, wish and reality. Moreover, her misgivings were reenforced by a narrator who casts doubts upon her "shaded" dream by his frequent interventions and by juxtaposing her fantasies to those of the Beadsman and Angela. There are no such narrator and no such subsidiary characters in "Porphyria's Lover." As in the companion-piece to this poem, "Johannes Agricola in Meditation," we are from start to finish within the "madhouse cell" of the Lover's screened-off mind.

As an exercise in the subjectivism of projection, "Porphyria's Lover" thus raises certain questions that validate the earlier contention that Browning devised a parody of the Romantic quest for a Female Other. Who is the Lover addressing? Where is he located? Given the absence of a verifiable interlocutor and a verifiable setting such as Browning was to provide six years later in the poem usually considered to be his first bona fide dramatic monologue, "My Last Duchess," how trustworthy, ultimately, is the Lover's account? We have the authority of Keats's narrator that Porphyro entered Madeline's chamber and exploited her dream. We cannot at all be sure that a Porphyria actually sought out the egocentric speaker who, at the very outset of his monologue, projects his internal turmoil on the "vexing" storm outside.[15] Has this speaker, whose very identity depends on his act of projection (the poem was originally called, quite simply, "Madhouse Cell, No. II"), truly killed Porphyria? Indeed, does a "Porphyria" really exist in a shape other than in his mind?

The similarity in the names of "Porphyro" and "Porphyria" may, after all, involve more than the reversal traced above. It may well suggest that, not only Browning but also the deranged speaker whom Browning animates is a latter-day Romantic who knows his Keats. The "story" of "Porphyria's Lover" could hence be read as a pure fantasy told by a reader of "The Eve of St. Agnes" who, after identifying with Madeline's desire for the phantasm of a lover, does not want to share her disenchantment. That male reader thus not only feels free to reverse the gender of Keats's protagonists but also to devise a different outcome to gratify his crazed need for "pure" possession. In this sense, the Lover's confident assertion, "No pain felt she; / I am quite sure she felt no pain" (ll. 41–42), actually would be true. The strangling of a purely imaginary object of desire can cause no pain to an actual human being "cased in flesh and blood."

By the untrustworthiness of his speaker, Browning teases the readers of

"Porphyria's Lover" into trying to provide a "story" of their own. But the scenarios we may concoct are just as untrustworthy. We may want to visualize a murderer who, surprised by the guard, still hovers gleefully over the body of an actual victim; or, if we accept the murder as imaginary, we may prefer to glimpse a madman in a cell. We may also be tantalized into furnishing some antecedent narrative of star-crossed lovers or one in which a passive visionary who has seen a nameless, high-born lady from afar (one "born in purple," a "porphyrogenite") dreams that this "She" will visit and worship him. The possibilities are multiple, but all such conjectures are destined to remain futile. Our need to entertain them, despite that futility, only helps to sharpen Browning's ironic emphasis. Our mental narratives delude us into thinking that we can confer permanence and objectivity on what remains erratic and subjective. By inventing alternative "stories," we hope to distance ourselves from the grotesque Lover. Instead, however, we partake of the very same craving. To master a problematic instability we, too, yearn for some spurious form of permanence.

It is precisely such an assumption of a spurious godlike immutability that links "Porphyria's Lover" both to its 1836 pendant poem "Johannes Agricola" as well as to the 1842 "My Last Duchess," with its own dramatization of the displacement of a Female Other by a male figure playing the role of God. The last two lines of "Porphyria's Lover" jar the reader almost as much as the strangling acknowledged in line 41: "And all night long we have not stirred, / And yet God has not said a word!" (ll. 59–60). God's voicelessness recalls the Lover's own deliberate silence when "called" by Porphyria. He and God and now she remain unstirred, at one. If Johannes Agricola the Antinomian professes, "night by night," to be able to reach the abode of a deity who has exempted him from damnation, so does the Lover exult in newly gained invulnerability. In the seventeenth century, the theologian Ralph Cudworth had inveighed against those "Porphyrianists" (the followers of Arius and Porphyrius) who made "their Trinity a foundation for creature-worship and idolatry."[16] Though not a follower of Porphyrius, the third-century neo-Platonist, the Lover is nonetheless a "Porphyrianist" in his own way. His "creature-worship" of a woman of "flesh and blood" has resulted in her deanimation into a cold idol. By appropriating her mentally, he has become, he thinks, immune and immoveable, like God. In the "night" of his own mind, he has shaped a new triune Identity. Whether Porphyria is his dead victim or merely a figment of his imagination thus does not matter. She remains in either case an eidolon whose possession he regards, in true Romantic fashion, as licensing his elevation to godhead. Like the artist-figures in the later monologues, who can confer life as well as arrest it, Porphyria's Lover professes to be actuated by his desire for another. Yet his love stands exposed as a monomaniacal self-love.

A similar self-love obviously operates in "My Last Duchess," a poem discussed by Browning critics, and ably so, far more often than "Porphyria's

Lover," yet seldom seen in its own pendant relationship to the earlier poem. The similarities between the two works are significant; but so are the differences. The Lover who must dominate the "stooping" Porphyria by freezing her into a posture of submissive dependence resembles the Duke of Ferrara who chooses "Never to stoop" (l. 43). The Duke, too, deanimates a Female Other who threatens his need to remain in absolute control of his rigid mental world. But this calculating aesthete, though every bit as monstrous (and possibly more so), is not a crazed, improvising, pale Lover whose words are subject to doubt. Unlike that dehistoricized speaker's voice, his own carries the authority of a specific time and place, the staples of Browning's future monologues.

We do not know whom the Lover addresses and why, or whether he addresses anyone at all. We do know the identity of the Duke's interlocutor and know, moreover, that other viewers have previously been shown the portrait he ritually unveils "by design" (l. 6). Indeed, it is the Duke's compulsive need for repetition that belies his efforts at composure and control. A new Duchess may be his current "object" (l. 53), but his previous effort to objectify a living woman into a frozen painting still seems to unsettle him. The "curtain" he removes for the Count's emissary thus gradually unveils a mind that is more disturbed than it would admit. If the reader of "Porphyria's Lover" becomes a voyeur at Bedlam who ultimately can no more "dissever" truth from fantasy than the subjective Lover himself, the reader of "My Last Duchess" becomes a detective who wrests away the control the Duke desires by seizing on the "objective" clues that have been provided. These clues permit us to judge the Duke far more unequivocally than we could ever judge the Lover.

The chief clue is provided by the Duchess herself. Like Porphyria, she exists solely within the speaker's words. Yet Browning permits the reader to free the Duchess from the Duke's possessive "My" in ways that Porphyria could never be disengaged from her Lover's strident, "she was mine, mine." There is a further difference. It is his yearning for an Ideal that prompts the Lover to drain a woman's "flesh and blood." The Duke, however, has failed to grasp that such a feminine Ideal had actually animated his own world. If the blush on Porphyria's dead countenance was purely imaginary, the "spot of joy" preserved in Pandolf's painting still confounds the Duke's literalism (l. 21). He will never understand how "such a glance came there" (l. 12). Yet the details he furnishes carry symbolic meanings that continue to defy him. The "white mule" on which "my lady" was wont to ride, the offering of a "bough of cherries" brought to her by a worshiper, are iconographic details traditionally associated with the Virgin Mary. A democratic mediatrix, an earthly Madonna, has gone unnoticed by a mind determined not to stoop. The "approving speech" with which this kindly Madonna received all who greeted her has been extinguished, like her original "blush" (l. 31).

Empowered by Browning's art of inference, however, the reader can reactivate her receptivity, adopt the mediating role that she has lost, and thus restore to her what the Duke continues to deny.

Unlike the Duchess and Porphyria, Browning's later women are allowed to speak: of these, Pompilia, a full-blown version of the earthly Madonna, modelled, as Nina Auerbach shows elsewhere in this collection, after Barrett's Marian Earle (and Barrett herself), certainly remains the most notable. Even when dead or silenced, however, Browning's later incarnations of the Female Other continue to confound the male's attempts at mental possession. The fair "she" appropriated by that other art collector, the Bishop of St. Praxed's (a church named, significantly enough, after a female martyr) will find avengers in her sons. In "Andrea del Sarto" Lucrezia enacts the inconstancy that Porphyria's Lover had feared. But her behavior defiles her would-be possessor more than herself. She is an unchaste Cynthia whom he must share with others: "My face, my moon, my everybody's moon" (l. 29). Her mobility sets in relief the impotence of this "half-man." Although Andrea would, like Porphyria's Lover, dearly want to restrain the woman's movements, he can only paralyze himself. His self-loathing strangles his very dream of artistic immortality in a New Jerusalem where he, as the elected decorator of a fourth great wall, might join Leonardo, Raphael, and Michelangelo, "the three first without a wife" (l. 264). Sadly, he realizes that he remains walled in by the mental prison that Lucrezia can flee. If she acts as Andrea's foil, so does Fra Lippo Lippi, who also breaks out of the confinement of mental and physical cells, for Lippo knows that Ideal and flesh cannot be "dissevered." Accordingly, at the end of his monologue, he suddenly defers to the female voice of "the sweet angelic slip of a thing" whom he casts in the role of rescuer. She embodies the paradox he cannot resolve. She is an image, a Saint Lucy, a type in a painting; yet she is also the Prior's niece, a married woman, very much alive, and, as such, one who arouses Lippo's desire.

III

In *Jocoseria* (1883), one of his last volumes of poetry, Browning movingly recalls his dead mate in the fine lyric "Never the Time and the Place." The writer of dramatic monologues once more assays the Romantic lyrical mode he had been forced to relinquish. Whether consciously or not, however, he resorts to the same imagery he had used in "Porphyria's Lover" almost half a century before. And he does so now without the defensive ironies that had marked his earlier, seminal incursion into timelessness and placelessness. "Where is the loved one's face?" the speaker asks plaintively, and then proceeds to answer his own question:

> In a dream that loved one's face meets mine,
>   But the house is narrow, the place is bleak
> Where, outside, rain and wind combine
>   With a furtive ear, if I strive to speak,
>
> . . . .
>   Outside are the storms and strangers: we—
> Oh, close, safe, warm sleep I and she,
> —I and she!
>
> (ll. 5–9; 20–22)

James Lee had yet to mature before he could glimpse a female face like his own. But the seventy-year-old Browning was more than ready to exclaim, "'Tis She!" No "half-man" like Andrea, he had given expression to a feminine self. And in *Jocoseria* he once more strove to speak in the female voice. In his poem "Mary Wollstonecraft and Fuseli," Mary Shelley's mother utters an artistic credo that is unmistakeably Browning's own. Fuseli can sublimate emotions into his controlled compositions, but she toils "at a language" that in its very roughness retains her "strong fierce" passionate core. Elsewhere in *Jocoseria*, in the Talmudic tales of Balkis and Solomon, and Lilith and Eve, Browning blends his feminism with his growing philo-Semitism, the product of a similar identification with the victims of a cultural oppression that relied on mental projection as much as prejudice.

It is significant that *Jocoseria* was originally supposed to include "Gerousios Oinos," Browning's attack on the later Tennyson, Morris, Rossetti, and Swinburne. What prompted Browning to cast his contemporaries as "mere servingmen" unrestrainedly quaffing the diluted "true wine" of the elder English poets, thinking it "bettered and bittered" by mixing it with beer? He had become defensive about his own stature after Alfred Austin's attack; yet Tennyson had been just as shabbily treated by Austin, and, moreover, younger poets like Swinburne had indignantly rallied to Browning's side. As his letters to Isa Blagden show, Browning genuinely disliked the supposed dilutions of meaning in the later *Idylls of the King*, the later poems of Morris, and the verses of Swinburne and Rossetti, all marred by "the *minimum* of thought and idea in the *maximum* of words and phraseology."[17] Yet even this artistic difference seems insufficient to account for the excessive vehemence of Browning's attack in "Gerousios Oinos"—an excessiveness he seemed to acknowledge when he suppressed publication of the poem.

It was not mere difference that so disturbed Browning but a shocked recognition of kinship. Tennyson's "Lucretius," his most Browning-like dramatic monologue, had appeared in 1868. The trio of younger poets had also adopted Browning's central theme of the Female Other—from Morris' 1856 "The Defence of Guenevere" to Rossetti's 1870 "Jenny" and "A Last Confession." To be sure, his impact on these younger poets was far from exclusive. Their female portraits were also indebted to a Tennyson who had, after all, published "Mariana" and "The Lady of Shalott" even before Browning printed—and withdrew—his *Pauline* (which Rossetti was to rediscover), and who had written "Tithon," the original version of "Tithonus," around the very same time that Browning composed "Porphyria's Lover." Yet the Female Other whom the Pre-Raphaelites represented on canvas and in verse, like Swinburne's Proserpines and Sapphos, owed as much, or more, to Browning.

"One face looks out from all his canvasses," Christina Rossetti wrote in an implicit criticism of her brother's work ("In an Artist's Studio"). Whether queen or "nameless girl" or angel or saint, the Female Other now allowed a younger generation of artists to "feed" upon "her face by day or night." Browning agreed: "Yes,—I have read Rossetti's poems," he wrote Isa Blagden, "you know I hate the effeminacy of his school,—the men that dress up like women,—that use obsolete forms, too, and archaic accentuations to seem soft" (*Dearest Isa*, p. 336). Were not these lovers of the Female Other like his own Porphyria's Lover? Rossetti had even indulged in necrophilia by wresting his poems from Lizzie Siddal's corpse. Looking at the face that glanced at him from their paintings in pen and pencil, a shocked Browning saw not the flush of joy of a Last Duchess, as if she were alive, but the grimaces of ladies of pain, adulteresses, femmes fatales, prostitutes, and vampires. The younger nympholepts were not just "feeding" off the representations of England's elder poets. These hungry "servingmen" were also consuming the very substance of the elderly Browning's own poetry.

In "John Jones's Wife," a Swinburne who had become disenchanted with Browning did, in effect, just that. By writing a parody of "James Lee's Wife," the younger poet could openly appropriate Browning's mode and subject matter and go one better. In his attack on Browning in "The Chaotic School," the essay he left in manuscript, Swinburne denies Browning the skill of impersonating a true woman: "How does it fare with his Colombes, Constances, Mildreds, Phenes, who are visibly fleshless and senseless? Analyze the doings and sayings of the wife of Jules or the mistress of Norbert; the utter mechanical absurdity of the monstrous parts they have to play is equalled by the tight, hoarse, intermittent, hard, febrile manner of their utterances: as far from emotion as from reason."[18] Swinburne thus transforms the voice of James Lee's Wife into the voice of a Female Other wronged by Browning's art; his speaker's quarrel is not just with "John Jones," but with her original creator:

> My skin might change to a pitiful crone's,
> My lips to a lizard's, my hair to weed,
> My features, in fact, to a series of loans;
> Thus much is conceded; now, you concede
> You would hardly salute me by choice, John Jones?[19]

Like the Keats who wrests Psyche away from Cupid, Swinburne the parodist has become a rival lover. Yet his rivalry stems from an acknowledgment of the very kinship which the older poet so eagerly tried to suppress.

Browning had come to see himself as the jealous preserver of both the memory and the voice of his female "moon of poets." He could not accept this "effeminate" competitor, whose "florid impotence" he denounced (*Dearest Isa,* p. 333). And yet Swinburne's criticism was an act of generosity. "I do *not* count Browning a lyric poet proper," he wrote, "nor properly a dramatic, as he breaks down in dialogue; but his greatness as an *artist* I think (now more than ever) established to all time by his *monodramas.* I say *artist,* or poet, as well as thinker."[20] It is significant that this tribute should have come shortly after Swinburne's close reading of the monodrama of "James Lee's Wife." It was a tribute he was to extend in his elegiac "Sequence of Sonnets on the Death of Robert Browning" in 1889. There, he celebrated Browning for his capacity to "see / The heart within the heart that seems to strive" (*Complete Works,* VI, 148). And that innermost heart remained, for both poets, always essentially female.

This attempt at a chapter in literary history would not be complete without my calling attention to the centrality, in all Victorian poetry, of the patterns of projection I have described. In "The Voice" (1912), Thomas Hardy, that relic from the Victorian Age, still tried to animate a dead Female Other: "Woman much missed, how you call to me, call to me, / Saying that now you are not as you were." Browning's contribution to English poetry was both his attempt to give voice to a Female Other as well as his persistent skepticism about the process of projection that such a voicing involved. Like Keats, who might have become the greatest of Victorian poets, Browning knew that poetry, like all art, can distort the Other into what she is not. It was that skepticism which gave rise to the dramatic monologue and which led to a mode simultaneously ironic and idealistic that Browning came to perfect and to bequeath to later poets.

Notes

1. All citations from Browning's poetry are taken from *Robert Browning: The Poems,* ed. John Pettigrew and Thomas J. Collins, 2 vols. (Yale Univ. Press, 1981); the quotations from Romantic poetry in Section I are taken from *English Romantic Writers,* ed. David Perkins (New York, 1967).

2. Edmund Gosse, *Personalia,* quoted in George Willis Cooke, *A Guide-Book to the Poetic and Dramatic Works of Robert Browning* (Boston and New York, 1896), p. 204.

3. "On Exile and Fiction: the Leweses and the Shelleys," *Mothering the Mind,* ed. Ruth Perry and Martine Brownley (New York, 1984).

4. *Westminster Review,* 35 (1841), 330.

5. *Camera Lucida: Reflections on Photography,* trans. Richard Howard (New York, 1981), pp. 14–15.

6. *The Poetry of Experience: The Dramatic Monologue in Modern Literary Tradition* (New York, 1963), p. 28.

7. "Browning: Good Moments and Ruined Quests," *Poetry and Repression: Revisionism from Blake to Stevens* (Yale Univ. Press, 1976), pp. 175–204.

8. "Eliot, Wordsworth, and the Scenes of the Sisters' Instruction," *CritI*, 8 (1981), 224.

9. That skepticism is already in evidence as early as "Sleep and Poetry" in the deliberate infantilizing of the speaker who relies on "fancy" in order to catch the nymphs, to play with their fingers, and to touch merely "their shoulders white / Into a pretty shrinking with a bite / As hard as lips can make" (ll. 104–108).

10. Bloom holds that the all-machine " 'Childe Roland' " exposes the Romantic imagination" by the speaker's induction in a "visionary company of loss" (pp. 199, 200); his insight might have been borne out by a closer look at the identity of the speaker's two precursors in "The Band," Giles and Cuthbert.

11. Quoted in Richard Curle, ed., *Robert Browning and Julia Wedgewood: A Broken Friendship as Revealed in Their Letters* (New York, 1937), p. 109. Only the last italics are Browning's.

12. By adopting a female point of view, Browning attacked the weariness of a male Romantic egotist, much as Mary Shelley had done in *Frankenstein*, the novel which, significantly enough, always remained one of Elizabeth Barrett's favorites.

13. *The Letters of Percy Bysshe Shelley*, ed. Frederick C. Jones (Oxford Univ. Press, 1964), II, 434.

14. For these and subsequent connotations, see *The Compact Edition of the OED* (1971).

15. Like Keats, Browning seems acutely aware of Coleridgean antecedents: if the storm tends to "vex" the Lover by its unruliness, it is the opposite state of "calm," unhelped by "any wind," that "vexes meditation" for another cottage dweller in "Frost at Midnight" (ll. 8, 9). Coleridge's speaker moves from inward paralysis to a dynamic animation of the landscape he devises for his child; Browning's Lover draws Porphyria into the frosty stillness of his mental cell. "Dejection: an Ode," Coleridge's other "midnight" poem, is also recalled in "Porphyria's Lover." Unable to find fuel in "that inanimate cold world" his imagination projects, Coleridge's agonized speaker seeks vainly to remove the "viper thoughts, that coil around my mind" by listening "to the wind" (ll. 51, 94); Porphyria's Lover, beset by similar anxieties, prefers to relieve his agony by coiling his thoughts around Porphyria's "little throat."

16. The citation is from Cudworth's *True Intellectual System* (1678), quoted in the *Compact OED*, II, 2242. It is noteworthy that in the so-called "Porphyrian scale" or "tree" (also reproduced in the *OED*) the "Animate" should be identified, not with an "Incorporeal" substance such as the Christian soul, but with a "Corporeal" substance as much prized as its "Sensible" and "Rational" analogues. Long ago, C. R. Tracy ("Browning's Heresies," SP, 33 [1936], 618) pointed to the theological slant of the *Monthly Repository*, where "Johannes Agricola" and "Porphyria's Lover" originally appeared, in order to account for the religious satire of the former poem. The same case should be made for its companion piece, not usually recognized as a similar incursion into a heretical theology.

17. March 22, 1870, in *Dearest Isa: Robert Browning's Letters to Isabella Blagden*, ed. Edward C. McAleer (Univ. of Texas Press, 1951), p. 333.

18. *New Writings by Swinburne*, ed. Cecil Y. Lang (Syracuse Univ. Press, 1964), p. 53.

19. *The Complete Works of Algernon Charles Swinburne*, ed. Edmund Gosse and T. J. Wise (London, 1925), V, 268. The lines quoted are the conclusion of the poem.

20. To William Michael Rossetti, October 26, 1869; *The Swinburne Letters*, ed. Cecil Y. Lang (Yale Univ. Press, 1959), II, 46–47; Swinburne's italics. In the same letter Swinburne expresses his outrage at Austin's attack on Browning.

Browning's Female Signature

ADRIENNE AUSLANDER MUNICH

No Victorian has been so identified with the Perseus and Andromeda myth as Robert Browning; to many it seemed as if the poet had constructed his life to fulfill the promise encoded in the ancient myth. Allusions to it in his poetry precede his rescue of Elizabeth Barrett Barrett from the death grip of her father. William C. DeVane traced Browning's allusions to Perseus and Andromeda throughout his poetry and connected the romance in the myth to the poet's elopement yet failed to notice that the similarity between the poets' life and the myth did not end with marriage.[1] First the chivalrous rescuer, Perseus then became devoted husband and doting father who relinquished his throne when his son came of age. Browning, too, appeared willing to abdicate his eminence for the sake of his son's career. "Do you know," the poet confided to a friend "if the thing were possible, I would renounce all personal ambition and would destroy every line I ever wrote, if by so doing I could see fame and honor heaped on my Robert's head."[2] Browning apparently emulated his exemplar, Perseus, to the end.

Browning's many allusions to the Andromeda myth have been considered as presenting paradigms for proper human behavior. In *The Ring and the Book*, for example, frequent allusions to the mythological characters, Perseus, Andromeda, and the monster, represent absolute moral positions, counterbalancing the relativism of the differing viewpoints of the poem's monologuists. That Caponsacchi is a Perseus/St. George figure tells the reader to believe in his goodness; that she is likened to Andromeda confers upon Pompilia blameless victimhood. When regarded in this way Browning's interpretation of the myth reenacts a Victorian melodrama, complementary to Elizabeth Barrett Browning's sonnet on Hiram Powers's *Greek Slave*, complete with gender stereotypes. Politically liberal in the tradition of Shelley's redemptive vision, Browning's Perseus opposes tyranny of the strong over the weak, conforming to Victorian conventions of manliness. Browning also used the myth in less conventional, more complicated, ways.

Rather than rehearse the familiar story of saving man and saved woman by tracing rescue themes and allusions to the Andromeda myth in Browning's work, my focus will be on the emblematic interpretation of a specific Perseus

---

Adrienne Auslander Munich, "Celestial Emblems," *Andromeda's Chains: Gender and Interpretation in Victorian Literature and Art*. Copyright © 1989 Columbia University Press, New York. Used by permission.

and Andromeda etching which acted as a muse for Browning's poetry up to the time he actually rescued his wife. Many themes become attached to the idea of Andromeda during his career, culminating in his final invocation of the image in his last major work. Browning uses the etching from *Perseus et Andromede* by Polidoro da Caravaggio (figure 1) as the central image in a complex of signs he interprets as female. Making the Andromeda figure into an emblem of his poetics, he uses it as chivalric token to inspire great feats of poetry. As the sign of Browning's literary power, Andromeda is his aesthetic signature, a figure for his taking in, even taking over, female power.

An early letter to Miss Barrett illustrates how Browning incorporates the Andromeda figure into an emblematic image. Using the Andromeda etching in association with other personally meaningful objects, Browning describes the place at his parents' home where he wrote all his poetry. Out of his precious things, the poet makes an emblematic picture, the various scales of the objects contributing to a surreal portrait of his mind. His glosses the symbolic scene as emblematic of his own particular power to evoke a world of meaning mysteriously couched in personal objects:

> Who told you of my skull and spider webs—Horne? Last year I petted extraordinarily a fine fellow, (a *garden* spider—there was the singularity,— the thin clever-even-for a spider-sort, and they are *so* "spirited and sly," all of them—this kind makes a long cone of web, with a square chamber of vantage at the end, and there he sits loosely and looks about)—a great fellow that housed himself, with real gusto, in the jaws of a great skull, whence he watched me as I wrote. . . . Phrenologists look gravely at that great skull, by the way, and hope, in their grim manner, that its owner made a good end. It looks quietly, now, out at the green little hill behind. I have no little insight to the feelings of furniture, and treat books and prints with a reasonable consideration—how some people use their pictures, for instance is a mystery to me—very revolting all the same: portraits obliged to face each other for ever,—prints put together in portfolios . . . my Polidoro's perfect Andromeda along with "Boors Carousing," by Ostade,—where I found her,—my own father's doing, or I would say more.[3]

Browning makes an *impresa* of his writing place, glossing it to create an emblem of his poetic soul. The macabre scene contains a skull, a male (rather than a female) spider in a web, and Polidoro's perfect Andromeda. The objects require the emblem maker's explication in which he creates a composite image, associating Death, a predatory creature, Andromeda, false science, and art. Although the letter does not fully elucidate the meaning of his symbolic picture, Browning suggests that the power of art, personified by Andromeda, rescues the writer from the threat posed by the skull and the spider, suggestions confirmed by emblematic interpretations in two works appearing fifty-four years apart, in 1833 and in 1887.

A dream recounted in *Pauline* demonstrates how Browning connects gender identity to artistic power. The passage prepares for an emblem with Andromeda as central figure later in the poem. The speaker in *Pauline* confesses to dreaming of himself as a beautiful naked woman whom he calls a witch. Browning distances the dangers to his masculinity of imagining himself as a woman, first by reporting the story as the dream of a troubled speaker, and second by emphatically and repeatedly insisting that the speaker is not the poet.

The male speaker resembles a young poet like Browning in that he too is a Romantic quester with an evangelical conscience. He dreams that he is a beautiful female witch who draws down from the sky a male god and then ferociously diminishes him:

> I was a young witch, whose blue eyes,
> As she stood naked by the river springs,
> Drew down a god—I, watched his radiant form
> Growing less radiant—and it gladdened me;
> Till one morn, as he sat in the sunshine
> Upon my knees, singing to me of heaven,
> He turned to look at me, ere I could lose
> The grin with which I viewed his perishing.
> And he shrieked and departed, and sat long
> By his deserted throne—but sunk at last,
> Murmuring, as I kissed his lips and curled
> Around him, "I am still a god—to thee."
> (ll. 112–23)

Like Andromeda, the witch stands naked at the margin of earth and water, attracting a god-like man from the heavens as irresistibly as if she were a magnetic force. But there the similarity to the myth seems to end. Rather than the heavenly descender rescuing the naked young witch, she destroys him while he retains his power over her: "I am still a god—to thee."

The witch's spell turns the god into a dependent child sitting on her knees. Evoking primitive infantile emotions, the scene exemplifies Melanie Klein's concept of envy, involving not simply the desire to possess what the other has but the desire to harm the envied other. At the end of the passage the pronouns are sufficiently ambiguous that the "I" of the last line could almost refer to the witch. Confusingly and primitively merged, the witch curls around the god.

Admitting that the "I" is himself: "I was a young witch," the male dreamer gives a female gender to his own envious desire. While defining his desire as compelling, he sees it also as a destructive Other. Blissfully unaware of her envy, the god sacrifices his radiance to her. The dream confesses to vicious emotions, projected from the male self onto a female witch. Hannah Segal describes the emotion that incorporates the object as "envy fused with greed, making for a wish to exhaust the object entirely, not only in order to possess all its goodness but also to deplete the object purposefully so that it no longer contains anything enviable."[4] At the end of the dream, envy fails to overwhelm the dreamer's adoration; in more than one sense, the god has the last word. Diminished or not, he retains his divinity, even as the "I" curls around him, taking him in.[5]

The speaker bears the marks of guilt attendant upon his ferocious desires to incorporate the god and to deplete him. Like the poem in general, the dream is about the power of poetry, shown in the dream to be appropriative. The guilty dreamer confesses—the subtitle is *Fragment of a Confession*—to the murderous emotions he believes are required to make himself into a poet. By the end of the poem the speaker has discovered his life goal, "to be a lover and a poet, as of old," in the course of the poem confessing in various ways to the dangers of the poetic enterprise. To capture the radiant song of the god, the speaker believes that he needs a power identified with femininity, but that identification denotes a cultural diminishment. Aspiring to fame, the male poet gives up his culturally dominant masculine position to identify with the second sex.

Insofar as *Pauline* concerns Browning's exhilarating discovery and involvement with Shelley's poetry, the dream expresses the younger poet's attraction to the etherealized singer, who appeared as a "radiant god" to be emulated. The highly charged emotionality of the passage and its mythopoeic eroticism is Shelleyan.[6] Like a young god, Shelley sang to Browning who imitated Shelley's atheism and vegetarianism until, like the naked witch, he was forced to drive Shelley from his throne. Although Browning rejected his Shelleyan pose, the "Sun-Treader" was still a god to the younger poet, who fought to replace this "radiant form" with his Protestant God.[7] The witch both worships and destroys this Percy/Perseus.

Pauline's dream presents a paradigm of poetic appropriation, imagined in terms of taking over female power. This same paradigm is exemplified in the interpretative process whereby the poet constructs an emblem from the Perseus and Andromeda etching. The figure of Andromeda becomes an emblem of an expressive power associated with the feminine. Rather than make the characters in the Andromeda myth into dramatic figures, the poet uses them as emblematic ciphers, susceptible to the poet's interpretation. By interpreting the characters as if they were figures of an *impresa* Browning turns the image of Polidoro's Andromeda into a sign of male creativity. By using Andromeda's attributes—her chains, her nakedness, her hair—as emblematic objects, the poet gestures to elements in the myth and interprets their meaning as if he were an emblem writer. As an emblematic device, Andromeda becomes a sign of his poetic genius.

In *Pauline* the Andromeda picture becomes the *impresa* for an emblematic illustration of the plight of a young artist. Seeking a vocation, *Pauline*'s guilt-ridden speaker finds that looking at Polidoro's Andromeda gives him proof of a stability which steadies his own faltering identity. He discovers evidence of permanence in Polidoro's monumental Andromeda. At first emblematic of the poet's concern with poetic origins, Andromeda appears at that point in *Pauline* when the speaker, who desires a place in the company of great artists, has canvassed all arts, only to feel alienated, aging, and incapable of freeing himself from aspirations to be a god among poets.

The speaker ultimately chooses the goal of lover (later changed to poet) and prophet, but he has clearly wanted more of everything the world offers. Like many other of Browning's *personae*, this speaker confesses to insatiable desire, gnawing, infinite, and associated with hunger: "my hunger for / All pleasure, howsoe'er minute" (ll. 602–3). Awareness of mortality "chains" his desires. The speaker decides to moderate boundless desire, to focus upon "one rapture." His "still-decaying frame" forces him to be one person when he would be many, to concentrate upon one art when he would practice them all. He knows that such unity not only compromises his desires but lies about reality, limits full vision, and denies full pleasure. Withering into an acceptance of mortality, he settles for "Some pleasure, while my soul could grasp the world, / But must remain this vile form's slave" (ll. 616–17).

The poet's association to Andromeda emerges from the conflict of what he feels as his soul's capacity against his body's limitations. His restless passion lies within him, "a chained thing." Rather than conceiving himself as a slave to his passions, he imagines his passions as "my bright slave," hemmed in by the mortal coil.[8] His own too human condition resembles the picture of the chained maiden's plight. She represents his passion chained by the bondage of decaying flesh. Not only bound by the chains of mortality, flesh is also constrained by the monster, called in this poem a "snake," suggestive in this guilty poem of Miltonic Sin. Browning refers to the sea monster as "the snake" as he turns to Polidoro's etching:

> Andromeda!
> And she is with me: years roll, I shall change,
> But change can touch her not—so beautiful
> With her fixed eyes, earnest and still, and hair
> Lifted and spread by the salt-sweeping breeze,
> And one red beam, all the storm leaves in heaven
> Resting upon her eyes and hair, such hair,
> As she awaits the snake on the wet beach
> By the dark rock and the white wave just breaking
> At her feet; quite naked and alone; a thing
> I doubt not, nor fear for, secure some god
> To save will come in thunder from the stars.
> (ll. 656–67)

Browning describes Andromeda as monumental, earnest, and still, not as Kingsley's shivering girl nor as Hopkins' tortured one, but as a woman, solitary and proud. Indeed, Polidoro's Andromeda, who does not look helpless, dominates the picture plane. Starkly in the center of the composition, her hefty legs planted on the rock, her chin defiantly aloft, she neither importunes her descending deliverer nor gazes at her intended devourer. Meager in comparison to the damsel in distress, Perseus hovers in the air. The heroic slaying occurs in a corner; Perseus' cutlass descends airily upon the monster, a largish worm who seems almost to anticipate the slaying by curling up. The tenacious roots at the left, the ripples of waves curling around the rock, and the coiling dragon echo the hair motif, emphasizing the electric waves of Andromeda's flowing hair.

By ignoring the temporal sequence in the etching—Andromeda's parents in the left and Perseus who drops down from the sky like "some god"—Browning emphasizes Andromeda's solitude. He focuses on two of her attributes: hair (mentioned three times) and nakedness. Hair for Browning is a figure of mortality. The musing speaker in "A Toccata of Galuppi's," for example, uses the phrase "such hair" to remind himself of the poignancy of the decaying body's sexuality:

> "Dust and ashes!" So you creak it, and I want the heart to scold.
> Dear dead women, with such hair, too—what's become of all the gold
> Used to lie and brush their bosoms? I feel chilly and grown old.
>
> (ll. 43–45)

For the aging speaker hair signifies the gold of vital female sexuality. As in *Pauline*, his sigh, "such hair," evokes the skull looming behind such hair—dust and ashes.

Gold in conjunction with hair is directly associated with death in "Gold Hair: A Story of Pornic," where a dead woman's golden hair is a sign of her earthly vanity and greed, a counterpart of the golden coins which the dying maiden hid in her magnificent tresses as a refusal to acknowledge mortality:

> X
> And lo, when they came to the coffin-lid,
>   Or rotten planks which composed it once,
> Why, there lay the girl's skull wedged amid
>   A mint of money, it served for the nonce
> To hold in its hair-heaps hid!
>
> XI
> Hid there? Why? Could the girl be wont
>   (She the stainless soul) to treasure up

> Money, earth's trash and heaven's affront?
> Had a spider found out the communion-cup,
> Was a toad in the christening-font?
>
> (ll. 96–105)

As in Browning's letter to Elizabeth, skull and spider are emblematic objects. The skull peers atop the virgin's skeleton, surrounded by the unspent coins that eventually replaced her hair. The spider evilly lurks in the communion cup.

The historically true story of Pornic reveals the skull beneath the hair, whereas *Pauline*'s Andromeda portrays such hair as still moving in the eternity of art. Polidoro's Andromeda becomes an emblem of the artist's mission to create permanence from flux. To dedicate himself as an artist enables him to transcend the flesh, to "fling age, sorrow, sickness off, / And rise triumphant, triumph through decay" (ll. 674–75).

In its paradoxical formulation "Triumph through decay" resembles many emblem mottos, such as "Make haste slowly." The motto does not seem to refer to the Andromeda myth, but since Browning's emblem alludes to a specific work of art, the motto affirms the paradox of a mortal poet overcoming death through his art. Browning opposes the Andromeda emblem to the danger represented by the spider in the communion cup and the decayed Pornic maiden's body: "change can touch her not."

As a symbol of eternity Andromeda defends aesthetic interpretation against the challenge of scientific interpretation. The meaning of Andromeda as a representation of art's "recompense" for the artist's "still decaying frame" depends upon believing in a transcendent meaning of images, a meaning that challenges scientific discourse. Like Keats' urn, Browning's Andromeda contrasts eternal art to rotting flesh. The Andromeda figure, not the Perseus figure, rescues the poet from despair. The speaker gains hope and artistic purpose by his identification with Polidoro's perfect Andromeda. As an emblem Andromeda teaches Browning a lesson of feminine power, the reward for which, he believes, is the immortality of art.

At the beginning of Browning's career, Andromeda represents the timelessness of art. Toward the end of his life, in the *Parleyings with Certain People of Importance in Their Day* (1887), she represents a greater permanence but a greater abstraction than Art; she represents the imagination that makes art possible. Not recognizably autobiographical, *Parleyings* includes no facts about the poet's life. Perhaps, like Wordsworth's *The Prelude*, Browning meant to chart his poetic development, but unlike Wordsworth, Browning includes no scenes of youth, no faltering steps to manhood. The poet instead struggles with ideas divorced from incidents, conjuring seven silent figures from the dead who overhear the poet tell them what he thinks of their work. The title alludes to the mutability of fame, for the invoked shades of seven historical personages who had been important to the poet's intellectual development had become obscure. The poet's understanding at the end of his life further distances these figures from him; important in the past, their relevance has faded.

The etching of Polidoro's Andromeda returns in the longest and most complex of *Parleyings*, "With Francis Furini," a work differing from the other parleyings in that the Tuscan painter did not influence the poet's early intellectual development and, unlike the other six people, the artist wrote nothing. Most of what Browning knew of the painter's life came from the writings of the art critic Filippo Balducinni who complied a dictionary of the lives of Italian painters (1681–1728).[9] Balducinni clearly disapproved both of Furini's works and his character. A priest in his later years, Furini painted delicate and sensuous nudes—an *Andromeda* among them.

In "With Francis Furini" the Andromeda emblem appears in the context of seemingly irreconcilable themes. Defending his son against charges of painting nudes, opposing the epistemology of evolutionists, and attacking obtuse critics, Browning uses the emblem writer's gesture to evoke the Andromeda sign as a nondiscursive proof of his ability to convey the deepest truths. The Andromeda emblem attempts to unite irreconcilable but concurrent and mutually dependent ways of looking at the world.

"Parleying with Francis Furini" addresses a question of artistic propriety, specifically focused on nude painting. Should an artist paint naked women? If he does, what does the woman represent? It depends upon vision, Browning answers, and not optics. Both emblem-maker and scientist observe similar objects with a view to another meaning, a pattern outside the thing observed, but the emblematist finds a more exalted one. Evolutionists trace the exquisite female form back to simian origins. The emblematic artist observes a representation of an exquisite female form and ultimately finds God. That at least is Browning's uneasy claim.

What kind of seeing, he asks, is more profound, the view of a scientist such as an evolutionist, or the view of an artist such as the emblematist? In his search for an answer to his question, the poet explores Victorian concerns about art, science, and religion. Browning presents his final argument for an artist who trusted "signs and omens" (*Pauline*, ll. 301–2) contrasting that seer, who interprets voiceless signs, with an evolutionist who can only discern meaningless patterns, signatures without an author.

"With Francis Furini" expands upon Browning's concerns of 1835 when he constructed an imaginary biography for the philosopher/scientist Paracelsus (1493–1541), who could be considered a model for the Victorian scientist. By knowing the earth in its minute particulars, Paracelsus hoped to reach transcendent knowledge. The scientist traveled the world seeking traces and shadows of a unified truth, decipherable from the natural code written in the physical world. Browning's attraction to Paracelsus may have been based in part on the latter's theory of signatures, a theory of representation in which an object's appearance leads one to grasp its meaning. Every natural object is a signature, cipher, or character. If one understands the sign correctly and interprets it, one reveals the basic inner truth of the object.[10] Paracelsus' signatures structure the world as writing. Only a person who is chosen to decipher the code, to read the handwriting of objects, can gain a knowledge of transcendence. The world requires an emblem writer to read the meaning of the signature and to convey that essential meaning to his audience.

Paracelsus fails in his goal to decipher the signatures of the world. But he foresees the fulfillment of his goal in a future man who will be more perfect, more evolved. Browning considered that concept of human progress his version of evolution. In contrast, Darwinian evolution conflicts with a view of the textuality of nature.[11] Unlike Darwin's concept, Browning's notion of evolution is purposive, progressive, and hierarchical, more congruent with Lamarck than with Darwin.[12] Paracelsus describes Browning's Neoplatonic evolution:

> When all mankind alike is perfected,
> Equal in full-blown powers—then, not till then,
> I say, begins man's general infancy . . .
> Then shall his long triumphant march begin,
> Thence shall his being date,—thus wholly roused,
> What he achieves shall be set down to him.
>   (V, ll. 741–68)

Darwinian evolution conflicts with a Paracelsan view of nature as signatures. The purpose and meaning of the universe could dissolve if the signature did not signify anything beyond itself. Without signs that add up to something, there could be no plot to human existence. Paracelsus asserts the primacy of types to oppose a nihilistic threat:

>   Prognostics told
> Man's near approach; so in man's self arise
> August anticipations, symbols, types
> Of a dim splendour ever on before
> In that eternal circle life pursues.
>   (V. ll. 773–77)

Without the eternal circle, history tells no story, continuing without a pattern in an infinite evolutionary straight line. Types would be utterly self-referential as isolated and particular examples of multiplicity.

In trying to reject the evolutionist view, Browning seeks a language that will encompass the minute, the bizarre, the anomaly, uniting multitudinousness in a system of signs. Perhaps the world contains an infinite vocabulary, but it constitutes a language. To reconcile evolution with eternity is a Browning project continuing throughout his career, elucidated in his second, and final, Andromeda emblem.

As a step toward that reconciliation "Cleon" (1855) addresses the themes of evolution, extinction, and transcendence, polarizing them as a debate between aesthetic and scientific interpretation. A Greek polymath of the first century, Cleon's varied and successful endeavors promise to survive his death but leave him nonetheless with insatiable hunger to live forever. He believes in evolutionary progress on earth. His art improves upon earlier art; "one lyric woman," a slave, "refines upon the women of my youth"; the cultivated "suave plum" is better than the "savage-tasted drupe." He neither finds a pattern in the earth's evolutionary progress nor can he condescend to accept the barbarian Paul's Christian promise of immortality. The skull and the spider lurk at the corners of the poem, except a human reduces to less than bones and gold coins here; he is dust shut in an urn.

Without a signature that signifies, there is no meaning to evolutionary progress. Given evidence for evolution, for human improvement over the beast, why did the gods make consciousness concomitant with unfulfillable desire?

> Malice it is not. Is it carelessness?
> Still, no. If care—where is the sign?
> (ll. 267–68)

Like Paracelsus, Cleon cannot read the signatures of nature, but he seeks a sign that the world has meaning.

In "With Francis Furini" Browning presents the sign Cleon missed by using Andromeda as a Paracelsan signature. Against those with an analytical epistemology, represented in the poem by art critics and evolutionary scientists, he presents an emblematic reading of a representation of Andromeda. Critics resemble evolutionists, since both fail to grasp the transcendent meaning of the objects they scrutinize. Emblematic vision, on the other hand, both describes the object and finds its meaning. Whereas critic and scientist, literal-minded and ignorant of true signs, can only understand the material body, the emblem maker sees soul in the body. As a poet who can translate an object's silent meaning into language, Browning invokes the figure of Andromeda chained to a rock to challenge a world full of things but emptied of significance.

Developing the motto "triumph through decay" from *Pauline*, Browning defends the "Triumph of flesh" (l. 96) against critics who do not understand the transcendent meaning of nakedness. For emblem writers nakedness could signify a spiritual attribute. The depiction of naked women, the poet argues, is an artist's tribute to the supreme aesthetic power of the Creator. Furini's paintings, so regarded, are not scientific renderings but are a form of worship:

> pictures rife
> With record, in each rendered loveliness,
> That one appreciative creature's debt
> Of thanks to the Creator more or less,
> Was paid according as heart's-will had met
> Hand's-power in Art's endeavor to express
> Heaven's most consummate of achievements, bless
> Earth by a semblance of the seal God set
> On woman his supremest work.
> (ll. 126–34)

"Heaven's most consummate of achievements" refers both to the creation of woman by God and to the artist's imitation of her, an imitation that identifies the artist and God by female mediation.

Nude paintings imitate unfallen nature by honoring the Creator of naked Eve. Invoking the figure of Andromeda chained to the rock, as he had in *Pauline*, Browning argues about the permanence of art. His earlier argument, however, is now inadequate. It was too concrete, dependent on an etching on a piece of paper. Instead of Furini's or Polidoro's conception of Andromeda, he points to the firmament and to the Andromeda constellation.

God traced Andromeda with stars. Comparing an artist's delineation of the maiden to the Almighty's imitation of his supremest work in the heavens, Browning claims that representations are like the celestial Andromeda. They are ideas of woman, and the artist who saw that idea in the sky received authority from God. The truest artist imposes a pattern on otherwise arbitrary signs. Interpretation of those signs is the highest form of criticism.

Only certain imaginations can discern the heavenly Andromeda. To the uninitiated eye, the night sky looks like an unconnected mass of lights. Browning compares God's creation of woman with an artist's nude paintings. Then, as if in confirmation of the sacred nature of that kind of art, he invokes the Andromeda constellation:

> soul and body's power you spent—
> Agonized to adumbrate, trace in dust
> That marvel which we dream the firmament
> Copies in star-device when fancies stray
> Outlining orb by orb, Andromeda—
> God's best of beauteous and magnificent
> Revealed to earth—the naked female form.
> (ll. 137–43)

Like emblematic images, constellations comprise a language of signs requiring a decoder with divine inspiration. To know that an assemblage of lights visible to an ordinary eye means "Andromeda" requires special knowledge, leading to truth beyond flesh. Andromeda serves Browning's purpose not only because she is a figure in a myth but also because she is a constellation. As if he were a child playing a cosmic dot-to-dot game, the artist agonizes to "trace in dust" a figure of a woman. How does he know he has made the right connections? To make interpretation not merely "fancy" but "truth" Browning requires that the imagination receive external validation.

Evolutionists offer some sort of proof, but they look in the wrong place for their evidence. They "rack nature" and emerge with a tortured, reduced answer. Lofty scientists view the lowest forms of life—atoms, protoplasm (l. 270)—and argue from that to man. Since they emphasize descent, they close off the possibility of ascent: "Have you done / Descending?" (ll. 277–78) Browning's query echoes Darwin, but his demeaning tone indicates that the poet's perspective from the vastness of cosmic spaces exposes as paltry the evolutionist's painstaking survey of physical minutiae. *Homo sapiens* appears as the supreme creation on earth, but he could be dashed from the pinnacle in an instant:

> He's at the height this moment—to be hurled
> Next moment to the bottom by rebound
> Of his own peal of laughter. All around
> Ignorance wraps him,—whence and how and why
> Things are,—yet cloud breaks and lets blink the sky
> Just overhead, not elsewhere! What assures
> His optics that the very blue which lures
> Comes not of black outside it, doubly dense?
> (ll. 337–44)

Browning's skepticism doubts sense perception as he posits a black hole behind the blue sky. Like Shelley's Mont Blanc and Wordsworth's spots of time, the Andromeda constellation presents to mortals the possibility of some sort of transcendent knowledge. Echoing yet changing Wordsworth's idea of tranquillity, Shelley asserts, "Power dwells apart in its tranquillity." Then he adds what is important to Browning's Andromeda: "Remote, serene, and inaccessible." Browning's Andromeda is as much the space's blankness as the more reassuring stars. Andromeda's power, too, is remote and serene, but Browning's assertion of his faith in interpretation attempts to bring that power to earth. Closed to the critical, scientific, evolutionary mind, emblematic interpretation is mysterious, needing an artist not a scientist to discern; needing intuition and not microscopic observation to understand. Andromeda, an emblem of unrepresentable black nothingness, signifies for

Browning a female power unavailable to rational critics or scientists. Appropriating that power, the artist acts as a hierophant, conveying privileged information about heaven's hieroglyphics.

Browning's final vision of Andromeda refines representation to an almost pure semiotic sign. The celestial Andromeda is the opposite of Rossetti's Blessed Damozel whose breast warms the bar of heaven. She is colder than Keats' urn, the Cold Pastoral. Like Shelley's frozen Mont Blanc, she represents a terrifying blankness as well as a reassuring stability. Browning claims his own art plucks the veil of flesh to see the soul beneath. Yet, even the poet cannot be quite sure that what he showed was a permanent and not an evanescent truth:

> There did I plant my first foot. And the next?
> Nowhere! 'Twas put forth and withdrawn, perplexed
> At what seemed stable and proved stuff
> Such as the coloured clouds are:
>
> (ll. 402–5)

The artist tries to interpret what is not visible by looking at what is. But the poet's emblematic vision may be no truer than any necromancer's claim. Browning reassures himself by returning to the image of Andromeda, but now he imagines that he is a woman in a picture who stands on a rock, wearing chains. Seeking some proof of his vision, he identifies his essential knowing self with a representation of Andromeda:

> Who proffers help of hand
> To weak Andromeda exposed on strand
> At mercy of the monster?
>
> (ll. 489–91)

The Evolutionist is the "sea-beast," and poor Browning/Andromeda clings to the rock, needing a miracle to be rescued:

> Just here my solid standing-place amid
> The wash and welter, whence all doubts are bid
> Back to the ledge they break against in foam,
>
> (ll. 509–11)

To be rescued from speaking empty signs, words without truth, a signature signifying nothing, he needs to be able to prove the priority of symbolic reality over scientific fact. Browning turns the monster into an emblem of dangerous objective rationalism, such as evolutionists employ.

Evolutionists poke at nature to glean some minute fact as a sign of its ultimate meaning, but all they find is imitation. They scrutinize insects, for example, examining a moth with a star-pattern on its wings: "that on some insects' wing / Helps to make out in dyes the mimic star" (ll. 295–96). Looking downward from a height, evolutionists mistake the sign of a star on a bug for a signature. The emblematic imagination discovers symbolic reality, the real star, by looking from the frailty of its human condition up to the heavens:

> Look upward: this Andromeda of mine—
> Gaze on the beauty, Art hangs out for sign
> There's finer entertainment underneath
> (ll. 529–31)

The emblem maker turns the constellation, a sign of beauty, into a signature. "Andromeda of mine" in contrast to "utterances, not mine" is a powerful erotic enticement to consider a more essential female sign, discovered by the true visionary by looking at the sea-beast. It is that ability to transform evil into a sign of transcendent good that proves the emblem maker's power over the evolutionist's:

> But what if, all at once, you come upon
> A startling proof—not that the Master gone
> Was present lately—but that something—whence
> Light comes—has pushed Him into residence?
> Was such the symbol's meaning,—old, uncouth—
> That circle of the serpent, tail in mouth?
> Only by looking low, ere looking high,
> Comes penetration of the mystery.
> (ll. 540–47)

With the gesture of a necromancer, Browning the emblematist turns the serpent, earlier in the poem an emblem of false science, into the mystical sign of ourobouros, symbol of eternity. By invoking the ancient hieroglyph of a pre-Christian belief, Browning appeals to a proof beyond rationality old, unlettered but a valid signature. The sign of Andromeda beckons us to consider an older sign, an ancient symbol of womanhood, the circle in the form of a serpent (figure 2).[13]

Circles are female symbols, as Browning makes explicit in "Pan and Luna." The naked Luna, illuminated by an aura, escapes from Pan's pursuit into what she thinks is a cloud; as she flees, Browning describes her body as composed of circles:

> Orbed—so the woman-figure poets call
> Because of rounds on rounds—that apple-shaped

> Head which its hair binds close into a ball
> Each side the curving ears—that pure undraped
> Pout of the sister paps—that . . . Once for all,
> Say—her consummate circle . . .
>
> (ll. 41–46)

All circles are emblematic of that consummate circle which, according to the poet's mythmaking, is not an emblem or an imitation, but is the original place of creativity. As woman is the consummate achievement of the Creator (l. 132), so the sign of human creativity is the circle, symbol of female sexuality.

The ouroboros represents the magic female power of Browning's visionary ability. He has taken an evolutionary line and has turned it into an eternal circle. His ability to change a monster into a dual symbol of woman and eternity proves his knowledge superior to the scientists. Browning "penetrates" the old, uncouth, and mysterious female sign, and claims it as a sign of his own power.

By discovering the feminine in himself, Browning returns to the quest he initiated in *Paracelsus*. He finds a symbol for that "eternal circle life pursues"—not an aimless evolution that keeps on and on endlessly through time, without rhyme or reason. By means of the semiotic, he resolves for himself an epistemological riddle he posed in 1835. Knowledge in *Paracelsus* was imagined as coming not from the world outside but from the inner self. The repetition of "in" emphasizes his point:

> There is an inmost center in us all,
> Where truth abides in fullness; and around
> Wall upon wall, the *gross flesh* hems it in,
> This perfect, clear perception—which is truth.
> A baffling and perverting carnal *mesh*
> Binds it.
>
> (Pt. 1, ll. 728–33; my emphasis)

As in "With Francis Furini" imagery of clouds and mist represents the poet's difficulty in penetrating the mystery. But in the later poem the poet has resolved for himself the vexing dichotomy between what he calls "the dear fleshly perfection of the human shape" and the inner truth. The skull may be a reminder of the vanity of human wishes but the heavenly orb, like the circle, enables the poet to see beyond the baffling and perverting carnal mesh:

> the head of the adept
> May too much prize the hand, work unassailed
> By scruple of the better sense that finds
> An orb within each halo, bids *gross flesh*
> Free the fine spirit-pattern, nor *enmesh*

More than is meet a marvel custom blends
Only the vulgar eye to.
(11. 201–7; my emphasis)

By placing the crucial words of his earlier poem as end-rhymes, Browning creates closure. A nondiscursive proof, embedded in the signs and position of sounds, the rhymes create a truth beyond what the words say, appealing to magic, to a wisdom old and coarse, to spells, to charms, to chiming. As Andromeda's body deconstructs in a star sign, his defense of the signature transcends rational meaning of language.

Although the Andromeda and Perseus myth seems clearly to ascribe activity according to gender, Browning collapses the polarities: the monster turns into ourobouros, language turns into witch's chant, poet turns into naked woman. By dismantling oppositions, he appeals to the nonheroic, the nonrational, the passive, the silent. His poetics appropriates the uncouth power of the ourobouros, figured however as rescue, suggesting that the taking over improves, civilizes, articulates what had been inchoate, inexpressible, and indecipherable. But Browning also questions polarities—serpent and ourobouros, rescuer and victim, man and woman. In awe of the irrational sign that is the circle, symbol of the Other, he claims it as his own. The ourobouros and the chained maiden, like the orb (symbol of his wife in "My Star"), appeal to what Julia Kristeva and other French feminists describe as the force of the feminine, the yet unverbalized, beyond or beneath language, at the level of the unconscious.[14] The potent silent sign is Browning's female signature.

Notes

1. William Clyde DeVane, "The Virgin and the Dragon." *Yale Review* (1947), 37: 33–46.

2. Browning, *Cornhill*, 1902, p. 152, letter to Katharine Bronson, quoted in *Learned Lady: Letters from Robert Browning to Mrs. Thomas Fitzgerald, 1876–1889*, ed. Edward C. McAleer (Cambridge: Harvard University Press, 1966), p. 25.

3. No. 9. February 26, 1845,, *Letters of Robert Browning and Elizabeth Barrett Barrett*, vol. 1, ed. Elvan Kinter (Cambridge: Harvard University Press, 1969), p. 27.

4. Segal, "Envy," *Introduction to the Work of Melanie Klein*, (New York: Basic Books, 1974), p. 41.

5. The witch curling around the god is another of Browning's enclosures, described by Eleanor Cook, *Browning's Lyrics: An Exploration* (Toronto: University of Toronto Press, 1974) pp. 109–11.

6. See p. 1024 notes to Pettigrew/Collins edition for the identification "radiant form" with a Shelleyan locution. See also Harold Bloom on the relationship between Shelley and Browning. I find particularly useful Bloom's discussion of daemonization and negation of the precursor from the *The Anxiety of Influence*, (New York: Oxford University Press, 1973) pp. 100–3, although Bloom's own repression of female influence in general leaves out that crucial aspect of Browning's poetic identity.

7. In "Troops of Shadows," I argue that the title *Pauline* refers to Browning's replacing Shelley by means of Pauline typology. The pun on Percy exemplifies a similar transformation and replacement occurring in the poem. In his overdetermined use of the Andromeda myth, Browning also replaces the male Shelley with the female Andromeda/Elizabeth, a figure he can both reject and appropriate. Adrienne Munich, "Troops of Shadows: Browning's Types," in *Robert Browning: A Collection of Critical Essays* (Englewood Cliffs, NJ: Prentice-Hall, 1979), pp. 167–87.

8. Cook, p. 109, connects the chains in this passage to Browning's imagery of enclosure, thus giving imagistic support to the connection of the witch curled around the god and Andromeda's chains.

9. DeVane, *Browning's Parleyings*, (New Haven: Yale University Press, 1927), p. 167.

10. Lisalotte Dieckman, *Hieroglyphics: The History of a Literary Symbol* (St. Louis: Washington University Press, 1970) p. 68.

11. Georg Roppen, *Evolution and Poetic Belief: A Study in Some Victorian and Modern Writers* (Oslo: Oslo University Press, 1956) questions Browning's claims to be sympathetic with evolution and finds them in the Platonic tradition, pp. 171 ff.

12. Beer, *Darwin's Plots: Evolutionary Narrative in Darwin, George Eliot and Nineteenth-Century Fiction* (London: Routledge and Kegan Paul, 1983)

13. For a discussion of the ourobouros as a female sign, see Dijkstra, *Idols of Perversity: Fantasies of Feminine Evil in Fin-de-Siècle Culture* (New York: Oxford University Press, 1986) pp. 128–29, and passim. Dijkstra emphasizes the decadent uses of the symbol as "the circle of chaos with a woman's body" (p. 129) and the womanly desire to "physical self-reproduction." Browning uses the symbol as a transcendent healing one to stave off the masculine danger of the serpent. Although the ourobouros does not terrify Browning, it is a female sign, and one could not consider his resolution any less ambiguous or subtle than "resolutions" in his earlier poems. Claiming a female symbol for his own can never be an utter triumph.

14. Julia Kristeva on the semiotic in "The Bounded Text," in *Desire in Language: A Semiotic Approach to Literature and Art*, trans. Leon S. Roudiez, (New York: Columbia University Press, 1980); in addition to Kristeva see Hélène Cixous, "The Laugh of the Medusa," in Elaire Marks and Isabelle de Courtivron, eds., *New French Feminisms* (New York: Shocken Books, 1981), pp. 245–64; and Marguerite Duras, "From an Interview," in Marks and Courtivron, pp. 174–76.

Fig. 1
Etching by Volpato after Polidoro da Caravaggio.

Fig. 2
From *A Collection of Emblems* by George Wither. Photo used by permission of the Beinecke Rare Book and Manuscript Library, Yale University.

"Cleon" and Its Contexts

Antony H. Harrison

As Arnold begins to demonstrate in the virtual monodrama of act 2 of *Empedocles*, the dramatic monologue is a highly self-conscious and intellectual poetic form.[1] Since the intended targets of a monologue's author may be quite other than those of its speaker, a dramatic monologue inevitably and spontaneously evokes a subtextual question in most readers' minds: What is the poet as artificer attempting to accomplish by devising this elaborate mode of self-disguise? What values and beliefs does he (really) wish to support, criticize, or propound? And to what end?[2] Because such questioning and traces of anticipatory authorial response to it inhere in the operations of the dramatic monologue, this literary form that on its surface appears determined to suppress ideology, instead complexly draws attention—through its self-conscious elisions—to the subtle ways in which both poet and reader are entrapped in webs of ideology that demand interrogation or defense. Further, because of the inherent complexities of the dramatic monologue, discussions of intertextual relations in this poetic form can frequently yield surprising insights, especially with a master monologuist like Robert Browning, for whom the monologue becomes the most cerebral of poetic forms.

Roland Barthes has suggested that for every poem, every reader must be conceived as "une pluralité d'autres textes, de codes infinis"[3] because he bears a history of reading texts, some of which he perforce associates as intertexts with whatever work happens to be before him. It is thus the reader who "establishes a relationship between a focused text and its intertext, and forges its intertextual identity."[4] But, as is clear, readers are given guidance in seeking meaningful pre-texts for a poem that is demonstrably intertextual by the echoes and allusions embedded by an author in his text. Browning's monologues, informed by a wealth of (often obscure) allusions, repeatedly demand intertextual readings, and their ideological complications are—like metaphors drawn out to conceits—insistently extended in this way. Preeminent among such poems by Browning (as Harold Bloom has observed)[5] is "Cleon," a monologue whose speaker defiantly concerns himself with his own artistic and specifically poetic lineage, much as Browning does in his famous essay on Shelley (1852).

" 'Cleon' and Its Contexts," Chapter 2, *Victorian Poets and Romantic Poems: Intertextuality and Ideology* (University Press of Virginia, 1990). Reprinted by permission.

Composed in 1854, "Cleon" is a monologue in the form of an epistle written by a famed Greek poet and artist (invented by Browning) in response to a letter from King Protus (also fictitious).[6] Protus has asked Cleon the truth about his artistic accomplishments and his ability to "fear death less" because his poems and paintings will live immortally. In his letter Cleon describes his artistic lineage and supremacy, yet acknowledges the futility of his achievement in outstripping mortality and presents "the accurate view" of what constitutes joy in life. Cleon hastily concludes by acknowledging that he is unable to redirect a letter Protus has written to one "Paulus" and speculates that this person might be identical with another reputed "barbarian Jew"—Christus—whose "doctrine could be held by no sane man."[7]

Joy is the most important conceptual term—both philosophical and aesthetic—in "Cleon." Repeated in variant forms eighteen times, it is the key to the intertextual reaches of the work. As we shall see, it is the poem's most important link to Arnoldian, Wordsworthian, Keatsian, and Spasmodic pre-texts and the term that positions Browning's monologue on the front lines in mid-Victorian disputes about the value and function of poetry and, more specifically, about the precedence of particular "schools" of nineteenth-century poetry.[8] Cleon first uses the word *joy* early in the poem, when he describes himself disingenuously, as one "whose song gives life its joy" (l. 21). This boast is afterwards explained in his description of the eminence he has attained in all arts:

> I have not chanted verse like Homer, no—
> Nor swept string like Terpander, no—nor carved
> And painted men like Phidias and his friend:
> I am not great as they are, point by point.
> But I have entered into sympathy
> With these four, running these into one soul,
> Who, separate, ignored each other's art.
> Say, is it nothing that I know them all?
> The wild flower was the larger; I have dashed
> Rose-blood upon its petals, pricked its cup's
> Honey with wine, and driven its seed to fruit,
> And show a better flower if not so large:
> I stand myself.
> (ll. 139–51)

Cleon thus attempts to establish that he has a "greater mind / Than [his] forerunners, since more composite" (ll. 64–65). Only the product of such a mind can "give life its joy."

This passage from "Cleon" transposes into verse an important statement from the essay on Shelley ("Introductory Essay") that partially lays out Browning's understanding of the intertextual relations among poets. In his essay Browning speculates that the "two modes of poetic faculty"—the objective and the subjective—may possibly "issue hereafter from the same poet in successive perfect works, examples of which . . . we have hitherto possessed in distinct individuals only" (*Poems*, p. 1003). Browning proceeds to describe his concept of the historical process of evolution among poets and presents a virtually Hegelian theory of artistic cycles of poetic supersession, beginning with the demise of the "objective" poet:

> There is a time when the general eye has, so to speak, absorbed its fill of the phenomena around it, whether spiritual or material, and desires rather to learn the exacter significance of what is possesses, than to receive any augmentation of what is possessed. Then is the opportunity for the poet of loftier vision, to lift his fellows, with their half-apprehensions, up to his own sphere, by intensifying the import of details and rounding the universal meaning. The influence of such an achievement will not soon die out. A tribe of successors (Homerides) working more or less in the same spirit, dwell on his discoveries and reinforce his doctrine; til . . . the world is found to be subsisting wholly on . . . the straw of last year's harvest. Then is the imperative call for the appearance of another sort of poet, who shall . . . [get] at new substance by breaking up the assumed wholes into parts . . . careless of the unknown laws for re-combining them (it will be the business of yet another poet to suggest those hereafter), . . . shaping for their uses a new and different creation from the last . . . to endure until, in the inevitable process, its very sufficiency to itself shall require, at length, an exposition of its affinity to something higher.
> —*Poems*, pp. 1003–4

This long passage is crucial in understanding the intertextual and ideological operations of "Cleon." But these become fully visible only when we situate the poem in its most important historical contexts, one of which is the publication of *Empedocles on Etna* in 1852 and Arnold's retraction of it in 1853.

Since 1927 a number of critics and readers have extended A. W. Crawford's observation that a relationship between "Cleon" and *Empedocles on Etna* clearly exists.[9] That Browning had read Arnold's poem with enthusiasm and had been disappointed by its suppression in 1853 is certain. On August 19, 1867, shortly after Arnold had republished *Empedocles* in his *Poems*, Browning wrote to his close friend Isabella Blagden: "I should like to know something about Arnold's new volume: he told me he had reprinted therein ['Empedocles] on Etna'—with a pretty note saying that it was done thro' my request. I am really flattered at *that*—I like the man as much as the poems."[10] "Cleon" may in fact have been written as much in reaction to Arnold's retraction of *Empedocles* and his explanations for doing so in the 1853 Preface as in response to Arnold's poem itself. If this speculation is correct, then Browning's poem situates itself in the debates about Spasmodicism raging in the early 1850s as fully as Arnold's Preface does. "Cleon" may be seen as a kind of attack upon Spasmodicism (and all it represented to the Arnoldian mind) different from Arnold's earnest and theoretical Preface or William Edmondstoune Aytoun's parodic *Firmilian* (published in 1854), but a polemic, nonetheless, against the decadent poetic practices culminating in the early fifties with the publication of Sydney Dobell's *Balder* and Alexander Smith's *A Life-Drama*. These practices Arnold assaults directly in his Preface, as Browning would certainly have realized.[11]

At the center of Browning's poem, Cleon acknowledges his epistle's confessional tone. He tells Protus, "Nay, thou art worthy of hearing my whole mind" (l. 181). Indeed, this work, like so many of Browning's monologues, takes shape—with its elaborate, often obscure and convoluted conceits and symbols—as an allegory of the state of Cleon's mind, and thus as a representative history of the fate of the consummate, misguided artist. My phrasing here comes from Arnold's 1853 Preface, where Arnold misquotes J.M. Ludlow's recent critical review supporting specifically Spasmodic elements of contemporary poetry. Arnold responds: "The modern critic not only permits false practice; he absolutely prescribes false aims.—'A true allegory of the state of one's own mind in a representative history,' the poet is told, 'is perhaps the highest thing that one can attempt in the way of poetry.' . . . An allegory of the state of one's own mind, the highest problem of an art which imitates actions! No assuredly, it is not, it never can be so: no great poetical work has ever been produced with such an aim." After stressing the preeminent value in poetry of architectonics—"the power of execution, which creates, forms, and constitutes" rather than the "profoundness of single thoughts, [or] the richness of imagery, [or] abundance of illustration"—Arnold proceeds to criticize the stylistic excesses of much contemporary poetry. . . . He locates the most recent precedent for this malaise in the work of Keats, passing over *Endymion* as a negative model in favor of *Isabella*. *Endymion*—which explores an aesthetics of hedonism from its very first line, "A thing of beauty is a joy forever"—Arnold finds "so incoherent, as not strictly to merit the name of a poem at all." He concludes his essay, as he had begun it, insisting that the present "era of progress . . . commissioned to carry out the great ideas of industrial development and social amelioration" is wholly "wanting in moral grandeur" and therefore cannot contribute as a subject matter to the grandest goal of poetry: "to afford to [people] the highest pleasure they are capable of feeling," that is to say, the "highest enjoyment."[12]

From the very beginning of the Preface Arnold introduces into his discussion of the purposes of poetry this key term from the great poem whose retraction it is the function of the Preface to explain and justify. He does so by quoting Schiller's dictum that all art "is dedicated to Joy, and there is no higher and no more serious problem, than how to make men happy. The right Art is that alone, which creates the highest enjoyment" (*Prose*, 1:2). In the two paragraphs that follow Arnold analyzes the true sources of joy in poetry and, by extension, in life (if poetry constitutes—as Arnold later insists—a "criticism of life").

That Browning was, with "Cleon," participating in the ongoing Romantic debate concerning the true grounds and constitution of joy in poetry and in life at large—a debate that Arnold energetically enters into here—seems an inevitable conclusion, given these contexts. Further evidence for it emerges from a simple comparative analysis of "Cleon" and *Empedocles*, especially each poem's employment and interrogation of the term *joy* and each poem's implicit revision of its uses in seminal poems by Wordsworth and Keats.[13] These works—including the Intimations Ode, *The Prelude, Endymion*, and the "Ode on Melancholy"—establish a philosophical dialogue surrounding the term, one that has important implications for the politics of poetic achievement and supersession in the nineteenth century.[14]

Like Empedocles, Cleon is a philosopher-poet. Like Arnold's hero, too, Cleon confessionally laments the loss of joy in his life. This loss, and that of Empedocles, results from both poets' painful obsession with mortality. Both Arnold and Browning set up as the central dialectic of their respective poems the opposition between youth and age, though Arnold embeds that dialectic both within Empedocles (who wistfully recalls the "days . . . / When we were young" and "could still enjoy")[15] and between Empedocles and Callicles. Following Arnold's direction, Browning chooses to focus his poem, not in the modern world or on contemporary events, but—in defiance of mid-century calls for relevancy in poetry—in Greece, the cradle of Western aesthetic culture. Again like Arnold, Browning fastens upon the term *joy* as the pivotal conceptual and philosophic term in Cleon's epistle.

"Cleon" is a poem that finally despairs over the materialism of its titular hero's historical era, as does *Empedocles*. Arnold's drama instructs in the value of the "natural joy" and spiritual fulfillment that Empedocles had temporarily attained in his youth, while "Cleon" exposes the moral, intellectual, and spiritual deficiencies of its speaker, whose concept of joy is entirely hedonistic. Cleon serves the reader as a negative example. In *Empedocles*, as well as in poems like "The Buried Life" and "Stanzas in Memory of the Author of *Obermann*," *joy* clearly refers to an ideal state of spiritual fulfillment, self-completion, and affinity with Arnold's version of Wordsworth's "Immortal Sea," man's transcendent spiritual matrix (the "general life" of "Resignation"). In Browning's poem, however, *joy* and terms associated with it refer exclusively to the effects of sensory and aesthetic experience. Cleon has no conception of the "soul" beyond such experience. Hence, his inaccessibility to Christian truth and revelation. He is, philosophically, the most sophisticated and refined of materialists, for whom a belief in the value of Christian renunciation would indeed seem insane.

Before we can determine the significance of Cleon's moral, aesthetic, and spiritual failures, we must understand—as Browning did—the success of Empedocles in sustaining right moral, aesthetic, and spiritual values. This he can accomplish only through his suicide, thus (like Byron's Prometheus) making death a victory.[16] Empedocles' obsessive aim is to preserve what remains of his spirit's "self-sufficing fount of joy" (2. 23). He wishes to die

> Ere quite the being of man, ere quite the world
> Be disarray'd of their divinity—
> Before the soul lose all her solemn joys,
> And awe be dead, and hope impossible
> And the soul's deep eternal night come on.
> (2.31–35)

Empedocles is wrenchingly preoccupied with his "dwindling faculty of joy" (2. 273). Using grand and simple Wordsworthian abstractions, he associates "joy" with his early days, with the "shock of mighty thoughts" that derived from elementary, commonplace experiences. In those days, "on the road of truth,"

> . . . we could still enjoy, then neither thought
> Nor outward things were closed and dead to us.
> But we received the shock of mighty thoughts
> On simple minds with a pure natural joy;
>   . . . . .
> We had not lost our balance then, nor grown
> Thought's slaves, and dead to every natural joy.
> (2.240–43, 248–49)

For Empedocles the most sublime and valuable human experiences are these which reveal the "primary affections of the human heart," the spiritual affinities of men to which "the imperious lonely thinking power" (2. 375), when overindulged and overly refined, becomes antagonistic. The overactive intellect impedes access to spiritual fulfillment, to "being one with the whole world" (2. 372). Sophisticated intellectuals, from Empedocles' point of view, are blind to spiritual knowledge and impervious to communion with the ultimate truths of human nature and experience which are derived from the "smallest" things:

> The sports of the country-people,
> A flute note from the woods,
> Sunset over the sea;
> Seed time and harvest,
> The reapers in the corn,
> The vinedresser in his vineyard,
> The village-girl at her wheel.
> (1.2.251–58)

While Empedocles disparages excessive intellectual refinement, he also rejects most major schools of philosophical thought in the crucial concluding section of his homily in act I. Significantly, his attack culminates with a diatribe against hedonism that seems especially applicable to Cleon. Empedocles reminisces on "Our youthful blood" which inevitably "Claims raptures as its right" and has "Pleasure" in its "hot grasp" (1.2.352–53, 357), but which becomes discontented as we age:

> Yet still, in spite of truth,
> In spite of hopes entomb'd,
> That longing of our youth
> Burns ever unconsumed,
> Still hungrier for delight as delights grow more rare.
> (1.2.367–71)

And thus, as we age and our senses fail, we realize our mortality with increasing urgency:

> We pause; we hush our heart,
> And thus address the Gods:
> "The world hath failed to impart
> The joy our youth forebodes,
> Failed to fill up the void which in our breasts we bear."
> (1.2.372–76)

This is exactly Cleon's dilemma as he confesses to Protus his unsuccessful quest for fulfillment and the reasons for his failure. He is unable to satisfy his "joy-hunger" because he conceives of joy exclusively in terms of hedonistic and aesthetic experience. Browning's Rabbi Ben Ezra provides the perfect gloss on Cleon's fate. Cleon is the rabbi's "crop-full bird" or "maw-crammed beast," albeit disguised by his sophisticated intellect and aesthetic refinement. The rabbi comments:

> Poor vaunt of life indeed,
> Were man but formed to feed
> On joy, to solely seek and find and feast:
> Such feasting ended, then
> As sure an end to men.
> (*Poems*, 1:781)

Pathetically, Cleon's ultimate spiritual fantasy is merely an aesthetic and hedonistic one: to satisfy his "joy-hunger" in an afterlife that reminds us of Keats's "favorite Speculation": that "we shall enjoy ourselves here after by having what we called happiness on Earth repeated in a finer tone and so repeated."[17] Cleon craves

> Some future state . . .
> Unlimited in capability
> For joy, as this is in desire for joy,
> —To seek which, the joy-hunger forces us.
> (ll. 325–28)

    Ironies cluster around Cleon's use of the word *joy*, which appears always in the context of material accomplishments and physical sensations. As I have noted, it first occurs in the poem's second stanza as part of his initial self-description. Cleon believes one of the songs he is noted for "gives life its joy," and he immediately reveals his sense of kinship with Protus by juxtaposing that accomplishment of his own with a discussion of "the daily building of [Protus's] tower." Both the poet and the king, according to Cleon, recognize "the use of life," which is the enjoyment of sensory pleasures. Cleon assumes that Protus's goal is

> . . . some eventual rest a-top [his tower],
> Whence, all the tumult of the building hushed,
> Thou first of men mightst look out to the East:
> The vulgar saw thy tower, thou sawest the sun.
> (ll. 33–36)

Since Cleon mentions the "sun-god" fourteen lines later, it is probable that in these earlier lines he, nonetheless, understands Protus's quest to be more than the creation of a material monument and the acquisition of a sublime view. Protus wishes to "see" god's face; he is intent upon a material quest that will effect spiritual fulfillment. Cleon promises to celebrate Protus's aspirations, but the rest of the poem exposes his skepticism that spiritual fulfillment can be separated from material existence. One climbs the tower "just to perish there" (l. 236). Despite his polite expressions of admiration for Protus's perseverance, Cleon ultimately sees the king's quest as futile, like his own. Such a conclusion is implied shortly after Cleon describes Protus's tower and catalogues his own material accomplishments, *his* artifacts. One of them, an implicit critique of Protus's labors, is "The image of the sun-god on the phare," which, ironically, "Men turn from the sun's self to see" (ll. 51–52). For Cleon, who rejects the possibility of spiritual revelation (ll. 115–27), art and the sensational world it celebrates, *are* the ultimate "spiritual" reality.

    "Joy" for Cleon finally cannot exist without our material existence in which consciousness inheres, any more than it can be sustained, according to Empedocles' opposite view, as one's consciousness expands and intensifies. In the evolutionary pattern of Cleon's thought, the greatest joy would result from the most highly developed and sensitized consciousness. By "making [a creature] / Grow conscious in himself" (ll. 197–98), Cleon insists,

> . . . the more he gets to know
> Of his own life's adaptabilities,
> The more joy-giving will his life become.
> (ll. 217–19)

Were man immortal, his consciousness of action and sensation, of "his own life's adaptabilities" (l. 21), would bring man the joy of complete fulfillment. But because of death, "in man there's failure" (l. 225).

From Cleon's point of view, then, consciousness benefits man, not because it allows for the perception of moral or spiritual truth, but because, as "the sense of sense" (l. 224), it enables man to savor sensations in the fashion of the Paterian aesthete, for whom "experience itself is the end," being present "always at the focus where the greatest number of vital forces unite in their purest energy." Pater defines "success in life" as Cleon defines it: a "quickened, multiplied consciousness" generated by "forever . . . courting new [sensory] impressions."[18] However, unlike Pater, for whom—in the Keatsian tradition—knowledge of mortality makes sensory impressions infinitely valuable, Cleon finds the prospect of death "horrible" (l. 323). Cleon uses metaphors with decidedly materialistic associations to describe human consciousness. It is "the pleasure-house, / Watch-tower and treasure-fortress of the soul" (ll. 231–32). And the "soul" for Cleon is simply the repository of man's aggregate sensory pleasures enjoyed in life, in combination with the potential for further (ideally infinite) enjoyments of the same sort:

> . . . there's a world of capability
> For joy, spread round about us, meant for us,
> Inviting us; and still the soul craves all.
> (ll. 239–41)

Soul here becomes an illimitable appetitive organ, and as such, it is ultimately the source of Cleon's despair of life. Because we die, "life's inadequate to joy, / As the soul sees joy" (ll. 249–50).

Thus in the last section of his epistle, Cleon understandably laments his mortality and the inverse relationship that exists between the development of the soul's thirst for joy and the physical capacity to quench it:

> . . . every day my sense of joy
> Grows more acute, my soul (intensified
> By power and insight) more enlarged, more keen;
> While every day my hairs fall more and more.
> (ll. 310–13)

Envying one of Protus's oarsmen, a "young man, / The muscles all a-ripple on his back," Cleon laments that he himself is "grown too gray / For being beloved" (ll. 297–99), and with self-conscious irony he conceives an appropriate epitaph for himself, "The man who loved his life so over much" (l. 322). He is the antithesis of Empedocles.

In its intertextual relations with Arnold's poem, "Cleon" thus generates a powerful irony. For Empedocles the prospect of reincarnation—a "return . . . to this meadow of calamity" (2:365)—is excruciating. But for Cleon, who believes in progressive evolution rather than fruitless, repetitive cycles, such a prospect would constitute bliss and fulfillment. Empedocles' world of "bondage" to the flesh and mind (2. 375), if made eternal, would be a state "unlimited in capability / For joy" to Cleon (ll. 326–27). Through Cleon's arrogant but pathetic negative example, Browning directly condones Empedocles' early Wordsworthian quest, his "ineffable longing for the life of life" (2. 375), his implacable urge to escape sensation and consciousness in order to achieve unsullied spiritual fulfillment, to "feel the ALL" (2. 353). For Browning's aesthetic and philosophical values, the implications of his poem's tacit acceptance of the Wordsworthian definition of *joy*—and, indeed, of Wordsworth as a model to be remodeled—are extensive and intriguing, as we shall see, especially in light of Browning's persistent antagonism to Wordsworth during his mature years. A full understanding of what such acceptance signifies for Browning's poetic practice and his ambitions as a poet, however, requires some preliminary discussion of particular, extra-Arnoldian, literary-historical contexts of "Cleon."

If Cleon the poet is, ultimately, a misguided hedonist blind to the revelation he (falsely) believes he craves, he nonetheless embodies—as a refashioned Paracelsus—a number of Browning's own poetic traits and aspirations. These qualities had earned Browning little fame, mostly disappointing reviews, and frequent comparisons with the Spasmodic poets, whose popularity Browning envied even as he began to compose most of the poems of *Men and Women* in 1853.[19] In this year Sydney Dobell's *Balder* and Alexander Smith's *A Life-Drama* were published to extraordinary critical acclaim.[20] Herbert Spencer described Smith as "*the* poet of the age" and insisted that none better had appeared since Shakespeare, while George Meredith wrote a sonnet in Smith's honor. As Jerome Hamilton Buckley has explained, "no poem since *Childe Harold* had won its author such widespread acclaim."[21] *A Life-Drama* went through four editions in two years. Similarly, *Balder* earned Dobell accolades from many quarters. *The New Monthly Magazine* acknowledged that rarely "has such an ovation been offered to any modern poetical aspirant."[22]

Jerome Thrale has shown that Browning certainly knew the Spasmodics well. He had presented Elizabeth Barrett Browning with a copy of Bailey's *Festus* in 1845. Eight years later her letters demonstrate a serious interest in Alexander Smith's work and its fortunes. On April 12, 1853, she writes of having borrowed a copy of the *Athenaeum* in order to read a review of *A Life-Drama*. Smith is, she allows, "applauded everywhere." In June, apparently after both she and Browning had read Smith's work, she writes that "it strikes us . . . that he has more imagery than verity, more colour than form." In August she comments with some satisfaction on Tennyson's judgment of Smith's work, "*in the very words* we had given here—'fancy and not imagination.' Also, imagery in excess; thought in deficiency. . . . It is extraordinary . . . [that Smith] has met with so much rapid recognition." As Thrale observes, in such comments and elsewhere Barrett Browning's use of *us* and *we* suggests that her opinions were shared by her husband.[23]

Like the heroes of most Spasmodic epics, Cleon is an ambitious poet and, like the Spasmodics themselves, a successful and popular one. But the connections run deeper than this. Just as "Popularity" is Browning's satirical response to the superficiality and the success of Spasmodic poetry in 1853, "Cleon" constitutes his serious critique of the inadequate aesthetic, philosophical, and spiritual values of Spasmodicism.

Cleon—master of all arts—is a projection of Browning's own earliest fantasies, in good part realized by poets like Smith and Dobell. Even before his twentieth birthday, Browning had aspired to amaze the world by producing simultaneously and anonymously a play, an opera, a novel, and a poem. With each hailed as a brilliant success, he planned to "disclose his authorship to an astonished world."[24] Although in his correspondence through the forties, Browning claimed to disdain popular success, he strongly craved it,[25] especially after it became clear that, with Wordsworth's death and the laureateship vacant, Browning himself, after twenty years as a publishing poet, was not even a contender for the post. Whereas Cleon's works, like Smith's, are the center of popular attention, Browning's had on occasion become the butt of jokes. In 1840, for instance, *Sordello* had "brought notoriety, not fame" to Browning, with reviewers and acquaintances alike despising it as "obscure," "unreadable," "trash, of the worst description."[26]

Thus when preparing *Dramatic Romances and Lyrics* for publication in 1845, Browning was anxious that these poems become popular. And eight years later, with the poems of *Men and Women* underway, he explained to his friend Joseph Milsand: "I am writing—a first step towards popularity for me—lyrics with more music and painting than before, so as to get people to hear and see."[27] But the reception of *Men and Women* was generally unfavorable. With Aytoun's exposé of the excesses of Spasmodicism the year before, Browning's new monologues were disparaged particularly for their Spasmodic obscurity.[28] Responding to the reviews, Browning wrote in exasperation to Edward Chapman, his publisher: "As to my own Poems—they must be left to Providence and that fine sense of discrimination which I never cease to meditate upon and admire in the public: they cry out for new things and when you furnish them with what they cried for, 'it's *so* new,' they grunt. The half-dozen people who know and could impose their opinions on the whole sty of grunters say nothing to *them* (I don't wonder) and speak so low in my own ear that it's lost to all intents and purposes."[29] Despite his hopes for the success of *Men and Women*, Browning had, ironically, anticipated its poor reception in "Popularity," a poem that followed "Cleon" closely in the volume. (Only "The Twins" intervened.) The speaker in "Popularity" hails a true but neglected poetic genius, "a star," "God's glow-worm," whose essential artistry—which Browning figures in an elaborate conceit of Tyrian blue, the "dye of dyes"—is popularized by a group of feeble imitators, Hobbs, Nobbs, and Nokes: the "tribe of successors" described in the essay on Shelley (*Poems*, pp. 722–23). Meanwhile the "true poet" who "fished the murex up" is starved of fame. The poem's final line—"What porridge had John Keats?" (*Poems*, p. 724)—suggests that the work is a satire of popular Spasmodicism, which Browning, like so many of his contemporaries including Arnold, saw as a development from the work of Keats, who had been critically disparaged by his contemporaries but posthumously admired.[30]

Browning's relationship with Spasmodicism is complex and, it would seem, contradictory. Donald Hair has convincingly argued that *Pauline* is a proto-Spasmodic poem.[31] *Sordello* was denounced by some reviewers for its Spasmodic excesses. And by the mid-forties William Edmonstoune Aytoun, along with other critics, had positioned Browning in the "school" of Bailey.[32] The reviews of *Men and Women* demonstrate that Browning found it impossible to shake his association with the Spasmodics and evade the damage that association continued to do to his reputation even in the late 1850s. As Mark Weinstein has observed, an important reason for the adverse reception of *Men and Women* was the volume's "absorption . . . into the reaction against Spasmodic poetry."[33] In its commentary on *Men and Women*, for instance, the *Saturday Review* castigated Browning: "Can any of his devotees be found to uphold his present elaborate experiment on the patience of the public? Take any of his worshippers you please—let him be 'well up' in the transcendental poets of the day—take him fresh from Alexander Smith, or Alfred Tennyson's *Maud*, or the *Mystic* of Bailey—and we will engage to find him at least ten passages in the first ten pages of *Men and Women*, some of which, even after profound study, he will not be able to construe at all."[34] *Blackwood's* describes Browning as a "true brother" of Alexander Smith and Sydney Dobell; Browning is the "wild boy of the household—the boisterous noisy shouting voice."[35] Though this review was printed anonymously, Browning doubtless thought it the work of Aytoun, who was still on the offensive against the Spasmodics two years after *Firmilian* and who, in the January 1857 number of *Blackwood's* lambasted Elizabeth Barrett Browning's new *Aurora Leigh*. It is small wonder, then, that Browning maligned the "wretched organ-grinding Ayton and his like" in a letter to Edward Chapman shortly after these attacks appeared.[36]

Aytoun had been at the center of what Weinstein has aptly dubbed "the Spasmodic controversy" since its beginnings. In the early fifties the debate over poetic values and the ultimate value of poetry had fairly raged in the pages of British periodicals and, as we have seen, had engaged such luminaries as Arnold, Arthur Hugh Clough, Herbert Spencer, and Charles Kingsley, along with the lesser lights, George Gilfillan, and J. M. Ludlow. Browning in fact had entered the debate with his essay on Shelley, and the extent to which the poems of his 1855 volume extend his participation in the controversy has yet to be acknowledged. As Browning had promised Milsand, fully a fifth of these monologues (occupying a quarter of the pages of the volume) treat matters of aesthetic and poetic ideology.[37]

"Cleon" itself was composed at the climactic moment of the dispute over the proper subjects, settings, and functions of poetry in the modern age. Browning's 1853 letter to Milsand and his response to the reviews of *Men and Women* indicate that the previous year had precipitated a crisis for Browning—the serious, ambitious, but largely unappreciated poet. One factor in his reinvigorated quest for popularity may well have been the reception of Smith's *A Life-Drama* in 1853. But in May of 1854 Aytoun had delivered the coup de grâce to writers of the Spasmodic school by publishing in *Blackwood's* his effusive, parodic review of what he presented as the latest Spasmodic masterpiece, *Firmilian* by Percy Jones. (Poem and poet were both his own creations.) Shortly after, in the summer of 1854, Browning wrote "Cleon." Even if Aytoun's hoax is not viewed as the immediate occasion of Browning's poem, "Cleon" must be read, if read properly, in the context of the Spasmodic controversy. The poem follows the lead of Arnold's *Empedocles* and his Preface as a corrective response to the intense introspection, the dangerous self-absorption, and the obtuse pretentiousness of much recent Spasmodic verse, poetry extending what was universally accepted as the tradition of Keats.[38] Despite their frequent abstractions, the Spasmodics had taken Keatsian hedonism and materialism to their ultimate, absurd conclusions, especially in their works' stylistic excesses. As a serious exposé of the poetic and spiritual inadequacies of Spasmodicism, "Cleon" partially allies itself with the poetry of that school, only to subvert the poetic ideology its writers and George Gilfillan, its most important exponent among the critics, had propounded.

Browning's strategy of subversion is double-edged, involving not only the self-confessed failure of Cleon's value system, but also anti-Spasmodic elements that serve as implied correctives to Spasmodic practices. These include the Greek setting of "Cleon," its hero's overt intellectualism, and its disciplined blank verse. Since Spasmodicism embraced the critically popular insistence on contemporary settings and "relevance," the Hellenic setting of "Cleon" signals an interrogation of Spasmodic redactions of the Keatsian values Cleon propounds. This is especially the case insofar as its setting allies Browning's poem with *Empedocles* (which had been much criticized for the Greek rather than modern character portrait it presents). Nonetheless, like any number of Spasmodic poems, "Cleon" presents an intensely introspective monologuist discussing the value of poetry (and art) in its relations with religious belief and human mortality. Also in the tradition of Spasmodicism, the speaker has hedonistic propensities and self-indulgently employs elaborate and obscure metaphors. In the most prominent Spasmodic poems, as well, poetry becomes the particular medium of self-analysis through which a speaker ultimately intuits God's will and attains immortality, or attempts to do so. Such is the case, for instance, in Bailey's *Festus*, Smith's *A Life-Drama*, and Dobell's *Balder*. Dorothy Donnelly has succinctly explained how all these works

> have as their protagonist a poet-hero who is at once capable of transcendence and in the process of self-realization. In each . . . the poet-hero-prophet-savior speculates in long passages about his "God-given powers," his "spontaneous and inspired" thoughts, his "emotional" needs and desires, and his high "aspirations." Throughout the poems attention is focused on the protagonist's attempt to establish a relationship with his universe and in so doing to formulate what he experiences as a revelation of "truth," of the "secrets of the universe." In a dialogue with an interlocutor, each protagonist expresses his conception of himself and, because he is a poet, his "high purpose."[39]

Smith's poet-hero in fact preempts the specific aspirations Cleon delineates for himself as the evolved master-poet "with greater mind / Than our forerunners" ("Cleon," ll. 64–65). Smith's Walter envisions himself as

> A mighty Poet whom this age shall choose
> To be its spokesman to all coming times.
> In the ripe full-blown season of his soul,
> He shall go forward in his spirit's strength,
> And grapple with the questions of all time,
> And wring from them their meanings.[40]

But the thrust of Browning's poem is precisely to deflate such Spasmodic pretensions. The focus of Cleon's lament is, finally, that revelation and immortality are unavailable to him despite his genuine accomplishments. For him, as for all men, he insists, "life's inadequate to joy, / As the soul sees joy, tempting life to take." He craves a sign of

> Some future state revealed to us by Zeus,
> Unlimited in capability
> For joy, as this is in desire for joy,
> —To seek which, the joy-hunger forces us.

"But no!" he concludes, "Zeus has not yet revealed it; and alas, / "He must have done so, were it possible!" (ll. 325–35). For the composite artist with the most refined sensibilities possible, therefore, "Most progress is most failure" (l. 272).

In addition to this deliberate subversion of the dominant ideology of Spasmodic poetry, according to which the poet-hero will save the world, Browning also presents his poem as a critique of Spasmodic "failures" by eschewing in both the form and substance of "Cleon" many of the pretentious literary strategies of Spasmodic poetry. He especially repudiates the undisciplined and rambling epic form characteristic of works by Bailey, Dobell, Smith, John Westland Marston, and John Stanyan Bigg.[41] Browning further purifies Cleon of the intense passions typical of Spasmodic heroes, along with their demonic desire to exhaust experience. Cleon thus appears as an intellectually refined and Hellenized poet who shares many of the impulses and ambitions common to heroes of Spasmodic poetry, as those derive from Keats. He can be seen, in fact, as a Keats (or Callicles) who has survived into old age as an immensely successful poet. Yet his example serves finally to expose the failure of Spasmodic transcendental aspirations by acknowledging the inadequacies even of Cleon's own (putative) supreme achievement. Cleon cannot redeem the world, or even himself; he cannot satisfy his "joy-hunger" and attain assurances of immortality (taken for granted by heroes of Spasmodic verse).

In this he presents a contrast to the successful Romantic example provided—for both Browning and Arnold—by Wordsworth in his Intimations Ode. Wordsworth was, in fact, the Romantic poet (besides the unknown Blake) who was least influential on the Spasmodics and whose voice Browning in "Cleon" (emulating Arnold in *Empedocles*) echoes and reinvigorates. He does so by stressing Cleon's inability to attain Wordsworthian "joy" or any intimations of immortality when confronted with the "horrible" fact of mutability.

As all readers of Wordsworth's Intimations Ode know, *joy* is a crucial term in the poem, just as it is essential to Empedocles' recollections of his youth, and just as it is the pivotal term in "Cleon." Repeated eight times, it initiates the Ode's final movement, as the ecphonesis at the beginning of stanza nine. The poem's three final stanzas celebrate the recovery of the "glory and the dream" whose loss is mourned in stanzas one through four. In Wordsworth's poem, joy is in fact the emotional counterpart of idealized, visionary capacities designated by these abstractions, the emotional form in which possession of "the visionary gleam"—and certainty of immortality—expresses itself.[42] Thus, in stanza three the springtime birds sing "a joyous song"; the prelapsarian shepherd boy is a "Child of Joy"; the growing boy of stanza five beholds his originary spiritual matrix, his "life's Star," in joy; and in stanza nine all experiences and phenomena that threaten to undermine our consciousness of infinitude and immortality are "at enmity with joy." To argue that all such threats can finally be overcome is the raison d'être of this work that memorializes the permanent recovery of joy:

> O joy! that in our embers
> Is something that doth live,
> That nature yet remembers
> What was so fugitive!
> (stanza 9, ll. 133–36)

Through the pattern of experience it describes, the poem implies that the recovery is permanent, precisely because it is inscribed in an always accessible work of art that can, in future, preempt the agonized process of realizing loss and recovering joy that the poem delineates. The "palm" of assured knowledge of immortality is won forever by its memorialization in a poem that dependably "gives life its joy," as Cleon would have Protus believe his own song does, before he confesses the ultimate failure of his work.

That the Intimations Ode also has a political subtext (as Marjorie Levinson has recently argued)[43] is suggested by the fact that in the same year that Wordsworth was finally able to answer the questions that conclude stanza four of his Ode (1804), he also composed a well-known section of book II of *The Prelude* celebrating the promise of the French Revolution. Published as a separate poem in 1809, this passage—including the famous lines "Bliss was it in that dawn to be alive, / And to be young was very heaven!"—begins with an emphasis upon the Intimation Ode's key term, *joy*. "Oh! pleasant exercise of hope and joy!" introduces a paean to the utopian ideals of the Revolution, ideals that, of course, were brutally disappointed for Wordsworth in the event and whose loss still obsessed him in 1802 when he wrote the Ode's first four stanzas.

Unquestionably Browning was familiar with both the Ode and *The Prelude*, Wordsworth's final monument to his own immortality, first published and much discussed only four years before Browning composed "Cleon."[44] As a young man, Browning had greatly admired Wordsworth's poetry and had read him carefully. But Browning's relationship to Wordsworth is as complex as his relationship with the Spasmodics. Browning's poem "The Lost Leader" (1845) is a vicious attack on the laureate's political backsliding. Even thirty years after the publication of this poem, Browning could acknowledge that "the change of politics in the great poet," his "defection . . . was to my juvenile apprehension, and even mature consideration, an event to deplore."[45] And in a letter to Elizabeth Barrett the year after "The Lost Leader" appeared, Browning insisted that he would not even "cross the room" to obtain Wordsworth's distilled essence, a statement that has become notorious. But, as John Maynard points out, these slurs only partially reveal Browning's attitude toward this Romantic giant:

> To the president of the Wordsworth Society, which he joined in old age, he set the record straight: "I keep fresh as ever the admiration for Wordsworth

which filled me on becoming acquainted with his poetry in my boyhood." That his statement was not a hollow testimony is made clear in subsequent letters where he endorses as old favorites early works that even a Wordsworthian may pass over in rereading. . . . His repeated preference for Wordsworth's "first sprightly runnings" exceeds even the conventional view that the early poetry is best and suggests that Browning retained a personal and lifelong fondness for what he read as a boy.[46]

Indeed, the particular influence of the Intimations Ode on works by Browning written throughout his career has been convincingly established. Anya Taylor has recently made clear, for instance, that in stanza three of "Rabbi Ben Ezra" Browning goes so far as to repeat "not only the argument but [also the] sentence structure and meter" of the second sentence of the Ode's ninth stanza. And W. D. Shaw has observed how the "Prologue" to *Asolando* persistently echoes Wordsworth's poem, albeit with a corrective, orthodox thrust, when God himself emphatically responds to Asolo's vanished perception of the "glory" and the "alien glow" formerly projected by "Hill, vale, tree, [and] flower": "At Nature dost thou shrink amazed / God is it who transcends" (*Poems*, 2:896).[47]

It was Wordsworth's betrayal of his early political ideology that turned Browning against him. "The Lost Leader" makes clear both the extent of Browning's admiration for Wordsworth and his anguished disappointment in him:

> Just for a handful of silver he left us,
>   Just for a riband to stick in his coat—
>   . . . . .
> We that had loved him so, followed him, honoured him,
>   Lived in his mild and magnificent eye,
> Learned his great language, caught his clear accents,
>   Made him our pattern to live and to die!
> Shakespeare was of us, Milton was for us,
>   Burns, Shelley, were with us,—they watch from their
>   graves!
> He alone breaks from the van and the freemen,
>   —He alone sinks to the rear and the slaves!
>   —*Poems*, 1:410

These lines are, of course, reminiscent of Byron's condemnation of Wordsworth as a "shabby fellow" in the "Dedication" to *Don Juan*. By contrast with Milton, Byron makes plain, Wordsworth, along with the other Lakers, "belie[d] his soul in songs" and "turn[ed] his very talent to a crime."[48] As "The Lost Leader" and Browning's letters demonstrate, Browning had fully idolized Wordsworth before the laureate's "defection."

Significantly, however, even in repudiating Wordsworth, Browning follows exactly the pattern of idealization and disillusionment that informs much of Wordsworth's own poetry and is repeated in the Intimations Ode. Nowhere is this pattern more powerfully expressed than in book II of *The Prelude*. Browning's bitterness at Wordsworth's betrayal of his early political ideology, voiced in "The Lost Leader," is modeled upon Wordsworth's response in book II to France's betrayal of the revolutionary principles he had idealized in 1790. That response culminates at the end of the book with Wordsworth's description of the crowning of Napoleon as emperor:

> This last opprobrium, when we see a people,
> That once looked up in faith, as if to Heaven
> For manna, take a lesson from the dog
> Returning to his vomit.
> (ll. 361–64)

When reading *Empedocles on Etna*, and later Arnold's discussion of enduring poetic values in his 1853 Preface, Browning may well have thought of these lines and the hundred that follow to complete book II of *The Prelude*. This final passage is addressed to Coleridge, who is described as recuperating "Where Etna, over hill and valley, casts / His shadow stretching toward Syracuse" (ll. 377–78). In the following lines Wordsworth, in fact, claims to discover "solace to his grief" (a grief precipitated by recalling the events of the revolution and his painful disillusionment at its failure) in part by "giving utterance to a name / Of note belonging to that honoured isle, / Philosopher or Bard, Empedocles" (ll. 432–34).

For Browning, the Wordsworthian resonances of Arnold's *Empedocles* must have brought to mind the constellation of issues—literary, philosophical, religious, and aesthetic—surrounding the term *joy* which, as Browning well knew (having owned one of the first copies of *Endymion*),[49] was a most important term in Keats's poetry as well. But, as should by now be clear, far more than a conflict between Keats's sensual and Wordsworth's spiritual conceptions of *joy* operates in the language, structure, and argument of "Cleon." The term becomes the intertextual locus where historical issues of aesthetic and political ideology, as well as issues of poetic supremacy, intersect to accomplish multiple aims.

Thus, on one reading "Cleon" constitutes an implicit attack on the Keatsian extravagances, the pretensions to greatness, and the conceptual limitations of Spasmodicism and, as such, the poem is an extension of the aesthetic ideology of Arnold's *Empedocles* and his 1853 Preface. It accomplishes this attack in part by recalling the language and transcendental values of Wordsworth's great Ode, while suggesting, by extension, a critique of the later values of this most "composite" of Romantic poets, who was—as the

"Prospectus" to the *Excursion* (1814) makes clear—ambitious to supersede his greatest "forerunners," especially Milton. The Keatsian hedonism that blinds Cleon to true spiritual joy—a joy compatible with Christian religious values and evangelical ideas of revelation—is unquestionably at war with the transcendental intimations that are the subject of Wordsworth's internal monologue in the Intimations Ode. But Browning realized that the interrogatory mind-set that precipitated the revelations of the Ode, along with the profound and intuitive spiritual values generated for Wordsworth by the failure of political and social structures permanently to redeem mankind, ended with Wordsworth's "defection," his absorption into the Tory establishment, and finally his acceptance of the laureateship in 1843. Unlike Empedocles as Arnold depicts him (and perhaps as Wordsworth had envisioned him when composing the expanded *Prelude* in 1805), the poet of the great Ode to joy had betrayed the originary spiritual values that had made him the supreme Romantic philosopher-poet. This conclusion to Wordsworth's evolution, his progress as a poet, Browning denounces in "The Lost Leader."

But he also alludes to it through the language and elaborate evolutionary metaphors of "Cleon." These suggest an inverse relationship between the desirability of Wordsworth's early spiritual values and the trajectory of his career as a poet: "Most progress is most failure." Wordsworth attained the poetic supremacy of a Cleon only after his "defection" from the political ideology upon which his early spiritual values first depended. His complacent position atop the tower of fame during the first thirteen years of the Victorian period exposed his actual failure as the missionary of an aesthetic ideology that had profound political ramifications. During his tenure as laureate any possibility that the ideals of liberty, fraternity, and equality might continue to be transposed into popular poetry had given way to the solipsistic and hedonistic "evangelism" of the Spasmodics.

Through the intertextual ironies of "Cleon" and the example of its misguided speaker, nonetheless, Browning attempts to reconstitute, in a highly generalized form, the spiritual values of Wordsworth's early years and to do so implicitly in terms of early Christian history and doctrine. Complexly, with Wordsworth as the poem's haunting absent presence, Browning plays Paulus to the young Wordsworth's Christus.[50] In assuming the role of Wordsworth's disciple, as Arnold had provisionally done in *Empedocles* and his Preface, Browning accomplishes another goal as well. Read in the contexts established here, "Cleon" can be understood to serve, on a personal level, as Browning's preemptive denial of his own unyielding quest for popularity and poetic supremacy. Not to be positioned to become a "defector" like Wordsworth, it seems, required an anticipatory acknowledgement that "Most progress is most failure."

Notes

1. For the most helpful recent theoretical commentary on how the dramatic monologue operates, see Ralph Rader, "Notes of Some Structural Varieties and Variations in Dramatic 'I' Poems and Their Theoretical Implications," *Victorian Poetry* 22 (1984): 103-20.
2. Dramatic monologues have been the subject of much theoretical discussion in recent years. Among the best commentaries are: Dorothy Mermin, *The Audience in the Poem: Five Victorian Poets* (New Brunswick, N.J.: Rutgers Univ. Press, 1983); Linda K. Hughes, *The Manyfaced Glass: Tennyson's Dramatic Monologues* (Athens: Univ. of Ohio Press, 1987); and the essays in *Victorian Poetry* 22, no. 2 (1984) on *The Dramatic "I" Poem* (ed. Linda M. Shires), including Rader's cited in note 1, above.
3. Roland Barthes, *S/Z* (Paris: Editions du Seuil, 1970), pp. 16-17.
4. Owen Miller, "Intertextual Identity," in *Identity of the Literary Text*, ed. Mario J. Valdes and Owen Miller (Toronto: Univ. of Toronto Press, 1985), p. 21.
5. Harold Bloom, Introduction to *Robert Browning*, ed. Bloom (New York: Chelsea House, 1985), pp. 1-3.
6. Pettigrew says that "Cleon" was probably composed in 1854 (*Robert Browning: The Poems*, ed. John Pettigrew, supplemented and completed by Thomas J. Collins, 2 vols. [New Haven: Yale Univ. Press, 1981], 1:1140). William DeVane is more specific in positioning that the poem "was written in the summer of 1854, after Browning had written 'Karshish' and had meditated upon Arnold's *Empedocles* of 1852, and its omission from [the] volume of 1853" (*A Browning Handbook* [New York: Appleton-Century-Crofts, 1955], p. 265).
7. All citations to Browning's poetry and his essay on Shelley are from volume 1 of *Robert Browning: The Poems*, ed. John Pettigrew. "Cleon" appear on pages 712-20. The words I quote in text conclude the poem. Future citations of line numbers from this edition of "Cleon" will appear parenthetically in text as *Poems*. Other poems by Browning and his "Introductory Essay" (on Shelley) will be cited parenthetically in text to *Poems*, with page numbers.
8. For a generalized discussion of these influences on the composition of "Cleon," see Adrienne Munich, "Emblems of Temporality in Browning's 'Cleon.' " *Browning Institute Studies* 6 (1978): 117-36.
9. A. W. Crawford, "Browning's 'Cleon,' " *Journal of English and Germanic Philology* 26 (1927): 485-90. See also John Coates, "Two Versions of the Problem of the Modern Intellecual: 'Empedocles on Etna' and 'Cleon,' " *Modern Language Review* 79 (1984): 770-82; Park Honan, "Robert Browning and Matthew Arnold," *Studies in Browning and His Circle* 3 (1975): 123; and Munich, "Emblems of Temporality," pp. 124-26.
10. *Dearest Isa: Robert Browning's Letters to Isabella Blagden*, ed. Edward C. McAleer (Austin: Univ. of Texas Press, 1951), p. 278.
11. For discussions of Arnold's Preface as an oblique attack on the Spasmodics, especially Alexander Smith, see H. W. Garrod, "Matthew Arnold's 1853 Preface," *Review of English Studies* 17 (1941): 310-21, and Mark Weinstein, *William Edmondstoune Aytoun and the Spasmodic Controversy* (New Haven: Yale Univ. Press, 1968), pp. 99-108.
12. *The Complete Prose Works of Matthew Arnold*, vol. 1, ed. R. H. Super (Ann Arbor: Univ. of Michigan Press, 1960), pp. 8, 9, 15. Future citations to this edition in this chapter will appear parenthetically in text to *Prose*, with volume and page numbers.
13. See Munich, "Emblems of Temporality," pp. 119, 126-28.
14. With "Dejection: An Ode," now generally accepted as Colerdige's response to the firt four stanzas of the Intimations Ode, Coleridge also clearly participated in this dialogue, but his contribution is not as demonstrably fundamental to the operations of "Cleon" as the poems of Wordsworth and Keats.
15. *Matthew Arnold*, ed. Miriam Allott and R. H. Super (Oxford: Oxford Univ. Press, 1986), p. 102. Future citations to "Empedocles" in this chapter will appear parenthetically

in text with act, scene, and line numbers. Citations to other poems will appear by line numbers.

16. Jerome J. McGann makes this point in "Matthew Arnold and the Critical Spirit: The Three Texts of Empedocles on Etna," in *Victorian Connections*, ed. McGann (Charlottesville: Univ. Press of Virginia, 1989), pp. 146-71.

17. Keats to Benjamin Bailey, Nov. 22, 1817, in *The Letters of John Keats*, ed. Hyder E. Rollins, 2 vols. (Cambridge: Harvard Univ. Press, 1958), 1:185.

18. Walter Pater, *The Renaissance*, ed. Donald L. Hill (Berkeley: Univ. of California Press, 1980), pp. 188-90.

19. On composition dates see Pettigrew, ed., *Robert Browning: The Poems*, 2:1103. The only critic I know who has argued that Browning envied the success of the Spasmodics is Jerome Thrale in "Browning's 'Popularity" and the Spasmodic Poets," *Journal of English and Germanic Philology* 54 (1955): 353-54.

20. *A Life-Drama* appeared late in 1852 but was dated 1853. See Weinstein, *William Edmondstoune Aytoun*, p. 76. For the reception of *A Life-Drama*, see Thrale, "Browning's 'Popularity,' " pp. 348-52.

21. See Thrale, "Browning's 'Popularity,' " p. 351; *Life and Letters of Herbert Spencer*, ed. David Duncan (New York, 1908), 1:87; and Jerome Hamilton Buckley, *The Victorian Temper* (New York: Vintage Books, 1951), p. 52.

22. *New Monthly Magazine* 100 (March 1854): 292, quoted by Thrale in "Browning's 'Popularity,' " p. 351.

23. Thrale, "Browning's 'Popularity,' " p. 353.

24. "Introduction," *Browning: The Critical Heritage*, ed. Boyd Litzinger and Donald Smalley (London: Routledge and Kegan Paul, 1970), pp. 2-3.

25. Ibid., pp. 3-15.

26. Ibid., p. 6.

27. Browning to Joseph Milsand, quoted in DeVane, *A Browning Handbook*, p. 207.

28. Weinstein, *William Edmondstoune Aytoun*, pp. 184-86.

29. *New Letters of Robert Browning*, ed. William C. DeVane and Kenneth L. Knickerbocker (New Haven: Yale Univ. Press, 950), pp. 92-93.

30. For a full discussion of the Spasmodic and Keatsian contexts of "Popularity," see Thrale, "Browning's 'Popularity,' " passim.

31. Donald Hair, *Browning's Experiments with Genre* (Toronto: Univ. of Toronto Press, 1972), pp. 4-19.

32. Weinstein, *William Edmondstoune Aytoun*, p. 183. Theodore Watts later inverted that relationship and insisted upon Bailey's *Festus* as a work derivative from Browning's *Paracelsus*. But Weintein quotes a letter from Bailey claiming ignorance of *Paracelsus* when he composed *Festus*.

33. Weinstein, *William Edmondstoune Aytoun*, pp. 184-85.

34. Anonymnous review of *Men and Women*, *Saturday Review* 1 (1855): 69-70.

35. *Blackwood's* 79 (1856): 136-37.

36. Browning to Edward Chapman, Jan. 5, 1857, in *New Letters*, p. 99.

37. This group of poems includes "Fra Lippo Lippi," "A Toccata of Galuppi's," "How It Strikes a Contemporary," "Master Hughes of Saxe-Gotha," "Memorabilia," "Andrea del Sarto," "Old Pictures in Florence," "Cleon," "Popularity," " 'Transcendentalism: A Poem in Twelve Books,' " and "One Word More."

38. See Thrale, "Browning's 'Popularity,' " pp. 348-50.

39. Dorothy Donnelly, "Philistine Taste in Victorian Poetry," *Victorian Poetry* 16 (1978): 104.

40. Alexander Smith, *Poems* (Boston, 1852), p. 24.

41. For commentary on the formlessness and other weaknesses of poetry by these Spasmodics, see Buckley, *Victorian Temper*, pp. 40-65.

42. All citations to Wordsworth's poetry will appear by stanza and/or line number and are taken from *Wordsworth: Poetical Works*, ed. Thomas Hutchinson, rev. Ernest de Selincourt (London: Oxford Univ. Press, 1969).

43. Marjorie Levinson, "Wordsworth's Intimations Ode: A Timely Utterance," in *Historical Studies and Literary Criticism*, ed. Jerome J. McGann (Madison: Univ. of Wisconsin Press, 1985), pp. 48–75.

44. Eleanor Cook notes Sordello's debt to the "Intimations Ode" and echoes of *The Prelude* in "One Word More" (*Browning's Lyrics: An Exploration* [Toronto: Univ. of Toronto Press, 1974], pp. 27, 236). Cook also cites Browning's unpublished letter to Charles Eliot Norton (Florence, May 9, 1850): "Yet let us hope that your gift of the 'Prelude' is an excellent omen" (Houghton Library, Harvard University), a sentence that also suggests Browning's aspirations to the laureateship soon after Wordsworth's death in April. The post remained opened until November, when Tennyson was selected to fill it.

45. Quoted by Pettigrew, ed., *Robert Browning: The Poems*, p. 1091.

46. John Maynard, *Browning's Youth* (Cambridge: Harvard Univ. Press, 1977), p. 169.

47. Anya Taylor, "Religious Readings of the Immortality Ode," *Studies in English Literature* 26 (1986): 645–47. W. D. Shaw, "Browning's Intimations Ode: The Prologue to Asolando," *Browning Society Notes* 8 (1978): 9–10. Stanza two of the "Prologue" further reveals, through its metaphors, the inextricable inter-relationships among Wordsworth, Keats, and the Spasmodics that Browning apparently found inescapable when considering issues of poetic accomplishment and poetic supremacy. Writing verses that echo Wordworth to figure the inherent spirituality of natural objects, Browning uses the same image of dyes that he employs in "Popularity" to figure the essence of the poet's (specifically Keats's) genius—"that dye of dyes / Whereof one drop worked miracles"—which popular imitators (the Spasmodics) intrinsically lack (Pettigrew, *Robert Browning: The Poems*, p. 723.). In stanza two of the "Prologue" to *Asolando* Browning's titular hero laments:

> "And now a flower is just a flower:
>   Man, bird, beast are but beast, bird, man—
> Simply themselves, uncinct by dower
>   Of dyes which, when life's day began,
>   Round each in glory ran."
>   —*Poems*, 2:875

48. *Byron*, ed. Jerome J. Mcgann (Oxford: Oxford Univ. Press, 1986), p. 375. Byron's denunciations of Wordsworth began, of course, with *English Bards and Scotch Reviewers*. As Maynard observes, "Byron's influence on Browning was probably as great as that of any modern poet except Shelley" (*Browning's Youth*, p. 175).

49. See Maynard, *Browning's Youth*, p. 195.

50. Coincidentally, Wordsworth had just completed his thirty-third year when he finished writing the Immortality Ode.

Browning's *Sordello* and the Parables of Modernist Poetics

CHRISTINE FROULA

Sordello . . . Is a modern hieroglyphic and should be carved on stone. . . . It abounds in things addressed to a second sight, and we are often required to *see double* in order to apprehend its meaning.
—Richard Hengist Horne (1842)

When I began, Browning was the only thing to go on from—the only live form.
—Ezra Pound[1]

Robert Browning's *Sordello* has encountered a double reception. Many readers, including distinguished ones, have derided its opacity. Others, no less distinguished, have not only valued it highly but, even while acknowledging its obscurity, made great claims for its social importance. The poem's notorious unreadability has inspired such jests as Charles William Stubbs's "And did you once find Browning plain? / And did he really seem quite clear?"; Douglas Jerrold's mock-conviction that he had lost his mind when he found himself, while convalescing from a serious illness, unable to comprehend two consecutive lines of it; and the apocryphal retrospect attributed to Browning: "When I wrote it only God and I knew what it meant, and now only God knows."[2] But it was presumably something more than its unintelligibility that led Rossetti, who discovered it in 1850, to read fifty pages at a time to the Pre-Raphaelite Circle, and Swinburne, who described it as a scene of brutal violence upon language, to learn it by heart at the age of nineteen.[3] Pound, who deplored its obscurity, still judged it "the best long poem in English since Chaucer," the "live form" from which his *Cantos* could depart.[4] And Browning himself, fifteen years after publishing it, insisted that it was "my best performance hitherto" even as he labored over revisions that he hoped would "do justice to" it.[5]

The irony of *Sordello* is that it is at once a poet's poem—or, to be precise, a poet's poet's poem, for Landor, Kingsley, Tennyson, even Elizabeth

Reprinted from *ELH* 52 (1985): 965–92. Reprinted by permission of The Johns Hopkins University Press.

Barrett all found it unreadable—and a defense of the social importance of poetry.[6] Chesterton's mordant observation that *Sordello* is "the most glorious compliment that has ever been paid to the average man" recognizes that, however "few" readers Browning had to content himself with, in theory his audience had no limit.[7] But what kind of poem defends the social value of poetry in the highest terms, yet deliberately makes itself unintelligible? In this essay, I will explore the paradox of *Sordello*'s relation to its audience by attending to its internal explanation of its own difficulty. *Sordello*'s account of itself makes its linguistic obscurity contingent upon the problem of grounding poetic authority, of conceiving a foundation for language and ethics once the Christian and Romantic myths of poetic authority have failed.[8] Through *Sordello*'s engagement with the historical Sordello, Dante, and Shelley, Browning stages the earliest extended exploration of the situation and conditions of modernist poetics; he acts out the post-Romantic problem of poetic authority not only in the adventures of his poet-hero but also through his writing of *Sordello*, writing about writing *Sordello*, and offering *Sordello* to his audience. Browning's Sordello, and *Sordello*, inaugurate modernist poetics in all its re-creative aspiration, while Sordello's death, *Sordello*'s failure to reach its audience, and Browning's subsequent poetic development enact the collision of such visionary aspiration with history. *Sordello* captures a historical and literary historical moment that elucidates the linguistic difficulty of modernist poetics, Browning's later development of the dramatic monologue, and the high esteem in which many have held his modernist epic. *Sordello* is, indeed, a kind of "missing link" between Romantic humanism and modernist poetics.[9]

I

Pound considered *Sordello* "one of the finest *masks* ever presented."[10] "A poem about a poet writing a poem about a poet writing poems," as Stevenson characterizes it, *Sordello* allegorizes the young Browning's poet's progress in a tortuous and discontinuous narrative of a thirteenth-century troubadour poet-politician's career.[11] Yet Sordello is not Browning so much as the ghost of Browning's past, while Browning, like his narrator, is a Sordello who survives to write *Sordello*. Sordello's task as poet is also Browning's; his adventures and misadventures are Browning's own. But while Sordello fails and dies, Browning tells the tale and in such measure succeeds where Sordello fails. The breaks in the narrative in which Browning comments upon the poem and its story both in his own person and through the narrator do much to interpret not only the subject they frame but the fragmented telling that seems designed to obscure as much as to represent.

Much of Browning's narrative concerns Sordello's effort to define his relationship to his audience. *Sordello*'s structure is a spiral of episodes in which each abstract affirmation of the poet's power is undone by Sordello's failure to move an actual audience.[12] In this oscillating structure of poetic power and failure, vision and intractable history, it would seem that *Sordello* itself is the final term, for its ambitions coincide with the highest conceived by its hero while its reception recapitulates Sordello's most abject failures. Yet Browning, even before he begins this story, makes the problem of audience his own, and *Sordello*, not death, is his resolution. At the outset, he takes up a prominently antagonistic stance toward his audience, badgering and mocking the imaginary crowd before his fictive diorama booth. His first line, "Who will, may hear Sordello's story told," is not the conventional redundancy it seems, for he next ridicules his hearers' readiness to "believe." Describing them as sitting "fresh-chapleted to listen," Browning likens them to the faithful in a church pew; and he mocks his authority along with their credulousness by comparing his sighting of Sordello to Don Quixote's mistaking a dust cloud for "Pentapolin of the Naked Arm." When he musters a host of poet-spirits to join his living auditors, Browning taunts his audience further by confounding the living and the dead:

> My audience! and they sit, each ghostly man
> Striving to look as living as he can,
> Brother by breathing brother; thou art set,
> Clear-witted critic, by . . .
>
> (1.49–52)

In the context of such mockery, "Who will, may hear Sordello's story told" is not a truism but a challenge: Browning demands that his listeners be active, *will*ing creators—or, as may be, critics—of that story. He divests himself of the poet's privileged authority in order to elicit the exercise of authority from his audience, and in so doing, strives to bring into being a collaborative authority that puts in question the poet's traditional role as mediator between the audience and transcendence.

Browning's disturbance of the poet-audience relationship at the outset of *Sordello* implies his rejection of both the Judeo-Christian Logos and its Romantic translation, the Shelleyan "Power" that strums the poet as a lyre, as grounds for his poetic authority. His prologue bodies forth these Christian and Romantic paradigms in the images of Dante and Shelley, to both of whom Browning pays equivocal homage. Shelley appears only briefly: no sooner has Browning conjured him with the other poet-ghosts invoked to hear Sordello's story than he banishes him: "thou, spirit, come not near / Now—not this time desert thy cloudy place / To scare me, thus employed, with thy pure face!" (1.60–62). As Yetman has argued, Browning banishes Shelley not merely in order that his idol not witness his inferior poetizing but because he has in view the more aggressive project of subjecting Shelley's visionary poetics to a historical trial.[13] Sordello, indeed, is a Shelley skeptically plunged into history, his high claims for poets as unacknowledged legislators submitted to test in the world of events. In *Sordello*, Browning undertakes neither to imitate nor to honor Shelley but to test and revise the dream of "Imagination's" power.

To Dante, *Sordello* pays an homage no less equivocal. Browning's very choice of Sordello as his subject evokes Dante's portrait of him in *Purgatorio* 6, and both poets appear together in Browning's first statement of his theme. But Browning's apostrophe to Dante tinges admiration with a muted critique of his incorporative power:

> Sordello, thy forerunner, Florentine!
> A herald-star I know thou didst absorb
> Relentless into the consummate orb
> That scared it from its right to roll along
> A sempiternal path with dance and song
> (1.348–52)

While, he says, Sordello's star burns on in Dante's with no "disenfranchised brilliances," Browning proposes to

> approach the august sphere
> Named now with only one name, disentwine
> That under-current soft and argentine
> From its fierce mate in the majestic mass
> [and to] launch once more
> That lustre . . .
> I would do this! If I should falter now!
> (1.360–73)

Browning's avowed purpose is to disentwine the light of a lesser star from a greater one. But more is at issue here than his desire to honor a less renowned poet, for although Browning considers that Sordello's light still burns "prosperous and clear" in Dante's, he differentiates Sordello's poetics from Dante's in such a way as to criticize Dante's affinity with the imperialist aspects of Christianity. Dante's is the great orb that had "scared" Sordello's from its path and, "relentless," absorbed both its name and its light. Sordello, by contrast, held "right" to a different "path" of "dance and song." In light of this differentiation, strongly marked but as yet obscure, Browning's writing of *Sordello* becomes a kind of rescue mission, underscored by a sense of momentous consequence: "If I should falter now!"

II

But what is this mission and its consequence? John Grube has argued that *Sordello* must be read as "a Christian epic."[14] Yet much in Browning's poem manifests a dialectical and critical stance toward that paragon of Christian epics, *The Divine Comedy*, and the ethics it propounds. Browning's Dante is preeminently a righteous moral judge: a "pacer of the shore / Where glutted hell disgorgeth filthiest gloom," a "plucker of amaranths grown beneath God's eye / In gracious twilights where his chosen lie" (1.366–72). But whereas Dante underwrites his poetic authority with a myth of divine judgment, Sordello's moral sensibility has a different orientation, evoked by his childhood visits every evening to the baptismal font at Goito. Beneath this font, unbeknownst to him, Sordello's mother is buried; it thus figures a maternal origin for his poetics. The font is ringed by "shrinking Caryatides / Of just-tinged marble like Eve's lilied flesh / . . . Like priestesses because of sin impure / Penanced for ever" (1.412–26), and it recurs throughout the poem; indeed its Eves, whose burdens Sordello would lighten, become his muse. Sitting beside "each in her turn," he feels himself to be "the same / As one of them"; and he "begs / Pardon for them." So originates his task as poet: to forge a poetics that redeems rather than condemns human suffering, and that recognizes the poet's bonds with and likeness to sufferers without sacrificing the office of inspiration and revelation.

In the autobiographical interlude that concludes book 3, Browning intervenes in his narrative to expound such a poetics. Here he extrapolates the ideal that had embodied his hopes for Sordello midway through book 2, when Sordello has perfected his Shelleyan lyre but failed his audience, accomplishing nothing more than to "amaze / The multitude with majesties, convince / Each sort of nature that the nature's prince / Accosted it" (2.678–81). Sordello's songs were finely tuned, Browning judges,

> But the complete Sordello, Man and Bard,
> John's cloud-girt angel, this foot on the land,
> That on the sea, with, open in his hand,
> A bitter-sweetling of a book—was gone.
> (2.690–93)

Although the ideal of the poet here implied appears consonant with both Dante's Christian and Shelley's Romantic poetics, Browning gives it an ironic development in the autobiographical digression composed during his 1838 pilgrimage to the Italian scenes where *Sordello* is set. Taking Sordello's place at the center of the poem, he begins with an elaborate examination of his own conscience. As he muses "on a ruined palace-step" while watching the people in St. Mark's Square, Browning meditates on the aims and powers of poetry. He chooses from the "rabble" a peasant woman, a "care-bit erased / Broken-up beaut[y]" into whose exemplary "face / . . . The many faces crowd," and asks himself what he, the poet, could offer should she approach asking "alms" (3.747–68). In ironic answer, the many actual failures of poetry come to his mind. He has outgrown, he says, the Romantic notion that his poetry could enable "the whole race / [To] add the spirit's to the body's grace, / And all be dizened out as chiefs and bards" (3.719–21). He aspires instead, he tells the peasant woman silently, to a different form of redemption which would reclaim the lost souls that Dante damns:

>   we'll manage reinstate
> Your old worth; ask moreover, when they prate
> Of evil men past hope, 'Don't each contrive,
> Despite the evil you abuse, to live?—
> Keeping, each losel, through a maze of lies,
> His own conceit of truth? to which he hies
> By obscure windings, tortuous, if you will,
> But to himself not inaccessible . . .
> All men think all men stupider than they,
> Since, save themselves, no other comprehends
> The complicated scheme to make amends
> —Evil, the scheme by which, through Ignorance,
> Good labours to exist.'
>   (3.785–804)

Browning does not explicitly invoke Dante in this scene, but his judgment that it is "A slight advance / Merely to find the sickness you die through" (3.804–5) contrasts his treatment of evil with Dante's even as he himself, vacillating ironically in his claims for the poet's value to others, becomes one of the losels he describes. He mocks the poet's pretence of "dispensing without stint" the redemptive water of life, ridiculing the poet as a self-deluded Moses who "wonder[s] any one needs choke / With founts about!" even as he enslaves the Gibeonites (3.810, 824–25). Yet he also makes himself such a Moses, who "awkwardly enough . . . smites / The rock, though he forego his Promised Land / Thereby, have Satan claim his carcass, and / Figure as Metaphysic Poet" (3.826–29). The poet, Browning implies, is condemned to fail in the office of redeemer; and yet he maintains that the highest poet is the "Maker-see," the poet who "Impart[s] the gift of seeing to the rest" (3.868).[15] That Browning views his fantasy of awakening his audience to their own authority as utopian ("no-time," "no-place") does not diminish his conviction that this enterprise is of supreme importance:

> When at some future no-time a brave band
> Sees, using what it sees, then shake my hand
> In heaven, my brother! Meanwhile where's the hurt
> Of keeping the Makers-see on the alert,
> At whose defection mortals stare aghast
> As though heaven's bounteous windows were slammed fast
> Incontinent.
>   (3.925–31)

Browning's "Makers-see" would do more than make "heaven" visible to their audience. If, in their absence, heaven is not only closed off from view but *empty*, "Incontinent," then language, Browning implies, is not merely the medium but the very stuff of perception and of revelation alike. The task of the "Maker-see," then, is to give hearers a language conceived as power to see for themselves.

Browning next offers and defends his *Sordello* as such an endeavor by means of a remarkable parable addressed to two of his English readers and fellow poets, Walter Savage Landor and Euphrasia Fanny Haworth ("My English Eyebright"). He treats these readers with scarcely more gentleness than the rest of his audience, paying a most ambiguous homage to Landor's *Idyllia Heroica* and challenging, none too politely, what he represents as Haworth's expectations for his poetry in justifying his decision to write for the peasant woman in the Square:

> My English Eyebright, if you are not glad
> That, as I stopped my task awhile, the sad
> Dishevelled form, wherein I put mankind
> To come at times and keep my pact in mind
> Renewed me,—hear no crickets in the hedge,
> Nor let a glowworm spot the river's edge
> At home, and may the summer showers gush
> Without a warning from the missel thrush!
> (3.967–74)

Browning follows this aggressive turn on English pastoral by dedicating his poem to those who "flounder on without a term, / Each a god's germ / . . . In unexpanded infancy unless . . . / But that's the story" (3.981–84)—that is, to all those whom he would "make see"—and he admonishes his English readers to bear with his dull tale:

> There might be fitter subjects to allure;
> Still, neither misconceive my portraiture
> Nor undervalue its adornments quaint:
> What seems a fiend perchance may prove a saint.
> (3.985–88)

The parable by which Browning illustrates this platitude, upon which his defense of *Sordello* hinges, has for its subject St. John the Divine, author of Revelation, who was banished to the penal colony of Patmos "on account of the word of God and the testimony of Jesus" (Rev. 1:9). In it, "John the Beloved" visits the house of his disciple Xanthus on the eve of his departure for Patmos to bestow a final blessing upon "those his exile most would grieve." I quote from the point at which Browning describes the "touching spectacle" of Xanthus's house "in motion to receive him":

>   Xanthus' spouse
> You missed, made panther's meat a month since; but
> Xanthus himself (his nephew 'twas, they shut
> 'Twixt boards and sawed asunder), Polycarp,
> Soft Charicle, next year no wheel could warp
> To swear by Caesar's fortune, with the rest
> Were ranged; through whom the grey disciple pressed,
> Busily blessing right and left, just stopped
> To pat one infant's curls, the hangman cropped
> Soon after, reached the portal. On its hinge
> The door turns and he enters: what quick twinge
> Ruins the smiling mouth, those wide eyes fix
> Whereon, why like some spectral candlestick's
> Branch the disciple's arms? Dead swooned he, woke
> Anon, heaved sigh, made shift to gasp, heart-broke,
> 'Get thee behind me, Satan! Have I toiled
> To no more purpose? Is the gospel foiled
> Here too, and o'er my son's, my Xanthus' hearth,
> Portrayed with sooty garb and features swarth—
> Ah Xanthus, am I to thy roof beguiled
> To see the—the—the Devil domiciled?'
> Whereto sobbed Xanthus, 'Father, 'tis yourself
> Installed, a limning which our utmost pelf
> Went to procure against tomorrow's loss;
> And that's no twy-prong, but a pastoral cross,
> You're painted with!'
>   His puckered brows unfold—
> And you shall hear Sordello's story told.
>   (3:996–1022)

"What seems a fiend perchance may prove a saint," Browning says by way of introducing this parable. But is it a fiend that proves a saint that he depicts here, or the opposite—a saint that proves a fiend? Browning's source for this story is the apocryphal Acts of John 26–29, but his embellishments—the parade of Christian martyrs, the frame of John's banishment from Antioch, the character of Xanthus, and John's death-swoon—ironically transform it.[16] Whereas in the original story John takes his own image for a beautiful pagan god and says, upon his disciple's explanation, " 'You are teasing me, child; am I so (gracious) in form as your . . . Lord?' " in Browning's version John takes what his disciple had evidently considered a likeness for a hideous devil. This elaborate image of the saint taking his own portrait for a fiend dramatizes Browning's obsession with the potential violence of poetic authority; for the answer to John's question, "Am I [brought here to see the] Devil domiciled?" is evidently "Yes."

How, then, do we interpret this parable? Grube reads it as an exemplum of error: If the saintly John can err, how much more easily can Sordello himself.[17] But has John erred? Browning's grotesque memorial to the martyrs suggests that, although John does make the error of not recognizing himself in the portrait, his apprehension of it as a portrait of a devil is only too acute. For Browning has fashioned a parable of the danger of the poet's word to those who hear it. His John is a poet whose word, whose touch, brings death. Browning's rewriting of Revelation 1:1–2 is implicitly critical of John's authority. According to John's text Christ received the revelation from God, who "sent and signified it by his angel unto his servant John: who bare record of the word of God, and of the testimony of Jesus Christ, and of all the things that he saw." As the threatening injunction that closes Revelation confirms, it is not the authority of the "best" poets, the Makers-see, that John thus claims but that of the "worst" who merely "say they so have seen" (3.866):

> For I testify unto every man that heareth the words of the prophecy of this book, If any man shall add unto these things, God shall add unto him the plagues that are written in this book:
> And if any man shall take away from the words of the book of this prophecy, God shall take away his part out of the book of life, and out of the holy city, and from the things which are written in this book.
> (22:18–19)

Far from empowering the authority of his audience, John proscribes it. Hence Browning compares his ideal poet not to John but to the higher of the two intermediaries between transcendence and humankind: "John's cloud-girt angel" (2.690). In doing so, Browning denies the absolute authority that John's words claim. John exerts his authority against further authorship, or "augmenting," as such. In the terms of book 3, he bids his audience "take on trust" his visions—ironically compromised by his error concerning the painting (3.915). But the parable plays out the dangers of this kind of authority to Xanthus and to the martyrs whose deaths for such "trust" it details with gruesome irony. As Browning portrays him, John is not a redeemer, a "saint," but a death-dealing "fiend" whose authority foils the "Maker-see" authority by which Browning measures his hero and his *Sordello*.

In opposing the parabolic to the diabolic, Browning's revision of John's story continues his dialogue with Dante, restaging a scene from the origins of Christian history in such a way as to "disentwine" that authority from its institutions. John, who pictures himself as one in a chain of transmitters of the divine word, insists upon a "truth" which has only one form, that of his text. A parable, by contrast, cannot be fathomed by any amount of attention to its literal sense; its meaning depends upon faculties of interpretation rather than of recognition. It not only permits but *requires* translation into other words. Frank Kermode has pointed out that the parable may hold its own tyrannies, testing not the authority of its hearers but a prior imposition of authority: "only those who already know the mysteries—what the stories really mean—can discover what the stories really mean."[18] As Browning employs it here, however, the parable questions the poet's relation to force, and particularly, the interrelations of authority, faith, and moral force. What does it mean, in Browning's poem, to die for the faith—physically, as the martyrs do, or metaphysically, as Xanthus seems to have done? What does it mean for John to threaten his augmenters with exclusion from the book of life, or for Dante to enlist moral force (or advocate physical force) in the cause of a faith that would constitute the world's order in its own image? In the context of these questions, Browning's turn to parable—and this particular parable, an ironic revision of an *apocryphal* story of John—recursively illustrate his "Maker-see" poetics: not only its workings but, by virtue of the contrast with Dante and John, its metaphysical motives. An apocryphal text in an exaggeratedly apocryphal version, the parable at the heart of *Sordello* acts out Browning's poetics of recovering lost value, of recreating lost modes of authority and restoring them to his audience, the "losels" his poetics would redeem. Shrouding his meaning in a parable, Browning seeks to engage his audience in an act of reading that both dramatizes and subverts the violence of language, judgment, and authority. His "moral," that unquestioning faith can kill, requires the suspension of unquestioning faith in order to be understood. Following as it does upon his disquisition on the "losels," the parable strenuously counters the kind of moral authority exercised by John and Dante with another, and differently based, moral authority; and by doing so it illuminates Browning's larger project of disentwining Sordello's light from Dante's.

III

Browning closes book 3 by parodying his first line: "And you shall hear Sordello's story told," the emphatic *you shall* ironically testing the success or failure of Browning's parable. In the poem's second half, Sordello's career acts out the contradictions between Browning's ideal of poetic authority and its possibilities of realization in history; for, if the parabolic poetics of Browning, Sordello, and *Sordello* would dissociate poetic authority from violence, that poetics risks unintelligibility by its very conception. Browning explores the issue of poetic authority and force by continuing his dialectical comparison of Sordello with Dante, focusing on Sordello's dream of Rome.

In midcareer, Sordello abandons poetry for political action as a more direct means of serving "the Multitudes"; but he soon grows disillusioned with both Guelfs and Ghibellines, envisioning instead for humankind " 'A cause intact, distinct from these, ordained / For me, its true discoverer' "—figured as "the reintegration of Rome" (4.951–52). Sordello's vision of Rome recalls Dante's only to diverge from it, as begins to emerge in a curious dialogue in book 5, when Sordello loses hope of a world brought into harmony by poetry (5.74–79). Browning employs a *deus ex machina* to save his hero from despair, sending "a low voice . . . into his heart" to confirm his vision while explaining to him that he must be content to perform his part in a vast *collective* task (5.85–97). The voice conceives human history as a progress in which the poet's part is limited but crucial, and it affirms that Sordello is the poet to whom "fate wafts / This very age, her whole inheritance / Of opportunities" (5.298–300). Lest Sordello think the poet's share in shaping this collective history too small, the voice warns him that "all is changed the moment you descry / Mankind as half yourself—then, fancy's trade / Ends once and always" (5.250–52). From this perception of a bond with humankind there is no return to solipsistic dreaming; it plunges the poet into history, makes him share in "the rabble's woes," detailed in a long litany of the miseries of war (5.260–93).

The voice's exhortations translate the ethics rooted in Sordello's childhood visits to the font at Goito into a vision of the poet's work; and it is here that the difference between Sordello's dream of Rome and Dante's is located. Both poets inherit a world shaped by Christian history, but Browning distinguishes the "path" by which each continues that tradition. As Browning presents it, the origin of Christian history is a linguistic, and profoundly poetic, moment. Evoking this moment, the voice "disentwines" the powerful mystery of Christianity from its corrupt historical institutions, and it makes Sordello's poetic power continuous with that originating power. "Were you the first," it asks,

>   who brought—(in modern speech)
> The Multitude to be materialized?
> That loose eternal unrest—who devised
> An apparition i' the midst? The rout
> Was checked, a breathless ring was formed about
> The gold-rough pointel, silver-blazing disk
> O' the lily! Swords across it! Reign thy reign
> And serve thy frolic service, Charlemagne!
>   (5.124–32)

Since Browning identifies poetry as the wellspring of Christianity, his version of Christian history is fundamentally a *literary* history, continuous with his readings of Dante and John. The ambiguous image of the original "lily" crossed by Charlemagne's sword is elaborated in a dialectics of "Knowledge" and "Strength." The voice pictures the original Christian community as "A company amid the other clans, / Only distinct in priests for castellans / And popes for suzerains," and asks: "Dived you into its capabilities / And dared create, out of that sect, a soul / Should turn a multitude, already whole, / Into its body? Speak plainer! Is't so sure / God's church lives by a King's investiture?" (5.143–55). Speaking none too plainly, Browning seems to approve "God's church" even as he casts doubt upon the "Strength" by which Christianity, at first only one cult among others, "dared" to dominate them all. This covert critique of Christian imperialism continues as the voice states that Pope Hildebrand's investiture reforms are no advance at all on Charlemagne's sword: "Full three hundred years / Have men to wear away in smiles and tears / Between the two that nearly seemed to touch" (5.177–79). Yet, if the "Strength" of Charlemagne (motto: *Renovatio Roman. Imp.*) helped transform history into Christian history, the voice also asserts that history's "last step" must be to demolish the scaffolding of force upon which its lineaments are hung. The voice thus enjoins Sordello to imagine and dedicate himself to a genuine progress from "Strength" to "Knowledge," which, when accomplished, would make political force "a thing to spurn" (5.221–34).

With respect to political force, Sordello's idea of Rome at first appears to differ little from Dante's. For Dante, Rome was the historical city divinely designated to unify and govern the world, the capital at once of the Christian empire and of the Christian church. He venerated the city's glorious pagan past and grieved for its ignoble present; and in his *Divine Comedy* he dreamed that the imperial authority of the "Eternal City" might be restored, its papacy purged of corruption, and its divine destiny fulfilled.[19] Dante founded his epic authority equally upon Rome's past and future glories, forging his poem and his poetics from a myth of continuity between Virgil's ancient Rome and his vision of the Christian city no less than between a prophetic Virgil and himself. For Dante, literary history and Italian history alike followed a divine plan which justified not only his epic of judgment but also the political force which he, the exiled Florentine, could implore to besiege his native city and bind it again under the temporal power of Rome.

Sordello, like Dante, inherits Christian history and is implicated in its heritage of force; but the path by which his poetics and its politics would continue this history diverges from Dante's. Sordello's "voice" envisions history as a progress led by a poet capable of creating political unity through "Knowledge"—language—as Charlemagne had created it through "Strength." What distinguishes Browning's Sordello from Dante's, then, must be sought in the language through which he attempts to realize his dream of Rome. At the voice's instigation, Sordello meets with Salinguerra the Ghibelline leader, to urge him to take up "the People's" cause. Rebuffed, Sordello is stirred to an impassioned and eloquent defense of poetry in which he prophesies a "new structure" for poetry and, by extension, for politics. This language diverges from Dante's in the extent to which it makes history, and not a myth of a divine plan, the foundation of poetic and political authority. Like the parable of book 3, this poetics demands that the audience, not the poet alone, exercise authority; hence the important, reiterated point that the poet is one with the people, having a mind which is "finest" "All in degree, no way diverse in kind / From minds about it" (5.561–62):

> 'How I rose,
> And how have you advanced! since evermore
> Yourselves effect what I was fain before
> Effect, what I supplied yourselves suggest,
> What I leave bare yourselves can now invest.
> How we attain to talk as brothers talk,
> In half-words, call things by half-names, no balk
> From discontinuing old aids.[']
>
> (5.620–27)

Sordello's "brother's speech" is built upon the violent history outlined by the voice. But his turn from a myth of transcendence to that shared past as the basis for language bespeaks a radical skepticism which does not *assume* common ground and common authority but *tests* it, through a language of "half-words" and "half-names" that effects a meeting of minds as by two halves of a tally. This "new structure" of language ensures that agreement will not be presumed where it cannot be enacted. In this way, it functions doubly to prove and provide a common ground for ethics and politics where it succeeds, and to disprove claims for such authority where intelligibility fails. Even such failure is success: a negative success by which the greater moral failure of *imposing* authority is avoided.

At stake in Sordello's "new structure" is the construction not only of his poetic authority but of Browning's own, as he breaks into Sordello's speech to say: " 'Once more I cast external things away, / And natures composite, so decompose / That' . . . Why, he writes *Sordello*!" (5.618–20). Thus Sordello's new language too is a parabolic rather than a signifying one. Like the parables of the gospels, it presupposes the inheritance of Christian history in such a way as to diffuse rather than assert its authority; the very possibility of its comprehension rests upon the shared authority of speaker and interpreters. In the event that this collaboration does not work, meaning merely fails; it cannot impose itself. In the event that it does work, on the other hand, it attests to both translation and translatability, to difference within sameness and sameness within difference, to an eliciting of many voices rather than the preeminence of one.

In Sordello's envisioned language, then, Christian history is skeptically received, its authority perpetually tested and renewed in the collaborative ritual of language. The past is received not as binding tradition but as a heritage of "structures" to be interrogated and discarded, translated, or recreated:

> To-day
> Takes in account the work of Yesterday:
> Has not the world a Past now, its adept
> Consults ere he dispense with or accept
> New aids? a single touch more may enhance,
> A touch less turn to insignificance
> Those structures' symmetry the past has strewed
> The world with, once so bare.
> (5.628–35)

Sordello allegorizes his (and Browning's) shift from a poetics grounded in transcendence to one grounded in history in describing the highest stage of art, the "synthetist's," by analogy to St. Mark's Cathedral in Venice:

> Ends
> Accomplished turn to means: my art intends
> New structure from the ancient: as they changed
> The spoils of every clime at Venice, ranged
> The horned and snouted Libyan god, upright
> As in his desert, by some simple bright
> Clay cinerary pitcher—Thebes as Rome,
> Athens as Byzant rifled, till their Dome
> From earth's reputed consummations razed
> A seal, the all-transmuting Triad blazed
> Above, Ah, whose that fortune? Ne'ertheless,
> E'en he must stoop contented to express
> No tithe of what's to say—the vehicle
> Never sufficient. . . .
> (5.641–54)

St. Mark's, that triumph of the mosaicist's art of fitting many fragments into one transcendent image, is an eclectic monument that incorporates relics of past and alien cultures into a grand representation of Christian cosmology. As an image for Sordello's poetics, it evokes and seems to celebrate the imperialist history which the voice's speech had indicted; yet it also complicates and questions that history. St. Mark's embodies the political implications of Sordello's visionary language, its form symbolizing the reconciliation of many different worlds. The Libyan, Theban, Roman, Athenian, and Byzantine fragments, styles, and icons allude to cultures in themselves whole and entire. But the Cathedral composes these fragments into a single synthetic design: Sordello describes the mosaic on the great dome as though it were not merely the Christian representation of divinity but divinity itself blazing through the broken seal of heaven.

Although the image most obviously implies that the Christian iconography surmounts the other artifacts, the instability of this hierarchy is betrayed by the *trompe-l'oeil* metaphor that describes the Triad as though it were not an icon but an actual Trinity. It is as though St. Mark's mosaics raze the seal not of less authoritative representations but of representation as such. In fact, of course, if the mosaics "raze the seal" formed by the "reputed consummations," they also form another: they do not reveal heaven but shut out its light with solid stone. Here Sordello limits the authority of his art; for even this apotheosis, he says, expresses "No tithe of what's to say," and he ends by "cast[ing] aside such fancies" (5.653, 657). Even as he fuses the power of the Church and the power of art, he rejects the universal, total, and final authority that dared to raise a cult above the other cults. By virtue of this limitation, the Cathedral's status as a triumphant synthesis shifts: it is not for the supremacy of the Triad that it is to be valued but for its representation of diverse cultures harmonized in a single structure. Building "new structures from the ancient," Sordello implies both that he will imitate the Venetians' art of synthesis and that he will surpass it. Similarly, Browning creates in *Sordello* a new poetic structure that subverts the hierarchical construction of poetic authority, making meaning dependent upon the crossing, not the obliteration, of boundaries.

What is most striking about Sordello's dream of Rome as expressed in this speech is that it moves, figuratively speaking, to Venice. Sordello's is a Rome in every way different from Dante's: a place displaced, a center decentered, a capital decapitalized, a metaphor transported. Sordello's idea of Rome, like Dante's, evokes a unifying political and spiritual authority created through language. But the image of St. Mark's, like Browning's parable of John, rewrites the Eternal City as a temporal one whose authority is founded on human history rather than divine plan. Sordello's Venetian Rome is an image of many cultures brought into harmony. It stresses not one unifying political and spiritual authority executing "God's will" but the existence of many diverse histories and cultures; not the desirability of hierarchy but the problematic aspects of setting one cult above the others. Embodied in language, art and history, Sordello's is a centerless Rome that exists everywhere. Positing neither divine destiny nor temporal privilege, Sordello's Rome is that merely occasional place where Browning sat "on a ruined palace-step" and thought how poetry might "reinstate [the] old worth" of the disenfranchised souls he saw before him.

Sordello's Venetian Rome, with its speech of half-words and half-names "where an accent's change gives each / The other's soul," embodies not Dante's ethics of judgment but an ethics of sympathy derived from his childhood visits to the Eves of the font, where he felt himself "the same / As one of them" (1.430–31). In this respect, Browning's reading of Sordello both draws upon and diverges from Dante's presentation of him in *Purgatorio* 6. Teodolinda Barolini has argued that Dante's honorary treatment of the historical Sordello stems from the high value he placed upon Sordello's linguistic internationalism. In *De Vulgari Eloquentia*, Barolini points out,

Dante associates Sordello with the reversal of the political and linguistic fragmentation allegorized in the Tower of Babel legend; and in *The Divine Comedy* Sordello stands for the healing of the political rifts caused by Italy's fragmentation into many warring city-states, each with its own dialect. But whereas Dante's linguistic internationalism took shape as his creation of the Italian *vulgare illustre*, Sordello's was signified by his writing in a language not his own: Provençal.[20] Browning's reading of Sordello incorporates Dante's; but, as he rewrites John's story, he also rewrites Dante's by distinguishing between Dante's one language and Sordello's many, between *erasing* boundaries by annexation and centralization and *crossing* them by learning and using the language of another. For Browning as for Dante, Sordello stands for peacemaking: for "crossing over, bringing together, reuniting what has been torn asunder;" and he, like Dante, endows this lyric poet with "quasi-epic" status.[21] But whereas Dante's Sordello becomes, by virtue of his poetics, a foil to the emperor whom Dante castigates in Canto 6 for refusing to cross boundaries in order to unify Italy's warring factions by force, Browning's Sordello—and *Sordello*—offer a poetics which seeks to circumvent violence by replacing force with collaborative authority. This poetics designs reading and writing as symbolic acts of boundary-crossing that transcend difference without destroying it.

IV

Yet Browning's Sordello fails. When it is mysteriously revealed that he is Salinguerra's son, Salinguerra bestows upon him the imperial baldric, making him chief of the Ghibellines. Sordello now has his chance to become a revisonary Charlemagne, crossing boundaries by Knowledge rather than by Strength and using language to empower rather than the sword to conquer. But this chance is lost by Sordello's death, whereby the power reverts to Ecelin, who did nothing to heal the differences between the strife-torn factions. Sordello's death is ambiguous. He dies, it is usually thought, from a crisis of conscience when he must choose between the poet's part and the secular leader's. But when Sordello spurns his worldly heritage, trampling the emperor's badge underfoot, he dies as poet too; and this double death suggests a more complicated allegory of poetic failure which Browning's obituary comments support:

> The Chroniclers of Mantua tired their pen
> Telling how *Sordello Prince Visconti* saved
> Mantua, and elsewhere notably behaved—
> Who thus, by fortune ordering events,
> Passed with posterity, to all intents,
> For just the god he never could become.

>   As Knight, Bard, Gallant, men were never dumb
>   In praise of him: while what he should have been,
>   Could be, and was not—the one step too mean
>   For him to take,—we suffer at this day
>   Because of: Ecelin had pushed away
>   Its chance ere Dante could arrive and take
>   That step Sordello spurned, for the world's sake:
>   He did much—but Sordello's chance was gone.
>   (6.822–35)

As Browning puts it here, Sordello, because of his historical position, had a unique "chance" which had vanished by Dante's time. While Dante, he says, "did much," Sordello might have done more. And yet Sordello's death raises doubts about how much more he might have done. In the context of Browning's own ironic alternation of aspiring and self-critical meditations in book 3, his obscure death seems to allegorize the impossibility of the task Browning sets his poet: the contradictoriness, that is, of raising Sordello's lyric poetics into an epic poetics, of attempting to endow his local and lyric words with historical "Strength" as Charlemagne did the Christian word. Browning's elegy for his poet, even as it puts Sordello's potential brilliance higher than Dante's, qualifies that judgment by doubting the very possibility of its fulfilment.

How then does Sordello's death reflect upon the project *Sordello*? Browning's contrast of Dante and Sordello within the poem prefigures the modernists' sense of their difference from Dante. Dante, for the moderns, is the great example of a poet whose epic art is sustained by a collective ideology. Living in a period when Christianity, however corrupt its institutions, still appeared to have the power to bind all of Europe into a single social order, Dante could construct his epic upon the ethical scaffolding of Aquinas as upon another foundation, no less important, the European history represented by Charlemagne's "Strength." Whereas modern artists had to be difficult in order to comprehend the "great variety and complexity" of their civilization, Dante, Eliot wrote, is "easy to read" because his culture was "not of one European country but of Europe." He "thought in a way in which every man of his culture in the whole of Europe then thought," and his allegorical method was "not confined to Italy" but "common and commonly understood throughout Europe."[22] Pound, too, was well aware of the formal advantages that the coherent and widely-accepted medieval world view conferred upon Dante in contrast to his own time. "As to the *form of The Cantos*," he wrote to a correspondent in 1939, "*wait* till it's there. . . . I haven't an Aquinas-map; Aquinas *not* valid now."[23] And Pound may have remembered *Sordello* when he assessed Dante against Cavalcanti in the following terms:

> [Cavalcanti] shows himself much more "modern" than his young friend Dante Alighieri, *qui était diablement dans les idées reçues*. . . . Guido is eclectic, he

swallows none of his authors whole. . . . one can, at any rate, scarcely exaggerate the gulf between Guido's state of mind and that of Dante in the same epoch, or between it and Dante's willingness to take on any sort of holy and orthodox furniture. Dante's "heresies" are due to feeling, annoyance with Popes and so forth, rather than to intellectual hunger, or to his feeling cramped in the Aquinian universe.[24]

Had "Sordello dared that step alone," Browning writes, "Apollo had been compassed / . . . Had he embraced / Their cause then, men had plucked Hesperian fruit" (6.836–47). The narrator's judgment that "we suffer at this day" because of Sordello's failure is a startling criticism of all poetry from Sordello's day forward, including Dante's. Dante's *Divine Comedy* embodies a vision of community conceived in the hope that the accession of Henry VII would bring about peace, a unified Italy, and a cultural renaissance. The language he created—"a language, in itself music and persuasion, out of a chaos of inharmonious barbarisms," as Shelley described it—drew upon the historical Sordello's vernacular experiments and shares some of the aims of Browning's Sordello's "brother's speech." But Browning appears to see limitation in the very quality in which Eliot finds Dante's strength: in his situating his poem within the institution of the church rather than striving beyond the single creed toward a community defined by differences transcended, by boundaries not obliterated but crossed. Dante's Aquinian cosmos must either narrow the possibilities of community or achieve community by overpowering alien cultures and absorbing them into itself.

Sordello's temptation to force suggests that he is of his father's party without knowing it: that, like Xanthus, he is *diablement dans les idées reçues* and that he does not entirely trust his own dream of a revisionary "Rome" brought into being by his new structures of language. Yet when Sordello tramples the badge underfoot, he refuses force, even as he loses the opportunity to transform political force by his poetics. Thus, Browning's Sordello, like Dante's, remains a lyric poet though endowed with epic importance. Demanding that his audience "live," Browning's and Sordello's "Maker-see" poetics renounces the force of John's or Dante's authority; and, paradoxically, the same difficulty by which this poetics evades authoritative force also ensures that it must "fail."

V

Browning's modernism is intrinsic to his collaborative poetics, which limits the poet's authority as it attempts to awaken that of the audience. He crosses boundaries in *Sordello*, and, by his poetics of difficulty, he elicits such crossing from his audience as well. His gibing address to "My English Eyebright"

(3.967–74, quoted above) illuminates the sense in which *Sordello* is a poem for the peasants in the Italian piazza who will never read it. Although its language of "half-words" is elitist in effect, it originates as an effort to cross over the boundaries, ethical and linguistic, of the closed culture, for example, the English tradition which Browning embodies dialectically in Landor and Haworth. What Browning does in *Sordello*, insofar as he can, is to turn English into a foreign language and English poetry into a foreign affair. As, in his rendering, the aesthetics of St. Mark's expresses a community of diverse cultures, so *Sordello*'s poetics and themes propose an imaginative life that crosses the bounds of the closed culture. If Browning addresses his audience in terms which confound the living and the dead (1.49–51), he hopes by *Sordello* to inspire these materially breathing "brothers" to a body politic. The peculiar act of reading which Browning designs gestures toward an open and inclusive human community through a symbolic rejection of the force of convention that makes acquiescence "easy." The poem asks its readers to be not passive receivers of meaning but curious, doubting, *will*ing creators of it—not only readers but half-writers of the poem. As the poem is constituted by collaborative authority, Browning intends, so the community. Browning closes *Sordello* by again needling his audience:

> any nose
> May ravage with impunity a rose:
> Rifle a musk-pod and 'twill ache like yours!
> I'd tell you that same pungency ensures
> An after-gust, but that were overbold.
> Who would has heard Sordello's story told.
> (5.881–86)

To represent *Sordello*'s effect as a physiological sensation is to stress its continuity with breath and bodies, to make the connection between poetry and life palpable. Browning wants his words to be made flesh. He wants to make his audience "see" (or smell)—not any particular thing, but *for themselves*. Browning leaves his audience with a metaphysical ache, a discomfiting challenge; and he dares to imagine an "after-gust" as proof that his poem has crossed the boundary between letter and spirit.

With respect to Dante, Browning and his Sordello might be said to pursue a protestant poetics.[25] But with respect to nineteenth-century poetics, *Sordello* is also the inaugural *modernist* poem. For although *Sordello* does at points preserve enough of the Christian construction of transcendence to justify Grube's description of it as a "Christian epic," what is most striking about the poem is its radical stripping of Christian theology back to a poetic and linguistic origin. Sordello's concept of "brother's speech" assumes no transcendent ground for language, politics, and human history but rather attempts to *recreate* the poetic moment *Sordello* posits at the origin of Christian theology: the linguistic crossing of the boundary, the distance, between mind and mind. Browning's linguistic contortion, his half-written language of gaps and holes, is the means by which he attempts to renew this miraculous, because groundless, crossing; and, with the radical skepticism such a language implies, it is also the essence of his modernity. Revising his failed epic in 1856, Browning wrote cheerily to his American publisher that he was making it "as easy as its nature admits, I believe—changing nothing and simply *writing in* the unwritten *every-other-line* which I stupidly left as an amusement for the reader to do—who, after all, is no writer, nor needs be."[26] Here Browning makes clear even as he betrays the method, however quixotic, of *Sordello*'s madness: its desire to make the act of reading a symbolic and performative feat, a meeting of minds not by the ease of convention but by a strenuous effort of imagination. On such lines Browning had earlier justified his linguistic difficulty to Ruskin, who complained that his poems were "worse than the worst Alpine Glacier I ever crossed. Bright, & deep enough truly, but so full of Clefts that half the journey has to be done with ladder & hatchet."[27] Browning replied, "You ought, I think, to keep pace with the thought tripping from ledge to ledge of my 'glaciers,' as you call them; not stand poking your alpenstock into the holes and demonstrating that no foot could have stood there; suppose it sprang over there?" Ruskin, he thought, had missed the point: "You would have me paint it all plain out, which can't be; but by various artifices I try to make shift with touches and bits of outlines which *succeed* if they bear the conception from me to you."[28] When Ruskin cried, Help, Browning could only shout, Jump, because he had invented his treacherous linguistic surfaces for the very purpose of staging such a leap, in order to prove the possibility of a communion independent of transcendence and convention alike. His poetics designed a pointedly effortful ritual of communication which only a metaphysics of sympathy could underwrite and which only a language of holes could facilitate.

Finally, however, *Sordello* failed: Browning accepted the fact that his audience, even the few he had hoped to content, could not leap between his lines or fill in his language of holes. His later turn to dramatic monologue can be understood as a development from the impossible *Sordello*, translating *Sordello*'s project into a different and far more accessible form. In the monologues, the poet's voice vanishes behind the "losel's," who keeps

> through a maze of lies,
> His own conceit of truth[,] to which he hies
> By obscure windings, tortuous, if you will,
> But to himself not inaccessible;
> He sees truth, and his lies are for the crowd
> Who cannot see. . . .
> (3.789–94)

Telling their own stories in a form that puts conventions of judgment in strenuous conflict with sympathy in the reader's mind, the lost ones of the monologues succeed where *Sordello* could not. The dramatic monologue is also a language of holes; yet we can and do read between its lines, fulfilling Sordello's expectation that his audience leap where no foot could have stood: "What I leave bare yourselves can now invest." Ourselves supplying the "unwritten every-other-line," we readers cannot but ask wherein we differ from, and how we can judge, that which we can understand without need of being told. Browning's dramatic monologue subverts the alienated judgment that Dante's *Divine Comedy* cultivates even as it calls forth the act of identification without which it cannot be read.[29]

Sordello's modernity is evident not only in its relation to Browning's later development but in its instigation of an epic successor, Pound's *Cantos*. What is perhaps most interesting about the relationship between *Sordello* and *The Cantos* is the extent to which Pound's poem reenacts Sordello's aspirations, struggles, and paradoxical success-in-failure. Pound devised in his ideogrammic method a poetics of fragments, gaps, and holes not unlike that of *Sordello*, which similarly depends upon the reader's active and self-authorized perception for its legibility. The linguistic internationalism of *The Cantos* seeks, as Sordello and Dante sought, a language to register a diversity of cultures; and its unconventionality, like *Sordello*'s, originates in an obscure desire to transcend the arbitrariness of signs. But whereas Sordello spurns the temptation to political force even as he fails to make persuasive his dream of a common language, Pound, reaching what Hugh Kenner names the "fault line" of the Italian Cantos, falls prey to this temptation when his own "Maker-see" poetics fails.[30] In Cantos LXXII and LXXIII, he, like the historical Sordello, crosses into a language not his own.[31] But Pound's crossing is a desperate and drastic response to a world torn apart by war, and his model, crudely followed, for the dramatic form of these cantos and for the ethics they inscribe is *The Divine Comedy*, not as the lyric he had praised but as the epic of judgment which, following Browning, he had once censured.

Pound's epic struggle repeats *Sordello*'s darker lesson of a violence that can be neither mitigated by language nor cured and redeemed in the world. The problem that Browning explores in *Sordello*, one that its reception reenacts and that modern history, literal and literary, has inherited, is the problem of force in poetic and political authority. While Pound was writing the Italian Cantos and *The Pisan Cantos*, both dramatic monologues of the poet in *propria persona* and both in their different ways documents of barbarism, the thinkers of the Frankfurt School were articulating the problem of poetic authority, of linguistic violence, in terms given by the specifics of twentieth-century history deployed through two world wars: antisemitism, nationalism, Nazism, Fascism. Walter Benjamin's radical judgment that "There is no document of civilization which is not at the same time a document of barbarism" can be set beside Browning's revisionary representation of St.

John and of St. Mark's Cathedral.[32] Twentieth-century theorists of language have articulated the condition that Browning's, Sordello's, and Pound's poetics act out: that poetic language cannot entirely escape the arbitrariness of the sign and consequently the intersubjective violence that always, at some level, underlies acts of communication. Ruskin's complaint of Browning's untraversable, glacial wordscapes anticipates the common charge of the metaphysical coldness of modernist poetics, the bareness and scantiness of the garments its words supply. Modern poetry suffers, Barthes wrote, from a "Hunger of the Word."[33] In its radical doubt of language, *Sordello* is a quintessential modern poem. Yet it counters this hunger, this desolation, by staging an exemplary meeting of merely human minds in the glacial deserts of a language given by no supreme authority. Browning's poetics recognizes the violence that may lie buried beneath consensus, the hidden "Strength" that may enforce apparent agreement. He makes his poem illegible to all except those who "will" to hear its story through a poetics that is designed to circumvent this violence, that measures the distance between mind and mind and the costs of consent even as it asks, in its parabolic way, for a bridging of that distance, a leap of sympathy.

Notes

1. Pound's remark is quoted in Myles Slatin, " 'Mesmerism': A Study of Ezra Pound's use of the Poetry of Robert Browning" (Ph.D. diss.: Yale Univ., 1957), 263. Horne's "Robert Browning's Poems," originally published in *Church of England Quarterly* (Oct. 1842), 464–83, is reprinted in *Browning: The Critical Heritage*, ed. Boyd Litzinger and Donald Smalley (London: Routledge & Kegan Paul, 1970), 68.
2. See Philip Drew, *The Poetry of Robert Browning: A Critical Introduction* (London: Methuen, 1970), chap. 4; William Clyde DeVane, *A Browning Handbook*, 2nd ed. (New York: Appleton-Century-Crofts, 1955), 85–86; and Litzinger and Smalley, eds., 60–69, for these and other contemporary comments on *Sordello*.
3. DeVane, 86; Algernon Charles Swinburne, "The Chaotic School," *New Writings by Swinburne*, ed. Cecil Y. Lang (Syracuse, N.Y.: Syracuse Univ. Press, 1964), reprinted in Litzinger and Smalley, 216.
4. Unpublished letter to Homer Pound dated December 18, 1915, in the Letters of Ezra Pound transcribed by D. D. Paige, Beinecke Rare Book and Manuscript Library, Yale University. For Pound's critical response to *Sordello's* obscurity, see his review of Yeats's *The Grey Rock* in *Literary Essays*, ed. T. S. Eliot (New York: New Directions, 1968), 381. Pound's "Three Cantos," begun in 1915 and published in 1917, open with the line "Hang it all, there can be but one *Sordello*!" (*Poetry* 10 [June 1917]: 113).
5. Letters to James Thomas Fields, September 6 and October 9, 1855, in Ian Jack, ed., "Browning on *Sordello* and *Men and Women*: Unpublished Letters to James T. Fields," *Huntington Library Quarterly* 45 (1982): 190, 187.
6. See, for example, Lionel Stevenson, "The Key Poem of the Victorian Age," *Essays in English and American Literature Presented to Bruce Robert McElderry, Jr.*, ed. Max F. Schultz, William D. Templeton, and Charles R. Metzeger (Athens: Ohio Univ. Press, 1967), who judges *Sordello* the best post-Romantic defense of poetry, one that "still remains vitally

applicable" (289); Michael Mason, "The Importance of *Sordello*" in *The Major Victorian Poets: Reconsiderations*, ed. Isobel Armstrong (London: Routledge & Kegan Paul, 1969), 125-51, who sees *Sordello* as the most fully articulated exploration of a shift, or "revolution," in the poet's role, from Romantic soliloquist to a social being dynamically engaged with the audience; and John Lucas, "Politics and the Poet's Role," *Literature and Politics in the Nineteenth Century*, ed. John Lucas (London: Methuen, 1971), 7-43, who considers it "by far the finest of all the Victorian poems that deal with the nature of the poet" and "essential to any study of the post-Romantic development of the idea of poetry and its relation to life" (24).

7. G. K. Chesterton, *Robert Browning* (London: Macmillan, 1903), 38. For "the few," see *Sordello* 5.611-16, in *Robert Browning: The Poems*, ed. John Pettigrew, supplemented and completed by Thomas J. Collins (New Haven: Yale University Press, 1981), 1:149-296. All further citations are to this edition.

8. Morse Peckham, "Browning and Romanticism," *Robert Browning*, ed. Isobel Armstrong (Athens: Ohio Univ. Press, 1975), 47-76, discusses Browning's inheritance of the Romantic poet-prophet-priest role, analyzing the Romantic ethos as a translation of the failed Christian and Enlightenment myths of redemption—"verbal and political and final"—and tracing Browning's ambivalent affiliation with it in *Pauline* (61). On the translation of Christian theology into Romantic mythology, see Leslie Brisman, "Mysterious Tongue: Shelley and the Language of Christianity," *Texas Studies in Language and Literature* 23 (1981): 389-417.

9. While *Sordello*'s thematics of language and authority shows many continuities with Romantic poetics, particularly Shelley's, it is specifically its disruption of linguistic continuity and wholeness—the grammar of the *Logos*—that marks its poetics as "modernist." Jacques Derrida (*Of Grammatology*, trans. Gayatri Chakravorty Spivak [Baltimore: Johns Hopkins Univ. Press, 1976], 92) locates the "first break" with the Western Logos in the work of Nietzsche and Mallarmé, followed by the Pound-Fenollosa poetics; *Sordello*, by virtue of its own critique of language, has affinities with this company. For a discussion linking *Sordello*'s poetics to Pound's, see Ronald Bush, *The Genesis of Ezra Pound's Cantos* (Princeton: Princeton Univ. Press, 1976), 77 ff.

10. Ezra Pound, *Gaudier-Brzeska: A Memoir* (New York: New Directions, 1970), 86.

11. Stevenson, 278.

12. Stevenson provides a useful summary and discussion of this structure, 278-88. See also Mark D. Hawthorne, "Browning's *Sordello*: Structure Through Repetition," *Victorian Poetry* 16 (1978): 204-16, and Alan J. Chaffee, "Dialogue and Dialectic in Browning's *Sordello*," *Texas Studies in Language and Literature* 23 (1981): 52-77.

13. Michael G. Yetman ("Exorcising Shelley Out of Browning: *Sordello* and the Problem of Poetic Identity," *Victorian Poetry* 13 [1975]: 79-98) traces Browning's "shift away from his youthful belief in [the] unassailable Romantic bastion of the self" (97).

14. John Grube, "*Sordello*, Browning's Christian Epic," *English Studies in Canada* 4 (1978): 413-29.

15. See Daniel Stempel, "Browning's *Sordello*: The Art of the Makers-See," *PMLA* 80 (1965): 554-61, for a discussion of this poetics.

16. Grube identifies this source in his note 4; he remarks the "theatrical qualities" of Browning's rendering but does not comment on its import in *Sordello*. In the source, John says upon seeing the painting, " 'Lycomedes, what is it that you (have done) with this portrait? Is it one of your gods that is painted here? Why, I see you are still living as a pagan!' " and he delivers a gentle sermon against idolatry: " 'these are the colours which I tell you to paint with: faith in God, knowledge (*gnosis*), reverence, kindliness. . . .' " See Edgar Hennecke, *New Testament Apocrypha*, ed. Wilhelm Schneemelcher, English translation ed. R. McL. Wilson (Philadelphia: Westminster Press, 1965), 2:220-21.

Browning's St. John reappears, along with Xanthus, in his 1864 "A Death in the Desert," which may well have been inspired by his 1863 revision of *Sordello*. E. S. Shaffer, in her study of this poem in *'Kubla Khan' and the Fall of Jerusalem: The Mythological School in Biblical Criticism and Secular Literature, 1770–1880* (Cambridge: Cambridge Univ. Press, 1975), 191–224, argues that "Browning is a participant in, is implicated in the casuistry of his casuists. . . . Coleridge's late perception that Christian European civilization rests upon a lie is never far from Browning" (204); and that Browning embraced the idea of progressive revelation: "Revelation was seen by an increasing range of thinkers not as static or once-for-all, not as inspired dictation, but as . . . the development of mankind from its primitive response through a series of equally valid yet progressively more civilized and refined formulations of religious experience" (217–18). Shaffer interprets the multiple narrators and the uncertain provenance of the manuscript that records John's words in "A Death in the Desert" as conveying the conclusion of the Higher Criticism that "it is the tradition of the Christian community itself which becomes the guarantor of authenticity" (209). This position is convincing as far as it goes, but it begs the question raised by Browning's treatment of St. John in *Sordello*, of the violent impact the poet's vision (or revelation) may have upon an audience or community.

17. Grube, 418.

18. Frank Kermode, *The Genesis of Secrecy: On the Interpretation of Narrative* (Cambridge: Harvard Univ. Press, 1979), 3. Kermode extrapolates this idea from St. Mark's account of Jesus' explanation to the disciples of why he speaks in parables: "To you has been given the secret of the kingdom of God, but for those outside everything is in parables; so that they may indeed see but not perceive, and may indeed hear but not understand; lest they should turn again, and be forgiven" (4:11–12).

19. Charles Till Davis, *Dante and the Idea of Rome* (Oxford: Oxford Univ. Press, 1957), analyzes Dante's treatment of Rome and places it in the context of contemporary history. See also A. P. d'Entrèves, *Dante as a Political Thinker* (Oxford: Oxford Univ. Press, 1952).

20. Teodolinda Barolini, "Bertran de Born and Sordello: The Poetry of Politics in Dante's *Comedy*," *PMLA* 94 (1979): 395–405. See esp. 398–99, 401–3.

21. See Barolini, 402.

22. T. S. Eliot, "Dante," *Selected Essays* (New York: Harcourt, Brace & Co., 1950), 200–204. See Jewel Spears Brooker's fine discussion of Eliot's essay in "Common Ground and Collaboration in the Aesthetic of T. S. Eliot," *Centennial Review* 25 (Spring 1981): 225–38.

23. Pound, *Selected Letters, 1907–1941* (New York: New Directions, 1971), 323.

24. Pound, "Cavalcanti: Medievalism" (1934), *Literary Essays*, 149, 159. In an earlier essay, Pound reconciled his admiration for Dante's poetry with his impatience with his "orthodoxy" by noting Dante's "scant regard for the ecclesiastical lumber by which his philosophy is said by certain critics to be smothered," and by reading his Christian allegory as a "tremendous lyric" ("Dante," *The Spirit of Romance* [New York: New Directions, 1968], 146, 153).

25. See Barbara Melchiori, "Browning in Italy" in *Robert Browning*, ed. Armstrong, 168–83, for a discussion of "Browning's strongly prejudiced criticisms of the Catholic Church and of the Catholic religion" (177); and J. Hillis Miller, *The Disappearance of God: Five Nineteenth Century Writers* (Cambridge: Harvard Univ. Press, 1963), 81–156, for a discussion of Browning's as a protestant poetics.

26. Letter of February 4, 1856, to Fields, in Ian Jack, ed., 196.

27. Letter dated December 2, 1855, in David J. DeLaura, ed., "Ruskin and the Brownings: Twenty-five Unpublished Letters," *Bulletin of the John Rylands Library* 54 (1954): 326–27; cited in Betty S. Flowers, *Browning and the Modern Tradition* (London: Macmillan, 1976), 165.

28. Letter dated December 10, 1855, in W. G. Collingwood, ed., *The Life and Work of John Ruskin* (Boston: Houghton Mifflin, 1890), 1:232; cited in Flowers, 165.

29. See Robert Langbaum, *The Poetry of Experience: The Dramatic Monologue in Modern Literary Tradition* (London: Chatto & Windus, 1957), chaps. 2 and 3, for a discussion of the

dialectics of sympathy and judgment in the "relativist ethos" of Browning's poetics. Langbaum notes that "Browning's contemporaries accused him of 'perversity' because they found it necessary to sympathize with his reprehensible characters" (86). Langbaum studies Browning's poetics in the context of "Romanticism as a modern tradition" and thus does not relate the problem of reading the dramatic monologue to the specifically linguistic difficulty Browning builds into the form, or to its roots in the poetics of *Sordello*.

30. Hugh Kenner, *The Pound Era* (Berkeley: University of California Press, 1971), 469 n.

31. Ezra Pound, *Cantos LXXII & LXXIII* (Washington, D.C.: The Estate of Ezra Pound, 1973).

32. Walter Benjamin, "These on the Philosophy of History," *Illuminations*, ed. Hannah Arendt (New York: Harcourt, Brace & World, 1968), 256.

33. Roland Barthes, *Writing Degree Zero / Elements of Semiology*, trans. Annette Lavers and Colin Smith (Boston: Beacon, 1967), 48.

Genre and Poetic Authority in *Pippa Passes*

DAVID G. RIEDE

In a recent essay on "Victorian Poetic Genres" Avrom Fleishman argued that though Victorian poets were less overtly concerned with political issues than were their Romantic predecessors, and though they were apparently "the first of the moderns in putting themselves beyond politics," their formal experimentation indirectly reveals the complex relations in which they stood to the historical pressures of their time. Consequently, the Victorian "movement toward inventing new genres" ought to be understood as a "direct response to an historical situation and felt needs for personal standing-ground, rather than willed oppositions, either political or esthetic."[1] Fleishman's suggestions seem particularly apt for an understanding of Browning's early works, which rarely mention particular contemporary issues and which present themselves as a series of experiments in genre. In the first decade of his career, Browning attempted a quasi-Shelleyan Romantic "confessional" poem in *Pauline*, a Byronic closet drama in *Paracelsus*, a quasi-Shakespearian historical tragedy in *Strafford*, a wholly new form in his earliest dramatic lyrics, a bizarre form of epic narrative in *Sordello*, and an extraordinary medley of conventional drama, closet drama, narrative, and lyric in *Pippa Passes*. None of these works is overtly political in theme, but all of them formally reflect the historical uncertainties, the multitudinousness, of the early Victorian age, and they also formally imply a specifically political, in fact a specifically republican, critique of pretensions to authority. This is especially true of *Pippa Passes*, a poem apparently written in response to Browning's recognition, recorded in Book 3 of *Sordello*, that his art ought not to flatter the pretensions of the great, but to speak for the masses. As he described the incident in *Sordello* to Fanny Haworth, the "sad disheveled form" of an Italian peasant girl had been used to "typify and figure to myself Mankind, the whole poor-devildom one sees cuffed and huffed from morn to midnight, that, so typified, she may come at times and keep my pact in mind, prick up my republicanism and remind me of certain engagements I have entered into with myself about that same."[2] Though *Pippa Passes*, apparently written to fulfill this pact, hardly seems a particularly republican statement, it is republican in its generic experiments, in its formal concerns with the perni-

Reprinted from *Victorian Poetry* 27 (1989): 49–64, with permission.

cious effects of speaking to people in a seemingly authoritative voice, with the problems encountered when no authoritative voice is to be heard, and even with the problem of speaking for other people, the problem of demagoguery passing as representation. From this perspective, *Pippa Passes* can be seen as an extraordinary experiment in the politics of genre, an experiment that calls into question the moral authority of both lyric and drama.

The poems preceding *Pippa Passes* were explicitly concerned with what the speaker of *Pauline* self-mockingly calls "The vaunted influence poets have o'er men!" (l. 530). Though such influence, on the whole, is apparently to be desired, Browning hints even as early as *Pauline* that if achieved it could be tyrannical—though he foresees failure. Pauline's lover expresses an alarming ambition "to make / All bow enslaved" (ll. 543–544). Similarly Paracelsus, though he expresses a desire "To serve my race at once" (3.578), is characterized by his contempt for the rest of mankind, by a desire for knowledge which is power. And even though *Sordello* concludes with apparent contempt for the "sorry farce" (6.850) of its hero's ineffectual life, the poem as a whole seems to offer no very clear role for the poet in society. All of these poems, in short, consider what influence the poet may or may not have, and whether such influence is to be desired as a way to serve mankind, or to be feared as coercive and tyrannical.

The thematic concern with poetic authority is paralleled in Browning's highly self-conscious choices of genre. *Pauline*, for example, does not merely recapitulate the confessional mode, but problematizes it, calling into question the authority and value of the Romantic egotistical sublime. If *Pauline* were in the straightforward confessional mode that is generally assumed, one could hardly challenge John Stuart Mill's judgment that its author was morbidly self-conscious to the point of insanity—but the poem undercuts its arrogant speaker,[3] who is evidently a prototype of the lunatic speaker of "Porphyria's Lover," exhibiting the same destructive desire to be absolutely worshipped, to exercise absolute power and control. He longs for one worshipping look, "one look / As I might kill her and be loved the more" (ll. 901–902). But as Mill's response indicated, the dramatic undermining of the egotistical sublime could easily be mistaken for what it parodied, so when Browning next attempted to explore the moral issues raised by the quest for authoritative knowledge, he did so, in *Paracelsus*, within the Romantic genre of closet drama. The closet drama enabled Browning not only to maintain a distance from his central speaker, but also to introduce other speakers and other points of view, to reduce his central speaker to one voice among many. Further, the denial of clear authority to any one speaker resulted, as Browning saw, in ceding at least some authority to the reader:

> It is certain . . . that a work like mine depends more immediately on the intelligence and sympathy of the reader for its success—indeed were my scenes

stars it must be his co-operating fancy which, supplying all chasms, shall connect the scattered lights into one constellation—a Lyre or a Crown.
—Poems, 1:1030

The choice of genre insures that the poet-author will not make the same arrogant mistake as his poet-protagonists—he will not assume a position of authority and coercive rhetorical power, but will empower the reader to supply the chasms in his discourse. Further, as David Latané has observed, Browning's image is notable not only for its "insight into his rhetoric, but [his] 'constellation' is itself significant: the lyre or crown denotes the choice between song or power" that would become the central issue of *Sordello*.[4]

Sordello, indeed, seems a still more radical attempt to share the responsibility for making meaning with the reader, who must actively fill in the gaps left by the speaker: "what I supplied yourselves suggest, / What I leave bare yourselves can now invest" (5.623–624). These lines manifestly forego the authoritative, coercive role of the poet, and epitomize a sort of republican ideal of "brother's speech" (5.635), but they state only one position in the bewilderingly conflicted analysis in *Sordello* of the poet's role. Indeed, the poem opens with a plea for poetic faith in which the reader is not asked to share in the making of meaning, but to "Only believe me," (1.10), and the choice of narrative form is explicitly set forth as only a second best—resorted to because the poet fears his audience will not adequately understand if he adopts the best course, presenting Sordello

> By making speak, myself kept out of view,
> The very man as he was wont to do,
> And leaving you to say the rest for him.
> (1.15–17)

Consequently he takes the authoritative role of showman-teacher, "Motley on back and pointing-pole in hand" (1.30), and sets out to "play my puppets" (1.72). The passage about "brother's speech" only arises late in the poem, and is spoken not by the narrator, but by Sordello, who explicitly calls into question the narrator's mode of puppeteering. The puppet, in effect, arraigns the puppeteer, and according to the narrator, seems even to usurp his role: "Why, he writes *Sordello*!" (5.620). No matter who speaks in the poem, he seems to exceed his authority—Sordello would seem to be usurping the narrator's prerogative and, much more seriously, the narrator would seem to be appropriating Sordello's life for his own purposes. The difficulty has clear implications for Browning's choice of genre—to adopt a narrative mode is to stand pointing-pole in hand, superior to his puppets and to his audience both; to adopt a dramatic mode is to allow his puppets an autonomy that destroys any unified point of view. Moreover, the autonomy of the puppets is, of course, only apparent, and another problem that Browning faces in his early works is that to pretend to speak from within the consciousness of a speaker, to claim an impossible ideal of "negative capability," is to usurp the will and consciousness of that person entirely.

Such a concern might seem an exceeding delicacy of conscience, but in all of his early works Browning was attempting to depict, as he later said, "the incidents in the development of a soul: little else is worth study," yet he was well aware that no genuine access to another "soul" was possible.[5] His earliest attempts at dramatic lyrics make this point very clearly. In "Porphyria's Lover" the speaker himself attempts to enter into the consciousness of another, of Porphyria, but his appropriation of her consciousness reduces her to a mere puppet, figuratively at first, and then literally as he props up her murdered body. Such utter appropriation of another's consciousness, such desire to speak for another, is clearly insane, but of course Browning could not be unaware that he himself, claiming to speak from within the consciousness of the lunatic, was performing a similar act. As Richard Stein has recently pointed out, the dramatic genre here devised involves an appropriation of consciousness akin to "the model proposed by Michel Foucault; if we feel as if we are within the cell, we also seem to be peering into it with the intensity of a keeper."[6] Browning himself seems to have been conscious of the moral implications of the kind of penetrating gaze that Foucault has made a concern in our own age—throughout his career, those of his characters who claim to speak for others, to appropriate and control their consciousnesses, come in for harsh treatment. Clyde de L. Ryals points this out as a concern for Browning as early as *Pauline*,[7] but morally dubious claims to represent the thoughts and feelings of others are also examined in the Duke of Ferrara's representation of his Duchess, in Blougram's complacent account of Gigadibs' thoughts (ll. 34–44), and most especially in Mr. Sludge's claims to speak for the dead—claims that may have struck Browning as distressingly akin to his own.

The other major genre that Browning attempted in the decade preceding *Pippa Passes* was the drama, a genre in which any moral queasiness about speaking from the mouths of others would create serious problems. Nevertheless, in *Strafford*, his first attempt for the theater, he seems to have been content to accommodate himself to the traditional requirements of the genre, to take it on its own terms without much experimentation—though the play is at least passingly concerned with questions of who can legitimately speak for whom, as when Hampden chastises Vane for presuming to speak for Wentworth (Strafford): "Will you let him speak, / Or put your crude surmises in his mouth?"[8] But though Browning may at first have felt free to put his own surmises into the mouths of his historical personages, he must have been forced to reconsider the implications of doing so when he read the reviews. Herman Merivale, writing in *The Edinburgh Review*, not only argued that Browning was wrong to try to pluck out the heart of Strafford's mystery, but that he had grossly misrepresented the man, transforming the "bold, heady, and sagacious leader" into "a sort of monomaniac." In general, Merivale argued, "there would be little difficulty in showing how he has emasculated these vigorous characters—how what he affectedly calls 'the healthy natures of a great epoch,' have been rendered morbid, eccentric, *unnatural*; merely in order to produce those coarse effects of overstrained passion and sentiment which are necessary, we suppose, to please the historical taste of pit and gallery."[9] Merivale's arguments, of course, support the general post-Romantic literary separation of the essential human passions from historical contingency, and they may help us to understand why such attempts as Browning's to unite literature and history might have seemed questionable on both aesthetic and moral grounds. On aesthetic grounds, as Browning himself acknowledged, the attempt to represent the intricacies of a character's motivations had led him away from a clear and unified dramatic action. On moral grounds, it had led him to usurp the consciousness of another, to put his "crude surmises" into another's mouth, to impose if not to find what could be called a morbidly diseased consciousness. How, after all, could the author of *Strafford* be certain that his surmises about another's consciousness were any more legitimate than the surmises of Porphyria's lover?

By the time Browning came to write *Pippa Passes*, then, he had long been concerned to find a genre in which he could explore "incidents in the development of a soul" without engaging in morbid introspection, without bullying the reader with his pointing-pole, without tyrannically imposing his own consciousness on either his subject or his audience. Discussion of the genre of *Pippa Passes* has consisted for the most part of descriptions of its dramatic failure and defenses of its dramatic success, but it is better seen as a radical generic experiment that can hardly be called a drama at all—or if it is a drama, it is an uneasy cross between closet and conventional drama. The work consists of four disconnected scenes, interrupted by brief "talks by the way," and flanked by a hardly dramatic "Introduction" and "Epilogue." The unity of the work depends upon the passage of Pippa through each scene, singing a lyric that functions as a catalyst to action—but Pippa is, in these scenes, less a character than a disembodied lyric voice, so that in this strange medley of genres dramatic action seems to be dependent on the provocation of lyric. There is no central dramatic action at all, no semblance of Aristotelian plot, and even the sequence of scenes is strikingly anti-climactic as drama—scene I, between Ottima and Sebald, comes far closer to meeting the theatrical requirements of sharply delineated characters and issues than any of the subsequent scenes, and the close of the play, Pippa alone in her room inconclusively summing up, has no dramatic potential at all.[10] Browning, however, was not merely subverting conventional dramatic form, but devising an experiment in decentered form. He was, that is, devising a genre appropriate to a multitudinous age with no stable, central truths.

Yet although recent critics have begun to see the lack of an authoritative center in *Pippa Passes*, the traditional reading of the work has been just the reverse. Pippa has traditionally been taken as a bona fide messenger from God, and her songs have been regarded as morally regenerative, and spiritually authoritative. As Browning's friend John Forster said in an early review, "Whomever she passes, she cannot but do good to—opening generous hopes, suggesting cheerful thoughts, awakening virtuous impulses." Browning himself told Edmund Gosse that Pippa symbolized "the unconscious messenger of good spiritual tidings to so many souls in dark places."[11] From this perspective the work would seem almost exaggeratedly centered—indeed, the multiplicity of perspectives characteristic of dramatic form would be transcended by the monologic authority of the lyric voice. However multitudinous and confused the modern world may be, clear moral imperatives remain, and are transmitted through the unwitting innocence of the child, and the intuitive mode of lyric. Since Pippa's songs do unarguably have an immediate and decisive effect on the other characters, even some of the best recent readings argue that *Pippa Passes*—far from being an experiment in decentered form—is an experiment in cutting through the indeterminacies of a multitudinous world. Jacob Korg, for example, has argued that although "the world of *Pippa Passes* is a cryptogram" in which "its people cannot read the book of their experiences," Pippa can bring about meaningful resolutions "because her divine simplicity has the power to cut through any knot without undoing it."[12] And Herbert Tucker has suggested that Browning deliberately worked against the "current of his dominant creative impulse" in *Pippa Passes*, creating situations in which "psychological tangles of Gordian intricacy . . . receive sudden clarification, with the flash of a decisive judgment."[13]

To see Pippa as the authoritative moral center of the work is certainly tempting, especially since such a reading would seem to confirm the poem as an experiment in republican genre. As one earlier reviewer saw it, Pippa's moral authority enforces the message "which it were well the poor should learn,—and still better that the rich should ponder,—that the meanest of them all has his appointed value in God's scheme,—and a higher part may be cast to him who has to play it in rags, than to the puppet of the drama who enacts king, and walks the stage in purple. This despised little silk-weaver, like a messenger from God, knocks at the hearts of all these persons who seem to her so privileged,—and the proudest of them all opens to her."[14] Of course, this reading is consistent with the general Victorian notion that innocent women and children, uncorrupted by the world, are closer to God than worldly men, and may be channels for his benevolent messages, and is also consistent with Browning's avowed republican commitment in Book 3 of *Sordello*, where he had implied he would no longer allow "Sordello's Will" to "be queen to me," but would cede regal authority to the peasant girl, "make / A queen of her" (3.680–681, 689–690). Given God's own authority in the poem, Pippa would indeed "play a higher part" than "the puppet of the drama who enacts king."

Such a reading is finally more sentimental than republican, and hinges on acceptance of Pippa's authority, and particularly on acceptance of the truth of her New Year's hymn:

> All service ranks the same with God:
> If now, as formerly he trod
> Paradise, his presence fills
> Our earth, each only as God wills
> Can work—God's puppets, best and worst,
> Are we; there is no last nor first.
> —"Introduction," ll. 190–195

As Tucker notes, however, much depends upon this "if," which "deserves emphasis as a sign of the hypothetical experimental mode within which Browning has chosen to work" (p. 123). Indeed, if God's presence fills heaven and earth, and if it overflows in Pippa's song, the traditional reading of the work and of Pippa's lyric authority inevitably follows. And to be sure, Pippa does seem to be a channel for God's voice, a virtual embodiment of God's presence on this earth. Throughout the work she is associated with the break of day that she salutes in the opening lines, the sunrise that "grew gold" and, like God's presence, "overflowed the world" ("Introduction," l. 12). In Part I, for example, her song seems to restore moral value and truth to characters who had fallen so deeply into guilt that they were unable to see God's light, literally unable to say whether it was day or night. Indeed, before Pippa's passing the dialogue of fallen perception between the adulterous murderers Ottima and Sebald seems at times almost theater of the absurd as they try to get hold of truth in a world without God's presence. Sebald's song affirms it to be night, but Ottima challenges him: "Night? . . . We call such light the morning" (I.1–6). But to Ottima's comments on "the clear morning," Sebald responds "Morning? / It seems to me a night with a sun added. / Where's dew, where's freshness?" (I.28–33). Even after desperate attempts to achieve a complete objectivity, Sebald remains bewildered: "Off, off—take your hands off mine, / 'Tis the hot evening—off! oh, morning is it?" (I.113–114). The point of this dialogue would seem to be the extreme subjectivity of perception in a fallen world, a world without God's truth, and it would further seem that Pippa's song restores the morning, the dew and freshness, to this world by restoring God's presence:

> The year's at the spring
> And day's at the morn;
> Morning's at seven;
> The hill-side's dew-pearled;
> The lark's on the wing;
> The snail's on the thorn:

> God's in his heaven—
> All's right with the world!
> (I.221–228)

Sebald, at any rate, takes this as definitive: "That little peasant's voice / Has righted all again" (I.261–262). But though he claims cleansed perceptions now that God's in his heaven, he ends by threatening suicide, and his closing words suggest not lucidity but insanity:

> My brain is drowned now—quite drowned: all I feel
> Is . . . is, at swift-recurring intervals,
> A hurry-down within me, as of waters
> Loosened to smother up some ghastly pit:
> There they go—whirls from a black fiery sea!
> (I.277–281)

Pippa's effects in other scenes are equally problematic. Jules makes the noble choice to stay with Phene, but far from thinking he has heard God's voice in Pippa's song, he still longs "to hear / God's voice plain," and deludes himself with the notion that he had heard it previously, "before / They broke in with their laughter!" (II.303–305). In Part III, Pippa's song seems to bring back "the morning of the world / When earth was nigher heaven than now" (III.165–166) and helps to convince Luigi of his vocation as an assassin: "'Tis God's voice calls" (III.229). But it has been reasonably argued that his decision to commit a political murder even though he cannot articulate the reasons for it is at best morally dubious.[15] Arguably, at least, Luigi's enlightenment is, as his mother had suggested, only that of "a short-sighted man who sees naught midway / His body and the sun above" (III.128–129). Finally, even the Monsignor's sudden action may not signify a moral triumph—as E. Warwick Slinn and Ryals have both noted, his decision to gag Maffeo may well arise from a desire to forestall his public declaration of distressing facts (Slinn, p. 30; Ryals, p. 130). Evidently, though Pippa's songs may cut through the entanglements of the various scenes to bring about a crisis, the cutting of Gordian knots leaves a great many loose ends— the closure achieved in these scenes is not as complete and satisfying as the traditional readings have suggested.

There are other reasons to doubt Pippa's authority—her much quoted apostrophe to the sunbeam reflected and fragmented in her basin suggests that she has no more ability to see the pure white light of God's presence than anyone else:

> up, up, fleet your brilliant bits
> Wheeling and counterwheeling,
> Reeling, broken beyond healing:

> Now grow together on the ceiling!
> That will task your wits.
> —"Introduction," ll. 78–82

Throughout the play, such energetic descriptions of the sunshine as Pippa's (and Sebald's) tend to confirm the comment made by Paracelsus that "God's intimations rather fail / In clearness than in energy" (III.599–600). Further, to the very limited extent that Pippa is characterized at all, she seems to be morally compromised. Jacob Korg, who calls her "a favorite of God," is obliged to admit that her limited characterization demonstrates her "fallible humanity and her incapacity for doing good intentionally," so that "she is irrelevant, as a person, to the purposes she serves" (pp. 9, 17). Tucker observes that Pippa's "innocence is scarcely presentable," that Browning could present her at length in the "Introduction" "only by compromising her innocence to the extent of involving her in a primitive psychological economy" (p. 124). If Pippa is human at all, there is no reason to consider her any less fallible than the other characters in the play, no reason to assume that she speaks with the authority of God, or even with the authority of Browning.

Moreover, the other characters do not take Pippa's songs as authoritative revelations: they act on misrepresentations of these songs rather than on what they actually say. In this respect the work is rather like Arnold's somewhat later *Empedocles on Etna*, in which Empedocles consistently misinterprets Callicles' songs, persistently and wrongly hearing them as confirmations of his own point of view. The characters in *Pippa Passes* are not in fact transformed by Pippa's songs—each character accepts Pippa's song as somehow authoritative, but interprets it in such a way as to authorize his own limited and self-aggrandizing selfhood. In fact, the persistent misinterpretations of Pippa's songs may constitute an ironic commentary on Browning's occasional desire to cede the power of creative interpretation to his readers. The "cooperating fancy" may "connect the scattered lights into one constellation," but the result is not a dialectic collaboration between singer and auditor—it is simply a misreading that confirms the auditor's own narrow egotism. Sebald confirms his sense of honor, Jules his sense of power to assimilate and appropriate all things "through aesthetic transformations," Luigi his sense of noble idealism, and the Monsignor his sense of profound identification with the interests of the Church.[16] The responses to Pippa's songs, then, far from revealing the entrance of truth into the world, reveal the extreme subjectivity of perception—the apprehension, or rather misapprehension—of words and events as they are refracted through idiosyncratic consciousnesses. As Slinn has said, once we doubt Pippa's authority, the poem can no longer be read as a "parable about a moral universe supervised by God," and it becomes apparent that "the structure of *Pippa Passes* emphasizes the multitudinousness of life, which is more the raw material for irony than for theological optimism" (p. 20).

The irony revolves around the complex play with the symbolism of queens and puppets in the work. The crucial passage, of course, is Pippa's New Year's hymn, sung in the "Introduction" and recapitulated in an abbreviated version as a seemingly authoritative conclusion to the whole:

> All service ranks the same with God—
> With God, whose puppets, best and worst,
> Are we, there is no last nor first.
> (—"Epilogue," ll. 113–115)

If the hymn is indeed authoritative, the play offers a certain republican leveling, but it also reduces the characters to automata, and becomes, Slinn notes, an ironic representation of the "appearance of free egos in a deterministic universe" (p. 21). But again, much depends upon that "*if*" that has been elided in the final version of the hymn: *if* God's "presence fills / Our earth, each only as God will / Can work." If God's presence does not fill the earth, or at least does not fill it in any decipherable way, the characters may remain puppets, but not unambiguously God's puppets. Luigi, for example, may think himself an instrument of God's will, but like the "short-sighted man" who "sees naught midway / His body and the sun above," he fails to see that his strings are being pulled not by God—at least not directly by God—but by political writers characterized by his mother as demagogues. Further, if the various characters are not transformed, but only confirmed in their idiosyncrasies by Pippa's songs, they are the puppets of their own limited and deluded wills, particularly of their egocentric tendencies to interpret random lyrics as divine validation of their own wills. In this respect Browning's generic experiment should be seen not only as a critique of the presumption of the lyric voice to speak with divine authority, but as a critique of the readers who are willfully deluded by such a claim.

If, however, God is not the puppet master in this play, the ultimate puppeteer is the author. The analogy of the author to a puppet master is not uncommon in literature, and is not generally regarded as terribly problematic, but Browning's earlier works, as I have suggested, show that he was somewhat troubled by the claim of superiority implicit in the image. In *Pippa Passes*, of course, Pippa's prominent description of God as puppet master makes the author's puppeteering all the more suspect, his implicit claims of authoritative control all the more worrisome. The author who puts others into action, for example, is glanced at in writer A and writer B, who incite Luigi to an assassination. Indeed, Browning's evident doubts about the moral status of manipulating others with words may indicate why he, at least, did not attempt, like his Romantic predecessors, to write directly political verse.[17] Early Victorian writers may have avoided political incitement because the dangerous consequences of demagoguery were too evident in the still recent French Revolution and in continuing English fears of domestic unrest. In *Pippa Passes*, to be sure, the situations and characters are fictional, and Browning was not reducing actual people to puppets, or in any way stirring emotions about actual people, but it is precisely such fictionality that enabled him to explore the pernicious nature of any claims of authority.

In one way or another, every scene reflects Browning's interest in the dangers of playing puppet master. In Part I, the manipulative power of impassioned language is looked at in the extraordinary crescendo that precedes Pippa's passing:

> OTTIMA: Crown me your queen, your spirit's arbitress,
> Magnificent in sin. Say that!
> SEBALD: I crown you
> My great white queen, my spirit's arbitress,
> Magnificent . . .
>
> (I.217–220)

Ottima temporarily makes a puppet of Sebald, and more explicitly than anywhere else in the play shows the moral arrogance of putting words into someone else's mouth. Pippa's passing undoes Ottima's work, but only by putting yet another person's words into Sebald's mouth, for he immediately repeats her phrase, "God's in his heaven!," and takes its authority to reduce Ottima to a puppet, speaking of her as a mere object for the remainder of the scene. In Part IV, the difficulty of making puppets of others is emphasized—the Monsignor has brought forth his Intendant to force a confession, and is quite sure he will speak the right words, tell "the old story" (IV.134–135). But the puppet is rebellious: "So old a story, and tell it no better?" (IV.139). The Intendant has indeed been a puppet of sorts, the tool of the Monsignor's evil brother, but he has never been as easy to manipulate as his masters have supposed: "When did such an instrument ever produce such an effect?" (IV.139–140). The Intendant may be an instrument, but he is "not fool enough to put himself in his employer's power so thoroughly" (IV.141–142). Here and elsewhere in the work, Browning reverted to the problem he had glanced at in *Sordello*—the manipulation of others is no easy matter, and in the end the puppet may arraign the puppeteer. As Tucker has argued in a somewhat different context, "in spite of the overdetermination of the play's fable," some of the characters "assume a life of their own": "God's puppets exhibit an independent activity" (p. 127). But the liveliness of the puppets implies that the fable is not, in fact, as overdetermined as it would seem if we were to accept Pippa's account of the providential scheme. The unpredictability of the characters, their seeming autonomy, reflects

Browning's sense of the difficulties involved in manipulating people who refuse to become puppets.

The most complex parallel in the play to Browning's own role as puppet master is to be found in Part II, the episode in which Jules weds Phene, discovers she is not what she had seemed, and finally accepts her anyway. Jules is an artist, and like the author of *Sordello*, he has found a peasant girl, and chosen to "make / A queen of her." He has carved her, as he "imagined her"—as Hippolyta, a queen (II.54)—and in another sculpture he has "laboured to express [her] thought," as though anyone could fully express the thought of another. But Phene is more puppet than queen—her supposed thought is the invention of Lutwyche and the other students who have made her their instrument. Indeed, Phene is an obvious puppet in the work, a model appropriated as the subject of others' imaginings and art, and a mere mouthpiece for the words of the plotting students. But like the Intendant, she complicates matters by resisting such control—she speaks the lines, but only after revealing the plot to Jules. Yet it can hardly be said that she utterly resists being appropriated by others, for though Jules seems to take her as his queen, his spirit's arbitress, he actually makes a puppet of her. She almost seems one of his statues as he wonders "Where must I place you" among the others (II.16), and characterizes her as "like my very life's-stuff, marble—marbly / Even to the silence!" (II.80–81). He even, like the students, puts words into her mouth: "Read this line . . . no, shame—Homer's be the Greek / First breathed me from the lips of my Greek girl!" (II.41–42). And moments later he again says "But you must say a 'well' to that—say 'well!' " (II.78). Jules does not pause to let Phene obey these commands, but she nevertheless fails to be an effective puppet for the students only because she has been appropriated by Jules. She cannot at first speak their speech only because she cannot get Jules's speech out of her mind: "I shall find it presently / Far back here, in the brain yourself filled up" (II.146–147). When she finally does attempt to recite the speech, she mistakenly begins with the first words of Jules's speech to her (though she substitutes the word "love" for her own name): " 'Do not die, love! I am yours' " (II.177). When Jules finally chooses to accept Phene after hearing Pippa's song, he is merely, as Slinn has said, reinforcing the tendency he has already shown to appropriate her body and soul. But now he need no longer pretend she is queen to him, but boldly affirms that he will be queen to her:

>   If whoever loves
> Must be, in some sort, god or worshipper,
> The blessing or the blest one, queen or page,
> Why should we always choose the page's part?
> Here is a woman with utter need of me,—
> I find myself queen here, it seems!
>   (II.282–287)

But of course he has been "queen" all along—he has, as he now recognizes, "created" Phene, filled the "unshaped stuff" of her unformed being with a

> new soul
> Like my own Psyche,—fresh upon her lips
> Alit, the visionary butterfly,
> Waiting my word to enter and make bright,
> Or flutter off and leave all blank as first.
> This body had no soul before . . .
> . . . .
> Now, it will wake, feel, live—or die again!
> Shall to produce form out of unshaped stuff
> Be Art—and further, to evoke a soul
> From form be nothing? This new soul is mine!
> (II.288–300)

The imperial gesture of the last line only emphasizes the underlying point of the entire scene—the artist who claims to enter into the spirit of another, to be inspired by another and express her thoughts, is self-deluded. He is more likely to be imposing his own will on the other, making her a puppet. The episode clearly draws heavily on the myth of Pygmalion, suggesting that the artist who claims to be a soul-maker has only fallen in love with his own powers.

The parallels to Browning's own art are obvious. In *Pippa Passes* he seemingly made the peasant-girl queen, in terms of the apparent authority of her message, but actually made her the ultimate puppet of the play. To the extent that she is characterized at all, she reveals that she would like to see herself as a queen, and she reinforces the dubious notion that human relations must be described as a sort of power game in which one either worships or is worshipped, is either queen or puppet. Pippa wants to appropriate the happiness of the "Happiest Four" in Asolo, to be Ottima, Phene, Luigi, and the Monsignor, but of course she fails in this, and only manages to claim the worship of a flower: "I am queen of thee, floweret! . . . Love thy queen, worship me!" ("Introduction," ll. 95, 103). The lines are a sort of anticipatory parody of the aspirations of other would-be queens in the play and hint at the absurdity of puppets presuming to power. Pippa's status as a puppet within the plot of the play is clear—she has been deprived of her true identity as the rightful heir of vast wealth, has become the instrument of the Intendant, and, like Phene, she is to be appropriated also by the sordid students, betrayed into the squalid instrumentality of prostitution.

Pippa is the ultimate puppet in the play in terms of Browning's experiment in genre. She thinks she is God's puppet, but her mere instrumentality in the extreme artifice of the play makes it clear that she is in fact the author's puppet. She is repeatedly trotted out as a sort of regina ex machina to bring scenes to a climax; she is the string that moves the other puppets. Her lack of more than superficial characterization further signifies her mere instrumentality. She can hardly be said to have her own voice at all—the songs she sings, of course, are not of her own devising, and even when she speaks in her "own" voice in the "Introduction" and "Epilogue" she sounds far more like the author of *Sordello* than an adolescent silk-weaver. To the extent, then, that Pippa's lyric voice exercises power in this work, it is a power delegated by the author, the poet who fills the void of meaning if God's presence does not fill the world. That Browning was self-consciously examining this assumption of authority is evident not only by the attention he calls to such issues elsewhere in the play, but also by comparison to the exploration of similar concerns in *Sordello*. There the poet, in the absence of "External power" determines to "stand forth ordained . . . / Himself a law to his own sphere" (6.111–113), to speak to and for the people. But his gesture is strikingly demagogic: "The People were himself" (6.120). The parallel to *Pippa Passes* becomes evident when Sordello's egotism is conflated with a notion of service almost identical to Pippa's affirmation that "All service ranks the same with God: / If now, as formerly he trod / Paradise." For Sordello, when external power is lacking and God's authority is not evident, "All is himself; all service, therefore, rates / Alike" (6.127–128). In fact, Browning had made the point about the arrogance of the poet who mistakes the service of his own ego for the service of God as early as Paracelsus, when Festus had upbraided Paracelsus: "God's service is established here / As he determines fit, and not your way, / And this you cannot brook" (4.578–580).

Tucker is right to describe *Pippa Passes* as an experiment in genre that examines what happens if an authoritative voice is introduced into a drama to force closure. In this case the experiment seems to privilege lyric, as though to accept the romantic idea, later endorsed in Browning's essay on Shelley, that the lyric or subjective poet represents, at least partially, "not what man sees, but what God sees."[18] But Browning is also offering an implicit critique of lyric authority. As Ryals puts it, the presumed power of the disembodied lyric voice puts the poet "at a monologic remove from his listeners, exercising power over them but abnegating his obligation to love them and hence help them advance in the business of soul-making" (p. 137). Slinn, similarly, argues that "the source of Browning's success in the play lies rather in the ironies of the egotistical sublime than in negative capability. If Pippa as a singer of songs is to symbolize poetic creation, then Browning is well aware of the interfering ego in both artist and audience" (p. 33). I would go still further, and suggest that the parallels of the Sordello episode and, within the play, of the Jules-Phene episode, indicate that Browning had serious reservations about the notion that even love, or what passes for it, can help others in the "business of soul-making." J. Hillis Miller has said that Browning's aesthetics justifies the poet's appropriation of other souls only by affirming that the poet "has a commission from God," but *Pippa Passes* calls into question the whole basis of Browning's art by asking what happens if God's presence does not underlie the poet's power. In such a case the violence of language Miller uses to describe Browning's art of imitation would be fully justified: Browning "batter[s] his way to the secret center of the life of others." As Miller's language also suggests, the poet's assumption of divine right is not only theologically presumptuous, but implies also a kind of imaginative and cultural imperialism: "Like a world-conqueror moving from city to city, he goes with the utmost rapidity from man to man, always hungry to make new conquests, for his aim is to possess the whole creation."[19] Browning's experimental mode, however, indicates that at least early in his career he had serious reservations about the assumption of such power and authority. *Pippa Passes* undermines both the lyric (egotistical sublime) and the dramatic (negative capability), implying that both involve an illegitimate assumption of quasi-divine power. Further, in its presentation both of characters who present themselves as "queens" and of characters who submit to be "puppets" the work criticizes both presumptuous authors and submissive audiences.

Pippa Passes, then, is an experimental examination of both lyric authority and dramatic impersonation in a society without clear moral certainties. The lyric voice of Pippa foregrounds claims to divinely inspired truth, and the dramatic scenes hide the author behind his characters, but not completely enough to conceal the manipulations of the puppet master. In consequence the decentered form self-deconstructs in its ironic undermining of all seeming sources of authority. Indeed, it seems almost to have foreseen some elements of modern deconstruction by depicting the consequences of doing without a metaphysics of presence. The play examines what happens if God's "presence fills / Our earth," but it also examines the reverse, what happens if God's presence does not fill our earth. As an experiment in genre, the play does, as Fleishman would have it, inevitably reflect the historical mood of its time in its multitudinousness, its lack of a central authoritative truth. But it has more specific political implications as well. Written at a time when political reform and mass agitation were the dominant public issues, *Pippa Passes* examines the presumptions of autocratic authority in its representation of the authoritative lyric, and of demagogic claims to speak for the people in its dramatic enactments. *Pippa Passes* calls into question, that is, what it means to represent people at all, what it is to represent them aesthetically, and, by implication, what it is to claim to represent them politically.

Notes

1. "Notes for a History of Victorian Poetic Genres," *Genre* 18 (1985): 365, 373.
2. *The Browning Correspondence*, ed. Philip Kelley and Ronald Hudson (Winfield, Kansas, 1984–), 4:269.

3. For a fuller argument along these lines, see Clyde de L. Ryals, *Becoming Browning: The Poems and Plays of Robert Browning, 1833–1846* (Columbus, Ohio, 1983), pp. 9–30.

4. David E. Latané, Jr., *Browning's Sordello and the Aesthetics of Difficulty* (Victoria, Canada, 1987), p. 44.

5. See the prefatory letter to the 1863 publication of *Sordello*, in *Poems*, 1:150.

6. Richard L. Stein, *Victoria's Year: English Literature and Culture, 1837–1838* (New York, 1987), p. 33.

7. "Soul-making . . . involves us in a moral problem. For the self is restless and aggressive in its attempts to increase the soul's wealth. As it encounters the not-self, it may be overcome and thus live only as a reflection of the object encountered; or it may attempt to absorb the not-self into its own orbit of value, thereby robbing the not-self of its freedom and distinctiveness. In the case of human encounter, the will of the one violates the will of the other. Considered morally, action of this sort must be condemned. Yet if the self does not engage in such activity, the soul can never grow; which is to say, the self can never be a soul—a moral entity—unless it engage in immoral conduct. It is a paradoxical situation, the self being damned if it does, damned if it doesn't. The dialectic of self and other is the basic theme of *Pauline*, and the ironies that it entails are heavily informative of the early verse" (Ryals, p. 11).

8. *The Complete Poetic and Dramatic Works of Robert Browning*, ed. Horace E. Scudder (Boston, 1895), p. 51.

9. Herman Merivale, *The Edinburgh Review*, July 1837, pp. 132–151; reprinted in *The Browning's Correspondence*, 3:411.

10. For a discussion of the dramatic failings of the play, see Terry Otten, *The Deserted Stage: The Search for Dramatic Form in Nineteenth-Century England* (Athens, Ohio, 1972), pp. 122–140.

11. Forster's review appeared in *The Examiner*, October 2, 1841, and is reprinted in *The Browning Correspondence*, 5:399. Browning's comment to Gosse is quoted by J. M. Purcell, "The Dramatic Failure of *Pippa Passes*," *SP* 36 (1939): 85.

12. Jacob Korg, "A Reading of *Pippa Passes*," *VP* 6 (1968): 8.

13. Herbert Tucker, *Browning's Beginnings* (Minneapolis, 1980), p. 122.

14. Review in *The Athenaeum*, December 11, 1841, p. 952. Reprinted in *The Brownings' Correspondence*, 5:399–400.

15. Dale Kramer observes, for example, that "Luigi's bravado and his disregard for life are based more on egoism and youthful love of glory than on a reasonable, if not reasoned, basis that Browning could respect, however much he might sympathize with the cause of Italian freedom." "Character and Theme in *Pippa Passes*," *VP* 2 (1964): 247. See also E. Warwick Slinn, *Browning and the Fictions of Identity* (London, 1982), p. 29, and Ryals, pp. 127–128.

16. See Slinn, pp. 24, 28, 29, 30.

17. In the late poem "Why I Am a Liberal" Browning commented explicitly on these issues, praising liberty of thought and, with a rhetorical question, indicating why he did not write directly of political questions, even of a "brother's right to freedom": "If fetters, not a few, / Of prejudice, convention, fall from me, / These shall I bid men—each in his degree / God-guided—bear, and gaily too?" (*Poems*, 2:966).

18. *The Complete Poetic and Dramatic Works*, p. 1009.

19. J. Hillis Miller, *The Disappearance of God: Five Nineteenth-Century Writers* (Cambridge, Massachusetts, 1963), pp. 113, 118, 124–125.

Browning and the Primitive

Dorothy Mermin

One of the central organizing principles in Robert Browning's late poems—those written after *The Ring and the Book* and published from 1871 to 1890—is the opposition of primitive and modern, savage and civilized, nature and culture. Many of these poems form part of the great intellectual movement that had gathered strength in the preceding decade and was producing the beginnings of modern anthropology, best represented by Edward Tylor's *Primitive Culture* (1871), the developmental theories of myth inaugurated by Andrew Lang's attack on Max Müller in 1873, and the new approach to classical literature that culminated in *The Golden Bough*. Books on such subjects were numerous and extensively reviewed. Periodicals were filled with essays on exotic tribes and customs, contemporary superstitions, witchcraft, ghosts, myth, and folklore, as the Romantic interest in such matters developed in Britain by Sir Walter Scott, Thomas Percy, and others converged with more extensive and more scientific concerns. The Governor Eyre controversy of the late sixties, the Ashanti war of the early seventies, and many other matters of Empire brought alien cultures to the attention of the British and made attitudes towards them matters of significant practical consequence. Browning's poems reflect the intellectual trend of these decades with great precision. He shared the common attitude of mixed horror, contempt, and fascination, and his poems presuppose the evolutionary view that became current in the seventies: that primitive peoples and barbaric myths represent early rather than degenerate stages in the cultural development of the human race, and furthermore that fragments of primitive thought and behavior survive in higher cultures—even in modern England.[1]

I

Browning's interest in the primitive, like that of the intellectual world in general, developed over a long period of time and not always in the same direction. His earliest published works linked poetry to old notions of the

Reprinted from *Victorian Studies* 25 (1982): 211–239. Reprinted by permission of *Victorian Studies* and the Indiana University Board of Trustees.

occult, particularly the resuscitation of the dead—an idea that recurs in *The Ring and the Book* and provides a curious running link between Browning and spiritualism.[2] He also celebrated the noble savage: *Luria* is a play about a Moorish hero who ironically calls himself a "savage" (Act 3, 351, 353, 398), and brings "New feeling fresh from God" (Act 5, 265) to the crafty, overcivilized Florentines whose treachery causes his death. Pippa, the duke's last duchess, and Pompilia are Luria's female counterparts, figures of spontaneous insight and intuitive goodness; the Italian villains, in contrast, are the corrupt heirs of a highly sophisticated society, sometimes brutes but never savages: even Count Guido at bottom is not a primitive but a wolf. But Bishop Blougram in *Men and Women* (1855) had cited "cosmogony, / Geology, ethnology, what not" ("Bishop Blougram's Apology," [679–680]) as the sciences that worked against faith in the Bible—he had read in "a French book" (probably by Balzac) that "Philosophers" trace the idea of chastity to the behavior of savages with clubs (825–833). "Caliban Upon Setebos" in *Dramatis Personae* (1864) is an extensive study of primitive thought in relation to modern religious controversy; Huxley was reported to have said in a lecture "that it seemed to him a scientific representation of the development of such [religious] ideas in primitive man."[3] Two other poems from *Dramatis Personae*, "Mr. Sludge, the Medium" and "Gold Hair," also bring together primitive materials and religious topics. In *The Ring and the Book* (1868–69), however, the subject does not appear at all, and when Browning turns to it again in the later poems he uses it to chart murkier, less clearly defined depths of thought and feeling. The idea of the primitive appears directly in the late poems set in parts of rural France where druid monuments and traditions still survive; in pictures of contemporary life such as *The Inn Album* and "Bad Dreams," in which highly cultivated characters show that under stress their mode of thinking reverts to the level of savages; and in all the late poems on classical subjects. It also appears more generally as a sense of the opacity of individual souls and the dark roots of human civilization; like Freud, Browning objectifies the unconscious as mythic prehistory, which he sees as the arena of violence, superstition, and fierce sexuality.

Insofar as Browning's ideas may derive from the anthropologists' (rather than simply representing a concurrent development in the same wide intellectual stream), they probably reflect reading in periodicals. After returning to London from Italy in 1861 Browning became an assiduous reader of journals, going regularly to his club to see them. Our knowledge of his reading in these years however is scanty and comes largely from his poems; *La Saisiaz*, for instance, directs us fairly clearly (lines 163–164) to a series of essays in *The Nineteenth Century*. And the poems can be misleading when they suggest specific influence: Browning writes firmly and plausibly about evolution, but a letter inadvertently makes it clear that he had not read Darwin's books.[4] Tylor's subjects, like Darwin's, were unavoidably part of the intellectual atmosphere, available for anyone who was interested. The poems show that whatever obscure forces impelled John Lubbock, James Frazer, Tylor, and Lang and brought them their avid readers were at work in Browning too.

In one area related to primitive thought, however, we have extensive documentation of Browning's views. It was easy to find primitive survivals among peasants or the potentially violent masses, but more sophisticated English people were most often accused of thinking like savages when they practised spiritualism, which figures prominently in Tylor's *Primitive Culture* as an example of the survival of witchcraft.[5] Spiritualism was a matter of acute personal interest to Browning. His wife's belief in it still irritated him long after her death; he never mentioned it without exasperation and said he wished he could burn all her letters about it.[6] He detested the people who duped her and was at best contemptuous of others who were deluded. He thought, characteristically, in terms of psychological self-awareness: "The difference between me and the stupid people who have 'communications' is probably nothing more than that I don't confound the results of the natural working of what is in my mind, with vulgar external appearances" (McAleer, *Dearest Isa*, p. 201).[7] The Brownings' friends in Italy had encompassed a wide range of involvement in spiritualism and related phenomena. The spirits that communicated with Elizabeth Barrett Browning's high-minded circles were bland and innocuous, sometimes comically foolish, but fascination with the occult and other primitive phenomena often touched murky depths. Seymour Kirkup, whose credulity Barrett Browning herself thought rather silly, owned a library "famous for its assemblage of works on Demonology, Witchcraft, Alchemy, Astrology, Table-Turning, and other occult sciences."[8] William Wetmore Story, whom Browning liked and respected, also frequented spiritualist circles and wrote an essay on "The Evil Eye and other Superstitions," a long and apparently pointless catalogue of malice, fear, and error that he himself seems to have found somewhat unaccountable: "The subject of this essay, unprofitable as it may seem to many, aroused my interest and curiosity, and for several years I hunted it down from library to library." He hunted it with greatest success in Siena, where he and Browning walked and talked together daily; Browning corrected the proofs in 1863 and contributed at least one item from his own reading.[9] Both Story's collection of materials and the persistence with which he collected them were signs of the times that would have fed Browning's interest in the "natural workings" of the human mind; the "stupid" self-deception of his wife and so many of their friends, and their refusal to listen to reason—his reason— must have brought vividly home to him the obstinate persistence of primitive thinking.

When the Victorians looked at primitive culture as an object for study (and not as unconscious participants) they seem to have been fascinated chiefly by the examples of bizarre beliefs and savage behavior which both professional scholars and obsessed amateurs like Story provided in abundance. The evolutionary theory of cultural development could make such examples into matter for self-congratulation; thus although Sir John Lubbock apologizes in the preface to *The Origin of Civilization* (1870) for the distasteful material he finds it necessary to include, he can offer his readers as compensation the satisfaction of seeing how far the human race has progressed.[10] But such confident detachment does not really go well with the idea that the primitive represents, so to speak, the childhood of the race; Victorian autobiographers, after all, turned first to their own childhoods in the search for themselves. Henry Rowley, writing about contemporary Africa in the *Cornhill Magazine* in 1873, articulates the shock which awaited readers of ethnography and related subjects in the second half of the nineteenth century: "Nothing more astonishes an inexperienced traveller than the discovery that in all men, differ how much so ever they may in outward circumstances or acquired habits, our race still preserves its social character; that there are the same instincts, the same natural feelings . . . with the most degraded equally with the highest. . . ."[11] At least for amateurs and poets, ethnography was a form of self-confrontation through which they could see in their own apparent opposites images from prehistory of what might still be hidden within themselves. In Browning's late poems, this is what the primitive represents: on the one hand, dark psychic forces that civilization may conceal but has not eradicated; and on the other, the roots of human consciousness, and perhaps of poetry. Essentially the Victorian interest in the primitive is the idea of evolution, or progress, turned on its head to become an obsession with origins. The origin is both that which one must leave behind, in order to progress, and that which explains the nature of whatever derives from it; thus to most people the proposition that people descended from apelike creatures irresistibly meant that they *are* apelike creatures. To Browning the primitive suggested both innate savagery and, more disturbingly and excitingly, savage origins for poetry.[12]

The later poems tend to associate impulse and intuition with crude savagery rather than with virtue as the earlier ones did and repeatedly show the necessity for cultivation and reason as curbs on instinct. The formal concomitant of this shift in emphasis is that the late poems are essentially narrative rather than dramatic: instead of revealing character in a flash of certainty as the earlier poems do—as even *The Ring and the Book* does—they show the difficulty of knowing oneself or anyone else with any certainty at all. Often a narrator stands between us and the characters, analyzing and explaining them, so that it is hard to see the characters, at all. The narrator tells us how the story has been transmitted and advises us as to how much— if at all—we should believe it. If we judge the late poems by the degree to which they approximate the methods and ethos of "My Last Duchess," they will seem intolerably undramatic, rationalistic, rambling, and dull. But attention to the new concerns that form them will discover their coherence and may lead to a juster estimate.

II

In 1861 Browning's wife died, and he immediately left Italy to live in England. In the next years he spent several holidays on the coast of France where he delighted in remnants of an older and more savage culture than had appeared in his poems before. He liked villages that were "dirty, unimproved," "wild and primitive." "Croisic is the old head-seat of Druidism in France," he explained, "the people were still Pagan a couple of hundred years ago . . . and the women used to dance round a phallic stone still upright there with obscene circumstances enough" (McAleer, *Dearest Isa*, pp. 218, 243; Hood, p. 106).[13] This is more than tourist's gusto: druid stones and rites like these figure significantly in the later poems. Moreover Browning seems to associate primitive remains with the roots of poetry. In a letter to John Ruskin in 1855 he had defended his poems' obscurity with a surprising image: "In *prose* you may criticise so . . . but in asking for more *ultimates* you must accept less *mediates*, nor expect that a Druid stone-circle will be traced for you with as few breaks to the eye as the North Crescent and South Crescent that go together so cleverly in many a suburb."[14] Ruskin's friendly attack is couched in more traditional terms of Alps and crevasses; Browning's metaphor brings poetry down from sublime heights. Several of the later poems explore the connection between savage survivals and poetry's "ultimates," and the equation of poems with stone ruins recurs.

In *Fifine at the Fair* (1872), druid stones stand for the persistence of the primitive in a nonverbal text. The speaker, Don Juan, is engaged in a highly sophisticated analysis of life and himself, but it all ends at a druid monument: "a cold dread shape,—shape whereon Learning spends / Labour and leaves the text obscurer for the gloss, / While Ignorance reads right—recoiling from the Cross!" (2057–59). Like a poem, it is intelligible although nondiscursive (crudely translated, it says that human civilization is based on brute sexuality). The local Curé had offered a Christian gloss on it, but the peasants knew that "what once a thing / Meant and had right to mean, it still must mean" (2126–27). So the Curé had the stone thrown down. Someone "pert from Paris," however, smugly observes that it will "rise again," and that in fact the church spire is "just the symbol's self" (2152, 2151, 2154). The phrasing suggests that this reading of phallic symbolism—as easy then, apparently, as it is today—annoys Browning because it is reductive, not because he thinks it untrue. Meanwhile the peasants keep coming to the fallen stone, which still speaks "the prime authoritative speech" (2128). Don Juan has a rich and complex intelligence, great fluency, and an evident craving for self-knowledge, but he cannot speak with as much authority as the silent stones do. The stone's brutal message negates all his arguments, and when at the end of the poem he leaves his wife to return to the seductress Fifine, he shows that the stones speak truth.

In *The Two Poets of Croisic* (1878), Browning takes a lighter but similar view of the link between poetry and primitive culture, jokingly considering both under the guise of sun-worship.[15] First he describes ancient druid rites and their modern survivals. Long ago on May Day, he says, women "Unbuilt and then rebuilt" (98) a temple to the sun and tore "limb from limb" (103) whoever dropped a stone. Now the rites are less violent but recognizably the same: girls dance round the remaining stone and fall "with fisticuffs" (120) on anyone who touches it. Meanwhile boys "from door to door / Sing unintelligible words to tunes / As obsolete" (121–123) which scholars (here as in similar context the object of Browning's scorn) struggle vainly to understand. We see here, Browning says, "the story of our race / In little" (139–140), for human life developed the same way everywhere, "at Croisic as at Rome" (140). (This sounds very much like Tylor's theory of survivals and cultural development.) Le Croisic also produced two comically incompetent writers who illustrate both the poem's ostensible subject, the vagaries of fame, and its more essential theme, the relation of poetry to the primitive.

The first of these writers was René Gentilhomme, a comic version of the poet-prophet imagined by Thomas Carlyle.[16] Inheriting the poetic office from his father, René wrote "Rubbish unutterable" (233) for the Duke of Condé, his patron in the French court who was expected to succeed to the throne, until a thunderbolt struck. René understood this to foretell the birth of a Dauphin and wrote forty lines of verse urging France to turn from the "mock-sun" (310) of the Duke of Condé to "Sol's self, about / To rise" (311–312). This "actual sun" (344) did in due course rise and the descendant of druid sun-worshippers became royal poet. But success as a prophet did not make him a poet, and he quickly slipped into oblivion. He was not such a failure, however, as Paul Desforges Maillard, who tried to base his career more on sex than on worship (the two major aspects, as Browning sees it, of ancient religion). René sought fame in the Parisian literary world, which was ruled not by Louis the Sun-King but by Phoebus Apollo (611, 776, 966, 1007), an empty name from the dead mythology that was still thought fit theme for verse. He succeeded briefly through a sexual appeal as empty as Greek myths or René's claim to prophetic insight: his sister sent his poems as her own with seductive letters to an influential editor and to Voltaire. Paul let the secret out, however, not believing that "the envious crew" which "show their teeth" and "snarl" (1151–52) would ever bite; he was wrong. The sun-god of Greeks and druids was dead, but the spirit of violence survived. The moral of these parodic (and true) histories seems to be that poets should leave the primitive alone. One can "weigh / The worth of poets," Browning says in one of his most gnomically optimistic formulations, "By asking 'Which one led a happy life?'" (1234–40). The one, that is, who triumphed over pain, who rose most successfully above the primitive folly, violence, and gloom from which René and Paul never emerged.

Browning himself continued to use primitive materials, but as objects for conscious analysis. The *Dramatic Idyls* of the following year (1879) include several lower-class figures (infrequent in Browning), as well as Pan the goat-god and an altruistic dog. Martin Relph is an old peasant who publicly confesses every May Day (sacred in *Two Poets* to druid rites) an ancient crime. Halbert and Hob are the last of "the genuine wild-beast breed" (10). "Ivàn Ivànovitch" is the dreadful tale of a woman who, traversing the "monstrous wild" of the forest that surrounds a tiny enclave of civilization, threw all her children to the wolves and was killed, without recourse to law, by a righteous carpenter. Ned Bratts and his wife are lusty and hideous sinners who clamorously repent and insist on being hanged. These characters inhabit a borderland between civilization and savagery, nature and culture; the savage characters are visited by intimations of moral law which they obey with the crudity that characterizes the rest of their lives, while those who seem to stand for civilization are brutal too. The captain who shoots the girl Martin Relph loved and betrayed is a "brute / With the bloated cheeks and the bulgy nose and the bloodshot eyes" (73–74); the "gentry" in "Ned Bratts" amuse themselves by watching men on trial for their lives; Ivàn Ivànovitch's act of summary justice is, after all, murder. In general these four poems point to the need for Christian revelation to complete the inchoate moral stirrings of human nature. " 'Is there a reason in nature for these hard hearts?' O Lear, / That a reason out of nature must turn them soft, seems clear!" ("Halbert and Hob," 65–66).

The two remaining idyls complement the others by showing the virtues of nature itself when it is uncontaminated by human components. "Pheidippides" tells how Pan saved Athenian civilization, and "Tray" rather crossly asserts the moral superiority of the "mere instinctive dog" (19) that saves a child's life to the vivisectionist who wants to see "How brain secretes dog's soul" (45). "Tray" is a silly poem, but it locates *Dramatic Idyls* at a confluence of two streams of contemporary thought. The antivivisectionist movement and the fascination with primitive culture are related phenomena that run side by side not only in Browning's book but also, for instance, through the table of contents for the *Fortnightly Review* in the mid-seventies. The penultimate paragraph of Darwin's *Descent of Man* memorably illustrates the link between revulsion from savagery in people and admiration for the innocent virtues of animals:

> The main conclusion arrived at in this work, namely that man is descended from some lowly-organised form, will, I regret to think, be highly distasteful. . . . He who has seen a savage in his native land will not feel much shame, if forced to acknowledge that the blood of some humble creature flows in his veins. For my own part I would as soon be descended from that heroic little monkey, who braved his dreaded enemy in order to save the life of his keeper; or from that old baboon, who, descending from the mountains, carried away in triumph his young comrade from a crowd of astonished dogs—as from a savage who delights to torture his enemies, offers up bloody sacrifices, practises

infanticide without remorse, treats his wives like slaves, knows no decency, and is haunted by the grossest superstitions.[17]

Here is the distinctive note struck more feebly by "Tray" and again by "Donald" (1883), in which a man is horribly crippled in just punishment for his treachery to a stag. The significant difference is that Browning's ignoble savages are modern Europeans. The savage having been discredited as an example for the cultivated, his place is taken by noble animals.

It is only when Browning conceives of instinct and reason in such very simple terms, however, that the late poetry denigrates reason. From "Pippa Passes" to *The Ring and the Book* he had opposed simple instinctive virtue to artifice and intellectual corruption, but such oppositions came to seem less clear. The late poems show that noble instinct without strong reason guiding it ends in moral disaster, while intellectual sophistication may be a thin cover for primitive superstition. Many of these poems take place in a borderland where reason and instinct, cultivation and nature, and even good and evil seem to mingle and blur. Thus *Red Cotton Night-Cap Country* (1873) and *The Inn Album* (1875) tell long, sordid, violent tales based on actual recent events that show the persistence of primitive modes of thought and behavior in apparently civilized contemporary life and the moral and intellectual confusion that ensues.

Red Cotton Night-Cap Country demonstrates that the white nightcaps of rural Normandy are misleading symbols of the inhabitants' lives. The symbol is odd but efficient: a nightcap is a quaint traditional article associated with sleep, dreams, and the unconscious, and each church steeple, Browning says, is like the nightcap of a town (378). The speaker undertakes to prove that beneath the visible white is a fierce red ground. He tells the story of Miranda, a man whose craving for whiteness led him again and again to choose the red: to love a fallen woman as an idol of purity; to take her as his mistress and then expiate this offense against his dreadful, respectable mother by burning off his hands; to offer his ardent worship to the Virgin while he is living with his mistress again; and finally to test his faith and lose his life by attempting to fly from a high tower. Miranda always wants to choose the best, but he is not clever enough to find his way through the moral chaos of the modern world, strewn with "ravage of opinions" (1104) like a ruin overgrown with vegetation, neither renovated nor cleared away (1134–39). In particular he finds inadequate guidance for sexual and religious impulses, which his society generally tries to ignore. His country house is a mock paradise of artificial nature, a park, *"a l'Anglaise"* with "Grass like green velvet, gravel-walks like gold" (657–658); his religious guides are Catholics "in that second stage of things" (3032) with "dogma in the bottle" (3034) and diluted, rationalizing faith. But the red ground of nature remains. Miranda's soul is torn between the Virgin and a more elemental goddess, "a Power as absolute" (3306), "The unrobed One" (3312), naked, shameless, and silent. Clara de Millefleurs (so his mistress calls herself) is like a polyanthus: "out of simple came the composite / By culture: . . . the florist bedded thick / His primrose-root, in ruddle, bullock's blood, / Ochre and devils'-dung, for aught I know" (1505–08). The primitive is bad, but so is the suppression or denial of it: culture is necessary, but blood and dung on its roots make it disgusting.

This world of moral and intellectual muddle is too complicated for Miranda, whom the narrator firmly sums up as sane, good, but stupid. And yet his stupidity is partly his own fault: "The heart was wise according to its lights / And limits; but the head refused more sun" (4010–11). Towards this strange protagonist Browning displays the harsh, rather contemptuous pity that he felt for the spiritualists' earnest dupes. He even makes jokes about Miranda's horrible self-mutilation and his fatal attempt to fly. Levitation was part of the medium's bag of tricks in the 1870s, and Browning would have been amused by the jocular comment on "survivals" in a review of Tylor's *Primitive Culture*: "The exploits of Mr Home [Browning's Sludge the Medium] at the present day may fairly be considered to set gravity itself at defiance."[18]

The Inn Album (1875) focusses still more clearly on the survival of primitive modes of thought and behavior. *"Hail, calm acclivity, salubrious spot!"* (11)—a line from the album of an English country inn, frequently repeated, this sets the apparent tone of trite culture, rationality, ease. In the inn parlor everything is "vulgarized . . . comfortably smooth" (33). Wild nature is represented by "Sir Edwin's dripping stag" (35) on a "sprig-pattern-papered wall" (34) and *"Salmo ferox"* (39) mounted above the mantle. Visitors make neat drawings of trees and flowers. Outdoors one sees "The reign of English nature—which means art / And civilized existence. Wildness' self / Is just the cultured triumph" (62–64). But the characters have not reached this vapid equilibrium of nature and culture. The younger of the two men is a "good strong fellow, rough perhaps" (110), "A clumsy giant handsome creature" (255) with a "large red" hand (256). He is of low birth and very rich. The elder is an aristocrat, a "polished snob . . . refinement every inch / From brow to boot-end" (143–145). The elder man has polished up and preyed on the younger, although in his rage at having lost money that he cannot pay he reasserts the difference between them: "I polished snob off to aristocrat? . . . still silk purse . . . Roughs finger with some bristle sow-ear-born" (395–398).

But the elder man himself—cold, vicious, aristocratic, a collector of art and women like the duke of "My Last Duchess"—has the soul of a primitive. The unexpected appearance of the older woman, whom he had once seduced, startles him into superstitious horror. She is a devil, a witch; she has ruined him: "Well I knew what lurked, / Lay perdue paralyzing me,—drugged, drowsed / And damnified my soul and body both" (1420–22). Her sorcery is responsible for everything that has gone wrong with him since they parted: it has lost him money, opportunities, and position, and made him a worse and stupider man:

> fattened, fulsome, have you fed on me,
> Sucked out my substance? How much gloss, I pray,
> O'erbloomed those hair-swathes when there crept from you
> To me that craze, else unaccountable,
> Which urged me to contest our county seat
> With whom but my own brother's nominee?
> (1484–89)

His accusations of sorcery continue for quite a while until eventually he pulls himself together and becomes, so to speak, his own ethnologist:

> Well, I have been spellbound, deluded like
> The witless negro by the Obeah-man
> Who bids him wither: so, his eye grows dim,
> His arm slack, arrow misses aim and spear
> Goes wandering wide,—and all the woe because
> He proved untrue to Fetish, who, he finds,
> Was just a feather-phantom!
> (1856–62)

Fetishism, which Comte had identified as the first stage of religious development, and Sir John Lubbock dismissed as "mere witchcraft," was for the Victorians one of the most fascinating aspects of primitive culture (Lubbock, p. 164). "Obeah" is a term of Ashanti origin. In the 1870s British troops were fighting the Ashanti on the Gold Coast; the war, said Henry Rowley in the *Cornhill* in 1873, "is another link in the chain of events which of late years has brought Africa and the Africans more within the sphere of our knowledge," while "the worst features of their character and habits have received a wide publication" (*Cornhill Magazine*, 28 [1873], 679). Browning's elder man finds in the savage not evil so much as folly: thus he compares himself to an African king in a traveller's tale who thought a silver sixpence worth a ship's cargo (2578–95). To the reader he demonstrates that the highest intellectual and social culture is compatible with the most primitive stage of religious development.

The other three characters embody similar antithetical elements though in different ways. Country bred and with substantial intellectual and aesthetic culture, the woman has punished her own sin by marrying an old, poor, stupid, utterly insensitive parish priest who preaches to "brutalized" men (1679) the doctrine of eternal damnation—the theology Browning attributes in "Caliban" and "Ixion" to a very primitive stage of human development. Her self-sacrifice is as pointless—as superstitious—as Miranda's. The younger man and the girl, however, are in the process of developing toward genuine culture. The girl's fancies of fairyland and a "fairy marriage-tree" (1164) are childlike and playful, embellishments of a world whose evil she has not yet recognized. Conscious of her own inexperience, she asks the woman to advise her whether or not she should marry the young man. She rather likes his crudeness: "no polished steel / Somebody forged before me" (1217–18). The woman agrees: "*He's virgin soil—a friend must cultivate / I think no plant called 'love' grows wild . . .*" (3060–61). In the end the contrast is between true cultivation, which brings genuine spiritual growth, and false refinement, which allows the grossest savagery to survive within. Browning's defense of his portrayal of Guido in *The Ring and the Book* could apply to the elder man: "We differ apparently [he wrote to Julia Wedgwood] in our conception of what gross wickedness can be effected by cultivated minds,— I believe, the grossest—all the more, by way of reaction from the enforced habit of self denial which is the condition of men's receiving culture" (Curle, p. 175). *The Inn Album* differs from *The Ring and the Book*, however, in its portrayal of the elder man's "wickedness" as in large part a reversion to primitive thinking, and its firm insistence that cultivation is necessary. In an instinctive leap like that by which Browning's earlier heroes typically show their virtue, the young man kills the elder one to save the woman from his threats of blackmail, but this St. George is also a beast in his "tigerflash—yell, spring, and scream" (3015). " 'And that was good but useless' " (3023), says the woman rather deflatingly; she has already taken poison. The poem ends with the girl at the door. " '*Hail, calm acclivity,*' " she happily repeats from the opening lines of the poem—about to discover how primitive nature survived after all in that tamed, "salubrious" spot.

Browning's last poem on this theme is the fine, sharply drawn, witty, and enigmatic "Bad Dreams" (1889). This poem plays on the close connection between primitive culture and the sleeping mind which was widely recognized by contemporary writers on ethnology. Lubbock says:

> Dreams are intimately associated with the lower forms of religion. To the savage they have a reality and an importance which we can scarcely appreciate. During sleep the spirit seems to desert the body; and as in dreams we visit other localities and even other worlds, . . . the two phenomena are not unnaturally regarded as the complements of one another. Hence the savage considers the events in his dreams to be as real as those of his waking hours, and hence he naturally feels that he has a spirit which can quit the body.
> —Lubbock, p. 126

A similar mode of thinking appears in Browning's poem, in which a highly cultivated man and woman discuss their dreams, and the line between dream and waking, conscious and unconscious, gets increasingly blurred. The man's first dream is that the woman has lost faith, love, and "charm of face" (2[the phrase is evidence that the dreamer here is the man]), but he has "loved on the same" (8). He evidently believes that our dreams show us ourselves, since he is delighted to find that his best self, his love, persisted even in the depths of nightmare. In Part II, however, he has begun to fear that dreams show the truth about others too. He dreamed that he saw a weary and hateful dance, grim as the druid rites in other poems, of a devil's chapel and a strange "cult" (50) that he observed and tried to fit into his general knowledge of "guild and cult" (51)—an ethnologist in his sleep—until the woman joined the worship. Awake, like Young Goodman Brown he cannot exonerate her. His theory of dreams now is like that which Lubbock ascribes to savages: "Sleep leaves a door on hinge / Whence soul, ere our flesh suspect, / Is off and away" (78–80). The woman at first cannot take this nonsense seriously and replies rather indirectly by reminding him that he has been teaching her Greek but has carefully censored the texts. " 'You warned me to let alone / (Since our studies were mere philology) / That ticklish (you said) Anthology" (93–95). In sleep she comically associated "ticklish" Greek materials with an irreproachably pious writer on female education:

> "So, I dreamed that I passed *exam*
> Till a question posed me sore:
> 'Who translated this epigram
> By—an author we best ignore?'
> And I answered, 'Hannah More'!"
> (96–100)

She is reminding him that classical literature, the basis of British education and culture, is itself full of primitive materials which he has refused to acknowledge. What he has repressed—presumably sexuality—is returning in his dreams and suspicions. The situation is like that in *Middlemarch*: a prudish scholar of ancient culture and the ardent young wife to whom he teaches languages and whose vitality—and implicit sexuality—he comes to hate and fear.

In Part III the opposition between nature and culture, the primitive and the forces of repression, becomes still more intense. The man dreams of a grand primeval forest where only "some brute-type" (11) lives and of a city "too fine / For human footstep's smirch" (20). The dream ends with "each devouring each" (27) in a ruin like those in *Fifine, Red Cotton Night-Cap Country*, and *The Two Poets of Croisic*. The moral he draws is that nature and art are each good alone but "Both in one—accurst" (36); but it is worth noticing that the antithetical states equally exclude human life. He himself, like the elder man in *The Inn Album*, is a horrible example of how the extremes can come together in a deadly combination and make just such a ruin of a man, destructive of himself and others. The woman's last dream is that his chilly censorious culture has killed her. "Bad Dreams" shows primitive modes of thought and feeling surviving in the unconscious and surfacing both in dreams and in the response to dreams, and suggests, finally, that a mere fastidious recoil from savagery is as inhuman and destructive as savagery itself.[19]

"Bad Dreams" is Browning's most successful poem about primitive survivals, a concise distillation of the themes of the long works that precede it. It is short and genuinely dramatic rather than narrative, perhaps because Browning has these ideas sufficiently under control to be able to dispense with discursive analysis. But it is not dramatic in the way his earlier monologues were. For one thing there are two characters, not just one: we learn about the man not by our own reactions or by observing the responses of a silent auditor, but with the commentary provided by the woman's dreams. Furthermore, neither characters nor situations are clearly delineated: it takes place in an increasingly phantasmagoric world of uncertain times and places. Browning is not interested now in the way one individual deals with a particular situation—historical, social, marital, amatory—but with how that person deals with the unconscious impulses and the attitudes that link civilized people to the savage.

III

The Victorian fascination with the primitive not only opposes but works to undermine the traditional humanistic culture that the man in "Bad Dreams" so inadequately represents. *Culture and Anarchy* came out in 1869, and *Primitive Culture* appeared only two years later in 1871. In terms of Matthew Arnold's hierarchical, evaluative notion of culture, with its stress on conscious self-improvement and its dependence on the world of books, Tylor's title is a devastating oxymoron.[20] And students of the primitive took over some of the main territory of Arnoldian culture, too, finding new ways to interpret the classics. For Frazer and others the road to modern anthropology started from ancient Greece and Rome. When Browning began to use Greek materials extensively for the first time in the late sixties, he did not look for traditionally "classical" values—moral heroism, sanity, intellectual power, clarity, artistic control—but for primitive elements. Modern "comparative mythologists," Max Müller said in 1867, find rational meanings in ancient myth and explain away "some of the most revolting features": Müller's own explanation was linguistic error, a "disease" all languages contract in their infancy.[21] But in the seventies Müller's theories were attacked by mythographers more "modern" still, and the features that disturbed Müller were reborn with new vigor like figures in a vegetation myth. Browning's Greece is part of this revival. He translates Euripides and emphasizes his modernity, translates Aeschylus and emphasizes his obscurity, but passes by Sophocles, the embodiment of Arnold's luminous classical ideal. Although Browning, unlike Algernon Swinburne or Walter Pater or William Morris, unabashedly imposes the moral ethos of enlightened Protestantism on ancient myth, he is increasingly drawn to whatever is wild, strange, and anarchic in classical literature. He especially loves Euripides, who was thought to offend against "classical" canons of taste much as Browning himself did: Augustus Schlegel accused Euripides of sacrificing the whole to the parts, writing in a style too loose and a tone too familiar and ordinary, creating scenes like lawsuits, and celebrating amoral passions.[22] The central myth of Browning's earlier poetry is the story of Perseus saving Andromeda from the monster, but his later mythic heroes incorporate the monstrous too, and Bacchus and Pan are the ambiguous deities who preside over the later verse.

Browning published *Balaustion's Adventure* and *Prince Hohenstiel-Schwangau* in 1871, and a similar pair, *Aristophanes' Apology* and *The Inn Album*, in 1875. The two classical poems give a context of modern feelings and ideas to translations from Euripides, while the other two use classical references and models to present modern events. *The Inn Album* is a narrative framed as a classical tragedy, observing the unities and finding materials like those of Greek tragedy—passionate, violent, primitive—in contemporary life. Prince Hohenstiel-Schwangau (Napoleon III) uses classical myth to express what is dark, hidden, violent, and enduring in human nature. He starts by comparing himself to the sphinx, about to tell Oedipus his secret lest he appear to be a fraud like Home the medium (6–14)—thus immediately linking classical myth to modern superstition—and ends by recalling the priests of Nemi, who murdered their predecessors: "So it was once, is now, shall ever be / With genius and its priesthood in this world: / The new power slays the old" (2008–10). The final allusion, which sums up all forms of power and its transmission, is marked by a striking process of evasion and return, for the prince first locates the murderous rite by Clitumnus, "a mild river that makes oxen white" (1987). The 1888–89 edition adds nine lines of correction and comment without deleting the error: the prince says that he unconsciously needed "the ox-whitening piece of prettiness" (2142) to soften the "grim cult" (2138). By an elegant coincidence, the first of Browning's long late poems on contemporary themes comes reluctantly to rest where *The Golden Bough* was to begin, in the sacred grove of Nemi. For the prince, however, the grove is an impasse rather than a starting place, a dark image of social origins that leaves the would-be "Savior of Society" nothing more to say.

The poems based directly on classical literature consider ways of dealing with such apparently intractable material and move consistently towards simply taking that material as it stands. The first is *Balaustion's Adventure*, which vigorously analyzes, rationalizes, and reformulates Euripides's *Alcestis*, trying to subjugate that ancient story of death and rebirth to the moral imagination of nineteenth-century England. Balaustion says that myths can always be remade: "You, I, or anyone might mould a new / Admetos, new Alkestis" (2415–16). Her commentary points with gentle contempt to Admetos's selfishness; her own remaking—a drastic reinterpretation of the story—explains it away and eliminates both human weakness and superhuman intervention, which becomes unnecessary. The myth has been successively transformed: by Euripides's play, Balaustion's narration and commentary, and her own projected version. Morally, the poem seems clearly to say that each change is an improvement. But Balaustion's analysis is only the outline of what sounds rather like a sentimental comedy and in any event remains unwritten. The center and originative force of Browning's poem is the translation of Euripides's *Alcestis*, while the modern element is given by the frame.

The center of *Aristophanes' Apology* is also a translation from Euripides, but without interpolations or commentary. The *Herakles*, furthermore, is much darker and more violent than the *Alcestis*, showing not moral weakness and a happy ending but irremediable horror. Herakles, who is the embodiment of sanity and strength when he brings back Admetos's wife, now kills his own wife and children in a fit of madness. The frame consists mostly of Balaustion's report of her argument with Aristophanes and is related to the *Herakles* only indirectly, by a common concern with primitive elements in drama. Balaustion accuses Aristophanes, who has arrived with a crowd of drunken revellers, of celebrating "nastiness" (3399), "scurrility" (3401), "muck" (3403), "the base, / The brutish" (3435–36). But Aristophanes says that he stands up for "the common coarse-as-clay / Existence . . . solid vulgar life" (2683–85) and the good old notions of "what is good, right, decent" (2223) that Euripides's restless cleverness dissolves. Aristophanes, the bluff conservative, argues (among other things) that what seems brutish indecency to Balaustion is hallowed by the origins of comedy in ancient ritual. His comedy, he says, offers "appropriate worship to the Power / Adulterous, night-roaming, and the rest: / . . . that originative force / Of nature . . . Phales Iacchos" (2360–67). This is a standard Victorian argument, set forth at length for instance by J. A. Symonds in 1873. But Balaustion replies (in what has been called the poem's most significant contribution to the Victorian argument about the classics) that it is simply wrong.[23] Comedy is not a "prescription and a rite," "No growth of the blind antique time" (2908–09). It developed very recently from mere brutish country shows, and Aristophanes himself refined and improved it. The gross elements of comedy may be survivals—but of nothing so exciting or dignified as ancient ritual.

At the time the poem takes place, however, civilization is in fact regressing into barbarism. Balaustion tells the story as she flees from Athens, which is being destroyed by Spartans "who live hutted (so they laugh) not housed, / Build barns for temples, prize mud-monuments" (5525–26). Aristophanes, whose art is part of this retrogression, gives examples of two kinds of literary return to the past. One is the beautiful song of the early world, "Thamuris Marching," that he attributes to Sophocles. Aristophanes does not aspire to the joyous vision of Thamuris, who saw nature transfigured in "the ease of earth's fulfilled imaginings" (5229) and turned earth's music into song. He prefers the debased and easier version of primitive tradition represented by *The Frogs*:

> Bacchos did stand forth, the Tragic God
> In person! and when duly dragged through mire,—
> Having lied, filched, played fool, proved coward,
> . . . .
>
> (—Oh never fear! 'T was consecrated sport,
> Exact tradition. . . .)
> (5396–403)

Browning's poem, then, contrasts three ways of using primitive material: Aristophanes's brutish and false repetitions of barbaric ritual; Euripidean tragedy, which gives modern forms and meaning to old myth; and the joyous song of Thamuris, who sang the world when it was new and was punished for doing so by blindness and the loss of his memory.

In Browning's third and last translation, the *Agamemnon* (1877), ancient and modern elements hardly meet at all. There is no frame, and the poet has severely withdrawn his own mediating presence from a translation so rough and unaccommodating that some baffled readers have concluded that Browning simply meant to disprove Matthew Arnold's claims for the charm and clarity of Greek drama.[24] But the roughness and irreducible mystery are precisely what Browning wanted to capture, as his introduction (if we read it seriously) shows: "For, over and above the purposed ambiguity of the Chorus, the text is sadly corrupt, probably interpolated, and certainly mutilated; and no unlearned person enjoys the scholar's privilege of trying his fancy upon each obstacle whenever he comes to a stoppage, and effectually clearing the way by suppressing what seems to lie in it" (*Works*, VIII, 294). This mutilated text, through which the scholar proceeds as through an overgrown ruin, is like the phallic monument in *Fifine at the Fair*:

> Take my word, the deeper you explore
> That caverned passage, filled with fancies to the brim,
> The less you will approve the adventure! such a grim
> Bar-sinister soon blocks abrupt your path, and ends
> All with a cold dread shape,—shape whereon Learning spends
> Labour, and leaves the text obscurer for the gloss,
> While Ignorance reads right—recoiling from that Cross!
> (2053–59)

The monument is a "text" too, and retains the clarity of "the prime authoritative speech," "the arch-word," the text that scholars with their commentary just "efface." In his *Agamemnon* Browning tries to speak the arch-word and not efface it with either learning's gloss or the artist's desire to "beautify" it (*Works*, VIII, 297). Its unaccommodating roughness is part of its meaning. This is partly a strategy of desperation: the frames of the earlier translations had imposed not so much a gloss as a moral point of view, and Browning seems to have found it increasingly difficult to find a point of view that could accommodate the starkness of the primitive. The rough literalness of his *Agamemnon* reflects the impasse of revulsion and fascination at which his imagination found itself. It is an artistic impasse as well as a moral one, reaching the lowest limit of intelligibility and creation. In his later approaches to classical literature Browning takes a different and more promising line.

"Ixion" (1883) expresses Browning's abhorrence of the punitive deity of pagans, Caliban, and Calvinism. "Echetlos" (1880) celebrates a rough heroic ploughman who fought for Greece at Marathon. Both of these poems emphasize the primitive element in the classical tradition. "Apollo and the Fates" (1887) is a final comic-ironic word on the Alcestis myth, and the autobiographical "Development" (1890) reiterates Browning's dislike of learning's glosses—here, Wolf's deconstruction of the author of the Homeric poems. And "Pan and Luna" (1880) is the sublest articulation and perhaps the finest fruit of Browning's late confrontation with the primitive as expressed in the classics. Although his wife had announced the death of Pan in one of her most famous poems, years later Browning found him disturbingly alive. In "Pheidippides" (1879) Pan is grandly goatish, wholly good, saving Athens at Marathon to prove his right to be worshipped; he represents manly power, dangerous but benign. In "Pan and Luna," however, he is both more primitive and more terrifyingly attractive. The poem recapitulates the total argument of the three long translations, and offers at least for one moment and one poem a way out of the artist's dilemma. It begins by raising and setting aside the question of credence and interpretation; it ends with accepting, as in the *Agamemnon*, the bare facts of the old mysterious story, without gloss or extenuation. It enacts the artist's confrontation with the primitive, as subject matter for art, rather than a character's confrontation (or evasion) of dark forces within himself.

It approaches the god with wary indirection, beginning with an epigraph from Virgil's "strange three lines" (2) from *Georgics*, III—"*Si credere dignum est*"—that lets him assert his own belief in what he is to tell. The three lines are: "'Twas with gift of such snowy wool, if we may trust the tale, that Pan, Arcadia's god, charmed and beguiled thee, O Moon, calling thee to the depths of the woods; nor didst thou scorn his call."[25] But Browning does not give Virgil's words, with their mysterious assertion that Luna willingly followed lecherous Pan—the part of the tale that Browning found hard to believe—till the end. First he recreates the scene: the blackness of earth and sky, the naked moon's flight as in a nightmare of exposure, her entanglement in what seems a cloud that offers shelter, and Pan's rough embraces. It begins as a story of gleaming whiteness and darkness palpable, purity and lust: perfect opposites. A whole eight-line stanza tells how rams with any spot of black are pitilessly exterminated to preserve the whiteness of a flock. But the poetry presents each extreme as if from the point of view of the other. Overtly committed to whiteness, it is saturated with sensuality. The naked moon is described with vivid delectation, "that pure undraped / Pout of the sister paps—that . . ." (44–45)—the suggestive ellipses is Browning's. Pan's embraces are described with vivid horror. The poet imagines how the story might have continued: Luna "rips / The cloud's womb through" (93–94) to escape—but there is no moral "lesson for a maid" (95). So Browning repeats Virgil's words. "The myth / Explain who may!" (100–101). Instead of explaining Browning reduces the myth to its bare remaining elements, like the ruins in *Fifine*:

> Let all else go, I keep
> —As of a ruin just a monolith—
> Thus much, one verse of five words, each a boon:
> Arcadia, night, a cloud, Pan, and the moon.
> (101–104)

This monolith is like the druid stone or the *Agamemnon*, the "prime authoritative speech" that survives even learning's attempts to gloss it, the elemental matter in which, Browning seems to think, poetry might yet rediscover the primal energies of nature and of art.

Browning's last and fullest statement on classical myth and its present uses is the "Parleying" (1887) with Gerard de Lairesse, whose *Art of Painting* sets forth with relentless consistency a sub-Arnoldian "classical" ideal of grace, decorum, and nobleness in opposition to those who wish merely to imitate unidealized nature. Browning splendidly demonstrates that he too can see myths in landscapes if he wants to. But the great set-pieces of myth-making do more than show his powers or recapitulate de Lairesse: they draw out the primitive essence of the myths that had been appropriated for so long by humanistic culture. Whereas de Lairesse drew mostly on Ovid's sophisticated tales, Browning's sources are Greek.[26] De Lairesse uses myth for decoration and reads it as moral allegory, while Browning moves in every instance toward the darker side of his stories: from Prometheus's defiance to Jove's cruelty (viii); from Artemis's purity to her cruel and envious character as "queen / Of . . . strange and sudden deaths" (ix); from a furry satyr's lovesick sadness to the "greedy hands" and "hot eyes" of his lust (x); from a vision of mighty armies to Alexander and Darius rigid with hate (xi).

The main argument in the "Parleying" is that the "simply true" (130) facts of nature are better than these sad old feignings, just as Christian truth is better than Greek errors about the afterlife. Having splendidly recreated traditional myth from earlier and more vital roots than those to which de

Lairesse ever penetrated, Browning ends with a lovely lyrical demonstration of how one might replace the old myths with new and truer ones:

> Here's rhyme
> Such as one makes now,—say, when Spring repeats
> That miracle the Greek Bard sadly greets:
> "Spring for the tree and herb—no Spring for us!"
> Let Spring come: why, a man salutes her thus:
>
> Dance, yellows and whites and reds,—
> Lead your gay orgy, leaves, stalks, heads
> Astir with the wind in the tulip-beds!
>
> There's sunshine; scarcely a wind at all
> Disturbs starved grass and daisies small
> On a certain mound by a churchyard wall.
>
> Daisies and grass be my heart's bedfellows
> On the mound wind spares and sunshine mellows:
> Dance you, reds and whites and yellows!
> (421–434)

The tokens of nature's death, fertility, and eternal rebirth are not interpreted, hardly even described, but simply named. This is minimal, unidealized nature, apprehended in simple units—leaves, stalks, colors. And yet in this bare naming we see the myth-making process beginning anew. "Earth's young significance is all to learn" (391). Browning has moved through increasingly primitive aspects of classical literature and myth to a glimpse (at least) of the primal vision which once created myth, and can, he hopes, make poetry still.

The spring song has no living people in it. Myth and characterization are at opposite poles, one generally developing at the other's expense, and the more seriously Browning turned to myth the less often he created the clear-cut, brilliantly individualized characters that have been responsible for most of his popularity. He had used the Perseus and Saint George myths in *The Ring and the Book* and earlier as pattern and analogue and to illuminate character, but in the later poems myth represents something obscure and formless, the primitive element that lies beneath both culture and personality and differs very little from one individual to another. Instead of revealing a character in a flash of brilliant certitude, the late poems more often demonstrate the opacity of character, another's or one's own. Many of them show the difficulty of interpreting other people, especially women ("Adam, Lilith, and Eve," "A Forgiveness," "Appearances," "Solomon and Balkis," "Pan and Luna," "Bad Dreams," and many others). Prince Hohenstiel-Schwangau and Don Juan are only the most notable of the many characters who fail to reach self-knowledge or (to judge from the critical record) self-revelation, and their failure is largely due to their baffled withdrawal from the primitive depths their search discovers. The Prince's impasse is at Nemi, Don Juan's at the druid stone. The most striking of many such withdrawals comes in *La Saisiaz*, where Browning argues at length that religious certainty is based on subjective experience and then, astonishingly, says that he will not look too deeply within himself:

> Life is stocked with germs of torpid life; but may I never wake
> Those of mine whose resurrection could not be without earthquake!
> (615–616)

The late poems typically invite and then baffle our judgment: thus Prince Hohenstiel-Schwangau disarmingly sets out to reveal his true nature and discovers that he can not, and our bafflement is doubled when we discover at the end that the dramatic situation in which he has been speaking was entirely imaginary.

Uncertainty about characters is matched by doubts cast on the authenticity of the stories in which they appear. The narrative element predominates over the dramatic, so that characters do not simply impose themselves on us with self-validating force, and stories of primitive life and behavior are usually attributed to dubious, often oral sources. "Martin Relph" for instance resembles more than most of the late poems the sort of dramatic monologue Browning wrote before, but it is sharply marked as different by the narrator's prefatory stanza: "*My grandfather says he remembers he saw, when a youngster long ago, / On a bright May day* . . ." (1–2). This preface subsumes Martin Relph's speech into a legendary account of ritual behavior. The narrator of "Ivàn Ivànovitch" says that the story was told him by a Russian who introduced it as "a tale told children, time out of mind" (11): "I wager 't is old to you / As the story of Adam and Eve, and possibly quite as true" (15–16). To "Jochanan Hakkadosh" Browning appends a mock-pedantic authentication that points our attention to the poem's fabulous quality. The late volumes contain numerous legends of the supernatural, unlikely anecdotes of early Christian Rome, strange tales of the mysterious east; in contrast to the brilliant historical realism of Browning's early poems or his insistence on documentary evidence in *The Ring and the Book*, most of these candidly present themselves as fictions embodying moral truth. For "a myth may teach" those who "Look through the sign to the thing signified" ("Parleying with Bernard de Mandeville," 204, 192). But signs mislead, as "The Pope and the Net" and "Mucklemouth Meg" demonstrate, and the eponymous hero of "Pambo" finds that interpreting one line of a religious text is an occupation for a lifetime. *Ferishtah's Fancies* presents the life and teachings of an imaginary Persian sage whose subject is interpreting the world: reading the signs of the physical universe, finding the moral meaning of events, and then making stories that teach spiritual truth.

* * *

Questions about the authenticity of primitive moral or religious tales, the manner of their transmission, and the proper way to interpret them link these poems to the Higher Criticism and the growing tendency to read the Bible as myth. Years earlier the Brownings had agreed that the dead, classical mythology should be replaced by the living Christian one—but that did not mean that they approved of David Strauss and Joseph Renan. Browning explained that in the rather enigmatic "Fears and Scruples" (1876) he meant to defend "the genuine love of the 'letters' and 'actions' of [God],—however these may be disadvantaged by an inability to meet the objections to their authenticity or historical value urged by 'experts' who assume the privilege of learning over ignorance"; we are reminded of Browning's distaste for scholars who adduced unpleasant facts about primitive survivals and the classics.[27] Browning's St. John in "A Death in the Desert" (1864) had mocked "the wise" who dismiss the question of factual truth, say *"The fact is in the fable"* (534), and classify John's testimony to Jesus with the heathen poet's story of Prometheus. And yet "A Death in the Desert" sets out to prove a truth by a wholly invented fable, to validate the historical authenticity of one epistle by feigning another. In later poems Browning would be more likely to call our attention to such contradictions than to invite us by dramatic presentation to suspend our disbelief.

Browning's first and in many ways exemplary use of the primitive materials he found in France is "Gold Hair: A Story of Pornic" (1864), in which he explicitly relates his poem to the issues raised by the Higher Criticism. "Gold Hair" is the story of a girl "too white" (1) for earth, whose dying wish was to be buried with her beautiful hair untouched; after she died her purity became a legend, until a hoard of gold coins was found hidden in her hair. The poem forecasts the many later ones that reveal baseness underlying extreme apparent purity and explore the dark underside of mythic materials. Why, Browning asks at the end of the poem, does he "deliver this horrible verse" at a time when "our Essays-and-Reviews' debate / Begins to tell on the public mind, / And Colenso's words have weight?" Because, he replies, it supports Christianity, which "taught Original Sin, / The Corruption of Man's Heart" (136–150). The holy legend actually gains religious significance when it is exposed as false; the circumstances of its creation and collapse are intrinsic parts of the story as Browning tells it, not its mere antithesis. The making and decay of myth, that is, is part of its meaning. In the later poems Browning almost always uses myth, as he uses other manifestations of the primitive in man, to explore the heart's corruptions. Some of the best, like "Pan and Luna" and "Bad Dreams," find formal unity in dramatizing this exploration. And two marvellous poems—

"Thamuris Marching" and the spring song—emerge at the end of longer, more flawed, and diffuse works to offer a glimpse of the kind of myth Browning would like to be able to make: a song of the world both fallen and redeemed, deeply felt and deeply impersonal, primal and new.

Notes

  1. On anthropology and mythography in Victorian England see: Richard M. Dorson, *The British Folklorists: A History* (Chicago, Illinois: University of Chicago Press, 1968); *Peasant Customs and Savage Myths: Selections from the British Folklorists*, Richard Dorson, ed. (Chicago, Illinois: University of Chicago Press, 1968); John B. Vickery, *The Literary Impact of the Golden Bough* (Princeton, New Jersey: Princeton University Press, 1973), especially chap. 1; *The Rise of Modern Mythology*, ed. Burton Feldman and Robert D. Richardson (Bloomington: Indiana University Press, 1972); J. W. Burrow, *Evolution and Society* (London: Cambridge University Press, 1966); T. K. Penniman, *A Hundred Years of Anthropology*, 3d ed. (London: Macmillan, 1965). Morse Peckham suggests a link between Browning's relativism and historicism and the anthropological idea of cultural relativism, in *Victorian Revolutionaries* (New York: Braziller, 1970), pp. 189–190.

  2. See *Pauline*, epigraph and lines 21–23; *Paracelsus; Sordello*, I, 35–54; *The Ring and the Book*, I, 752 ff. These reference are cited by John Woolford in "Sources and Resources in Browning's Early Reading," in *Robert Browning: Writers and their Background*, ed. Isobel Armstrong (Athens: Ohio University Press, 1975). Browning's use of the occult and alchemical traditions is surveyed by Woolford and by Robert Preyer in "Robert Browning: A Reading of the Early Narratives," *English Literary History*, 26 (1959), 531–548. References to Browning's poetry are to *The Works of Robert Browning*, ed. F. G. Kenyon, Centenary edition, 10 vols. (London: Smith, Elder, & Co., 1912).

  3. Huxley's comment was quoted at a meeting of the Browning Society in 1884 ("Twenty-fourth Meeting," [Friday, 25 April 1884], *The Browning Society's Papers*, 1881–84, Part 5 [London: N. Trübner, 1884], p. 120). Barbara Melchiori analyzes the poem as an anticipation of both Frazer and Freud in "Upon 'Caliban Upon Setebos,' " in *Browning's Poetry of Reticence* (New York: Barnes and Noble, 1968). R. E. N. Dodge argues that the Bishop's French book was Balzac's *Physiology of Marriage* (*Times Literary Supplement*, 34 [21 March 1935], 176). C. R. Tracy suggests Stendhal (*Times Literary Supplement*, 34 [24 January 1935], 48). Oscar Maurer suggests Diderot ("Bishop Blougram's 'French Book,' " [*Victorian Poetry*, 6 [1968], 177–179).

  4. On Darwin, see *Browning's Trumpeter: The Correspondence of Robert Browning and Frederick J. Furnivall*, ed. William S. Peterson (Washington, D. C.: Decatur House, 1979), pp. 34–35. On reading journals at the Athenaeum Club, see *Dearest Isa: Robert Browning's Letters to Isabella Blagden*, ed. Edward C. McAleer (Austin: University of Texas Press, 1951), pp. 196, 226. When he went to the continent in 1881 he arranged to receive *The Academy, The Athenaeum, The Pall Mall Gazette, The Nineteenth Century*, and *The Contemporary Review* (*Learned Lady: Letters from Robert Browning to Mrs. Thomas Fitzgerald 1876–1889*, ed. Edward C. McAleer [Cambridge, Massachusetts: Harvard University Press, 1966], pp. 119–120). Mrs. Sutherland Orr says that in his later years he read few books but "absorbed almost unconsciously every item which added itself to the sum of general knowledge" (*Life and Letters of Robert Browning*, 2d ed. [London: Smith, Elder & Co., 1892], p. 383). It is hard to learn more than this. Browning had a book of Andrew Lang's (1881) with uncut pages and a note from Lang's wife saying he was "too shy" to send it himself, and one from Müller (1887) inscribed to "Robert Browning, from an old admirer and debtor" ("A Reprint of the Dobell Browning Catalogue," *Browning Institute Studies*, 2 [1974], 97, 99, 112). In a book that

appeared after this essay was completed, Samuel B. Southwell suggests that Browning was probably influenced by Tylor, noting both general resemblances and verbal parallels between *Primitive Culture* and *Fifine at the Fair* (*Quest for Eros: Browning and "Fifine"* [Lexington: University Press of Kentucky, 1980], pp. 246–247.

    5. See Edward B. Tylor, *Primitive Culture*, 2 vols. (Boston: Estes & Lauriat, 1874), I, 143–168. See also Katherine H. Porter, *Through a Glass Darkly: Spiritualism in the Browning Circle* (Lawrence: University of Kansas Press, 1958), p. 20.

    6. See *Letters of the Brownings to George Barrett*, ed. Paul Landis and Ronald E. Freeman (Urbana: University of Illinois Press, 1958), p. 320.

    7. When Browning had what seemed a premonition about the discovery of a murdered man he explained it psychologically: "I attribute no sort of supernaturalism to my fancy. . . . By a law of the association of ideas—*contraries* come into the mind as often as *similarities*—and the peace and solitude readily called up the notion of what would most jar with them" (McAleer, *Learned Lady*, p. 152).

    8. "Book Sales," *The Athenaeum* (1871), 837. For an amusing description of Kirkup's experiences with clairvoyance, see *Elizabeth Barrett Browning: Letters to Her Sister*, ed. Leonard Huxley (London: John Murray, 1929), pp. 212–213.

    9. See William Wetmore Story, *Castle St. Angelo and the Evil Eye* (London: Chapman and Hall, 1877), p. iv; *Browning to His American Friends*, ed. Gertrude Reese Hudson (London: Bowes and Bowes, 1965), p. 116; *Letters of Robert Browning*, ed. Thurman L. Hood (New Haven, Connecticut: Yale University Press, 1933), p. 70; Huxley, pp. 190, 249.

    10. Sir John Lubbock, *The Origin of Civilization* (New York: Appleton, 1870), pp. v–vi, 114.

    11. [Henry Rowley], "The Ashantees," *Cornhill Magazine*, 28 (1873), 684.

    12. This old idea, put forth by Thomas Babington Macaulay and others, was being revived as part of the new science. Tylor says: "In so far as myth, seriously or sportively meant, is the subject of poetry, and in so far as it is couched in language whose characteristic is that wild and rambling metaphor which represents the habitual expression of savage thought, the mental condition of the lower races is the key to poetry" (Tylor, II, 447).

    13. On Ste. Marie, see McAleer, *Dearest Isa*, p. 223.

    14. For Browning's letter, see *The Works of John Ruskin*, ed. E. T. Cook and Alexander Wedderburn, 39 vols. (London: George Allen, 1909), XXXVI, xxxiv–xxxv. For Ruskin's, see David J. DeLaura, "Ruskin and the Brownings," *Bulletin of the John Rylands Library*, 54 (1972), 324–327.

    15. Browning may have had in mind Max Müller's theory that solar myths are the source of all mythologies; the theory was now being discredited, and Browning was not apt ever to have liked it. Julia Wedgwood asked him ironically in 1864: "What do you think of Max Müller finding out that the siege of Troy is a mythical representation of the Dawn, Helen is the morning twilight, stolen by the Sun, and only to be restored after a long siege!" (*Robert Browning and Julia Wedgwood: A Broken Friendship as Revealed by their Letters*, ed. Richard Curle [New York: Frederick A. Stokes, 1937], p. 50). (Browning's reply speaks of Helen [pp. 60–61] but not Müller.)

    16. Clyde de L. Ryals finds "the vatic poet" to be the poem's "main subject" (*Browning's Later Poetry: 1871–1889* [Ithaca, New York: Cornell University Press, 1975], p. 160).

    17. Charles Darwin, *The Descent of Man*, 2 vols. (London: John Murray, 1871), II, 404–405. Arthur O. Lovejoy and George Boas classify "animalitarianism" as "a sort of ultra-primitivism" (*Primitivism and Related Ideas in Antiquity* [Baltimore, Maryland: Johns Hopkins University Press, 1935], p. 19). Victorian sentimentalism about animals' virtues was among other things an attempt to make the beast within man seem tamer; see James Turner, *Reckoning with the Beast* (Baltimore, Maryland: Johns Hopkins University Press, 1980), pp 67–73.

    18. Review of *Primitive Culture*, *Athenaeum* (1871), 559. The episode is also, as Roma

A. King says, "an obvious parody of the second temptation of Christ" (*The Focusing Artifice* [Athens: Ohio University Press, 1968], p. 191.

19. There is some continuity but more change from the speaker in "Two in the Campagna" who finds thoughts of natural passion in the "primal naked forms of flowers" (28) by a ruined tomb and wants to be "unashamed of soul" (32). But that speaker is not repelled by nature's sexuality, does not associate it with the human primitive, and thinks about it in a rational civilized way.

20. On the complex relations between Tylor's idea of culture and Arnold's, see George W. Stocking, Jr., "Matthew Arnold, E. B. Tylor and the Uses of Invention," *American Anthropologist*, 65 (1963), 783–799, reprinted in *Race, Culture, and Evolution* (New York: Free Press, 1968). See also Patrick Brantlinger, *The Spirit of Reform* (Cambridge, Massachusetts: Harvard University Press, 1977), pp. 248–258.

21. "Greek Legends," (1867), in Max Müller, *Chips From a German Workshop*, 2 vols. (New York: Charles Scribner, 1869), II, 159, 160.

22. Augustus William Schlegel, *A Course of Lectures in Dramatic Art and Literature*, trans. John Black, rev. ed. (London: Bohn, 1846), pp. 111–121. On the Victorian poets' use of classical mythology, see Douglas Bush, *Mythology and the Romantic Tradition in English Poetry* (Cambridge, Massachusetts: Harvard University Press, 1937), and James Kissane, "Victorian Mythology," *Victorian Studies*, 6 (1962), 5–28. Robert Langbaum argues in a rich and persuasive essay, "Browning and the Question of Myth," (*PMLA* 81 [1966], 575–584), that Browning followed the "mythic method" adumbrated by T. S. Eliot. Browning uses classical myths negatively or parodically as a principle of allusive organization in the speech of the lawyer Bottinus (*The Ring and the Book*, IX), who continually puts the story into inappropriate mythic contexts. In Bottinus's telling, all myths are more or less anti-Christian, base, and lewd.

23. John Addington Symonds, *Studies of the Greek Poets* (London: Smith, Elder, & Co., 1873), pp. 238–241, 276 ff; Frederick Monroe Tisdel, "Browning's *Aristophanes' Apology*," *University of Missouri Studies*, 2 (1927), 11.

24. Mrs. Sutherland Orr broached this theory: see p. 308. It has been frequently approved, notably by Roma King, (p. 207).

25. *Virgil*, trans. H. Rushton Fairclough, rev, ed., 2 vols. (London: Heinemann-Loeb Classical Library, 1935), *Georgics* III, 390–392. On Pan as he appeared to the Brownings and other Victorian poets, see Patricia Merivale, *Pan the Goat-God* (Cambridge, Massachusetts: Harvard University Press, 1969). There are suggestive readings of "Pan and Luna" by Donald S. Hair and W. David Shaw in *Browning Society Notes*, 4 (July 1974): see Donald S. Hair, "Browning's 'Pan and Luna': An Experiment in Idyl," 3–8; and W. David Shaw, "Mystification and Mystery: Browning's 'Pan and Luna,' " 9–12.

26. William C. DeVane points this out in *Browning's Parleyings* (New Haven, Connecticut: Yale University Press, 1927), p. 231.

27. William G. Kingsland, *Robert Browning, Chief Poet of the Age*, new ed. (London: J. W. Jarvis, 1890), pp. 32–33. On Browning and the Bible critics, see William O. Raymond, "Browning and Higher Criticism," in *The Infinite Moment*, 2d ed. (Toronto: University of Toronto Press, 1965), and Elinor Shaffer, *Kubla Khan and the Fall of Jerusalem* (Cambridge: Cambridge University Press, 1975).

Browning's *Strafford* and the History of the Present

DAVID E. LATANÉ, JR.

> Prithee, Vane, a truce
> To Eliot and his times, and the great Duke,
> And how to manage Parliaments!
> —*Strafford*, III, i, 41–43[1]

We are living in an age of literary reformation in which "historical" is a graced word, especially when preceded by "new." But the celebration of centennials is an *old* historical endeavor—in 1837 when he wrote and saw performed his verse drama *Strafford*, Browning was engaged in a particular historical act, commemorating, as he says in his preface, the bicentennial of the Ship-Money Trial—a momentous event in the history of resistance to tyranny. *Strafford*, which struck its first and most influential reader, the actor William Macready, as "too historical,"[2] has been well considered from the point of view of "history," especially the history of its sources, its conception, and staging. Like its companion *Sordello*, it also has been examined as a work that is only incidentally historical. An examination of the English theater of political discourse in the 1830s, however, suggests that *Strafford* invokes the past in the service of a history of the present.

In his discussion of Browning's career to 1841, Lawrence Poston argues that "Through poetic engagement with the middle ground of history . . . Browning's early career represents . . . an attempt to construct a bridge between imagination and fact, between a perception of the eternal and an immersion in everyday experience. For this purpose, what serves him best are figures like Paracelsus and Sordello who have historical identities but about whom little is historically known; in them we sense the pressures of an age, while at the same time we participate imaginatively in the poet's freedom to reconstruct them as persons, a reconstruction untrammelled by an excess of biographical data."[3] *Strafford* I believe presents a different problem, though a natural tendency has been to align the play with the poems, and to judge its success by Browning's ability to resurrect the individual man

This essay is published here for the first time by permission of the author.

Strafford from the murk of history. Many critics have found, consequently, that in *Strafford* Browning's chief interest lay in the development of a soul[4]— the subject he proclaims later in his preface to *Sordello*; De Silva, for instance, discovers "a private world, which history cannot know. That is Browning's comfort, and the basis of his creative engagement with the past."[5] Browning's shift from the public to the personal world, compounded with an impractical theory of drama, thus led to a failed play, the chief defects of which, summarized by Katherine Gleason in 1927, are 1) poverty of action, 2) lack of clearness, 3) lack of humor, 4) lack of plot. As an acting play, according to this line of thought, *Strafford* shows too many of the poetic features of Browning's closet-drama *Paracelsus*, published two years before, and of *Sordello*, published three years after.[6] Many contemporary reviewers, however, noted the almost entire *lack* of fine "poetry" in the play, and, while most approved, some thought that Browning had erred too much in adapting his language to the practicalities of the theater.

Strafford may legitimately be seen as a privatization of history under the rubric of Love, as an ironic character study, and as an expression of skepticism about politics in general. It is also an example—subtle and sharp—of the way in which discursive threads spiral in and out of the text of history. Mary Ellis Gibson has usefully framed Browning as a "contextualist poet" for whom "the best presentation of history is not a straightforward narrative; the interconnections of the historical web require that many threads be followed, if possible at once."[7] In a way that I do not think is true for Browning's other works of the period, *Strafford* does more than follow with an ironic eye the warp and woof of the past and present; Browning's choice of Strafford for the subject of a Covent Garden tragedy is a self-contemplating but actual intervention in the discursive history of the present. Rather than argue from the poems to the play, noting the play's failure to represent clearly the complexities of individual psychology, it is possible to move from the play, with its overt concern with the discourse of contemporary politics, to the poems, where such concerns are buried in the more obscure, foreign figures of a German pseudo-scientist and an Italian troubadour.

To begin, it is important to mark Browning's moment of decision with regard to *Strafford*. Browning's opportunity to produce a play is often depicted as the beginning of an unfortunate detour into the theater. At the time, though, it must have been regarded by the twenty-four-year-old Browning and his friends as a golden opportunity to make his name, and to effect a change in the history of the nation's literature. A play at either Covent Garden or Drury Lane reached an immediate audience of three thousand, supposing a soldout first night (which Browning had); subsequent performances and readers of the printed book added many more. In comparison, Browning's first poem, *Pauline*, apparently failed to sell a single copy. Plays were also widely reviewed—*Strafford* received twenty-five notices, while

Sordello, Browning's next book, garnered only nine, and several of them were single dismissive paragraphs. The theater was the only place that a poet, as opposed to a novelist, could reach the many rather than the few.

While critics and readers in the 1830s accepted as a commonplace that current poetry was derivative, stale, and dying, the drama was cited as a lone spot of hope. Though there were quite a few Jeremiads about the state of popular taste in theater, many articles called for a rebirth of poetic drama, and many heralded a Renaissance. The "dramatic" in literature enjoyed an immense vogue; as a writer in the *Athenæum* puts it, critics, "whenever they have no distinct idea of a work's real excellence, declare it, in the straits of their criticism, very *dramatic*. Every pet work is dramatic now."[8] For a young author, however, to break into the theatre was conceived a difficult thing. In a *Monthly Repository* article of 1836, a critic asks, suppose a young "dramatic genius . . . writes a genuine tragedy—[but] he has no interest with influential people, and is not a man of wealth; what on earth can he do with it? Offer it to some of the managers?—nonsense!—to some of the publishers?—nonsense! . . . The fact is, there is no chance at all for such a production." At the same time, many agreed with this writer that "We should hail the appearance of a great tragedy founded on true principles, as one among the signs of the times, which combine to promise the purification and exaltation of society and nature itself."[9] Most new dramas were historical.[10] Browning was the author of *Paracelsus*, a dramatic poem praised by John Forster in his "Evidence of a New Genius for Dramatic Poetry." When Browning found that his new interest with influential people—Forster, Talfourd, Macready—gave him the chance to write a tragedy for Covent Garden, he may have felt as though he was carrying the weight of English Literature on his shoulders.

A central question, then, is what did Browning have in mind when he decided to make his mark in this atmosphere with a play about Strafford? The choice of Strafford is normally accounted for by circumstances. After the publication of *Paracelsus* Browning and John Forster became close friends, and Forster introduced Browning into Macready's circle at Covent Garden. Forster had been commissioned by Dionysius Lardner to write a series of lives for *The Cabinet Cyclopædia*—his subjects were Eliot, Pym, Hampden, Sir Henry Vane the Younger, Henry Marten, Cromwell, and Strafford. Forster completed the first volume, the *Life of Eliot*, then fell ill, and Browning finished *The Life of Strafford* for him. When Macready, after the first-night party for Talfourd's *Ion*, said, "Write me a play, Browning, and keep me from going to America," Browning replied, "Shall it be historical and English? what do you say to a drama on Strafford?" (Jack and Smith, 6–7). Presumably, if Forster had been writing a life of Narses, the eunuch General of sixth-century Byzantium who reconquered Italy from the Goths, Browning would have said, "what do you say to a drama on Narses?"

In fact, we know from Macready's diary that Narses was indeed Browning's first choice for a play—he proposed it to Macready on 16 January 1836, when he went backstage with Forster to compliment the actor on his performance of Othello. Browning's reading and interests were so varied, and the possibilities for theatrical subject matter so wide-open, that I think we must consider Strafford a deliberate choice for reasons not entirely tied up with the accident of Forster's illness and Browning's involvement with the *Life*. Indeed, with Bulwer publicly working on a play about Cromwell, Browning might have had an incentive to avoid direct competition with the most popular author of the decade. It is unlikely in this atmosphere that Browning settled on the subject of *Strafford* by mere chance.

Browning is usually portrayed as a sheltered young man, introspective and poetic, but there can be little doubt that he was keenly attuned to the times. *Strafford* is an oblique history of the present that should be read in the context of its own public staging in the wake of the Reform Bill, and as part of a discourse which faced a triple mirror. English writers in the 1820s and 1830s held their own revolutionary moment before a glass that gave them three reflections: the handsome, peaceful change of 1688, the lean, yet heroic fanaticism of the English civil war, and the horrific distortions of the French Revolution.

Whigs, Tories, and Radicals all saw their times in this triple glass, each group finding their own reflected meanings. In *The Victorian Mirror of History*, Dwight Culler argues that, in his speeches and writings in the five years before the Reform Bill, Macaulay suppressed the parallel with the ancien régime and evoked the period before the civil war. Culler argues that for Macaulay and other reformers, "The extreme Tories of the 1820s correspond to the intransigent followers of the early Stuarts. Lord Eldon is interchangeable with Laud. The Philosophic Radicals and Benthamites show the same fanatic adherence to political doctrine as did the Puritans to theology infected with politics, and they manifest the same aversion to literature and the fine arts." "The Tories, on the other hand, pushed the parallel with the French Revolution—most notably in Archibald Alison's interminable "On Parliamentary Reform and the French Revolution," which ran for almost all of 1831 in *Blackwood's*. Alison cried out that "the march of revolution has been much more rapid than that which preceded the Reign of Terror";[12] he makes numerous references, also, to England's civil war. After reviewing the details of the trial of Strafford, Alison concludes that "if the system of concession to popular demands were ever destined to be successful, here it was tried on the greatest scale, and with the fairest prospect of success. What were its consequences? . . . it inflated to madness the ambition of the Commons . . . and excited an universal frenzy throughout the nation" (Alison, 30). For the Tories, Strafford's execution was the prime example of the dangers of appeasement.

How much of this context is still operative four years after the Bill, when Browning begins work on his play? I think almost all of it. England was still in a very unsettled state, with short-lived ministries by Gray, Melbourne, and Peel, and the beginning of the end for the Whig party. As Patrick Brantlinger notes, for the reformers and radicals, "by 1836 or 1837 . . . utopian expectations were yielding to disillusionment",[13] caused in great measure by the conservative nature of post-Reform Parliament and the beginning of economic depression in 1836. William Lovett's formation of the Working Men's Association in 1836 was but one sign that the lower classes were stirring towards Chartism. The Tories, meanwhile, regarded the post-Reform Parliaments as little better than the Long Parliament, bent on the destruction of Old England. The *Times* leader for 2 November 1836 (when Browning was hard at work on his play) makes an implicit parallel: "The rump of the Whigs has become the scorn of the country, because it has been used on all occasions as a footstool by English Radicals, or Irish Papists, and kicked about by each in whatever direction suited the purpose of the time. The Whigs now in office—it can never be too emphatically dwelt upon or too often repeated—have identified themselves with the extirpation of Protestantism from Ireland, and with the subversion of Throne and Peerage in Great Britain" (p. 2). Of course, one thinks of Marx's famous tragedy/farce dictum when one discovers in the same month the thundering claim that "the Conservative meetings which . . . it has been our grateful duty to record and observe upon, constitute the most formidable barrier against revolution that ever existed in any society on earth" (1 November 1836, p. 2). The "West Kent Conservative Dinner," reported in January of 1837, was indeed a barrier to revolution; many Kentish men were well fed, and after a robust meal, the reporter recorded the gist of the speeches: "They would have an hereditary King and an Hereditary House of Lords. (Loud cheers.) The men of Kent would besides insist on having an established church (cheers). . . . They would not consent to lose the parent tree which, for so many ages, had been planted amongst them, for some sapling of a newer and more fashionable stock (cheers); or, to change the allusion, and borrow one from the repast they had lately partaken of, how would they like to exchange their good English fare for an indifferent Irish stew? ('Hear, hear,' and laughter); or to a less satisfactory dish—a death's head and cross-bones?" The political metaphors of the night are instructive; Clarendon was the first, I believe, to refer to the radicals of the Long Parliament as "root and branch men"—here the English "parent tree" is threatened, after uprooting, with some new sapling, which I believe calls to mind the "Liberty Tree" of the French Revolution, still appearing on working class banners in the 1830s. The Irish stew's chef is of course Daniel O'Connell. One might notice, though, that the speaker doesn't dare to ask his listeners if they would prefer French cooking, but instead raises the specter of the cannibalistic terror with the "death's head and cross-bones."

Every morning's newspaper, more or less, contained references to the triple mirror, reflected back to the tripartite party structure of Tory, Whig, and Radical. A utilitarian journalist notes with scorn in 1837 that "the oligarchical effusions of a Conservative dinner, reported in this evening's *Standard*, are records of the past" that use history as political capital.[14] To choose Wentworth, Earl of Strafford, as a subject guaranteed an audience with prejudices; to invoke the civil war was to draw party lines, to define the essential divisions of the nation. It was an article of political faith among both Whigs and Tories that their parties represented not faction, but eternal contraries in the ongoing story of English liberty and the English constitution, and that these lines were first drawn clearly during the seventeenth century. In his "A Tory's Account of Toryism, Whiggism, and Radicalism, in a Letter to a Friend in Bengal," Thomas De Quincey finds the essential principles of the modern parties, as crystalized in 1688, already "latent in the Parliamentary war" (495). The gist of his information for the Bengalese, however, is the answer to his question: "Toryism I understand, and Whiggism I understand; but what is Radicalism?" (511). The Radicals, on the other hand, defined the Tories and Whigs not through essential principles, but only as factions of "Aristocracy"; the difference was that the Tories were honest about their class interest, while the "mean, dirty set" of Whigs, in John Stuart Mill's youthful phrase, were hypocrites.[15] Radical thought firmly placed theory or principles ahead of historical example: as the author of "Principles before History," a *Monthly Repository* essay of 1837 puts it, "the importance of the narrative of particular cases is annulled when we possess their essence . . . compressed into general laws" (L.D., 285). Arguments from historical precedent are to be mistrusted, because "The falsification of History is a favorite engine of the oligarchy" which takes the records of the past as a material for the "manufacture of fictitious political credit" (L.D., 288). Depending on the political stance of the reader in 1837, a work about Strafford might mirror back a Tory martyr, a Whig villain, or be perceived by the philosophical radical as a duplicitous use of historical example to discredit theoretical political science.

Given the liberal sentiments of the author's one published work, *Paracelsus*, and the well-known political views of Macready, the manager, leading actor, and chief adviser to authors, the three thousand or so folks who crowded into Covent Garden might have expected a play that reflected the standard Whig view of Strafford's character. Strafford and Laud had become the stock villains of the tale; in the words of a well-known Whig historian, "Charles had . . . two counsellors who seconded him, or went beyond him, in intolerance and lawless violence, the one a superstitious driveller, as honest as a vile temper would suffer him to be, the other a man of great valour and capacity, but licentious, faithless, corrupt, and cruel".[16] Macaulay's "Essay on Hampden," which appeared in the *Edinburgh Review* in 1831, casts a powerful shadow over representations of the chief men of the 1630s in the discourse of the 1830s.[17] Strafford's character is hardly ambiguous:

> He abandoned his associates, and hated them ever after with the deadly hatred of a renegade. High titles and great employments were heaped upon him. He became Earl of Strafford, Lord Lieutenant of Ireland, President of the Council of the North; and he employed all his power for the purpose of crushing those liberties of which he had been the most distinguished champion. His counsels respecting public affairs were fierce and arbitrary. His correspondence with Laud abundantly proves that government without parliaments, government by the sword, was his favorite scheme. . . . In Ireland, where he stood in place of the King, his practice was in strict accordance with his theory. He set up the authority of the executive government over that of the courts of law. He permitted no person to leave the island without his licence. He established vast monopolies for his own private benefit. He imposed taxes arbitrarily. He levied them by military force. . . . When the violent acts of the Long Parliament are blamed, let it not be forgotten from what a tyranny they rescued the nation.
> —Macaulay, 1:121

The man who rescues the nation, in Macaulay's vision, is John Hampden, the simple "Mister" or "Esquire"—he is the precursor of the Whigs, a gentleman who loves liberty. And he dies a tragic and heroic death.

So why doesn't Browning write *Hampden: A Tragedy*?

Browning had been thinking of Shakespeare's *Henry V*, and Hampden would seem to be the perfect hero for the post-Reform stage. There was even a book (advertised in the *Metropolitan Magazine* in 1837) called *Hampden in the Nineteenth Century*. Browning's choice of Strafford, and his decision to foreground Pym instead of Hampden, seems rather curious—especially when one remembers that Hampden really was an early friend of Wentworth's while Browning's friendship between Pym and Strafford is by virtue of Browning's poetic license. Many of the next morning's newspaper reviews of Browning's play commented on Hampden's unimportance; *The Morning Post* said, "he cuts a sorry figure here. Whenever he appears he seems but a poor, unnoticed, and to all appearance, unknown, hanger-on upon the scene."[18] *The Sun* was disappointed in the shabby treatment, saying that in Browning's play the great patriot is "little better than a walking gentleman" (Kelley and Hudson 390). Browning's avoidance of the obvious may be part of a strategy to defeat his audience's stock interpretations and force them to engage with the ambiguities of historical mirroring.

Strafford's preface, as Clyde Ryals has noted, contains an irony (Ryals, 55). Browning begins, "I had for some time been engaged in a Poem of a very different nature, when induced to make the present attempt; and am not without apprehension that my eagerness to freshen a jaded mind by diverting it to the healthy natures of a grand epoch, may have operated unfavourably on the represented play, which is one of Action in Character rather than Character in Action" (Jack and Smith, 500). The irony exists in the discrepancy between the "healthy natures of a grand epoch" and the chief characters of the play, such as the fanatic Pym, the irresolute, craven Charles, and Strafford himself, willfully blind to the King's character. There may be a further complexity when one considers that, for most readers, the diversion of the "jaded mind" would have been understood as a movement back into history from the 1830s, whereas Browning, his friends, and subsequent readers know that it was also forward in time from the late-medieval setting of *Sordello*. Finally, Browning's irony extends to the relative absence of the healthiest nature of the grand epoch, John Hampden. Macaulay gushes over Hampden's character, finding, in Browning's terms, both "Character in Action" and "Action in Character": "We can scarcely express the admiration which we feel for a mind so great, and, at the same time, so healthful and so well proportioned, so willingly conducting itself to the highest, so contented in repose, so powerful in action. Almost every part of this virtuous and blameless life which is not hidden from us in modest privacy is a precious and splendid portion of our national history." Macaulay argues that Hampden's "history . . . is the history of England" (Macaulay, 103, 102).

What then is Strafford's history? In choosing to make Strafford a sympathetic hero—to make him a failed Henry instead of an evil, imposing Richard—Browning unsynchronizes the standard mirroring of the events of the 1630s. The broken links are what clearly puzzled Forster about the play; whereas his *Life of Strafford*, as finished by Browning, stayed within the bounds of the common discourse, Browning's play seemed to be a distortion, which Forster in his *Examiner* review ascribed to the error of a "pure poetical temperament." Forster argues that "in a tragedy, where the author places the popular cause in the very front of all our sympathies, the criminality of *Strafford* should have been made equally prominent with his grandeur. The catastrophe should have been the triumph of patriotism over the antagonist principle of tyranny; and this we do not feel as it stands" (Kelley and Hudson, 3: 400).

Browning's understanding of the dynamics of history, however, doesn't require a criminal or an apostate Strafford. When we consider the first act, we can see how Browning unsettles the audience's expectation of a play with conventional political content. Browning conflates biography with history—a process already outlined in a different way by Carlyle in his numerous periodical essays; he illumes the central power struggle of the 1630s, with complex implications for the 1830s as well.

The parliamentarians are gathered in a house near Whitehall, and the action opens *in media res*:

> *Vane.* I say, if he be here—
> *Rudyard.*   (And he is here!)—
>
> *Hollis.* For England's sake let every man be still.
> Nor speak of him, so much as say his name,
> Till Pym rejoin us! Rudyard! Henry Vane!

> One rash conclusion may decide our course
> And with it England's fate—think—England's fate!
> Hampden, for England's sake they should be still!
>   *Hollis.* For England's sake let every man be still.
> It is indeed too bitter that one man,
> Any one man's mere presence, should suspend
> England's combined endeavour: little need
> To name him!
>   (I, i, 1–11)

The dynamics of this opening defers the name, which once uttered will affect England's fate—that "one man" who can "suspend / England's combined endeavour." Rudyard's parenthetic "And he is here!" raises another question: how do you speak a parenthesis? Spoken as an aside to the audience, Rudyard reminds the playgoers that "He" must not be named.

If on the way to the theater that night, the playgoer of 1837 had overheard a similar, fragmentary conversation, I think he would have guessed that the "one man" still capable of suspending the combined endeavour of political reform was the Duke of Wellington. Wellington's battle cry during the Reform debates was "How is the King's government to be carried on?" Like Strafford, he was loyal first to his King, in this case the sailor William IV, even when the King supported Reform. During the agitation surrounding the Bill, appeals were made to Wellington to take command—in language always heavily charged with military metaphor. In *Blackwood's*, Alison accused the Tory troops in the Commons of deserting Wellington: "It was not by conciliation and concession that he resisted the invasion of Portugal in 1810. The Whigs then strenuously recommended the same submission to the French which they have since made to the Radicals." Tories in Parliament, he argues, should stand firm alongside Wellington, "the British Hero" (Alison, 20). A scene from Disraeli's *Coningsby* captures the mood among the Tories during the crucial "days of May" in 1832:

> " 'I think, Lord Monmouth,' said Mr. Rigby, 'we must ask permission to drink one toast to-day.'
> 'Nay, I will myself give it,' he replied. 'Madame Colonna, you will, I am sure, join us when we drink, THE DUKE!'
> 'Ah, what a man!' exclaimed the Princess, 'What a pity it is you have a House of Commons here! England would be the greatest country in the world if it were not for that House of Commons. It makes so much confusion!' "[19]

Many commentators of the 1830s, drawing on the example of the French Revolution, argued that military despotism was the inevitable result of experiments with Democracy.[20] The unstamped press in 1832 fantasized about the Duke and the Czar leading Cossacks into London to dissolve the parliament and slit "English Throats with Russio-Wellington swords."[21]

Throughout the 1830s, "The Duke," usually not denoted by a more specific name, was a force of reaction to be reckoned with; Carlyle writes, in a letter of 1835, that "Politics run mountain-high . . . the prophecy I give is black. What were the wager that Wellington lived yet to lose his head?"[22] In the third act, Browning makes a direct reference to Wellington. Vane begins to speak of Eliot and the parliaments of the 1620s, and Savile cuts him off with "Prithee, Vane, a truce / To Eliot and his times, and the great Duke, / And how to manage Parliaments!" (III, i, 40–42). Savile speaks of the Duke of Buckingham, but since he is not otherwise named, the audience, I believe, would only think about the current "great Duke" who singularly failed to manage parliaments.

Browning's play, dodging the censorship that forbade contemporary political reference in the legitimate drama, powerfully evokes the current situation. But the opening deflects any prepackaged interpretations of familiar historical analogy. This is because the events are less important than the language; Browning is interested in discursive conflict rather than physical action, and in the self-propagandizing nature of political rhetoric as much as its meaning. The focus on language, before either character or action, certainly led a number of the reviewers, though not all, to complain that the plot was "somewhat obscurely developed to those unread in English history" (*Metropolitan Magazine*, in Kelley and Hudson, 3: 386). Browning chooses to introduce the bicentennial topic of ship-money, for instance, through a fleeting reference by a minor character only in line 254. Instead of a beginning exposition that situates the action in relation to the main events, and the standard interpretations of those events, the two scenes of the first act present antithetical descriptions of historical forces, parleying discourse from historical figures through the actors on the stage into the present.

In the first scene, for instance, Browning illuminates the language that ironically connects the parliamentary party of the 1630s and the philosophical radicals of the 1830s. The McGuffin here, to borrow a term from Hitchcock, is the discourse of religion. Ryals has wittily noted that the "Puritan who appears and reappears like a character in *Hellzapoppin* is forever quoting scripture" (Ryals, 61). Strafford is typed by this puritan as a "Philistine" from the Book of Samuel; but the parliamentary party, through Browning's implication of its proto-historicist thinking, is connected with the philistinism of the utilitarians; Vane, for instance, thinks "on all that's past / Since that man left us, how his single arm / Rolled the advancing good of England back / And set the woeful past up in its place, / Exalting Dagon where the Ark should be" (I, i, 30–35). Vane's attack on Strafford's tyranny recalls the standard Whig view, but buried within it is the March of Mind, the "advancing good." The Radicals of the 1830s, alone among the parties, reject historical precedent and condemn the woeful past (just like the Jacobins, according to their critics). What is historically unimportant is the conscious belief by Vane that his actions conserve the Ark of Religion.

Browning makes us aware that to use the mirror of the past is to be subjected to mirrored reversals that mock the language of both eras. The first two scenes inscribe—not always in connection to individual speakers—the play of ideological formations around three key words: "England," "King," and "the People." Some variation of the word "England" or "English" is spoken by the parliamentarians some thirty times in the first scene alone. They appropriate the national name through repetition, and this again calls to mind the debate of 1832. The clearly felt will of the nation was the chief argument used to carry a Reform Bill through both Houses, with fear of Revolution providing the punctuation marks. De Quincey notes with scorn in 1835 how the Reformers still used this argument: "As a party opposed to a party, they would lie under the common presumption of error; but, as the nation opposed to a party, they have a dispensation from argument, and an immunity from error."[23] In Browning's first scene, the parliamentarians create themselves as "England," and are immune from error. From the perspective of 1837, this opening works variously. It reminds the audience of the power of the Duke, thus awakening both the fear of a military takeover and the fear of the mob that would necessitate such action. Perhaps it also mocks claims of the radicals to be above party/faction, to act disinterestedly for the public good. The claim to speak for England in 1637 ended in civil war, and the threat of such a war hangs over the theater.

In the second scene, Strafford enters the play. Macready's costume on the first night was apparently designed after the portrait of Strafford by Van Dyke. In Macaulay's essay on Hampden, the portrait is the occasion for an ekphrastic set piece. "But Wentworth, who ever names him without thinking of those harsh dark features . . . of that brow, that eye, that cheek, that lip, wherein, as in a chronicle, are written the events of many stormy and disasterous years, high enterprise accomplished, frightful dangers braved, power unsparingly exercised, suffering unshrinkingly borne; of that fixed look, so full of severity, of mournful anxiety, of deep thought, of dauntless resolution, which seems at once to forbode and to defy a terrible fate, as it lowers on us from the living canvas of Van-dyke?" (Macaulay, 1:120). Interestingly, it is Forster, in his review of Browning's play in *The Examiner*, who directly quotes Macaulay: "The most striking thing of the evening was Mr. Macready's first entrance upon the stage. It was the portrait of the great and ill-fated *Earl*, stepping from the living canvas of Van Dyke!" (Kelley and Hudson, 3: 401).

The first appearance of the hero, then, matches expectations of a liberty-usurping but forceful Earl, and Browning then proceeds to work changes upon these expectations. In this second scene the word "King" is used about twenty-five times, in opposition to "England" of the first scene. In between these two terms, mediating and in contestation, is the word "people"—the most highly charged term for the 1830s. Strafford complains to Lady Carlisle about the nibbling of the members of the court, and then asks

>   What 's Pym about?
>   *Lady Carlisle.* Pym?
>   *Wentworth.* Pym and the People.
>   *Lady Carlisle.*   Oh, the Faction!
>   Extinct—of no account: there'll never be
>   Another Parliament.
>   (I, ii, 61–63)

Strafford here cedes, perhaps sarcastically, the term "People" to Pym's faction, while Lady Carlisle's premature obituary for the "faction" foreshadows its more powerful resurrection in the Long Parliament, speaking the will of the people.

Wentworth's soliloquy in the scene immediately prior to his first meeting with Pym puts all three key terms in play in a field of multiple ironies and contemporary reverberations:

>   *Wentworth.* Heartless! but all are heartless here.
>   Go now,
>   Forsake the People!
>   I did not forsake
>   The People: they shall know it, when the King
>   Will trust me!—who trusts all beside at once,
>   While I have not spoke of Vane and Savile fair,
>   And am not trusted: have but saved the throne:
>   Have not picked up the Queen's glove prettily,
>   And am not trusted. But he'll see me now.
>   Weston is dead: the Queen 's half English now—
>   More English: one decisive word will brush
>   These insects from . . . the step I know so well!
>   The King! But now, to tell him . . . no—to ask
>   What 's in me he distrusts:—or, best begin
>   By proving that this frightful Scots affair
>   Is just what I foretold. So much to say,
>   And the flesh fails, now, and the time is come,
>   And one false step no way to be repaired.
>   You were avenged, Pym, could you look on me.
>   PYM *enters*
>   *Wentworth.* I little thought of you just then.
>   *Pym.*   No? I
>   Think always of you, Wentworth.
>   *Wentworth.*   The old voice!
>   I wait the King, sir.
>   (I, ii, 88–108)

The broken speech here—ascribed by the critics to a desire to favor Macready's style of pauses and gasps—is full of Browningesque gaps, amphibologic muddle, and intertextual self-allusion. Strafford reminds himself of his internal consistency—he rebuts the charge of apostasy towards the people's cause; if the King will trust me, he argues, I will hold faith with the people. As the Queen becomes "English," Strafford will be able to speak the "one word" that will rid the court of the "insects" who plot against him, the King, and the people. When Strafford interrupts himself to say "The step I know so well" he refers to audible footsteps which he thinks are those of the King.

The "one word," though, doubles back against Strafford's knowledge of himself. It represents a "step" towards centralizing, autocratic power such as Strafford exercised in Ireland. As he hears footsteps, though, he frets about his appearance before his beloved King, which summons the thought of Pym, who enters in place of the expected King. Here is the usurpation by King Pym, whose "old voice" is also the voice of the people whom Strafford has just proclaimed he will not forsake. Browning's play, like *Sordello*, is in good measure about the "steps" to power.

While the autocratic King is the "one man" who stands in for the nation, Browning explores the falling arcs of great men who sense their own presence on the world-historical stage. In *Victoria's Year*, Richard Stein argues that Browning's theme is the absence of heroes in the first year of Victoria's reign: "The victory of the Parliamentarians marks an end to the last heroic era in British history, or such is the view of the hero and his author."[24] This makes *Strafford* sound a bit like a dramatic parallel to Tennyson's "The Epic"—but I think Browning's play is both more skeptical and more hopeful about the possibility of individual action. The unpredictable interplay of history and hero and the strange fates that offer ordinary men the stage are Browning's subjects. What interested Browning in the story of Narses, I surmise, is that "A feeble diminutive body," according to Gibbon, "concealed the soul of a statesman and warrior"; Narses was trained in "the cares of the household . . . and the service of female luxury,"[25] but when given a chance he took command, led the forces that recaptured Italy from the Goths and Franks, and ruled for fifteen years (Gibbon, 4: 407). Dramatic irony abounds in the story of a eunuch ousting the barbarian; the "hero" can come from the least likely place. But who is to be the hero of *Strafford*?

The opening of *Strafford* broaches the hero in the guise of the "single arm" that can strike down the people; the real hero, however, will be the "one name," in Hampden's phrase, "dearer than all names" (I, i, 175) that will be remembered as the people's savior. Pym asks, "Who'd give at any price his hope away / Of being named along with the Great Men?" (I, i, 172–173). One man will save England, and Pym asks "What if Wentworth's should be still / That name?" (I, i, 178–179). Pym and Strafford share the ambition to have their biography become conflated with the history of England, making them joint predecessors of heroes and hero worship; at least, the idea of the "one man" adumbrates Cromwell and, perhaps, Wellington, while the "one word," implicitly theological, offers an always deferred escape from the many words of history and dogma.

Strafford, though, reverses the pattern Carlyle will trace in his "Hero as King" lecture, in which the love of the first king-man is transferred to the office. In the second act, realizing that his path diverges wide from "England's path" (II, ii, 272), Strafford discovers he is acting out of a love for the man and not the King: "Whose fault? / Did I make kings? set up, the first, a man / To represent the multitude, receive / All love in right of them—supplant them so, / Until you love the man and not the king—" (II, ii, 288–292). Strafford goes on to a fit end for a hero—foreshadowing Charles' execution as well—while Pym, despite his later unheroic death, changes history by not "diverging wide" from England's path. In *Sordello*, a low voice comes to the troubadour and whispers "Read the black writing— that collective man / Outstrips the individual" (V, 103–104). While Sordello is a self-doubter who rejects the "one step," Pym outstrips the people by reaching their destination ahead of them, by making his name their name. Browning's play narrates the stories of Strafford and Pym for an England in which power, metonymically noted as "King," "England," "People," is once more on the move. Effectual political action is possible with the grain; tragedy is inevitable against the grain.

Strafford thus presents a paradox for political interpretation, as much to the modern new historical critic as to the Victorian audience. In his introduction to a special issue of *Critical Inquiry* on "Politics & Poetic Value," Robert von Hallberg states that new-historical interpretive strategies decenter poems that veil the author's self-interest, while texts that express progressive political positions are salvaged from neglect. "Either way," he comments, "self-interest is now thought of as the most authentic motive an interpreter can divulge in a text."[26] While *Strafford* is a rich and overtly political work, unmasking in it either a self-interested stance or lauding in it an orthodox progressiveness is interpretive work that risks misprision or willful misinterpretation. Browning illuminates historical moments when the individual subject becomes unbound from the usual limits imposed by the discursive laws of an era. In 1837 any narrative of Strafford would be bathed in politics and ideologies, but Browning is strangely uninterested—perhaps even "disinterested"—in conveying a prefabricated political message. Patrick Brantlinger argues that *Strafford* is about neither history nor politics, and that "instead of suggesting that one side is right and the other side wrong, the play suggests that politics is dangerous—it destroys friendships and kills both body and soul" (Brantlinger, 165). Is Browning then, after all, only concerned with the development of a soul? Only, I think, the soul in history who speaks to the history of the present, and is prepared to move with— and perhaps a little before—the tide of history.

Browning writes at a time in which it is taken for granted that the impeachment of Strafford was a turning point in history, and that this event has a peculiar consonance with the events of the present. In his essay "On History," Carlyle argues that the "conflict of testimonies" of contemporary records rarely take note of the most important events; it is only much later that "it is settled, by majority of votes, that such and such a 'Crossing of the Rubicon,' an 'Impeachment of Strafford,' a 'Convocation of the Notables,' are epochs in the world's history, cardinal points on which grand world-revolutions have hinged."[27] Browning's play cannot be charged with an escapist or sentimental attitude towards history and politics. In it he dramatizes the collective man—or the will of the people—outstripping the individual—and he makes a tragedy about the cost of such a realization at a turning point in world history to the individuals involved. Browning's play is in part reparation for such cost—late in the play the King says "We have done / Less gallantly by Strafford. Well, the future / Must recompense the past" (IV, iii, 3–5)—and in part preparation for the tragic narratives that must attend any era of sudden change.

Foucault calls for "effective history," for events described in their most unique and acute manifestations. "An event," Foucault says, "is not a decision, a treaty, a reign, or a battle, but the reversal of a relationship of forces, the usurpation of power, the appropriation of a vocabulary turned against those who had once used it."[28] Events are not the work of destiny, though it is Foucault's faith that they are or can be made intelligible. Browning makes Strafford's trial into an event of this nature. In Carlylean terms, Browning strives to represent the past to reveal the "transaction" of history as something other than the chronicled battles of Dryasdust. He asks us to imagine the action of history in the character of the men who made it. Browning's works of the 1830s are often about destiny foiled, or ironic historical turning points in which the turn is missed. He inquires, like Teufelsdröckh, "Wilt thou know a Man . . . by stringing-together beadrolls of what thou namest Facts? The Man is the spirit he worked in; not what he did, but what he became" (*Works*, 1: 161). Strafford and the discursive field of England, King, People, however, have not "become," but are still "becoming," and Browning's play joins this activity. *Strafford* is an event in the political history of 1837, and we should consider Browning's play first as a brilliant parallel drawn between the struggles of the 1630s and those of the 1830s. Through its implicit ironic commentary on the struggle to control political discourse in the 1830s, it illuminates and makes intelligible the power relations of both eras.

Notes

1. All quotations from Browning's works are from *The Poetical Works of Robert Browning. Vol. II: Strafford, Sordello*, Ian Jack and Margaret Smith, eds. (Oxford: Clarendon Press, 1984). Hereafter cited as Jack and Smith.
2. William Charles Macready, *The Diaries of William Charles Macready: 1833–1851*, 2 vols., William Toynbee, ed. (London: Chapman & Hall, 1912). This entry was made on 19 March 1837.
3. Lawrence Poston, "Browning's Career to 1841: The Theme of Time and the Problem of Form," *Browning Institute Studies* 3 (1975): 85–86.
4. Donald S. Hair, *Browning's Experiments with Genre* (Toronto: University of Toronto Press, 1972), 49. Clyde De L. Ryals, *Becoming Browning: The Poems and Plays of Robert Browning, 1833–1846* (Columbus: Ohio State University Press, 1983), 53. Hereafter cited as Ryals.
5. D. M. De Silva, "Salvation, Politics, and Truth in History; A Reading of Browning's *Strafford*," in James Hogg, ed., *A Salzburg Miscellany: English and American Studies, 1964–84* 2:42.
6. Katherine Florence Gleason, *The Dramatic Art of Robert Browning* (1927; Folcroft Press, 1970).
7. Mary Ellis Gibson, *History and the Prism of Art: Browning's Poetic Experiments* (Columbus: Ohio State University Press, 1987), 265.
8. Anonymous, *Athenæum* No. 482 (21 January 1837): 21.
9. " 'Ion,' and the *Athenæum*," *Monthly Repository* 10 (1836): 446, 449.
10. As Bulwer states in his prologue to "The Duchess de la Valliere," the aim was "To paint the Past, yet in the Past portray / such shapes as seem dim prophets of To-day" The most important new long poem, Henry Taylor's *Philip van Artevelde*, (1834), was dramatic in form and specific in its historical reference.
11. A. Dwight Culler, *The Victorian Mirror of History* (New Haven: Yale University Press, 1985), 35.
12. Archibald Alison, "On Parliamentary Reform and the French Revolution. No. VII. What should the Peers do?" *Blackwood's* 30 (July 1831): 19. Hereafter cited as Alison.
13. Patrick Brantlinger, *The Spirit of Reform: British Literature and Politics, 1832–1867* (Cambridge: Harvard University Press, 1977), 12. Hereafter cited as Brantlinger.
14. L. D., "Principles Before History," *Monthly Repository* 11 (1837): 287. Hereafter cited as L. D.
15. Stefan Collini, Donald Winch, and John Burrow, *That Noble Science of Politics: A Study in Nineteenth-Century Intellectual History* (Cambridge: Cambridge University Press, 1983), 109.
16. Thomas Babington Macaulay, *Critical and Historical Essays*, 2 vols., A. J. Grieve, ed. (London: Dent, 1907), 1:119. Hereafter cited as Macaulay.
17. Macaulay's essay was in the form of a favorable review of the extreme Whig Lord Nugent's *Some Memorials of John Hampden, his Party, and his Times*. Robert Southey argued the Tory line on the book and Hampden in the *Quarterly*, and a pamphlet war between Southey and Nugent ensued, with both sides developing extensive parallels to contemporary politics.
18. Philip Kelley, and Ronald Hudson, eds., *The Brownings' Correspondence* (Winfield, Kan.: Wedgestone Press, 1984–), 389. Hereafter cited as Kelley and Hudson.
19. Benjamin Disraeli, *Coningsby, or The New Generation*, Sheila M. Smith, ed. (Oxford: Oxford University Press, 1982), 28.
20. Walter E. Houghton, *The Victorian Frame of Mind* (New Haven: Yale University Press, 1957), 54–58.
21. "Murderous Plans of the Insatiables," *The Cab* No. 19 (7 July 1832): 82.
22. Thomas Carlyle, and Jane Welsh Carlyle, *The Collected Letters of Thomas and Jane*

Welsh Carlyle, Charles Richard Sanders, K. J. Fielding, Clyde de L. Ryals, et al., eds. (Durham, N.C.: Duke University Press, 1970), 8:6.

23. Thomas De Quincey, *Politics and Political Economy*, (Boston: Houghton Mifflin, 1877), 521.

24. Richard L. Stein, *Victoria's Year: English Literature and Culture, 1837–1838* (New York: Oxford University Press, 1987), 89.

25. Edward Gibbon, *The History of the Decline and Fall of the Roman Empire*, 6 vols., Notes by Dean Milman, M. Guizot, and Dr. Wm. Smith (New York: Harper, 1905), 4:393. Hereafter cited as Gibbon.

26. Robert von Hallberg, "Editor's Introduction," *Critical Inquiry* 13 (1987): 415.

27. Carlyle, Thomas, *The Works of Thomas Carlyle*, Centenary Edition, H. D. Traill, ed., 30 vols. (London: Chapman & Hall, 1896–99), 27:87. Hereafter cited as *Works*.

28. Michel Foucault, "Nietzsche, Genealogy, History," rpt. in *Language, Counter-memory, Practice*, Donald F. Bouchard, ed., Donald F. Bouchard and Sherry Simon, trans. (Ithaca: Cornell University Press, 1977), 154.

"The Englishman in Italy": Free Trade as a Principle of Aesthetics

ROBERT VISCUSI

Dante Alighieri, whom Chaucer could read with pleasure and Byron with delight or even identification, has not always been so well-met in England. Horace Walpole found him "absurd, disgusting, in short a Methodist parson in bedlam."[1] The line is often cited as an example of how limited were the literary tastes of the eighteenth century. But I must confess that Walpole's reaction does not seem strange to me. Whether one may sympathize with it or not, I expect, depends upon the degree of one's experience with Christian zealots. D. H. Lawrence, in his depressing book *Apocalypse*, draws a vivid picture of the gleeful ease with which such persons come to employ the millenarian poetry of the New Testament.[2] To consign one's enemies to immortal tortures while reserving for one's heroes all the delights of a tropical resort constructed largely out of diamonds and emeralds is not a subtle pleasure. Its appeal can reach the crudest minds. So urbane and elegant a fellow as Walpole, confronted by the self-righteous hymn-singing disciples of John Wesley, not only recoiled in disgust but quite properly recognized in the scheme of the *Commedia* something of the same primitive spirit. In every age, there will be persons to whom the blunt simplicity of this arrangement, say what you will for the profundities and revisions in Dante's handling of it, will be repulsive. Nowadays, perhaps, we are so hermeneutically splintered, so historically well-nourished, that we can entertain sympathies for Dante and for Walpole, for Byron and for Chaucer, for Eliot and even for Pound, all at the same time, always keeping in mind that our understanding of the one sets some kind of boundary upon our understanding of another. We do not close our eyes to Walpole or to Dante, though perhaps we find both of them at times in one way and another more than a little out of reach. It is in the spirit of this hermeneutical splintering that I wish to take up an element in the writings of Robert Browning which is, on the face of it, if not absurd and disgusting (to use Walpole's bold language), then at least dissonant and troubling.

---

§ Reprinted from *Browning Institute Studies* 12 (1984): 1–28, with permission.

I

The young author of *Sordello* writes to Elizabeth Barrett that he has been impressed by Hans Christian Andersen's *The Improvisatore*. "That a Dane should write so," he all but exclaims, "confirms me in an old belief—

> that Italy is stuff for the use of the North—and no more: pure Poetry there is none, nearly as possible none, in Dante even—materials for poetry in the pitifullest romancist of their thousands, on the contrary—strange that those great black wide eyes should stare nothing out of the earth that lies before them."[3]

A more unlovely counterpoint of mercantile colonialism and settled racism would be hard to imagine. In the days when Austria and France were constantly plotting to extend their Italian hegemonies, when England forever was dreaming of naval bases in Naples and Leghorn, "stuff for the use of the North" was no innocent phrase. And surely, only a pair of light eyes well narrowed by several centuries of Protestant propaganda could pile upon the synecdoche "those great black wide eyes" the outright nonsense which completes the sentence. But we need not, perhaps, make too much of this. Browning was young, provincial even, when he wrote it. Against it we may place the years that he and Elizabeth Barrett spent in Italy. The best part of their creative lives occurred there. Most of Browning's greatest poems have Italian themes, Italian themes, Italian characters, Italian settings. The home he shared with his wife is today quite properly a museum not only of their spectacularly productive marriage, but equally of their intense devotion to Italian politics, history, literature, art, and life. Surely the decades spent among the monuments of Italy's long centuries in the van of civilization did much to soften the prejudices of the English expatriate who wrote "Fra Lippo Lippi" and "Pippa Passes." Consider the subtleties in "Andrea del Sarto" and "The Bishop Orders His Tomb at St. Praxed's Church." These works appear to spring from intricate understandings of the interplay of finance, ambition, politics, perception, and craft—the whole cultural and social ecology, in fact, which supports so extensive a flowering as the Rinascimento. Such explorations, though inevitably they are bounded by the narrow walls of a Congregationalist church, nonetheless would seem to remove us very far from the thoughtless bigotry and ignorance so much in evidence in the letter to Elizabeth Barrett. And yet, after all of this, after her death and his subsequent return to England, we find him writing to his confidante Isabella Blagden, in tones which suggest very strongly that some things had not changed:

> I agree with you and always did, as to the uninterestingness of the Italians individually, as thinking, originating souls: I never read a line in a modern Italian book that was of use to me—never saw a flash of poetry come out of

an Italian *word*: in art, in action, *yes*—not in the region of ideas: I always said, they *are* poetry, don't and can't *make* poetry . . . my liking for Italy was always a selfish one,—I felt alone with my own soul there.[4]

What are we to make of this? A letter written on a bad morning? The repetitions of *always* and *never* indicate that Browning was expressing opinions held steadily through a long course of years. Ian Jack, one of Browning's more alert critics, seems to think so. Citing this passage, he comments:

> Precisely. Italy provided Browning in his prime with what he needed as a poet, a refuge from the distracting pressures of Victorian England from which Tennyson was fated never to escape. Italy saved Browning from becoming just another eminent Victorian. . . . the play of his imagination was never again to be so untrammelled or so audacious as it had been when he wrote 'The Bishop Orders His Tomb' and 'Fra Lippo Lippi'. . . .[5]

This is perfectly fine so far as it goes, but it must be a little startling to most readers, as it certainly is to me, that Professor Jack finds nothing whatever to say of the blind and suffocated smugness which informs Browning's opinions in this letter. "I always said, they *are* poetry, don't and can't *make* poetry"—surely this offhand racism, the very pomp of a defensive ignorance, calls for some notice.[6] That a contemporary English critic should write so confirms *me* in an old belief—that Italy is *not* stuff for the use of the North, and that perhaps it is time for the North to attend instead to what it actually is. But, in fact, it is never Italy itself which is the object of such remarks. The opinions are English, and the concerns they reflect are English as well. Italy here, as in so much English writing on that country, assumes the role of Caliban's mirror. What in fact we face here is a formidable double knot of contradictions at which it is necessary to pick patiently if we are to arrive at a simple—which is to say, comprehensible—account of the violent complexities in Browning's attitudes to Italy. In knot-picking, a little bit of method avoids frustration. We must, for our purposes, separate here from Browning's the general mass of English notions about Italy which he inherited. This will allow us to see his approach in a larger frame. (In discussing Browning, perhaps more than most poets, such a frame is needful. His own metapoetics speak such a variety of jargons from Shelley, from Shakespeare, from liberal theology and liberal politics, that one is driven to seek some more familiar coign of vantage, whether that be provided by Freud or feminism or any other coherent account of social and linguistic reality.)

II

There are, one might say for the sake of quickly surveying a large tract, four huge English Italies before Browning's. There is Chaucer's, where one went for the latest in creative banking and for Boccaccio.[7] There is the Protestant's Italy of Spenser and Shakespeare and Webster and Milton. This is an exciting place. The libraries are full of good books. Elegant people ride horses and quote Seneca in the act of spitting a quail on a Cellini fork. Hunch-backed geniuses wearing poison rings write Papal bulls in defense of incest, rape, simony, and innovative tortures designed to suppress virtue, intelligence, originality, and conscience. There is the Imperialist's Italy of Addison and Gibbon, where one goes to derive the moral of Roman history. Dead bureaucrats in bedsheets ennoble a landscape otherwise repulsively littered with paupers, monks, and pigs. Finally, there is the Romantic Italy of Byron, Shelley, and Samuel Rogers. In the art gallery, the Carbonari whisper in code as the incredibly beautiful rich young widow passes out to her gondola, leaving behind her a cloud of perfume and a palpable sense of ineffable greatness. Everywhere, one encounters Alps, storms, deathbeds, manifestoes. These four Italies, one might say, for Browning did not *succeed* one another so much as they lay about at random in mounds upon the Campagna. An English reader in his time might readily sample all of them in the texts of contemporary writers. Gibbon's Italy is alive to Macaulay and Bulwer-Lytton. The Machiavel of Elizabethan mythology skulks in the confessionals of Ann Radcliffe. The Ugolino episode in Dante, which had touched Chaucer, found new life in Joshua Reynolds, William Blake, Henry Fuseli, William Hayley.[8] And, of course, the Romantics' Italy, the graveyard of Keats and Shelley, the rostrum of Alfieri and Byron, is the one to which Robert and Elizabeth Browning have often been supposed to have traveled after their marriage in 1846. In fact, however, it would be more accurate to say that the newlyweds, and Robert in particular, went to all four of these Italies at once.

The number four is a convenience of exposition. No one can separate and count all the discrete Italies to which Robert Browning made his many returns. It is enough to say that they were many, they were English, and they were *written*. What Browning visited when he visited Italy was an incommensurable mass of inscriptions in English. Italy, it sometimes seems in reading him, is the very scene of English literature. When the powerful folk traditions rise from the fens and marshes and come to London, it is not so likely to be the King they see as it is Punchinello rampant among the orange-girls. Indeed, in Browning's time, if they do arrive at the court, what they meet is a Queen inscribing the interminable record of her abundant life *in italics*. Is it surprising that the intrusion of emotion, of desire, of *will* into a line of writing should be signified by the word *italic*?[9] By the mid-nineteenth century, there existed a huge library of works of the imagination which implied that the Italian frame was the one thing needful to give the illusion of full life to the English character. Browning, who owed so much of his dramatic method to the author of *Othello* and *The Tempest*, was not the man to challenge this implication. Rather, as one might say, he made the most of its possibilities, not only for "objective" portrayal of characters other than his own but even, and especially, for the heightening and intensification of the meanings in his own enterprise. Italy in Browning's work has many functions. But chief among them, in the event, was its place in endowing with emotional consequence the mythological marriage which he chose to inscribe as the chief significance of both his life and his work. Long before that marriage, he had found the source-book of his nearest attempt to "R.B.—a poem," the ill-fated *Sordello*, in Muratori's *Rerum Italicarum Scriptores*.[10] And it was in fact to be that he after his wife would enter English literary history, and Italian as well, as a *writer of things italic*. Indeed, reading the Brownings' letters and the bizarrely heated epics upon which they rested so much of their claims against posterity, we see them, it would be precise to say, against the page as *italic characters*.

This pun allows us to disentangle the first knot before us, the complication in English attitudes to Italy and things Italian. For this play on words has a meaning thoroughly clear in the history of English typography, and it summarizes very plainly the problems which arose from the persistence of Italy in the unwilling English literary attention. Old English type disappeared before the elegance of Roman faces in the first full flush of the Renaissance. By a strange and lovely irony, it was the Puritans who preferred the Roman type, associated as it was with the new respect for antique texts; the last English bible to be printed in black-letter, as the English face was called, appeared in 1640; Cromwell's New Jerusalem announced itself in the very fonts designed to please the worldly Popes. Italic type, first devised by Aldus in 1501 for an edition of Vergil, was meant for an ultimate refinement of Roman clarity; and it carried for a while its association with literary art of the highest kind. But this reputation did not last long. "The relegation of Italic to a secondary role had been completed by the middle of the sixteenth century. It came about, it would seem, as a result of alternating Roman and Italic for decorative effect."[11] That this alternation has more effects than merely decorative may be suggested by the opening sentence of Fowler's entry on the word *italic*, which offers very clearly a wisdom on this theme which had become standard in England by the end of the eighteenth century. "Printing a passage in italics," Fowler begins, "like underlining one in a letter, is a primitive way of soliciting attention."[12] This, no doubt, was precisely the effect Virginia Woolf had in mind when she chose to have the thematic jointures of her masterpiece *The Waves* printed in that sloping cursive which so startles the eye and so sharply intrudes these passages upon the flow of conscious striving and perception which constitutes the bulk of the narrative.[13] *Primitive* indeed is a word which associates itself for the British reader with such words as *italic, Italian, Italianate*. The association is a key, simple no doubt but nonetheless of use, to the whole fabric of English attention to Italy, from Spenser's *Duessa* to Norman Douglas' *Nepenthe*, where the Italian and the italic signify forever the intrusion of what a more stoic British, imperial, and Roman frame of mind would certainly have wished to set aside. The alternation of Roman and italic is much more than decorative. The violence of the passage from, say, Gibbon to Shelley ought to be enough to suggest, to the suggestible reader at least, how the alternation of these two faces might come to signify.[14] Particularly of interest in the work of Robert Browning, and particularly our object here, is the alternation in one body of these two sharply distinguished modes. And thus we come to our second, more tightly-knit conundrum.

III

What great poet is more confusing, confused, and frustrating to the elucidator than Robert Browning? Was he a Puritan or an atheist? Was he spiritual or worldly? Was he an artist or a bourgeois? These are thrilling questions, fragrant with reminiscence for the expeditionary in the hill country of Browning commentaries. To these, I add now the further question, was he an Italic or a Roman? My excuse for this apparent compounding of the trouble is that these were the terms, with all their English meanings hanging heavy in their arms, by which the confusion presented itself to the poet in his wanderings. And, even more important, these were the terms in which he received his reply.

These are, it is important to recognize, emphatically *not* a pair of theoretical counters which Browning himself would, or could, have employed. And this for the simple reason that all the repression—ideological and theological and sexual and economic—which Betty Miller and Barbara Melchiori,[15] prime among their peers, have taken such pains to excavate, all the forcible digestion in Browning of what the mind made out so plainly and yet the man refused to acknowledge, couched itself for him, and dramatically so, in terms of this particular alternation. For *Italian* never ceased to signify *primitive* to Browning, while *Roman* sustained something as much more respectable as it was devoid, correspondingly, of energy and vision, so that one may descry neatly aligned in the frame of this opposition the whole display of contrarieties which turned him so vividly round and round throughout his long, busy, noisy life:

	Italian	*Roman*
1.	feminine	masculine
2.	father	mother
3.	Catholic	Protestant
4.	atheist	believer
5.	artist	burgher
6.	black	white

7.	nakedness	dandyism
8.	solitude	society
9.	Elizabeth Barrett Barrett	Edward Moulton-Barrett
10.	Penini	Robert

The list, admittedly, might be a good deal longer. But perhaps the oppositions specified are adequate to suggest how lucid a topography may emerge here.

What grows from such a list is a very keen sense of the *drama* of Browning's poetry. By this I mean not the often only-too-evident staginess of his monologues, but rather the force and clash of innumerable opposing positions mingling and battling word-to-word and phrase-to-phrase in line after line: the confusion, as of battle, which gives to Browning's verse, graceless and even brutal as it sometimes can be, its startling vitality. This vitality and drama make a puzzle. Drama must be clear. Browning's verse is often notoriously murky. And yet we find it dramatic. I believe the reason for this is that we *do* find a clarity about the struggles it evidences. It is this clarity which we may begin to see, at least in outline, by means of our list.

At the left are ranged the forces of *Italy*. Italy is, as most nineteenth-century writing seems to have agreed, a woman. The woman in Robert Wiedemann Browning, if by woman we mean the person who corresponded to all the stereotypes of the passive, the victim, and the hypersensitive, was his father, that tendersouled Robert Browning who gave up a promising career in the West Indies because he could not stand the spectacle of slavery, who elected instead a quiet life in a modest position at the Bank of England, consoling himself and lightening his boredom with a vast library that rambled through the little house where he sat with a sketchpad which he filled with terrifying faces. The womanly man in the poet Browning, all feeling and ancient literature and pictures, is the one who understands only too well the affectional life of the Roman Catholic Church, particularly as this plays itself out in the piazzas and basilicas of Pisa and Asolo and all those other lovely places which, being Italy, are never Rome. These refuges of the imagination are, by one of history's finer paradoxes, the very places which the Congregationalist Browning must associate with his impossibly, his unattainably, ideal precursor, the atheist Shelley, who found Florence and Livorno and Pisa, in all their liturgical extravagance, the perfect homes for his godless anarchy. Italy again, by grace of antique stereotype, is the haven of the artist, where Mr. Justice Story's fortunate boy and clerk Browning's fortunate boy may play in the shadows of Michelangelo and Leonardo at the sculptor's trade. Italians are dark: "those great black wide eyes." To them attaches for Browning the servility in those days associated with blacks. Barbara Melchiori remarks that he often writes of them in the same way that E. M. Forster's characters talk of "natives."[16] To them also attaches the obscure moral splendor of the victim, a feeling not ever too far from the son of Robert Browning's father, appalled veteran of the slave trade as he was. *Nakedness*: it is hot in Italy, and, as we shall see presently, there was evident in the sunshine more tanned flesh than Mr. Browning, who did not even suppose that there was a need for his wife ever to lay eyes on him nude, knew quite how to manage. *Solitude*: most commentators seem to agree, and I with them, that it was the long hours alone in a thousand quiet places in Italy which provided Browning with that fund of meticulous observation and that access to obscure emotions which give his greatest poems their greatest moments. To this we may add, for the honor of our list, that his solitude occurred in a paradise of "feminine" color and feeling, where the boredom of the servant whose weariness he sometimes felt often turned itself into the calm of the mind exquisitely susceptible to the subtlest, some might say the divinest, influences. And, for the sake of drama, we may conclude by recalling that all which was in Italy most Italian and most *italic* seemed to roll itself up and take human form in the miraculously transfigured body of his bride and the ludicrously distorted character of his son. Elizabeth, as she returned from living death during the Italy of their honeymoon to a florid and thrilling life, became more Italian than English. She wrote, in *Aurora Leigh*, the epos of nineteenth-century English womanhood and made it, in the process, into the epos of the Risorgimento, providing herself, along the way, with an Italian genealogy which looked to a thoroughly Italian posterity.[17] This posterity, of course, took its most vivid shape in her only son, Robert Wiedemann Barrett Browning.[18] Wiedemann was the maiden name of Browning's mother, who had died at the time her only grandchild was born. *Wiedemann* with all its Northern, strict, and, in our terms, *Roman* virtues implied in it, was what they called the boy. But Elizabeth insisted upon raising him as a speaker of Italian. The toddler could not pronounce his own name. He corrupted it (they said) to Penini. *Penini*, at least, was what they heard. And this, italic and absurd together, shortened itself to *Pen*. Italic Pen, dressed as if he belonged to both sexes at once for as long as his mother lived, found himself when she died rather remarkably transformed.

For with Elizabeth died in that household the very body of Italy, and the forces of Rome, as they formed themselves in Robert Browning, took hold, if not entirely, then certainly most of the time and for a long time too. Let us read the right side of the list from the bottom up. Robert Browning, in respect of Italic Pen, grew more English than he had ever dared to be while Elizabeth Barrett lived. The fanciful child in ringlets and silks, charming burbler in the dialect of Tuscany, suddenly found himself in the fogs and glooms of London, had his hair cut and a new regime imposed, designed to prepare him for Balliol College, where Benjamin Jowett was to be his tutor, that English don more Roman than the Romans, who trained successive generations of imperial lords to regulate the Raj and subjugate the wily

Turk. Poor Pen. It was as if, at the age of twelve, he had joined the Marines. All which in Elizabeth Barrett had responded to the stringent puritan jealousy of her monster-father Edward Moulton-Barrett, whom Browning never met and whom, perhaps in consequence, he found at the very doorway of his dreams—all Elizabeth's exaggerated femininity, all her Italian fancy, all which was there precisely because it so distinctly was *not* her father, all of this provoked in Browning just those pursings of the lips and strokings of the beard which, always evident in him, had from the start of their peculiar intercourse wrapped up for Miss Barrett Barrett his miraculous sensitivity and thrilling *Italianita* in a rigid bolt of Sunday black which alone, we cannot but feel, allowed him to pass through the gates as the ideal successor to the dragon-father on his cloudy throne in Wimpole Street. Browning, too, possessed the virtues of these limitations. One did not see in him at Pisa or even Florence what so startlingly emerged during the winters the couple passed in Rome. The solitary poet of Asolo and Venezia there became a social tornado. Three parties in one single night, and every night something someplace. Charming, voluble, upright, English as a grocer, and, what always surprised the readers of his tortured poems when first they saw him plain, a fop. Lemon-yellow kid gloves, the gloss impeccable and innocently gleaming on the top hat, and the ritual black and white from glistening shoes to foaming collar, all according to the rubrics, presented the front not of some slouching Shelley nor even of this fabled man whose fabled wife reclined at home among the iambs and the jugs of morphia, but of a banker, finicky and elegant, full of talk and politics and sociable lust—agreeable, to be sure, but this *that* poet! and this *that* poet's groom and sainted lover! That this was a White Man, a Burgher, and a stoutly believing Dissenter, one had no need to wonder for an instant. Now this person, this clothes-wearing and sober *farfallone*, had always been there when Robert Browning went out in the world. He was no new invention. His whiteness, for example, had its intricate genesis in the moral history of his father among the slavers. Some ferocious inherited guilt born of that ancient mariner's decisive shrinking back played its way into Browning's wild lunge, as of a man who finally finds the thing he seeks, at Elizabeth Barrett, that victim of a father who, so different from Browning's own, rested firm upon a Caribbean pyramid of slaves. Guilty, white, and comfortable Robert Browning, who never worked a day in his life, could not bear to have his fingers seen in public naked. Afloat upon his father's labor and his bride's embarrassment of unearned increment, he eased the gloves upon his hands and, leaving her with Pen, went talking through the vast *salone* of the Papal capital. How strange a peregrination this was may be gauged perhaps in Book x of *The Ring and the Book*, where the poet contrives to present Pope Innocent XII as a liberal Protestant. For Browning associated all which hung imaginatively to Rome, as against Italy, with the fine, firm, clear religion of masculine restraint to which he had sacrificed his youthful atheism: the paternal church, as it were, of his sainted mother. Rome, at the affectional level where our topography locates itself, must be masculine, motherly, and Sunday go-to-meeting.

Italy against Rome. It was not mere phantasmagoria. This was, even in the newspapers, the shape of peninsular politics during the years of the Brownings' marriage (1846–61). More than that, it must be seen, it has always, one way and another, been the shape of Italian history ever since the Latins raised their standards against Etruria, the Oscans, and the Umbrians. Browning's dichotomies of feeling, and England's as well, towards the places and the themes of Italy grafted themselves onto long roots which run back through the poems of Dante and Vergil and Lucan and who knows truly how far beyond. What was particular and peculiar in Browning was blossom of the graft, which included among its lurid striations of color the vivid white of the dissenter and the vivid black of the slave, the paradoxical mauve of the new-made feminist and, perhaps newest of all, the intricately brindled spermatomorphography of bourgeois English poetry. Not only newest, but most important was this last, for it will provide some way to deal with the thorniest question which the list of opposites can pose: how in the world and with such air of ease did Browning sustain so wild a set of contradictions?

The answer, fortunately, can be simply put. He was a liberal.

IV

Browning on *why* he was a liberal:

> "Why?" Because all I haply can and do,
> All that I am now, all I hope to be—
> Whence comes it save from fortune setting free
> Body and soul the purpose to pursue,
> God traced for both? If fetters, not a few,
> Of prejudice, convention, fall from me,
> These shall I bid men—each in his degree
> Also God-guided—bear, and gaily too?
> But little do or can the best of us:
> That little is achieved through Liberty.
> Who, then, dares hold—emancipated thus—
> His fellow shall continue bound? Not I
> Who live, love, labour freely, nor discuss
> A brother's right to freedom. That is "Why."[19]

What did it mean for a poet thus to be liberated as a liberal? Nineteenth-century liberalism is so far removed from the political stances and cultures of our own time that this question has no obvious answer.

There *is*, of course, however, a standard reply, which we must briefly rehearse before we turn to the question at hand. The great codifier of Victorian liberalism, John Stuart Mill, put its basic principle succinctly when he wrote that "all restraint, *qua* restraint, is an evil."[20] This implied, in practice, an elevation of *liberty* to a position of unprecedented grandeur, where another age might have put *justice* or *love* or *wisdom*, at the very summit of human values. And this elevation implied much. In England, it implied the powerful devotion to the abolition of slavery as an institution which perhaps will finally be judged to have been the chief glory of Victorian politics. In Italy, it implied a passionate desire to see all traces of feudal servitude, theocratic empire, and foreign domination wiped away; the participation of the Brownings in this political crusade stands high among the jewels in their moral crowns. More familiar, perhaps, among the implications of liberalism's valuation of liberty is the set of individual freedoms to which it offers so firm a foundation. "There is," Mill writes, "a sphere of action in which society, as distinguished from the individual, has, if any, only an indirect interest."[21] This is a much-cited line, drawn from a passage in *On Liberty* which amounts to the Nicene Creed of this belief. Having so sharply excluded society from the individual's private sphere, Mill goes on to define triumphantly the "appropriate domain of human liberty." This is no small country:

> It comprises, first, the inward domain of consciousness, demanding liberty of conscience in the most comprehensive sense, liberty of thought and feeling, absolute freedom of opinion and sentiment on all subjects, practical or speculative, scientific, moral, or theological. The liberty of expressing and publishing opinions . . . , being almost of as much importance as the liberty of thought itself and resting in part on the same reasons, is practically inseparable from it.[22]

Now these freedoms—of thought, of speech, of the press—have remained so much a part of contemporary liberal belief that we are only too likely to read such a passage with the same glazed approval we accord to the Declaration of Independence. Doing so, however, we miss its enormous consequences for a poet of Browning's peculiar gifts and ambitions.

Nothing is for nothing in this world. These magnificent freedoms bear, for a poet in particular, a very heavy price. When thought, speech, and publication become *rights* of an *individual*—instead, as they had always been to some extent before the Enlightenment, the province of society—then they become also the *responsibility* of the individual. Nothing in the realm of language seems any longer to bear the assurance of divine or royal or even contractual authority. Those bets are off. One must devise for oneself systems of coherent meaning. Some poets—Blake is the most obvious example—can be seen to rise mightily to the task. No major poet can count himself or herself exempt from it. The gradual recognition of what these freedoms implied for poetry is one of the major themes in the history of that art since the beginning of the nineteenth century. Among Browning's contemporaries, this recognition produced a variety of manners and matters which remains to this day one of the more intricate puzzles in literary history. One key to that puzzle is that the leading poets and painters of that time—Christina Rossetti and her lurid brother no more than such household names as Lord Tennyson and Holman Hunt—followed Mill directly to the "inward domain of consciousness," where they found themselves staring into a mirror which was also a photographer's plate. Their work, like so many of the lesser products of their time and place, exhibits an obsessive attention to the data of sense-perception, a willingness to suppose that the eyes and ears and hands and nose and tongue, belonging as they do so fully to the individual who employs them, must somehow therefore be the veriest channels through which what is in the human situation most profound, most wonderful, most *true*, communicates itself to the human mind. This willingness produces some astonishing results. Pre-Raphaelite painting at its sensory zenith, in such a work as Millais' *Mariana*, possesses a richness of texture so full as to make one believe that the particolored autumn leaves upon the table are, in themselves and not in the painter's able hands, as fully communicative and intentional as the strict geometries and postures in the stained glass or the luxurious bend of the back, an ache of desire, by which Mariana herself gives force to the sheen of her dress and the brilliance of the light that falls upon the red velvet of her bench. Since the "inward domain of consciousness" had such great responsibilities and powers, its chief ministers, the avenues of the sensorium, rose mightily in value. And since the senses acquired such authority, there was an inevitable focusing upon those objects which seem, even as they meet the senses, to have their messages ready formed. Faded leaves. Buds. Seeds. Waterfalls. Birds. From the numbness through which John Keats heard a nightingale to the pained receptivity with which Father Hopkins beheld a brindled cow, there never lacked during these years for persons ready to be addressed directly by whatever is greatest and most important through the medium of something with a clear outline, a lively surface, a peculiar music, a strong aroma, or a complicated taste. Such attention, naturally, was difficult. Even more difficult, however, was the effort of extracting a notion of justice from a waterlily or an adequate idea of divine love from the predatory habits of a falcon. That Victorian poets succeeded so well as they sometimes did under such constraints need not blind us to the narrowness of the discipline. Nor to its failures. Royalty, in a liberal age, makes a poor subject for epic: even *Idylls of the King* has a hollow look of mere glamor and sentimentality when we place it next to *The Faerie Queene*. A vast library of Jacobean plays did not enable Swinburne even once to match Webster as a poet of treachery. Free speech, for Browning as for his contemporaries, meant the opportunity to exploit the ravishing landscape of perception but it also meant, since "society" has little place in that private world, that such "social" notions as love and wisdom and kingship and loyalty became difficult, even impossible, themes to address directly.

A full contemplation of both the licenses and the disabilities of that "inward domain of consciousness" takes us a long way towards understanding Browning's ability to write, with apparent ease, out of a set of contradictory values which seems to us both stunning and confusing. *Liberty*, as liberalism conceived it, gave so little room to any other political desiderata and so very much space to the apparently divine testimony of the senses that the reality of social claims tended to disappear in the seductive blizzard of seeming-significant *things*. Things, objects of desire, take the place of love, of wisdom, of indeed any other ideas of order, when the senses come freely to rule discourse. Thus free speech is, for Victorian poetry at least, a paradox. Allowing expression to any ideology, it effectively dethrones *all* ideologies except its own rigidly empirical program.

This, then, is the reason that Browning can so comfortably sustain what appears to be a wild mélange of opinions and stances which would seem often to be mutually contradictory: none of them matters so greatly as the sheer pleasure of entertaining them all. Nor is even that delight so great as the yet more disorderly attraction of yielding oneself, like Mariana at the window, to the rainbow conversation of the mighty Scirocco, the articulated underside of the starfish, or the pedantic shadow of a dome as it progresses through the afternoon across a cathedral's roof, pointing up the colors of the slates and the curved teeth in the lesser gargoyles, as if the whole world were a string of tutors engaged by an indulgent parent for a spoiled but precocious and attentive only son. The freedom awarded to the "inward domain of consciousness" by liberalism cooperated in him with the authority long enfiefed to that same demesne by liberal theology: if the reader and the scripture are everything, then everything—every *thing*—is scripture for the reader.

But freedom of speech, interpretation, thought, and publication, though they are in themselves enough to explain Browning's curious placidity in the face of profound self-divisions, will not take us the whole way towards understanding the strange mixture in him of a desire to see Italy "free" and an unbridled contempt for actual living Italian persons. To approach this very crucial and revealing problem in Browning we must first look at an equally crucial, and equally revealing, problem in liberalism: the embattled policy of *free trade*.

Free trade stood at the very center of the liberal program in practical politics. But its position in liberal philosophy was very uneasy indeed. Mill goes so far as to admit that "the principle of individual liberty is not involved in the question of free trade."[23] And he is quite clear about why this is so:

> . . . trade is a social act. Whoever undertakes to sell any description of goods to the public does what affects the interests of other persons, and of society in

general; and thus his conduct, in principle, comes within the jurisdiction of society. . . .[24]

Subsequent liberals of course have recognized that this is the case. For this reason liberal democracies nowadays devote a good deal of attention to regulating traffic in food, medication, machinery and appliances of every kind, and indeed all manner of things. Individual freedom may be desirable, but there are limits to any good. So liberals believe nowadays. Not so Mill:

> . . . it is now recognized, though not till after a long struggle, that both the cheapness and the good quality of commodities are most effectively provided for by leaving the producers and sellers perfectly free, under the sole check of equal freedom to the buyers for supplying themselves elsewhere. This is the so-called doctrine of "free trade," which rests on grounds different from, though equally solid with, the principle of individual liberty. . . . Restrictions on trade, or on production for purposes of trade, are indeed restraints . . . but . . . are wrong solely because they do not really produce the results which it is desired to be produced by them.[25]

This argument is so blatantly wrong that one almost gasps for air while reading it. Is freedom so absolutely valuable, we ask, as to blind us to the numbers of persons who have compounded fortunes by selling adulterated milk and dyed wine? Will not restrictions on trade sometimes prevent an ambitious entrepreneur from putting forth placebos and narcotics under the guise of medication? Of course they will. And why is John Stuart Mill, so studious and so sensitive a man, not able to see this obvious fact?

The truth is that free trade, free speech, and "liberty" itself all rest upon the same powerful historic force. We might call it the rise of the middle class. Or we might simply call it the rise of *money*. The great diagnostician of Victorial liberalism, Karl Marx, makes perfectly plain the deep connection between the abstract power of money and the flowering of the notion of free expression of the self:

> That which is for me through the medium of *money*—that for which I can pay . . .—that am *I*, the possessor of the money. The extent of the power of money is the extent of my power. . . . Do not I, who thanks to money am capable of *all* that the human heart longs for, possess all human capacities? . . .
> If *money* is the bond binding me to *human* life, is not money the bond of all *bonds*? Can it not dissolve and bind all ties? Is it not, therefore, the universal *agent of divorce?*
> . . . .
> That which I am unable to do as a *man*, and of which therefore all my individual essential powers are incapable, I am able to do by means of *money*. Money thus turns each of these powers into something which in itself it is not—turns it, that is, into its *contrary*.[26]

That is, to recapitulate the argument thus far: money, freely flowing and completely separated from all which produces it and all which it procures, makes possible an imaginative elevation of the individual, *any* individual, unthinkable without it. Money, reproducing in the void according to its own mysterious alchemy along its own magical progress of geometry, lifts up the powers of the individual who possesses it—lifts that person far beyond the power of any mere object, any absolutely priceable *other*, to hold that person down or back. Money transforms personal powers into impersonal powers, their "contraries," making of each moneyed person a possible empire.

Free trade in the world of politics is exactly what free speech is in the "inward domain of consciousness": the spectacular transforming force of money. Free trade is the empire of money, just as money is the empire of free thought and expression. Free trade as a policy began with the "cessation of the bans on the export of gold and silver and the beginning of the trade in money," and this produced, according to our doctor, "world history for the first time, insofar as it made all civilised nations and every individual member of them dependent for the satisfaction of their wants on the whole world, thus destroying the former natural exclusiveness of separate nations."[27] The free circulation of money, what is called free trade, initiated an order of empire as grand in scale—though not, in the event, of nearly so long duration—as that of Rome.

The magic of money, its psychology and its aesthetics, is the theme which joins together the striking dissonances in Browning and brings out of them a terrible calm of clarity. It is money which, first of all, makes possible the celestial elevation of the individual beyond all claims society may have to put. Making available *"all* the human heart longs for," money is what gives life to that inward liberty, speculative and wild, which Mill praises in tones so reminiscent of a Protestant divine, that "absolute freedom of opinion and sentiment on all subjects" which so confounds and troubles us in Browning's verse. Similarly, this imperial status of the individual, in all his possible roarings and soarings, gives the theoretical, even the theological, underpinning of Browning's great technical innovations in the use of the dramatic monologue. It is no accident that speakers of these monologues display, as Barbara Melchiori has conclusively demonstrated, an almost universal preoccupation with money, with gold.[28] Gold it is which clasps these solitary dukes and visionary artists, each upon the frosty eminence of his own freedom, securely in place—fragments, as who should say, of a *Commedia* which cannot be written because *liberty*, when it is the liberty to buy, is so much less of freedom than love. Love, in Dante's sense, is all the claims of the *other* which money, like an *aqua regia*, so perfectly dissolves. Browning cannot write a *Commedia*. What he *can* produce is what Chesterton, taking one of his customary dead shots, pronounced "the epic of free speech."[29] And free speech, by the magic of money, becomes as an aesthetic protocol nothing less or more than free trade.

Mill's great costive grunt in drawing trade apart from society is, we might say, *the* Victorian gesture *par excellence*. It leaves money free to circulate eternally separated from all it may contain of human labor, pain, division, loyalty, conception, thought, or love. It is the invention, nothing less, of a sacrament. And, on a slightly less etherial plane, it is the ideological prophylaxis which enables so committed an anti-slaver, so great an apostle of human emancipation, as Robert Browning to live as he lived, live on what he lived on, and, most to our purpose, write as he wrote, the herald of liberty sustained throughout his long existence on someone else's labor, someone else's unearned income, fed by servants ("Italians"), dressed by tailors ("I always said, they *are* poetry, don't and can't *make* poetry"), paid and paid for in the name of freedom. *Whose freedom?* That simple question, the answer to volumes of Mill, would also open for us the charms of attack against a dead man for the crime of belonging fully to his own moment. We can resist these charms. But the aesthetic question is one we cannot avoid. Browning is so often proffered to us as the poet of all that is good and holy in the popular theology of his time and place, that it is hardly unimportant for us to reach far down into that bin of bunting and heroic pamphlets and poems in two volumes and to find there at the bottom, among the broken bits of pages the acid has eaten and strands from flags the moths have destroyed, to find there—what? This:

>   Do you see this Ring?
>   'T is Rome-work, made to match
>   (By Castellani's imitative craft)
>   Etrurian circlets found, some happy morn,
>   After a dropping April; found alive
>   Spark-like 'mid unearthed slope-side figtree-roots
>   That roof old tombs at Chiusi: soft, you see,
>   Yet crisp as jewel-cutting.[30]

This is the opening of Browning's epic. Commentators, always seeming to be anxious to get to the "Old Yellow Book" which was its source, tend to hurry past these lines. But, as Browning knew perfectly well, it is the first lines, by ancient custom, which announce the theme and purpose of an *epos*. What do these tell us?

"*Do you see this Ring?*" The force of that question has yet to be truly measured. The Ring is to reveal itself, we learn eventually, as "the golden ring between Italy and England" which Elizabeth Barrett Browning was said to have forged in her verse. It is to inspire a long analogy, a little later on, between making a poem and making a golden ring.[31] But these are not the first things we read. Before anything else, we are struck by the blunt, even rude, gesture of beginning an epic with a question aimed directly at the reader—a question which the reader can in no way answer in the affirmative.

This gesture carries all the gross force of possession, of boasting, of desire, and of demand. It speaks with perfect fidelity the vast assurance of the individual who holds it in his putative demonstrating hand.[32] That initial hemistich sails into view, as one turns the first page, with a lonely and absolute profile. This is the figure of the speaking poet determined we shall not avoid the sound of his voice. (He afterward spends a good deal of space hectoring us, whom he calls the "public," about our refusal to give him what he has been wanting.) He is in fact offering the reader what he supposes, on the strength of long experience, no "public" can refuse: gold. And what gold it is! Exactly the gold of the free-trade empire, which does its "Rome-work" in dissolving and possessing Italy, here in the very shape of Rome's first Italian victim, according to Vergil: "Etrurian circlets."

Rome-work. *The Ring and the Book*, if it is a *Commedia* of sorts, is the epos of this Rome-work, this power of gold to dissolve the particular, making of a local circlet in Etruria the pattern of a vast and universal unity. This is a harmony, a Vergilian theme drawn from the eighth book of *The Aeneid* and here, through the liberal's theology of money, transformed into a moral for the world-order of the moment through which Robert Browning passed. "Owing to the pathological estrangement which the insanity of nationality has induced," Nietzsche wrote, ". . . *Europe wants to become one.*" "Think!" he wrote. "What you hear is *Rome—Rome's faith without the text.*"[33] Browning portrays the very texture of this Rome-work in his epic, interweaving everywhere and anywhere the clearest possible signs of how the golden ring is to be forged through the acid (as in his famous metaphor) of money. Barbara Melchiori points out how careful, for example, Browning is to draw the parallel between the golden ring and the Book it parallels, a book whose greatest attractions so very emphatically included its price:[34]

> Do you see this square old yellow Book, I toss
> I' the air, and catch again, the twirl about
> By the crumpled vellum covers,—pure crude fact
> Secreted from a man's life when hearts beat hard,
> And brains, high-blooded, ticked two centuries since?
> Examine it yourselves! I found this book,
> Gave a *lira* for it, eightpence English just. . . .
> (I, 33–39)

These humble details bristle with consequence. How cheap things are in Italy! "A man's life when hearts beat hard / And brains high-blooded"—all for a *lira*, eightpence, think! *"Do you see this Ring?" "Do you see this square old yellow Book?"* This ring is what buys this book. This is the Rome-work of free trade, which subsumes, in crossing the boundaries of *lo scambio*, the discarded inexpensive heap of pamphlets into the very Ring which Browning holds out to tempt the reader.

There was a sense in which the ring very exactly bought the book. There was a wedding-ring in question; for it was Elizabeth Barrett Barrett's money which, weighing so heavy upon his puritan conscience that he never would use it to pay for the rent of a riding-horse, floated Robert Browning along through so many Roman and Italian years. And of course, notoriously, Robert's Rome-work Ring, such perfect imperial splendor as it was, carried the argument with Italian Elizabeth beyond the grave, superscribing her "*aureo anello fra Italia e Inghilterra*" with one of his own make, and superseding, as he so candidly dared to hope towards the end of the poem, her charms for the "British Public, who may like me yet" (XII, 831). One can, in this connection, only praise the absolute literality with which Browning took the imperial responsibilities implied in the freedoms both of expression and of trade; for if we read this poem as an *examen de conscience du mari*, as the opening and especially the closing lines quite bluntly invite us to do, then its candor is heroic to a stunning extent. May a man, it asks, who marries a rich woman who is also a saint, find some excuse to murder her? When Browning first discovered the old book, we are not surprised to learn, "Elizabeth was perfectly repelled by its unexampled sordidness and . . . quite refused to 'inspect the papers.' "[35] The Ring, finally, is identified with Art, and Art with a power of confession which commands respect, even awe:

> But Art,—wherein man nowise speaks to men,
> Only to mankind,—Art may tell a truth
> Obliquely, do the thing shall breed the thought,
> Nor wrong the thought, missing the mediate word.
> So may you paint your picture, twice show truth,
> Beyond mere imagery on the wall,—
> So, note by note, bring music from your mind,
> Deeper than ever the Andante dived,—
> So write a book shall mean, beyond the facts,
> Suffice the eye and save the soul beside.
> And save the soul! If this intent save mine,—
> If the rough ore be rounded to a ring,
> Render all duty which a good ring should do,
> And, failing grace, succeed in guardianship,—
> Might mine but lie outside thine, Lyric Love,
> Thy rare gold ring of verse (the poet praised)
> Linking our England to his Italy!
> (XII, 854–870)

This, then, is the heady justification of free speech and free trade, that, speaking to mankind instead of to man, they may reinvent some general truth. It is the old argument for Rome, as good and as bad as ever it was, but very tightly wound upon the particular of the poet in question, and, with that tensile power so particularly his, still stretched across the empty space between the woman Italy and Rome, the man.

V

There is perhaps some final clarity to be won by ending where we began, during the year of Browning's courtship of Elizabeth Barrett, before their years of marriage brought the question down to the pitch of complication, "Deeper than ever the Andante dived," which we find in *The Ring and the Book*. "The Englishman in Italy: Piano di Sorrento," a poem of 1845, has not been very much read, nor very carefully.[36] The closest examination of it, by William Harrald, finds a good deal in the poem by reading it alongside "The Italian in England," a work which in 1849 Browning offered as a companion-piece to the first.[37] For reasons which shall shortly appear, I do not intend to imitate this perfectly plausible strategy. "The Englishman in Italy" is a monologue whose eponymous speaker addresses a young Italian girl whom he is attempting to amuse. It is harvest-time, and he describes as he goes some very remarkable, very memorable, pictures of what is to be gleaned and consumed in the neighborhood of Vico Alvano. There he sees not only "The white skin of each grape on the bunches, / Marked like a quail's crown" (ll. 15–26) and all manner of prickly-pear and fig, but also the *frutti di mare*:

> No seeing our skiff
> Arrive about noon from Amalfi,
> —Our fisher arrive,
> And pitch down his basket before us,
> All trembling alive
> With pink and grey jellies, your sea-fruit;
> You touch the strange lumps,
> And mouths gape there, eyes open, all manner
> Of horns and of humps,
> Which only the fisher looks grave at,
> While round him like imps
> Cling screaming the children as naked
> And brown as his shrimps;
> Himself too as bare to the middle
> —You see round his neck
> The string and its brass coin suspended
> That saves him from wreck.
> (ll. 52–68)

This is Browning at his most Pre-Raphaelite, the whole 292 lines of it rippling with the startled attention which must believe that every blessed detail, every glistening hump and shadow of color ("the heavy blue bloom on each globe" in a bunch of grapes, l. 103), every breath of the breeze and snail in the trees has its powerful message to convey. And what messages are these?

The poem has a peculiar conclusion. After enough of such sketches in oil to satisfy even a Madox Brown, after an elaborate description of a liturgical procession and nighttime celebration, we find, without apparent preparation, this *envoi*:

> —'Such trifles!' you say?
> Fortu, in my England at home,
>   Men meet gravely to-day
> And debate, if abolishing Corn-laws
>   Be righteous and wise
> —If 't were proper, Scirocco should
>   vanish
> In black from the skies!
>
> (ll. 286–92)

Though Elizabeth Barrett thought this ending gave "unity to the whole . . . just what the poem wanted,"[38] it is not immediately apparent why this should be so. Harrald, reading this poem as a companion piece to "The Italian in England," an imaginary monologue which most readers put into the mouth of Mazzini contemplating his suffering homeland, arrives at the notion that Browning here is actually praising England, "since in England the democratic system of debate and voting is used to settle the injustice, whereas in Italy revolution and bloodshed seem to be the only ways to overthrow tyranny."[39] This is very seriously beside the point. Indeed, the only way to read these lines is against the preceding lines to which they are, as Elizabeth quite rightly perceived, intended to give a shape. What shape?

What messages and what shape? The messages are exceedingly direct: Italy is the land of appetite. All that is missing in England, all that exquisite food and sunshine and random ancient religion, is there. All that is missing in Browning, likewise: the naked, the brown, "Himself too as bare to the middle." And the shape is, as in *The Ring and the Book*, the following: all of this is there to be bought, and cheaply. "'T is a sensual and timorous beauty," he writes. "How fair! but a slave" (ll. 195–96). It is not insignificant, for every detail here is meant to *tell*, that the fisherman's talisman is but a "string and its brass coin." These are delectable places, delectable persons, to be had almost for the asking, a *lira* at most, "eightpence English just." In this light, the ending of the poem indeed makes more sense than one can readily gaze upon. Abolishing the Corn Laws, those final bastions between the great landlords and the flood of inexpensive European produce and grain, would make this vast catalogue of the delicious, as indeed it did do, part of the everyday English bill of fare. These were the days, recall, of the potato famine. People starved in the British Isles. Browning's political motive cannot have been more unexceptionable. Still, the poem is, to put it bluntly, an advertisement. Its dialect is precisely the mouth-watering diction of advertisement:

> We shall feast our grape-gleaners (two dozen,
>   Three over one plate)
> With lasagne so tempting to swallow
>   In slippery ropes,
> And gourds fried in great purple slices,
>   That color of popes.
> Meantime, see the grape bunch they've brought you:
>   The rain-water slips
> O'er the heavy blue bloom on each globe
>   Which the wasp to your lips
> Still follows with fretful persistence:
>   Nay, taste, while awake,
> This half of a curd-white smooth cheese-ball
>   That peels, flake by flake,
> Like an onion, each smoother and whiter. . . .
>   (ll. 95–109)

So, finally, we have before us the clothes-wearing man with nothing on. This is the language of desire, bare, untrammelled, even furious. We can glimpse the fury in this poem's true companion-piece, the one written just after it, and very much out of the same wordlist, the much-misunderstood masterpiece, "The Bishop Orders His Tomb at Saint Praxed's Church."[40] There the language of appetite and the language of money merge altogether in such lines as these:

> Peach-blossom marble all, the rare, the ripe,
> As fresh-poured wine of a mighty pulse.
> —Old Gandolf with his paltry onion-stone,
> Put me where I may look at him! True peach,
> Rosy and flawless: how I earned the prize!
>   (ll. 29–33)

Here are all the English Italies drawn down, through the mysteries of gold and the oculars of a parasite's bad conscience, into a piece of fruit, an onion, and a glass of wine. This is the free-trade empire's Italy, the simple object of desire, from which the English Roman never can detach himself, despite his virtues and his Titan sympathies, despite his horror that his own pale flesh might catch the sun, because, at last as at the start, there is a charm in slaves, there is in them as the rich man looks at them, all the loveliness which has been bought and paid for, which he has supposed he owns, but which in owning knows he loses unless, like Browning, he resigns himself always, like the murderer to the scene of the crime, to make his many returns.

Notes

1. Cited in William De Sua, *Dante into English, 1750–1950* (Chapel Hill: University of North Carolina Press, 1964), p. 8.
2. D. H. Lawrence, *Apocalypse* (1931, rpt. New York: Viking Press, 1966).
3. *The Letters of Robert Browning and Elizabeth Barrett Barrett*, ed. Elvan Kintner (Cambridge: Harvard University Press, 1969), 1, 50 (30 April 1845).
4. *Dearest Isa*, ed. Edward C. McAleer (Austin: University of Texas Press, 1951), pp. 238–39 (19 May 1866).
5. Ian Jack, *Browning's Major Poetry* (Oxford: Clarendon Press, 1973), p. 272.
6. William Irvine, in William Irvine and Park Honan, *The Book, the Ring, and the Poet* (New York: McGraw-Hill, 1974), p. 415, inclines to a version of the bad-morning explanation. Referring to the same letter without citing the offensive passages, he excuses Browning on grounds of creative stress: "His problem as he saw it was to transmute history into poetry, to cause once-living Italians to speak for themselves again within his own gigantic, revitalizing, blank-verse framework. If *The Ring and the Book* was composed consecutively, as he later claimed, he had just finished resurrecting Giacinto de Arcangeli and Giovanni-Battista Bottini. His weary letter to Isa is filled with exasperation for Italians, both dead and living." In its tacit admission that there is indeed something here to explain away, perhaps this is preferable to Jack's comment.
7. The assertions in this paragraph, breezy as they may seem, rest upon a very considerable amount of scholarly endeavor. The reader interested in the large subject of English literary relations with Italy should consult, first among all, the one classic on this theme: Mario Praz, *The Flaming Heart: Essays on Crashaw, Machiavelli, and Other Studies in the Relations between Italian and English Literature from Chaucer to T. S. Eliot* (Gloucester, Mass.: Peter Smith, 1969). Also of use are A. Lytton Sells, *The Italian Influence in English Poetry* (1955; rpt. Westport, Conn.: Greenwood Press, 1971); Roderick Marshall, *Italy in English Literature* (New York: Columbia University Press, 1934); and Kenneth Churchill, *Italy and English Literature, 1764–1930* (London: Macmillan, 1980).
8. See Praz, pp. 23–24.
9. On the history of italic type, see Harry Carter, "Supplement on Italic," in *A View of Early Typography* (Oxford: Clarendon Press, 1969), pp. 117–26.
10. See Jacob Korg, *Browning and Italy* (Athens: Ohio University Press, 1983), p. 18. See also Stewart W. Holmes, "The Sources of Browning's *Sordello*," *Studies in Philology*, 34 (July 1937), 467–96. Korg's painstaking survey and Barbara Melchiori's exemplary article "Browning in Italy" (see below, n. 16) have been of the greatest use to me in preparing to write this essay.
11. Carter, p. 125.
12. H. W. Fowler, *A Dictionary of Modern English Usage*, ed. Sir Ernest Gowers, 2nd ed. (Oxford: Oxford University Press, 1965), p. 313.
13. Virginia Woolf, *The Waves* (London: Hogarth Press, 1931).
14. Sound surveys of this territory can be found in Churchill, *Italy and English Literature*, and in Marshall, *Italy in English Literature* (see above, n. 7).
15. Betty Miller, *Robert Browning: A Portrait* (New York: Scribner's, 1972) is so bold

a book that subsequent biographers seem never to tire of arguing with its lapidary assessments of Browning's contradictions; Barbara Melchiori, *Browning's Poetry of Reticence* (New York: Barnes & Noble, 1968), and "Browning in Italy," in *Robert Browning*, ed. Isobel Armstrong (Athens: Ohio University Press, 1975), pp. 168–83, along with Maisie Ward, *Robert Browning and His World* (New York: Holt, Rinehart and Winston, 1967) and John Maynard, *Browning's Youth* (Cambridge: Harvard University Press, 1977), have been the works most to my purpose in compiling the list which follows.

16. "Browning in Italy," pp. 170–71.

17. See, for this, two extraordinary recent essays. Flavia Alaya, "The Ring, the Rescue, and the Risorgimento: Reunifying the Brownings' Italy," in *Browning Institute Studies*, 6 (1978), 1–41, opens anew with brilliance and elegance the whole question of the political groundwork of the Brownings' poetry. Sandra M. Gilbert, "From *Patria* to *Matria*: Elizabeth Barrett Browning's Risorgimento," *PMLA*, 99 (March 1984), 194–211, offers itself as a continuation of Alaya's initial inquiry, focusing particularly on the gender politics so thoroughly inwoven in nineteenth-century discussion and imaging of Italy.

18. See Maisie Ward, *The Tragi-Comedy of Pen Browning* (New York: Sheed and Ward, 1972).

19. Robert Browning, "Why I Am a Liberal," in *The Works of Robert Browning*, ed. F. G. Kenyon (London: Smith, Elder, 1912), ix, 351. Good general assessments of Browning's liberalism are in G. K. Chesterton, *Robert Browning* (1903; rpt. London: Macmillan, 1951) and Trevor Lloyd, "Browning and Politics," in Isobel Armstrong, ed., *Robert Browning* (Athens: Ohio University Press, 1975), pp. 142–67.

20. John Stuart Mill, *On Liberty*, ed. Currin V. Shields (New York: Liberal Arts Press, 1956), p. 116.

21. *On Liberty*, pp. 15–16.

22. *On Liberty*, p. 16.

23. *On Liberty*, p. 116.

24. *On Liberty*, p. 115.

25. *On Liberty*, pp. 115–16.

26. Karl Marx, *Economic and Philosophic Manuscripts of 1844*, trans. Martin Milligan, in Robert C. Tucker, ed., *The Marx–Engels Reader* (New York: Norton, 1972), pp. 103–04.

27. Karl Marx, *The German Ideology*, trans. S. Ryazanskaya, in *The Marx–Engels Reader*, pp. 184–85.

28. *Browning's Poetry of Reticence*, pp. 40–89.

29. Chesterton, p. 173.

30. Robert Browning, *The Ring and the Book*, ed. Richard D. Altick (New Haven: Yale University Press, 1971), 1, 1–7.

31. See. *The Ring and the Book*, 1, 18–31; see also Paul A. Cundiff, "The Clarity of Browning's Ring Metaphor," *PMLA*, 43 (1948), 1267–82.

32. So vividly does this person intrude himself that William E. Harrald, *The Variance and the Unity* (Athens: Ohio University Press, 1973), p. 118, with excellent results compares him with the "host for a diorama, pointing-pole in hand, ready to guide his audience through the exciting scenes and action."

33. Friedrich Nietzsche, *Beyond Good and Evil: Prelude to a Philosophy of the Future*, trans. Walter Kaufman (New York: Vintage Books, 1966), pp. 196, 198.

34. *Browning's Poetry of Reticence*, p. 71.

35. *The Book, the Ring, and the Poet*, p. 409.

36. Citations will be from the text in *Browning: Poetical Works 1833–1864*, ed. Ian Jack (London: Oxford University Press, 1970), pp. 421–29. For dates of composition and publication, see William C. DeVane, *A Browning Handbook*, 2nd ed. (New York: Appleton-Century-Crofts, 1955), pp. 157–59.

37. See Harrald, pp. 67–77.

38. Cited in DeVane, p. 158.
39. Harrald, p. 69.
40. Citations from text in *Browning: Poetical Works*, pp. 432–35. On this poem, its relationship in time to "The Englishman in Italy," and the history of its misunderstandings, see Korg, pp. 58–62.

Index

♦

Abrams, M. H., 29
Acts of John, 168
advertisement, diction of, 263
Agamemnon, 217–18
alienation, 80, 83, 93, 94. See also subjectivity
Alison, Archibald: "On Parliamentary Reform and the French Revolution," 229
Altick, Richard, 9, 10, 65
"Andrea del Sarto," 42–43, 66, 103, 115
Andromeda, 102–3, 120–35, 215; constellation, 130–33
antivivisectionist movement, 208
"Any Wife to Any Husband," 85
"Apollo and the Fates," 218
Aristophanes' Apology, 215, 216–17
Arnold, Matthew, 13, 217; *Culture and Anarchy*, 15, 214; "Dover Beach," 38, 43, 47–48; "Empedocles on Etna," 55–56, 139, 141, 143–45, 151, 194; Preface, 141–43
Asolando, 155
Athenaeum, 4, 148
audiences, Victorian and contemporary, 2–8. See also Browning, Robert Weidemann: audience of; readers
Auerbach, Nina, 115; "Robert Browning's Last Word," 12
authority, political and poetic, 170, 172–82, 186–200
Aytoun, William Edmondstoune, 150–51; *Firmilion*, 142, 150

Bacchus, 215
"Bad Dreams," 212–14, 222
Bailey, Benjamin, 150, 153; *Festus*, 148–49, 152
Balduccini, Filippo, 127
Balustion's Adventure, 215–16

Barolini, Teodolinda: *De Vulgari Eloquentia*, 175–76
Barthes, Roland, 139, 182
Benjamin, Walter, 181
Bigg, John Stanyan, 153
"Bishop Orders His Tomb at Saint Praxed's Church, The," 42–43, 70, 76–77, 103, 115, 263–64
Blackwood's (periodical), 150, 151
Bleich, David, 70
Bloom, Harold, 104, 106
"Blougram's Apology," 70
"Bold Lover" (of Keats's Urn), 107, 111
Book, the Ring, and the Poet, The (Irvine and Honan), 10
Boynton, Robert W., 31
Brady, Ann: *Pompilia: A Feminist Reading of Browning's* The Ring and the Book, 12
Brantlinger, Patrick, 230, 239
"brother's speech" (*Sordello*), 173, 178, 179–80, 188
Browning, Elizabeth Barrett, 2–3, 6, 11, 12, 102–3, 120, 204; *Aurora Leigh*, 250; and Italy, 244, 250–52, 258, 260; *Sonnets from the Portuguese*, 3; and the Spasmodics, 148–49, 150
Browning, Robert (father), 249
Browning, Robert Weidemann: and Arnold, 141–45, 156; audience of, 11, 12, 72–73, 149–50, 162–63, 178–82, 227; centenary of death of, 10–11; contradictory values of, 248–52, 255; and cultural criticism, 14–16; and Dante, 164–82; on the dramatic monologue, 82; and Elizabeth Barrett Browning, 2–3, 11, 12, 102–3, 120, 148–49, 204, 244, 250–52, 260; "Essay on Shelley," 107–8, 139, 140–41, 199; feminine side of, 100–118, 120–35, 249–50;

267

Browning, Robert Weidemann (*cont.*)
and feminism, 15, 116; as fop, 251;
and Greek culture, 214–21;
individuality of, 14; and Italy,
243–64; and Keats, 106–7, 109–13;
later poetry of, 10, 202, 205, 214,
220–21; as liberal, 231, 252–61;
modernism of, 177, 178–82; and
nationalism, 15; obscurity of, 4–7,
72–73, 180, 206; poetic language of,
6–7; and politics, 7–8, 170, 172–82,
186–87, 200, 227, 229–40; and
Pound, 181; and Pre-Raphaelites,
116–18, 161, 254, 261–62; as
reader, 203–4; recent criticism of,
8–13; and Rome, 251–52; and
Shelley, 102–3, 106, 107–9, 123,
163, 249; and *Sordello*, 162; and
Spasmodics, 5, 13, 141–42, 148–53,
156, 157; specialist vocabulary of,
6–7; and spiritualism, 203; and
Swinburne, 117–18; and Tennyson,
14, 15, 16, 21–23; and the theater,
189–90, 227–28; un-Englishness of,
5–6, 14–15; as versifier, 16, 84;
Victorian and contemporary audiences
of, 2–8; and Wordsworth, 148,
153–57. *See also* Arnold, Matthew;
character; Dante; Keats, John; Pound,
Ezra; Shelley, Percy Bysshe; readers;
Tennyson, Alfred Lord

POETRY
Agamemnon, 217–18
"Andrea del Sarto," 42–43, 66, 103,
115
"Any Wife to Any Husband," 85
"Apollo and the Fates," 218
Aristophanes' Apology, 215, 216–17
Asolando, 155
"Bad Dreams," 212–14, 222
Balustion's Adventure, 215–16
"Bishop Orders His Tomb at Saint
Praxed's Church, The," 42–43, 70,
76–77, 103, 115, 263–64
"Blougram's Apology," 70
"Caliban Upon Setebos," 203
"Childe Rolande to the Dark Tower
Came," 67, 85, 108
"Cleon," 11, 129, 139–57
"Death in the Desert, A," 222
"Development," 218

"Dîs Aliter Visum," 106
"Donald," 209
Dramatic Idylls, 207–8
Dramatic Lyrics, 103
Dramatic Romances and Lyrics, 103
"Englishman in Italy, The," 70, 261–64
"Echetlos," 218
Ferishtah's Fancies, 221
Fifine at the Fair, 206
"Fra Lippo Lippi," 25–26, 39, 103, 115
"Gold Hair: A Story of Pornic,"
125–26, 222
"Gerousios Oinos," 116
"Halbert and Hob," 208
"Home Thoughts from Abroad," 16
"House," 28
"In a Gondola," 103
Inn Album, The, 209, 210–12, 215
"Italian in England, The," 261
"Ivan Ivanovitch," 208, 221
"James Lee's Wife," 100–1, 106, 108,
109, 117–18
"Jochanan Hakkadosh," 221
Jocoseria, 115–16
"Johannes Agricola in Meditation," 22,
24, 74, 112
La Saisiaz, 221
"Lost Leader, The," 154, 155
"Lost Mistress, The," 103
"Love among the Ruins," 85–86
Luria (play), 203
"Martin Relph," 208, 221
"Mary Wollstonecraft and Fuseli," 116
Men and Women, 82, 102
"Mr. Sludge, 'the Medium'," 67
"Mucklemouth Meg," 221
"My Last Duchess," 102; and the
divided subject, 81, 83–84, 91; as
dramatic monologue, 27–28, 38,
42–43, 75; and the female other,
103–4, 113–15
"Ned Bratts," 208
"Never the Time and the Place,"
115–16
"One Word More," 25, 82, 92–93,
102, 107
"Pambo," 221
"Pan and Luna," 133–34, 218–19, 222
Paracelsus, 22, 72, 128, 134–35, 186,
187, 231
"Parleying with Bernard de Mandeville,"
221

"Parleying with Christopher Smart," 10
"Parleying with Francis Furini," 127, 128
"Parleying with Gerard de Lairesse," 219–20
Parleyings with Certain People of Importance in Their Day, 126–27
Pauline: A Fragment of a Confession, 21–22, 101–2, 186, 187; and Browning's female signature, 121–24, 129–33
"Pheidipides," 208, 218
"Pictor Ignotus," 66, 81, 85, 96
Pippa Passes, 13, 22, 186–202
"Pompilia," 106
"Pope and the Net, The," 221
"Popularity," 149, 150
"Porphyria's Lover": as dramatic monologue, 22, 24, 43–46, 74; and the female other, 102, 103–4, 106, 107–8, 109–115; and poetic authority, 187, 189
"Prince Hohenstiel-Schwangau," 15, 215
"Rabbi Ben Ezra," 145, 155
Red Cotton Night-Cap Country, 209–10
Ring and the Book, The, 10, 23, 93, 120, 212, 220, 251, 258–60
"Saul," 94–95
Sordello, 1–2, 11, 72, 73, 81, 186; and modernist poetics, 161–82; and poetic authority, 170, 172–82, 188–89, 196, 199
Strafford (play), 13, 186, 189–90, 226–42
"Thamuris Marching," 216–17, 222
"Toccata of Galuppi's, A," 86–91, 125
"Tray," 208
"Two in the Campagna," 54, 60–66
Two Poets of Croisic, The, 206–7

Browning, Robert Weidemann Barrett (son), 250–51
Browning: The Critical Heritage, 4
Browning Institute Studies, 14
Browning Society, 72–73
Buckley, Jerome Hamilton, 148
Byron, George Gordon, Lord, 105–6; *Don Juan*, 106, 155

Cadbury, William, 85
"Caliban Upon Setebos," 203
Cameron, Sharon, 24
canons, 6

Carlyle, Thomas, 207, 233, 235; "Hero as King," 239; "On History," 240; *Sartor Resartus*, 80–81
Carravagio, Polidoro da. *See* Polidoro
Cavalcanti, Guido, 177–78
character and characterization, 8; Browning's vs. Shakespeare's, 92; and dramatic lyric, 47–48; and dramatic monologue, 23–24, 26, 28, 29, 33, 46–47; in the later poems, 205, 220–21; in "My Last Duchess," 27–28
Chartism, 230
Chesterton, G. K., 162, 257
"Childe Rolande to the Dark Tower Came," 67, 85, 108
Christensen, Jerome, 25
circle, eternal, 128, 133–34
class interest, 96–97
"Cleon," 11, 129, 139–57
closet drama, 187
Coleridge, Samuel, 29, 105, 156
comedy, 216
communication, 56–57, 61, 64, 65, 66, 97
consciousness: appropriation of, 189 (*see also* female other); developed and sensitized, 57, 146–47; "inward domain" of, 254–55, 257; as writing, 54–55, 56–67. *See also* subjectivity
contradiction, 96. *See also* doubleness
Cook, Eleanor: *Browning's Lyrics*, 10
Corn Laws, 262–63
couplet convention, 83–84
Covent Garden, 228
Crawford, A. W., 141
criticism: in context, 2–8; cultural, 14–16; recent, 8–13
Cudworth, Ralph, 113
Culler, Dwight: *The Victorian Mirror of History*, 229

Dante, 163–64, 243, 257; *The Divine Comedy*, 164–66, 169–79, 181, 243; *Purgatorio*, 164, 175
Darwin, Charles, 94; *Descent of Man*, 208–9. *See also* evolution and evolutionists
de Man, Paul, 71
De Quincey, Thomas, 236
death, 66, 88, 89, 106, 126, 147; and art, 90, 126; for Arnold's Empedocles, 56, 60, 144, 148

"Death in the Desert, A," 222
deconstruction, 33, 70, 71, 200. *See also*
    Derrida, Jacques
demagoguery, 187, 196, 199, 200
Derrida, Jacques, 54, 56–60; "Freud and
    the Scene of Writing," 58–60. *See
    also* deconstruction
desire, 61, 62–64, 66, 107, 122. *See also*
    projection
DeVane, William C., 120
"Development," 218
"dialectics of discourses," 7
differentiation of consciousness, 61, 63, 65
"Dîs Aliter Visum," 106
discernment, 63, 65
Disraeli, Benjamin: *Coningsby*, 234
Dobell, Sydney, 153; *Balder*, 142, 148, 152
"Donald," 209
Donne, W. B., 5
doubleness, 65, 66, 82–83, 84, 90–91, 93, 94
drama, 189–90, 200. *See also* dramatic
    monologue; *Strafford*
Dramatic Idylls, 207–8
Dramatic Lyrics, 103
dramatic monologue, 13; and divided
    subject, 79–81; and the female
    epipsyche, 103; and intertextuality,
    139; and the lyric, 25–34, 37–39,
    47; and money, 207; and New
    Criticism, 72–73; prototypes of, 74;
    and *Sordello*, 180–81; two levels of
    language in, 84. *See also* lyric
Dramatic Romances and Lyrics, 103
dreams, 212–14
druid stones, 206
duality of awareness, 46. *See also*
    doubleness; dramatic monologue: and
    divided subject

Ecelin, 176
"Echetlos," 218
Eclectic and Congregational Review, The, 6
Edinburgh Review, 189, 234
egotistical sublime, 187, 199, 200
Eliot, George, 5
Eliot, T. S., 30, 92, 177; "The Love Song
    of J. Alfred Prufrock," 39
Elizabethan playwrights, 92, 93
emblemist and emblems, 123, 126, 127, 129–35

Empedocles, 56, 66, 67. *See also* Arnold,
    Matthew: "Empedocles on Etna"
"England" (in *Strafford*), 236, 239, 240
English civil war, 229
"Englishman in Italy, The," 70, 261–64
epipsyche, 101, 103, 105, 109. *See also*
    female other
Erickson, Lee, 4; *Robert Browning: His
    Poetry and His Audiences*, 11
"Essay on Shelley," 107–8, 139, 140–41, 199
Euripides: *Alcestis*, 215–16; *Herakles*, 216
ethnology, 205, 212, 213
evolution and evolutionists, 54, 127,
    128–29, 131 34, 204–5
experience, 57, 147

Fascism, 181
female other, 102–18, 122, 123
feminist criticism, 12, 15
Ferishtah's Fancies, 221
fetishism, 211
Fifine at theFair, 206
Fish, Stanley, 70, 71, 74
Fleishman, Avrom, 186
formal principles, 41–42. *See also* dramatic
    monologue; lyric; New Criticism
Forster, E. M., 249
Forster, John, 191; "Evidence of a New
    Genius for Dramatic Poetry," 228
Foucault, Michel, 189, 240
"Fra Lippo Lippi," 25–26, 39, 103, 115
Frankfurt School, 181
Frazer, Sir James George: *The Golden
    Bough*, 202
free speech, 255, 257, 260
free trade, 255–57, 260
French Revolution, 154, 196, 229
Freud, Sigmund, 58–60
Frost, Robert, 30, 72
Froula, Christine, 4, 13
Furini, Francis, 127, 130
Fuson, B. W., 82

gathering of characters, 92–93, 95
"Gerousios Oinos," 116
Ghibellines, 170, 172, 176
Gibson, J. J.: *The Senses Considered as
    Perceptual Systems*, 48
Gibson, Mary Ellis: "The Criminal Body in
    Victorian Britain," 15; *History and the
    Prism of Art*, 12, 227

Gleason, Katherine, 227
God, 74, 113, 127, 130, 191–200
"Gold Hair: A Story of Pornic," 125–26, 222
Greenough, Horatio, 94
Grey, Thomas: "Elegy," 38, 47
Grube, John, 164, 168–69
Guelfs, 170

hair, 125–26
Hair, Donald, 150
"Halbert and Hob," 208
Hallam, Arthur, 28, 49
Hampden, John, 232, 233
Hardy, Thomas: "Darkling Thrush," 38, 47–48; "The Voice," 118
Harrald, William, 261, 262
Harrison, Antony, 9, 13
Haworth, Euphrasia Fanny, 167, 179
hedonism, 145, 151, 157
"hero," 238–39
Higher Criticism, 10, 32, 222
Hirsch, E. D., 70
history and historicity, 12, 24, 34n4, 128, 172, 174, 226–42
Holland, Norman, 70, 71
Homans, Margaret, 105
"Home Thoughts from Abroad," 16
Honan, Park: *Browning's Characters*, 9, 10
Hood, E. P., 6
Hopkins, Gerard Manley: "Windhover," 38
"House," 28
Hunt, Holman, 254

ideology, 96, 139, 177, 255
imagist school, 30
individualism, bourgeois, 79–81. *See also* consciousness; selfhood
"In a Gondola," 103
Inn Album, The, 209, 210–12, 215
intellect, 144, 209. *See also* scholarship
interpretation, 71–78
intertextuality, 139, 140–41
Introduction to the Poem (Boynton and Mack), 31
Irvine, William, 10
Iser, Wolfgang, 70, 74
"Italian in England, The," 261
italic type, 246–48
Italy, Browning's, 243–64
"Ivan Ivanovitch," 208, 221

Jack, Ian, 245
"James Lee's Wife," 100–1, 106, 108, 109, 117–18
Jerrold, Douglas, 161
"Jochanan Hakkadosh," 221
Jocoseria, 115–16
"Johannes Agricola in Meditation," 22, 24, 74, 112
Jonson, Ben, 93
Jowett, Benjamin, 250–51
joy, 140, 142–43, 146–48, 152–54, 156
Jules, 193, 197

Keats, John, 28, 102, 106–7, 126, 132; Arnold and, 142; "The Eve of St. Agnes," 106, 109–13; "Isabella," 103; and "joy," 145, 156; "Ode to a Nightingale," 38; and the Spasmodics, 142, 150, 151, 156, 157
Kenner, Hugh, 181
Kermode, Frank, 169–70
"King" (in *Strafford*), 236, 239, 240
Kirkup, Seymour, 204
Knoepflmacher, U. C., 13
Knowledge, 134, 172, 176, 187
Korg, Jacob, 191, 194
Kristeva, Julia, 135

La Saisiaz, 221
Lacan, Jacques, 82
Landor, Walter Savage, 161, 167, 179
Lang, Andrew, 202
Langbaum, Robert, 40, 46; *The Modern Spirit*, 9; *The Poetry of Experience*, 9, 75, 92, 104–5
language, 80–81; in *Sordello*, 172; specialized, 83, 93–97. *See also* consciousness; linguistic internationalism
Latané, David, 9, 13, 72, 188; *Browning's Sordello*, 4, 12
Lawrence, D. H.: *Apocalypse*, 243
levitation, 210
Lewes, George Henry, 102
liberalism, 252–64
Liberty. *See* liberalism
linguistic internationalism, 175–76, 181
listeners in Browning's monologues, 74–75, 76
losels (*Sordello*), 166, 170
"Lost Leader, The," 154, 155
"Lost Mistress, The," 103

272 ♦ INDEX

Loucks, James, and Richard Altick: *Browning's Roman Murder Story*, 9, 10
"Love among the Ruins," 85–86
Lubbock, Sir John: *The Origin of Civilization*, 205, 212
Luria (play), 203
lyric, 21–22, 24–25, 199, 200; dramatic, 47–52; expressive, 39, 40–41; mask, 39–40

Macaulay, Thomas Babington: "Essay on Hampden," 231–32, 233, 236
Mack, Maynard, 31
Macready, William, 226, 228–29
Maillard, Paul Desforges, 207
"Maker-see" poetics (*Sordello*), 166–67, 169, 170, 178
Marston, John Westland, 153
Martin, Loy: *Browning's Dramatic Monologues and the Post-Romantic Society*, 6–7, 9, 12
"Martin Relph," 208, 221
Marx, Karl, 256; *Eighteenth Brumaire of Louis Bonaparte*, 15; *The German Ideology*, 96
Marxian criticism, 36n14
"Mary Wollstonecraft and Fuseli," 116
Mason, Michael, 82
Masson, David, 5–6
materialism, 143, 146, 151
May Day, 207, 208
Maynard, John, 2, 9, 13; *Browning's Youth*, 10, 154–55
meaning, 11, 14, 70, 71, 86, 91. See also message
Mehlman, Jeffrey, 59
Melchiori, Barbara, 248, 249, 257, 259
Men and Women, 82, 102
Meredith, George, 148
Merivale, Herman, 189–90
Mermin, Dorothy, 13
message, 83, 84. See also meaning
meter, 87–88
Michaels, Walter Benn, 59–60
middle class, 256
Mill, John Stuart, 21, 23, 94, 187; "On Liberty," 253, 255–56; "The Spirit of the Age," 80; "What is Poetry?", 23
Millais, Sir John Everett: *Mariana*, 254
Miller, Betty, 248
Miller, J. Hillis, 73; *The Disappearance of God*, 9, 10, 199–200

Milton, John, 28
"Mr. Sludge, 'the Medium'," 67
modernism, 9, 30, 177, 178–82
money, 256–60
Morazé, Charles, 97
Morris, William, 116
Moulton-Barrett, Edward, 251
"Mucklemouth Meg," 221
Müller, Max, 202, 214
Munich, Adrienne, 9, 13, 15; *Andromeda's Chains*, 9
music, 88–90, 94–95
"My English Eyebright," 167, 178–79
"My Last Duchess," 102; and the divided subject, 81, 83–84, 91; as dramatic monologue, 27–28, 38, 42–43, 75; and the female other, 103–4, 113–15
Mystic Pad, 58–60, 66
myth, 219–21, 222–23. See also Perseus-Andromeda myth

nakedness, 122, 127, 129–30, 250
Napoleon III, 15
Narses, 228–29, 238
nature, 208, 217
nationalism, 15, 181
Nazism, 181
necrophilia, 111, 117
"Ned Bratts," 208
negative capability, 73, 111, 189, 199, 200
"Never the Time and the Place," 115–16
New Criticism, 2, 11, 25, 31, 32, 69–70, 72
New Monthly Magazine, 148
"new structure," poetic (*Sordello*), 172–74, 175
Nietzsche, Friedrich, 56–57
nude painting, 127, 129–30

"One Word More," 25, 82, 92–93, 102, 107
Othello, 65
Other. See female other
Ottima, 192, 196
ouroburos, 133, 134

"Pambo," 221
Pan, 215, 218–19
"Pan and Luna," 218–19, 222
parable, 168–70, 173
Paracelsus, 127–28, 194. See also *Paracelsus*

Paracelsus, 22, 72, 128, 134–35, 186, 187, 231. *See also* Paracelsus
"Parleying with Bernard de Mandeville," 221
"Parleying with Christopher Smart," 10
"Parleying with Francis Furini," 127, 128
"Parleying with Gerard de Lairesse," 219–20
Parleyings with Certain People of Importance in Their Day, 126–27
Pater, Walter, 147; *The Renaissance*, 79–80
Pauline: A Fragment of a Confession, 21–22, 101–2, 186, 187; and Browning's female signature, 121–24, 129–33
Peirce, Charles Sanders, 59–60, 65
"People" (in *Strafford*), 236–37, 239, 240
perception as representation, 58–59, 64. *See also* experience; consciousness: "inward domain" of
Perrine, Laurence: *Sound and Sense*, 31
Perseus and Andromeda myth, 102–3, 120–35, 215
phallic symbolism, 206, 217
"Pheidipides," 208, 218
Phen, 193, 197
"Pictor Ignotus," 66, 81, 85, 96
Pippa Passes, 13, 22, 186–202
Polidoro: *Perseus et Andromede*, 121, 123–24, 125, 126, 127, 130, 137 (fig. 1)
politics. *See* Browning, Robert Weidemann: and politics
"Pompilia," 106
"Pope and the Net, The," 221
"Popularity," 149, 150
"Porphyria's Lover": as dramatic monologue, 22, 24, 43–46, 74; and the female other, 102, 103–4, 106, 107–8, 109–115; and poetic authority, 187, 189
Porphyrius, 113
Poston, Lawrence, 226
Pound, Ezra, 13, 30, 161, 162, 177–78; *Cantos*, 177, 181
power relations, 7, 238, 239
Pre-Raphaelites, 116–18, 161, 254, 261–62
Preyer, Robert: "Two Styles in the Verse of Robert Browning," 9, 10
primitive, the, 202–23; the Italian as, 247, 248
"Prince Hohenstiel-Schwangau," 15, 215

projection, 91, 100–18
puppets and puppeteers, 188–89, 195–200
purism, fin de siècle, 30
Pygmalion, 198

"Rabbi Ben Ezra," 145, 155
Rader, Ralph, 13, 83, 95
Radicals, 229, 231, 235
Ransom, John Crowe, 31
readers, 72, 73–78, 85, 139, 179, 187–88, 190, 195
Red Cotton Night-Cap Country, 209–10
Reform Bill, 229, 236
Renan, Joseph, 222
René Gentilhomme, 207
Revelation, 167, 169
rhythm, 87–88
Riede, David, 13
Ring and the Book, The, 10, 23, 93, 120, 212, 220, 251, 258–60
Roman type, 247–48
Romantic poetics, 165; and the lyric, 29; and subjectivity, 55–56, 104–5. *See also individual Romantic poets*
Rome, 170–76, 251–52, 259, 260–61
Rossetti, Christina, 117, 254
Rossetti, Dante Gabriel, 116, 117, 132, 161, 254
Rousseau, Jean Jacques, 94
Ruskin, John, 180, 182, 206
Ryals, Clyde, 10, 11, 193, 232, 235

St. George, 103
St. John the Divine, 167–69, 181–82
St. Mark's Cathedral, 174–75, 179, 182
Salinguerra, 172, 176
Saturday Review, 4–5, 150
"Saul," 94–95
Schiller, Friedrich, 142
Schlegel, Augustus, 215
scholars, 70, 207, 217, 218, 222. *See also* intellect
Scholes, Robert: *Elements of Poetry*, 31
Sebald, 192–93, 196
Segal, Hannah, 122–23
selfhood: as compromise, 65–66; erasure of, 60, 66; and the female other, 100–118; Romantic, 55–56; and Victorian poetry, 55. *See also* subjectivity
self-interest, 239
Shaefer, Herwin, 93–94

Shaffer, Elinor: "A Death in the Desert," 10
Shakespeare, William, 65, 92
Shaw, W. David, 155; *The Dialectical Temper*, 9, 10
Shelley, Percy Bysshe, 131, 132, 163–64, 249; *Epipsychidion*, 108–9; and the female other, 101, 102–3, 105, 106, 107–9; and *Sordello*, 163–64, 165
Ship-Money Trial, 226
signatures, theory of, 127–28, 129
skull, 121, 126, 129, 134
slavery, 249–50, 253, 263–64
Slinn, E. Warwick, 11, 13, 71, 77, 193, 194
Smith, Alexander, 153; *A Life-Drama*, 142, 148–49, 151, 152
Socrates, 24
solitude, 250
Sordello, 1–2, 11, 72, 73, 81, 186; and modernist poetics, 161–82; and poetic authority, 170, 172–82, 187–89, 196, 199
soul, 147, 189, 199, 201n7, 227, 239. See also character; selfhood
spacing, 58, 64
Spasmodics, 5, 13, 141–42, 148–53, 156, 157
speaker: absence of, 56–57; and poet, 30–32, 82–83
Spencer, Herbert, 148
Spenser, Edmund: *The Faerie Queene*, 28, 254
spider, 121, 129
spiritualism, 203, 204
Stein, Richard, 189; *Victoria's Year*, 238
stornelli, 26
Story, William Wetmore: "The Evil Eye and Other Superstitions," 204
Strafford (play), 13, 186, 189–90, 226–42
Strauss, David, 222
strength, 172, 176, 177, 182
structuralist or archetypal theories, 41
"structured collection," 12
Stubbs, Charles Williams, 161
subjectivity, 22, 32; dangers of, 107; divided, 25, 79–99; of perception, 192, 194; Romantic, 55–56, 104–5; as system, 59–60, 64–65. See also consciousness; selfhood; soul
sun-worship, 207
Swinburne, Algernon, 116, 117–18, 161; "John Jones's Wife," 117–18; "Sequence of Sonnets on the Death of Robert Browning," 118
symbolist movement, 30
Symonds, J. A., 216
Symons, Arthur: *The Symbolist Movement*, 30
"sympathy and judgment," Langbaum's, 40, 46, 75

taste, 5–6
temporality as spacing, 58, 64
Tennyson, Alfred Lord, 14, 15, 16, 21–24, 28, 116–17, 254; "The Epic," 238; "In Memoriam," 42, 49–52, 66; *Maud*, 5, 67; *Poems, Chiefly Lyrical*, 28; "St Simeon Stylites," 22; "Tithonus," 23, 40; "Ulysses," 23
Teufelsdröckh (Carlyle's), 80, 240
text and textuality, 32–34, 57, 70–73; of poetic objects, 217, 219; of nature, 128; readers as, 139. See also writing
textual mobility, 57, 67
"Thamuris Marching," 216–17, 222
Thrale, Jerome, 148–49
"Toccata of Galuppi's, A," 86–91, 125
Tompkins, Jane, 70
Tories, 229–31, 234
Tower of Babel legend, 176
traces, 60, 61, 79
"Tray," 208
Traugott, Elizabeth, 96
"Triumph through decay," 126, 129
Tucker, Herbert F., 13, 71; *Browning's Beginnings*, 11, 13, 191, 192, 194, 196
"Two in the Campagna," 54, 60–66
Two Poets of Croisic, The, 206–7
Tylor, Edward: *Primitive Culture*, 202, 214

unconscious, 135, 203, 213–14
union, ideal, 61, 63, 66
Urn, Keats's, 126, 132

Veblen, Thorstein, 94
Vergil: *Georgics*, 218
Verlaine, Paul, 30
Victorian: alienation, 80, 93–94; class interest, 96; poetics, 66–67, 92; poets and politics, 186, 196; view of

evolution, 54; view of the primitive, 204–5
Victorian Literature and Culture, 14
Victorian Poetry, 10
violence, 170, 182. *See also* authority, poetic and political; strength
Viscusi, Robert, 7, 13, 15
Vogler, Abt, 25
voice: idiosyncratic vs. common language, 95–97; the low, in *Sordello*, 171–72, 239
von Hallberg, Robert, 239

Walpole, Horace, 243
web of communication, 56–57, 61, 64, 65, 66
Weinstein, Mark, 150
Wellington, Duke of, 234–35
Wesley, John, 243
Whigs, 229–31, 234
Wilde, Oscar, 29, 30
Williams, Raymond, 97

Woolf, Virginia: *The Waves*, 247
Woolford, John, 4, 12
Wordsworth, Ann, 57, 67
Wordsworth, William, 28, 92, 101, 105, 126, 131; Intimations Ode, 153–54, 155, 156, 157; and "joy," 143, 144, 148, 153, 156; political "defection" of, 155, 157; *The Prelude*, 154, 166; "Tintern Abbey," 40–41; "With Ships the Sea Was Sprinkled Far and Nigh," 39, 40
writing: as consciousness, 54–55, 56–67; and authority, 176; world as, 127–28. *See also* emblemist and emblems

Xanthos, 167–69

Yeats, William Butler, 30; "Ego Dominus Tuus," 23; "Leda and the Swan," 42, 48–49; "The Magi," 49

47.00